JUST
LOVE

JUST LOVE

A Framework for Christian Sexual Ethics

Margaret A. Farley

continuum

NEW YORK • LONDON

2006

The Continuum International Publishing Group Inc
80 Maiden Lane, New York, NY 10038

The Continuum International Publishing Group Ltd
The Tower Building, 11 York Road, London SE1 7NX

www.continuumbooks.com

Printed in the United States of America

Library of Congress Cataloging-in-Publication Data

Farley, Margaret A.
    Just love : a framework for Christian sexual ethics / Margaret A. Farley.
      p. cm.
    Includes bibliographical references and index.
    ISBN-13: 978-0-8264-1001-6 (hardcover : alk. paper)
    ISBN-10: 0-8264-1001-4 (hardcover : alk. paper)
    1. Sex – Religious aspects – Christianity. 2. Sexual ethics. 3. Sex –
Religious aspects – Catholic Church. I. Title.
BT708.F38 2006
241'.66 – dc22

                                          2006014494

For Patricia and Robert Hammell,
John and Elizabeth Farley, Mary Farley Valenti,
and their cherished children and grandchildren

CONTENTS

PREFACE

❖

I never intended or planned to write a book on sexual ethics. When I began teaching, I did not plan to teach a course in sexual ethics. Agendas in ethics, however, are seldom set by ethicists; they are set by the questions that arise not only among students but in the wider society. I developed the notions of "just love" and "just sex" long ago in response to these questions. But the fuller considerations and proposals that constitute this book were forged through many years of listening, teaching, counseling, studying, and pondering. What I have taught has been shaped by what I have co-learned; what I have lectured on in many contexts has been influenced by interchanges with diverse groups; what I have previously written has gained from the many people who have shared with me not only their questions but their experiences, insights, and concerns.

All along I have been struck by the urgency of contemporary issues in sexual ethics, not in spite of but along with the many other urgent ethical issues that demand our attention today. What happens in the sexual sphere of human life is not isolated from what happens in other spheres — whether familial, religious, social, political, or economic. The possibilities for human flourishing in general are nurtured or hindered by the ways in which we live our sexual lives. Everyone is aware of not only the fulfillment and joy promised through human sexuality, but the harm, violence, and stigma that unjust actions, relationships, and attitudes bring to our sexual selves. Perhaps never before have words of healing and hope been so needed, especially from the churches. This book offers a challenge in this regard, even as it attempts to provide ways of thinking about sex and sexuality that will be useful for individuals and social institutions.

Although the aim of this book is ultimately more practical than theoretical, I have tried to show that genuine knowledge and understanding, discernment and deliberation, are essential for sorting out our choices in regard to sex. In a search for insights into our questions of today, I look to the past of Western culture as well as to cultures other than Western. I try to probe the many meanings of embodiment, gender, and sexuality. I attempt also to explore the meanings of love and desire, in an effort to demonstrate the relationship between love, sex, and justice. In addition, I consider what sorts of person we want and need to be in order to love justly. I argue that the key to what and how we should love — in the sexual sphere as in any other sphere of human life — lies in the justice of our loves, our desires, and our actions. The search for wisdom about sex and sexuality is complex; this book aims not to simplify the search but to open new possibilities. What I propose is a framework for Christian sexual ethics. However, I have attempted not only to incorporate major Christian beliefs and concerns, but also to render the framework intelligible and persuasive as part of a more general sexual ethics. In doing so, I have not avoided the issues raised by historical and cross-cultural approaches. My collaboration in recent years with African women theologians responding to the AIDS pandemic has reinforced my conviction that the questions of sexual ethics are to some extent common to people, despite the boundaries of time and space. Nonetheless, I have taken seriously the role of social and cultural construction in all of our understandings of body, gender, and sexuality.

The complexity of the issues to be addressed may appear as an obstacle to some readers. It is possible, however, after the introductory material in chapter 1 to go straight to the proposals for a framework for sexual ethics in chapter 6. Should anyone choose this route, I hope it will generate enough interest for them to look back, then, to chapters 4 and 5. For those who want more specific answers to questions about patterns of sexual relationships, it may be useful to begin with chapter 7. The book proceeds from one step to another, across time and across cultures (chapters 2 and 3), making each step in each chapter significant in understanding the whole. Nonetheless, it is possible to begin in more than one place.

It is also possible to read this book and to ignore its multiple notes. Insofar as notes are a distraction, attending to them should be avoided. The text should stand on its own — with appropriate attributions, of course. I have, however, included many notes sometimes as a way to elaborate on more technical points, and sometimes as a way to provide extensive bibliographical resources for those who want to pursue particular questions in greater detail. The search for insights on troubling and intriguing questions belongs to us all.

In addition to the many students, colleagues, and other conversation partners who have made this book possible, I want to acknowledge my gratitude, in particular, to: Leslie Griffin — who first proposed my writing such a book; Marie Fortune, whose invitation to me to speak at a regional gathering of her denomination in the mid-1970s provided the first occasion for my working out in broad strokes the framework that is detailed here; Mary Rose D'Angelo, Gilmary Bauer, Letty M. Russell, David Hollenbach, Francine Cardman, Alice Kearney, Christiana Peppard, and Jennifer Seaich, whose responses to specific chapters provided me with invaluable challenges and suggestions; my family members, friends, and co-workers who supported me in countless ways through the long process of writing this book. I am grateful to my editor, Frank Oveis, whose advice and sustained pressure made me finally put most other things aside and finish the book; and to Justus George Lawler, my longtime editor, whose careful reading of the text helped to make it more readable for others.

Chapter 1

OPENING THE QUESTIONS

═══ ❖ ═══

T HERE IS NOTHING NEW about questioning the meaning of human sexuality or the criteria for its incorporation into a moral view of human life. Plato responded to his times by exploring the relation of sex to love and the possibilities of homosexual as well as heterosexual relationships. The Stoics put forth arguments for the taming of sex in a context of human reproduction. St. Augustine analyzed the mixed motivations that he thought characterized even marital sex. Martin Luther defied a view of sexual desire that made celibacy, rather than a settled commitment to spouse and family, the generally better option for Christians. Sigmund Freud radically challenged a whole culture's interpretation of sex and its place in the psychological development of the individual.

There may be nothing new about questioning human sexuality, assessing its psychological and social significance, defending or defying judgments of its moral possibilities. Yet the questioning that goes on today is decidedly different from most of what has preceded it in the history of Western culture. As studies of sex proliferated in the latter half of the twentieth century and continue into the twenty-first, all sorts of perspectives have emerged. With many of these we seem far removed from the lyrical explorations of Plato's *Symposium*, or from the calm arguments of Seneca and Marcus Aurelius, or for that matter from the strong polemics of Augustine or Luther. Even the metapsychology and clinical theory of Freud's *Three Essays on the Theory of Sexuality* are now quite distant from our view. Today the mood of questioning is at once contentious and indifferent, defiant and tentative. Advocates of tradition clash with advocates of modern enlightenment on sex, and each of these is countered by

1

postmodern voices that reject any point of view that claims objectivity and a stable set of rules. The heat of the conflict between "right" and "left" frequently becomes lukewarm because it is tempered by a radical skepticism that undercuts both traditional and nontraditional methods in a search for new insights. All of this presents us with a situation regarding sexual choices that is different indeed from the situations of the past.

Finding the Way

The history of ethical standards for sexual behavior in Western societies is largely a history of unambiguous rules or at least ideals. There have, of course, been theoretical disagreements about sexual mores in the past, and history is replete with discrepancies between societally recognized rules and general practice. At different times and places societies have varied in their formulations of ethical norms for sexual relationships and activities. Moreover, cultural and class differences within societies have frequently been reflected in significantly varied sexual norms and practice. Yet overall, clarity and apparent continuity have marked the development and understanding of many of the guidelines governing our sexual lives.

Today, however, in Western culture (and others as well) nearly every traditional moral rule for sexual behavior is under some kind of challenge. Longstanding positive obligations as well as negative prohibitions have become problematic enough for governments to debate legal changes and for religious traditions to struggle with increasingly controversial beliefs and rules. New freedoms are celebrated, and new fears arise. The problem is more than traditionalism versus radical change. The shaking of the foundations of sexual mores has brought not only conflict and not only the repudiation of past sexual rules. It has also brought confusion and a genuine concern for moral wisdom about truly troubling human issues. Convictions long taken for granted have grown into questions. These range from how the human race should responsibly reproduce itself, to how we can eliminate destructive elements in sexual relationships; from how to integrate sexuality into the whole of human life, to how we may ensure the healthy psychosexual development of children. We are concerned as never before about the consequences of sexual violence, the proliferation of sex industries, sexual harassment and gender domination, the breakdown in committed relationships, and an apparent widespread powerlessness in a search for intimacy. Although some individuals and groups seem certain of the answers to these questions and the remedy for these concerns, many are not.

Multiple factors help to explain the sea changes in contemporary attitudes toward previously assumed sexual norms (standards, rules and principles, ethical guidelines). It will not do to lay all blame at the feet of so-called liberalism and its supposed offspring of materialism and hedonism, or for anyone to claim all praise for sexual revolutionary movements as if they had no parentage and no perplexities of their own. Threaded through the massive economic, political, and social shifts in twentieth- and twenty-first-century culture has been access to new knowledge and practical possibilities that have specifically influenced sexual choice and behavior. Without simplifying these factors too much, it is possible to identify representative developments. We who have become used to a torrent of studies about sex (not only scientific, but philosophical, historical, psychological, anthropological, literary) and accustomed to all sorts of behaviors and patterns of relationship, tend to take these developments for granted. We forget how recent many of them are and how complex as shapers of human experience. At the risk of belaboring the obvious, it is worth reminding ourselves of what some of these developments are.

Why We Are Here

There is, for example, the quite astonishing (relative to past ignorances and distortions) increase in scientific knowledge about sexual response as such and about the human reproductive process. While the ovum was discovered as early (or as late, depending on one's point of view) as 1828, little was known until the next century about the physiologically active contribution of the female partner in the reproductive process. In prior centuries it was possible to sustain an image of male "seed" and female "ground" for reproduction, which in turn supported a view of the male as essentially active and the female as passive in reproduction and in sexual relations overall.[1]

The twentieth and twenty-first centuries have brought new information not only from biology but psychology, anthropology, and sociology,[2] and not only regarding male/female interaction but many other matters as well. In what is sometimes called the new discipline of "sexology,"[3] many more traditional disciplines combine to explore the meaning and practice of sex, its economic and political implications, the causes and consequences of a variety of sexual behaviors. On the basis of laboratory and field research, analysis of psychiatric cases and the amassing of comprehensive data regarding sexual practices, social scientific research has proliferated. However disputed some of the studies have been, they successfully repudiated previous pseudoscientific beliefs in, for example, the danger of insanity from masturbation, the "unnaturalness" of homosexual activity in animals (and therefore in humans), the unlimited fecundity of women throughout their menstrual cycles, and so forth. None of this information by itself could overturn traditional sexual norms, but it seriously loosened their hold. If, for example, Alfred Kinsey was right (or anywhere near right) that ninety-five percent of the male population in the United States, and seventy percent of the female population, engage in autoerotic acts, the evil consequences of masturbation can hardly include inevitable insanity and disease (as was

---

1. The predominant tradition until the nineteenth century was based on Aristotle's "one-seed" theory: only male semen produced an embryo, and a female was needed only to provide "matter" in the sense of blood. There were other theories, however, even in antiquity. Some proposed a "two-seed" theory, in which both male and female produced seed that mixed for conception. The two-seed theory had at least two versions: some maintained that although both male and female produced seeds, the female seed was inferior to the male; others held to a more neutral view. See Wayne A. Meeks, *The Origins of Christian Morality: The First Two Centuries* (New Haven, CT: Yale University Press, 1993), 139.

2. Despite the critiques of early studies, it is nonetheless difficult to overestimate the impact of the work of, for example, Henry Havelock Ellis, *Studies in the Psychology of Sex*, 7 vols. (Philadelphia: F. A. Davis, 1900–1928); Alfred C. Kinsey et al., *Sexual Behavior in the Human Male* (Philadelphia: W. B. Saunders, 1948), and *Sexual Behavior in the Human Female* (Philadelphia: W. B. Saunders, 1953); William H. Masters and Virginia E. Johnson, *Human Sexual Response* (Boston: Little, Brown, 1966).

3. Sexology refers to the study of human sexual behavior. It sometimes is broadened from psychological and physiological approaches to include many of the social sciences as well as philosophy.

previously thought or at least proclaimed). And insofar as William Masters and Virginia Johnson accurately recorded the physiological responses of both males and females, an ideal of male activity and female passivity becomes no longer tenable. Moreover, as the biology of human fertility has grown clearer, claims for procreation as the fundamental moral justification for all sexual activity have also become more and more assailable.

Cross-cultural studies have revealed large variations in patterns of sexual behavior among different cultural groups. What was considered deviant in Western society was found to be permitted and even socially accepted in other societies. Mid-twentieth-century reports, for example, showed that in forty-nine of seventy-six societies studied, homosexual activities of one kind or another were considered normal for certain members of the community. Masturbation appeared among both sexes in almost every society anywhere studied. There were no consistent norms for premarital or extramarital sex.[4] Again, such information did not by itself overturn traditional Western norms, but it did tend to relativize in the minds of many the norms they had previously assumed to be absolute and universally adhered to by all persons. With each passing decade, cross-cultural studies have contributed to a growing belief in the social construction of sexual norms — norms shaped and conditioned not by the "essentially human" but by the forces within a given society.

Historical studies of Western sexual norms have also contributed to the relativization and weakening of these norms. The very disclosure that sexual prescriptions have a history has revealed the contingency of their sources and foundations. To see, for example, that a procreative ethic arose as much from Stoic philosophy as from the Bible has allowed many Christians to question its ongoing validity. And it is not only the history of ideas about sex that has been important in this regard. It is also the initial historical excavations of the moral attitudes and actual practices of peoples of the past, and an identification of the shifting centers of influence on the sexual mores

---

4. See, for example, Clellan S. Ford and Frank A. Beach, *Patterns of Sexual Behavior* (New York: Harper & Row, 1951).

of different times and places.[5] In an effort to make sense of present beliefs, historians have searched for the roots and developments of these beliefs, and the result has seldom been a reinforcement of the original rationales.

In addition to developments in theoretical disciplines, the rise in self-consciousness among women, especially in the last three decades of the twentieth century, has been a significant factor in the loosening of traditional sexual ethical norms. Women's new self-understandings have had an extraordinary effect on the perception of sexual norms. Long centuries of the kind of failure of vision that allowed sexism to flourish in spite of the seemingly best moral insights of major religious and philosophical traditions have made many women doubt the validity of almost all past teachings regarding the morality of sex. Women have recognized firsthand the irrationality of sexual taboos whereby, as Freud commented in regard to beliefs in the defilement of menstruation, pregnancy, and childbirth, " ... it might almost be said that women are altogether taboo."[6] Economic and social changes have interacted with various forms of consciousness-raising to give women new perspectives on old issues. Double standards, oppressive and repressive gendered social and political patterns, male interpretations of female sexual capacities, medical and social experts' identification of impossible ideals and destructive roles — women's experiences of all of these have led many to a radical questioning of traditional sexual beliefs and behaviors.

Besides the women's movement, the rise of the gay rights movement made an enormous difference in public perceptions of the morality of sexual practices previously considered unacceptable.

---

5. See, for example, the work of John T. Noonan Jr., *Contraception: A History of its Treatment by the Catholic Theologians and Canonists*, enlarged ed. (Cambridge, MA: Belknap Press of Harvard University Press, 1986); John Boswell, *Christianity, Social Tolerance, and Homosexuality* (Chicago: University of Chicago Press, 1980); John D'Emilio and Estelle B. Freedman, *Intimate Matters: A History of Sexuality in America* (New York: Harper & Row, 1988); John C. Faut, ed., *Forbidden History: The State, Society, and the Regulation of Sexuality in Modern Europe* (New York: Vintage Books, 1992); Kathy Peiss and Christina Simmons, eds. (with Robert A. Padgug), *Passion and Power: Sexuality in History* (Philadelphia: Temple University Press, 1989).

6. See Sigmund Freud, "The Taboo of Virginity (1918)," *The Collected Papers of Sigmund Freud*, ed. Philip Rieff, 8 (New York: Collier Books, 1963), 75.

What was largely hidden has become visible, and the presence of self-identified gay men and lesbians in families, communities, places of work, churches, has made possible a strong peripheral support for what might otherwise have been a small movement.[7] What was scorned by many is still scorned by some, but reluctant public recognition of gay rights (from nondiscrimination rights to the rights of civil unions and gay marriages) reflects not only a new toleration of alternative views of human sexuality, but a shaking of previous convictions regarding sexual morality in general. The volatility of public sentiment over issues surrounding same-sex relationships reveals perhaps better than anything else the depth to which foundations have been jarred.

It is difficult to overestimate the importance, for all of these developments, of the technologies resulting from scientific and medical knowledge. The widespread availability of effective contraceptives allowed for the first time a general practical separation of heterosexual intercourse from pregnancy. Despite failures regarding AIDS, medical technologies of prevention and treatment have also allowed some reliable separation between sexual activity and infectious disease. The development of reproductive technologies has given to previously infertile couples, and also to fertile individuals, possibilities of childbearing heretofore unimaginable. Sexual dysfunctions of many kinds have become treatable, whether through pharmaceutical or other forms of therapy.

Interesting as it is to speculate on these and other factors in the relativization of sexual norms, by themselves these factors do not resolve the questions that continue to worry us about human sexual relationships and activities; rather, they set for us an ethical task.[8] None of them represents self-evidently negative developments

---

7. What I mean by this is that movements become powerful when they are not dependent only upon the core participants but when they resonate in and are bolstered by large numbers of supportive persons.

8. My use of the terms "moral" and "ethical" may need some clarification here and throughout the chapters that follow. I, like many others, often use the terms interchangeably, a practice justified by the lack of consistent differentiation between them in either philosophy or theology. Insofar as they are differentiated, however, "moral" and "morality" tend to be closer to the concrete than "ethics" or the "ethical." "Moral" refers to real action, choice, judgment, experience; "ethical" refers to systematic reflection on moral action and character. Hence, "morality" has to do with life, and "ethics"

in human awareness or in practical options. They have all held an important potential to move us toward genuine freedom and well-being in the sexual sphere. It is, after all, a good thing to move beyond fear and shame generated by irrational taboos and beyond complacency built on ignorance. It is even better to gain clarity about patterns of sexual relationships insofar as they are harmful and unjust. Still, these developments have led us inevitably to further questions. We need good biology and psychology, useful anthropology, sociology, economic theory and history; we need liberating social movements. But we need more than these. Individuals and societies keep pressing the questions: Where do we go from here? How will we address the problems we still have in the sexual sphere? Can we incorporate our new knowledge and many new options into the worldviews that have provided meaning for the whole of our lives? No longer able to count solely on the compass of traditional insights and norms, or at least not on our agreement about them, what will anchor us or provide promise of moral wisdom and guidance? These questions have not been pondered historically only by scientists and empirical researchers. They have been the responsibility of lawmakers and courts and of communities of faith. Each of these, in turn, has depended to a great extent, and for better or for worse, on the insights and arguments of philosophers and theologians. To understand where we are and why, we need therefore to look at developments in these disciplines as well.

New Maps

Important philosophical and theological proposals have emerged in the last quarter of the twentieth century and in the beginning of the twenty-first. Just as theologies and philosophies of sex have in the past depended importantly on the best biology available, so contemporary revisions have responded to the demands of new biology and psychology, the advent of new technologies, and the impact of

---

is a discipline that tries to understand the moral life. Nonetheless, "ethics" can be equated with either or both "moral philosophy" and "moral theology," depending on one's sources and historical preferences. If there is a reason in a given context to differentiate these meanings explicitly, I do so; if not, they may be interpreted herein as interchangeable, with the sometimes vague and noncrucial difference I have just identified.

social movements. Indeed, there is widespread (if not unanimous) recognition of the necessity of interdisciplinary approaches. After World War II, Western philosophers like Jean-Paul Sartre, Maurice Merleau-Ponty, and Simone de Beauvoir, attempted to construct new meanings for human sexuality not only in the light of new scientific data but of new philosophical theories of freedom and interpersonal love.[9] The work of Michel Foucault may be as yet unsurpassed in influence on questions of sex and sexual desire.[10] Key studies by analytic philosophers have also appeared on issues such as gender, marriage, family, homosexuality, and pornography.[11] Feminist philosophers, in particular, have produced groundbreaking work not only on questions of sexual behavior, but on the large philosophical questions of human embodiment, gender identity, the nature of sexual desire, justice in familial relationships, modes of human parenting.[12]

Theology, too, has offered important insights regarding human sexuality and behavior. Some of this work in North America began among Christian theologians in the 1960s with the Roman Catholic

---

9. See Jean-Paul Sartre, *Being and Nothingness: An Essay on Phenomenological Ontology*, trans. Hazel E. Barnes (London: Methuen, 1958); Maurice Merleau-Ponty, *The Phenomenology of Perception*, trans. Colin Smith (New York: Humanities Press, 1967); Simone de Beauvoir, *The Second Sex*, trans. H. M. Parshley (New York: Alfred A. Knopf, 1971).

10. Michel Foucault, *The History of Sexuality*, trans. Robert Hurley, 3 vols. vol. 1: *An Introduction* (New York: Pantheon Books, 1978); vol. 2: *The Use of Pleasure* (New York: Vintage Books, 1990); vol. 3: *The Care of the Self* (New York: Vintage Books, 1988). I say this despite the serious critiques that have been made of Foucault's work in this regard.

11. See, for example, Robert Baker and Frederick Elliston, eds., *Philosophy and Sex* (Buffalo: Prometheus Books, 1975); Alan Soble, ed., *The Philosophy of Sex*, 2d ed. (Savage, MD: Littlefield Adams Quality Paperbacks, 1991). See also the historical work of Jeffrey Weeks, *Sexuality and Its Discontents: Meanings, Myths, and Modern Sexualities* (London: Routledge & Kegan Paul, 1985).

12. See, for example, Alison M. Jaggar and Susan R. Bordo, eds., *Gender/Body/Knowledge: Feminist Reconstructions of Being and Knowing* (New Brunswick, NJ: Rutgers University Press, 1989); Judith Butler, *Bodies That Matter: On the Discursive Limits of 'Sex'* (New York: Routledge, 1993); Susan Moller Okin, *Justice, Gender, and the Family* (New York: Basic Books, 1989); Sara Ruddick, *Maternal Thinking: Toward a Politics of Peace* (Boston: Beacon, 1989); Luce Irigaray, *An Ethics of Sexual Difference*, trans. C. Burke and G. C. Gill (Ithaca, NY: Cornell University Press, 1993). See also Domna C. Stanton, ed., *Discourses of Sexuality: From Aristotle to AIDS* (Ann Arbor: University of Michigan Press, 1992).

debate on artificial contraception.[13] Soon after, significant publications by Anthony Kosnik and his colleagues in the Roman Catholic
tradition, and James Nelson in the Protestant traditions, marked
the start of a whole new era for Christian sexual ethics.[14] The contributions of Charles Curran, André Guindon, Philip Keane, Giles
Milhaven, Lisa Sowle Cahill, Beverly Wildung Harrison, Carter Heyward, Christine Gudorf, and many others have been invaluable in
the search for sexual understanding within Christian communities.[15]
Biblical scholars have joined with theologians in attempting to interpret the tradition. Phyllis Trible, Mary Rose D'Angelo, William
Countryman, Robin Scroggs, Richard Hays, and Dale Martin, among
others, have provided approaches to exegesis and interpretation important for questions of sexual ethics.[16] Jewish theologians, too, have
provided significant studies on many of the same issues. Writers such

---

13. See, for example, Charles E. Curran, ed., *Contraception and Holiness: The Catholic Predicament* (New York: Herder & Herder, 1964); Dietrich von Hildebrand, *The Encyclical Humanae Vitae: A Sign of Contradiction* (Chicago: Franciscan Herald, 1969).

14. Anthony Kosnik et al., *Human Sexuality: New Directions in American Catholic Thought* (Mahwah, NJ: Paulist, 1977); James B. Nelson, *Embodiment: An Approach to Sexuality and Christian Theology* (Minneapolis: Augsburg, 1978).

15. See, as examples, Charles E. Curran, *Contemporary Problems in Moral Theology* (Notre Dame, IN: Fides, 1970) and *Tensions in Moral Theology* (Notre Dame, IN: University of Notre Dame Press, 1988); André Guindon, *The Sexual Creators: An Ethical Proposal for Concerned Christians* (Lanham, MD: University Press of America, 1986); Philip S. Keane, *Sexual Morality: A Catholic Perspective* (New York: Paulist, 1977); John Giles Milhaven, "Christian Evaluations of Sexual Pleasure," in *The American Society of Christian Ethics Selected Papers 1976*, ed. Max Stackhouse (Scholars, 1976); Lisa Sowle Cahill, *Sex, Gender, and Christian Ethics* (Cambridge: Cambridge University Press, 1996); Beverly Wildung Harrison, *Making the Connections: Essays in Feminist Social Ethics* (Boston: Beacon, 1985); Carter Heyward, *Our Passion for Justice* (Cleveland: Pilgrim, 1984); Christine E. Gudorf, *Body, Sex, and Pleasure* (Cleveland: Pilgrim, 1994). These authors and works constitute only a small sampling of the count-less works, by the individual authors listed above and by many others, that are now available from both Catholic and Protestant theologians and ethicists.

16. See Phyllis Trible, *God and the Rhetoric of Sexuality* (Philadelphia: Fortress, 1978); Mary Rose D'Angelo, "Women in Luke-Acts: A Redactional View," *Journal of Biblical Literature* 109 (1990): 141–61; L. William Countryman, *Dirt, Greed, and Sex: Sexual Ethics in the New Testament and Their Implications for Today* (Philadelphia: Fortress, 1988); Robin Scroggs, *The New Testament and Homosexuality* (Philadel-phia: Fortress, 1983); Richard Hays, "Relations Natural and Unnatural: A Response to John Boswell's Exegesis of Romans 1," *Journal of Religious Ethics* 14 (1986), 184–215; Dale B. Martin, "Heterosexism and the Interpretation of Romans 1:18–32," *Biblical Interpretation* 3 (1995): 332–55.

as Eugene Borowitz, David Feldman, David Novak, Judith Plaskow, David Biale, and Elliott Dorff,[17] have critically engaged the questions of sex and sexuality in ways of immense importance for the Jewish community and beyond.

And where have we come? Not everyone evaluates recent philosophical and theological proposals in the same way. Nonetheless, significant new insights can hardly be ignored, and paths that lead in heretofore unseen directions for exploration must be taken seriously. Some theoretical analyses of the meanings of human sexuality are as critical to our understanding as are the scientific discoveries that preceded them. New philosophical links between sex and freedom, sex and power, sex and history, gender and just about everything else, are in some respects so important that there can be no turning back to simpler ways of interpreting human experience.

Theological critiques of anthropological dualism and of an emphasis on sin and shame have made possible new perspectives on sexuality in the context of beliefs about creation, incarnation, and eschatology. Critical biblical exegesis has unsettled previously accepted sexual norms, and it has shed new light on the place of sexuality in the human community and in the call of human persons to God. Critiques of religious traditions have led in some cases to creative reconstruction of important aspects of traditions. Even where new theological perspectives on human sexuality are greeted with disagreement and controversy, the maps for theological discourse on matters of sex have been irrevocably altered. Theology, like philosophy, has come along some ways from which there is no turning back.

Hence, although major questions have been probed, and key directions have been charted for a contemporary philosophy, theology, and ethics of human sexuality, what we have overall is a work in

---

17. See Eugene B. Borowitz, *Choosing a Sex Ethic: A Jewish Inquiry* (New York: Schocken Books, 1969); David M. Feldman, *Marital Relations, Birth Control, and Abortion in Jewish Law* (New York: Schocken Books, 1974); David Novak, *Jewish Social Ethics* (New York: Oxford University Press, 1992); Judith Plaskow, *Standing Again at Sinai: Judaism from a Feminist Perspective* (San Francisco: Harper & Row, 1990); David Biale, *Eros and the Jews: From Biblical Israel to Contemporary America* (New York: Basic Books, 1992); Elliot Dorff, *Love Your Neighbor as Yourself: A Jewish Approach to Modern Personal Ethics* (Philadelphia: Jewish Publication Society, 2003)

progress. On some issues dissension still rages in the churches and synagogues. The very nature of other issues (such as the meaning of human sexuality, desire, and embodiment, and the structures of human relationships, both personal and public) makes them perennial problems for each generation to probe. It is therefore more important than ever to continue explorations, to engage the relevant disciplines, and to offer ethical frameworks for evaluating relationships and activities in the sexual sphere.

Problems with the Terrain

In addition to the usual difficulties of reflection on complex human experience, efforts at ethical analysis in the sexual sphere face particular reasons for skepticism regarding the enterprise as such. First, past failures haunt it: if it took so many centuries to "get it wrong," how many will it take to "get it right"? This, of course, presumes that there is no wisdom whatsoever retrievable from religious, philosophical, and cultural traditions regarding human sexuality. It also presumes that there can really be "nothing new under the sun," no new insight that is trustworthy at all, not even for a specific time and place. On the face of it, this seems an exaggerated rejection of both the past and the present. Even if the "last word" can never be in, the incremental gains of retrieval and reconstruction may be worth the effort. Whether they are judged so or not may depend on how urgent we perceive our questions to be. Insofar as we continue to harm and to hurt one another in our sexual lives, or fail to affirm the potential of one another; insofar as we hold ourselves in any way responsible for future generations; insofar as fear and confusion still qualify our sexual choices; insofar as we do not understand one another in these choices and cannot agree on either our own or those of others; insofar as our yearnings for pleasure or happiness or fulfillment seem unnecessarily hindered; insofar as any and all of these situations appear to us to be real, the questions of sexuality remain to be probed — no matter what form of skepticism might be otherwise appealing.

There is, however, another reason for skepticism that gives us caution. In Western culture, at least since its Christian formation, there has been a perduring tendency to give too much importance to the morality of sex. The sexual has threatened to take over the moral focus of whole generations of persons. Everything about the "sexual" is considered "moral" or "immoral," and "morality" is almost reduced to "sexual morality." All of this is to the detriment of concerns about economic injustice, the oppression of whole peoples, political dishonesty, even theft and the taking of life. Ironically, much of what constitutes the sexual sphere may not be a matter of morality at all, or only indirectly so. Relationships — with others, ourselves, God — always have moral elements; but the sex or lack of sex in them may be of less genuine moral significance than are elements such as respect, trust, honesty, fairness, and faithfulness. Still, we do frequently harm or betray ourselves and one another precisely as sexual human beings. Despite the risk, then, of escalating the moral significance of sex, the need for a sexual ethic cannot be completely dismissed.

The other side of the tendency to equate morality with sex is the tendency to see the sexual sphere as isolated from the rest of human life. Hence, while on the one hand we have given too much emphasis to sexual morality; on the other, we may now give too little. Skepticism of this sort takes the form of a complaint that sexual ethics is, after all, a minor enterprise, frivolous or obsessive, and a diversion from the truly urgent moral concerns of racism, hunger, homelessness, poverty, and war. While there may be some truth to this claim, it nonetheless misses the connections between social structure and sexual relations, between political struggles and gender bias, between sexual sanctions and social policies. Feminists have not always met with comprehension when they have insisted that the "personal is political"; but especially in the sexual ethical sphere the private is as likely to be institutionally determined as it is personally discerned. In a century that has seen rape as a part of military strategy, poverty as the result of lack of reproductive choice, industries based on the economic exploitation of sex, race joined with gender and class to determine the employment options of groups, the development of a sexual ethic cannot be a trivial concern.

A last, but twofold, source of skepticism comes from the wide range of experience that is included in our understanding of the "sexual sphere," and from our growing contemporary doubts that moral norms will make any positive difference in our sexual lives. Here

questions abound. The very idea of ethical standards for sexual relationships and activities implies that there is a way to generalize
about them. But is there? Even apart from considerations of cultural
differences, is it possible to develop an ethic that is useful for our
sexual lives? Take only the experience of romantic love, shaping and
shaped by sexual desire. How many forms does it take? Are there
really moral criteria that will apply to relationships of painfully unre-
quited love as well as to relationships where passion grows gracefully
into mature and mutual love in a shared and settled life? Will ethical norms determine whether loves will find fulfillment? Whether
unfulfilled loves will prove tragic, or simply sad, or fortunate losses
along a better way? Are ethical principles and moral rules the solution
to impossible loves, the roadmap to possible and beautiful relationships? Can ethical norms prevent our being harmed or our lives from
being disrupted? Can moral rules help us to navigate the fragile ways
of intimacy?

Are there ethical perspectives that can comprehend both erotic
love in romantic relationships and passionate desire for sex without
relationship? What about relationships that are neither romantic or
passionate? Can moral boundaries be the same when love has endured a long time (or become embittered along the way), and when
love is new, uncertain, filled with power and danger? Are ethical
norms more plausible when sex and love are institutionally regulated
by structures of marriage and family, and by professional boundaries,
categories of age, self-sustaining traditions, self-contained cultures?
In other words, can enough be said about the human experience of
sex to generate universal, or even local, guidelines for its practice?
What can the experience of moral obligation do for sexual experience
that will be protective or liberating? When sex fits peacefully into
the order of life, does it need ethical norms? When sex is disruptive,
contradicting the order of our life, will ethical norms help? Is the
problem with sexual ethical norms merely the problem of abiding by
them, or does it include a prior problem of discerning them at all?

No one would argue that ethical standards can determine or resolve or even illuminate all of the possibilities and problems of sex.
Few persons today are likely to insist that moral rules always have
good effects on our sexual and relational lives. Yet it is difficult to

conclude finally that our sexual lives should not be informed and governed by ethical guidelines and moral wisdom. However disparate our sexual experiences, however diverse the contexts for our sexual desire, however indifferent to ethical standards our sexuality may seem, we do still make judgments of right or wrong, experience moral claims in response to these judgments, and assume some freedom of choice in the face of moral claims. All of this may prove illusory, a mistake, a hold-over from longstanding but no longer credible taboos. Yet we do experience genuine ethical confusion, seek moral guidance, and experience moral outrage in relation to some sexual activities, some sexual relationships. Whatever our intellectual theories about sex and morality, moral questions do emerge at the heart of our sexual lives. Hence, skeptical or not, efforts to develop or at least refine a sexual ethic are inevitable.

The Task

It is clear by now that the development of an adequate contemporary sexual ethic requires paying attention to a number of related explorations. Cross-cultural situations must be taken into account; historical perspective must be achieved; social analysis needs to be made of contemporary experience. Moreover, some metaethical issues (or what may be called "large questions") must be addressed: the meanings of human embodiment and sexual desire, the meanings and purposes of "sex" itself, the relevance of gender, and the universality or particularity of any moral norms. And since ethical frameworks do not come out of a moral vacuum, a sexual ethic will have to draw on (if only to repudiate) some tradition, whether philosophical, theological, cultural; or draw on many traditions, testing whatever critical and constructive relationships they can achieve. Sexual ethics will need to assess human actions and possibilities, asking about discernible contradictions or harms, looking for patterns of relationship that promote individual and social well-being. Beyond this, it will be important to consider not only norms for actions and relationships, but questions of character or virtue as they relate to our sexual lives. No doubt this already large task can be expanded to include other useful or even necessary endeavors.

This book does not aim to provide a complete or specifically comprehensive sexual ethic. It will not address all of the issues crucial to sexual ethics, nor all of the promising frameworks. It is largely limited to issues facing contemporary Western culture (though there is no assumption that all of these are irrelevant for other cultures). It is further limited to providing a framework for sexual ethics that draws upon resources important to the Christian tradition, and that aims primarily, though not solely, to make sense within that tradition.

The more modest task of this book, then, includes some of the elements for a comprehensive sexual ethic. Succeeding chapters aim to provide an historical perspective for Western culture (chapter 2), an examination of issues of cross-cultural differences (chapter 3), and explorations of the meanings of human embodiment, gender, and sexuality (chapter 4). In chapter 5, I address questions that are preliminary to the formulation of a framework for sexual ethics: questions of methods and sources, alternative frameworks, and the relation of justice to human love. Chapter 6 contains my proposal for a framework for a human and Christian sexual ethics. The final chapter, chapter 7, considers three of what might be called "patterns of relationship" that involve our sexuality — because they are important for our lives, and because they may be illuminated within the framework for sexual ethics I will have proposed.

Chapter 2

THE QUESTIONS
AND THEIR PAST

═══ ❖ ═══

T HE HISTORY OF SEXUAL ETHICS provides an important perspective for understanding current ethical questions regarding
human sexuality. Historical overviews of sexual ethics are not without difficulties, however, as recent critical studies have shown.[1] While
it is possible to find a recorded history of laws, codes, treatises,
sermons, and other forms of moral instruction regarding sexual behavior, it is much more difficult — if not impossible — to determine
what real people actually believed and did in the distant past. Important historical research in this regard is under way, but it is
still fragmentary and often tentative. Second, ethical theory regarding sex (what is to be valued, what goals are worth pursuing, what
reasons justify certain sexual attitudes and activities) has been predominantly theory formulated by an elite group of men in any given
society. Women's experience, beliefs, values, are largely unrecorded
and, until recently, almost wholly inaccessible. The same is true for
men who do not belong to a dominant class. Third, what we do find
through historical research is necessarily subject to interpretation. It

---

1. See, for example, Peter Brown, *The Body and Society: Men, Women, and Sexual Renunciation in Early Christianity* (New York: Columbia University Press, 1988); Martin Duberman et al., eds., *Hidden From History: Reclaiming the Gay and Lesbian Past* (New York: Penguin Books, 1989); Susan K. Cahn, "Sexual Histories, Sexual Politics," *Feminist Studies* 18 (Fall 1992): 629–47; John C. Faut, ed., *Forbidden History: The State, Society, and the Regulation of Sexuality in Modern Europe* (Chicago: University of Chicago Press, 1992); Thomas W. Laqueur, "Sexual Desire and the Market Economy During the Industrial Revolution," in *Discourses of Sexuality: From Aristotle to AIDS*, ed. Domna C. Stanton (Ann Arbor: University of Michigan Press, 1992), 185–215.

makes a difference, for example, if one is looking for historical evaluations of human sexual desire or historical silences about sexual abuse of women.

All of these difficulties notwithstanding, it is possible to survey (with appropriate caution) a history of norms and theories in Western sexual ethics and to gain thereby some insight into contemporary beliefs and questions.[2] Before attempting this, however, we can illustrate the difficulties involved, as well as the rich possibilities, by looking briefly at three interpretive theories, all directed primarily at historical sources and trends within Western culture and some of its subcultures. These theories provide vastly different perspectives not only on the history of thought about sexuality and its institutionalized norms, but also on what is sometimes referred to as the history of sexuality.

Sex, Morality, and History: Theories of Interpretation

As suggested in chapter 1, no thinker may have been more influential in determining current questions about sex and sexual desire than the French philosopher Michel Foucault. His study of the history of sexuality in antiquity yielded ideas that continue to permeate much of the work of other sexual historians as well as of philosophers and theologians. Yet his is not the only formative study of the past, and his conclusions have provoked both positive and negative responses.

Michel Foucault: The Historical Constitution of Desire

Foucault originally planned to write a history of what he called "the experience of sexuality" in modern Western culture. In the course of his work, he became convinced that what was needed was a history of desire, or of the desiring subject. At the heart of this conviction was the premise that sexuality is not an abstract, ahistorical constant.

---

2. What follows in this chapter represents an expanded and heavily revised version of my earlier attempt at historical overview. See Margaret A. Farley, "Sexual Ethics," in *Encyclopedia of Bioethics*, ed. Warren Thomas Reich, rev. ed. (New York: Simon & Schuster Macmillan, 1995), 5:2363–75.

More radically, neither is sex a concrete natural given, a biological referent that simply expresses itself in different experiences of sexuality, molded historically by changes in moral attitudes and norms. With these premises, Foucault was turning upside down many traditional theories of sex and sexual desire. Sex in his view is not something "in itself," reducible to a bodily minimum of organ, instinct, and goal,[3] whose mysterious meaning needs to be examined and whose relentless "drive" needs to be controlled. To understand sexual desire, it is necessary to understand (in this order) power, sexuality, and, then only, sex. For power shapes the experience of sexuality, and sexuality constitutes and structures sex. In other words, "sex" and "sexuality" are historical social constructs, dependent on a particular configuration of power in a specific historical context. Hence, any insight into sex must come out of historical study.[4]

Underlying Foucault's view of sex, then, is a theory of human forces or power. Power as such, for Foucault, is diffused through a field of multiple "force relations immanent in the sphere in which they operate."[5] Thus religious, political, medical, psychological forces have been at work at various times in the past both in the form of "procedures ... to make us detest the body" and "ruses ... to make us love sex";[6] in short, mechanisms to discipline sexuality but also

3. Michel Foucault, *The History of Sexuality*, vol. 1, *An Introduction*, trans. Robert Hurley (New York: Pantheon Books, 1978), 151–52. Foucault's convictions regarding the role of discourse in the social construction of "realities" are recognizably in line with other postmodern philosophical theories of knowledge. However, his particular alignment of social construction with an analytics of power and a turn to history differentiates him from many postmodernists. It is this combination that has proven to be so influential in the subsequent work of sexologists and, in particular, feminist theorists.

4. Foucault, *The History of Sexuality*, 1:72. The history that Foucault studied was primarily a history of "discourse," or "discursive practices." That is, he focused on what he considered "serious speech acts," the thought in various disciplines and public documents that actually served as social norms and practices.

5. Foucault, *The History of Sexuality*, 1:92. Foucault's theory of power is not operative only in the context of his study of sexuality. For other contexts, both theoretical and practical, see Foucault, *Madness and Civilization: A History of Insanity in the Age of Reason*, trans. Richard Howard (New York: Mentor Books, 1965); *The Archaeology of Knowledge*, trans. A. M. Sheridan-Smith (New York: Harper & Row, 1972); *The Birth of the Clinic: An Archaeology of Medical Perception*, trans. A. M. Sheridan-Smith (New York: Vintage Books, 1973); *Discipline and Punish: The Birth of the Prison*, trans. A. M. Sheridan-Smith (New York: Pantheon, 1977); *Power/Knowledge: Selected Interviews and Other Writings*, ed. Colin Gordon et al. (Brighton, Sussex: Harvester, 1980).

6. Foucault, *The History of Sexuality*, 1:159.

to arouse and excite it.[7] Sexuality is a "transfer point" for relations
of power — between women and men, parents and children, teachers and students, clergy and laity, the young and the old, rulers and
people ruled.[8] In Foucault's view, what counts as "sex," as well as
how we interpret its meaning, is determined by complex and — without meticulous deconstructive historical analysis — largely invisible
forces. Power therefore creates, produces, sexual desire as well as represses it; and in Foucault's view, power produces and constitutes
sexual desire much more than it represses it. What this means is
that cultural and social forces shape our sexual desires, so that what
is sexually charged (whether thin bodies or plump ones, uncovered
breasts or covered, broad shoulders or great height or whatever) in
one era or place may not be in another.

Foucault rejected, then, the so-called "repressive hypothesis" as an
explanation of the eighteenth- and nineteenth-century Western experience of sexuality. He denied that the Victorian era had been an era
of sexual repression and socially enforced silence about sex. He argued, on the contrary, that it had been a time of a veritable explosion
of discourse about sex and an expanding deployment of sexuality.
This is why the questions that interested him were not "Why are
we repressed?" but, "Why do we say that we are repressed?" and
within this, not "Why was sex associated with sin for such a long
time?" but, "Why do we burden ourselves today with so much guilt
for having made sex a sin?"[9] Since the key to these questions was,
Foucault thought, to be found in a study of the history of discourse,
he began with an examination of what he considered a Western impulse to discover the "truth" about sex. In his view, this included a
striking Western compulsion to self-examination and self-reporting
about sexual experience, whether in the language and discourse of
religion, medicine, psychiatry, or criminal justice.

To make sense of the connections between power, sexuality, and
truth in the modern period, Foucault revised his project to include
a study of the variations on sexual themes in other historical peri-

---

7. Ibid., 1:151.
8. Ibid., 1:103.
9. Ibid., 1:8–9.

ods. His move to the past began with the thesis that a forerunner of modern discourse on sex was the seventeenth-century Christian ecclesiastical emphasis on confession. To put this in perspective, he reached further back in history, undertaking studies of pagan antiquity and of Christianity prior to the seventeenth century. Thus, volumes 2 and 3 of his *History of Sexuality* address the sexual mores of the fourth century B.C.E. Greeks and the first and second century C.E. Romans.[10] His thus far unpublished fourth volume, *The Confessions of the Flesh*, examines developments within Christianity. The contrasts he identified (and, as it turned out, the continuities) between the different historical periods shed some light on each other and on the overall Western pursuit of the kind of knowledge that promises power in relation to sex—what Foucault called the *scientia sexualis.*

Foucault came to the conclusion that the sexual morality of the Greeks and Romans did not differ substantially from Christian morality in terms of specific prescriptions. He rejected the commonly held view that the essential contrast between sexual ethics in antiquity and in early Christianity lay either in the permissiveness of Greco-Roman societies as distinguished from the strict sexual rules of the Christians, or in the ancient positive attitude toward sex as distinguished from a negative Christian assessment. Both traditions, he argued, contained prohibitions against incest, a preference for marital fidelity, a model of male superiority, caution regarding same-sex relations, respect for austerity, a positive regard for sexual abstinence, fears of male loss of strength through sexual activity, and hopes of access to special truths through sexual discipline. Nor were these basic prescriptions very different, he thought, from what could be found in post-seventeenth-century Western society.

Yet Foucault insisted that there were clear discontinuities, even ruptures, between these historical periods. The very reasons for moral solicitude regarding sexuality were different. On his reading, the ancients were concerned with health, beauty, and freedom,

---

10. Foucault, *The History of Sexuality*, vol. 2, *The Use of Pleasure*, trans. Robert Hurley (New York: Vintage Books, 1990); vol. 3, *The Care of the Self*, trans. Robert Hurley (New York: Vintage Books, 1988).

while Christians sought purity of heart before God; and bourgeois moderns aimed at their own self-idealization. The Greeks valued self-mastery; Christians struggled for self-understanding; and modern Western individuals scrutinized their feelings in order to secure compliance with standards of normality. Eroticism was channeled toward boys for the Greeks, women for the Christians, and a centrifugal movement in many directions for the Victorian and post-Victorian middle class. The Greeks feared the enslavement of the mind by the body; Christians dreaded the chaotic power of corrupted passion; post-nineteenth-century persons feared deviance and its consequent shame. Sexual morality was an aesthetic ideal, a personal choice, for an elite in antiquity; it became a universal ethical obligation under Christianity; and it was exacted as a modern social requirement under the power of the modern family and the management of the modern professional.

Foucault's study of the history of sexuality left open the question with which he had become preoccupied: How did contemporary Western culture come to believe that sexuality is the key to individual identity? How did sex become more important than love, and almost more important than life? Foucault exposed the lack of freedom in past constructs of sexuality, and he critiqued past formulations of sexual prescriptions. But his presentation of current strategies for sexual liberation yielded no less skeptical a judgment. He suggested, rather, that however historically relative sexual ethics may be, moral solicitude regarding sexuality is not in every respect a mistake.

Catherine MacKinnon: Historical Silences/Gendered Violence

Many Western feminists have shared Foucault's convictions that sexuality is socially constructed and the body is a site of power. Like Foucault, they have exposed the relentless influences of medicine, education, and psychology in determining post-eighteenth-century sexual mores. With Foucault, they have emphasized discourse as a key to identifying underlying forces that link power, sexuality, and identity. But many feminists fault Foucault for not extending his analytics of power to gender. Legal scholar Catherine MacKinnon, for example, opposes a Foucault-style history of desire on the grounds that his unacknowledged desiring subject is male.[11] A history of sexuality that emphasizes sexual desire and change misses the stark enduring aspects of history—that is, the unrelenting sexual abuse of women. History, then, remains silent regarding sexual exploitation, harassment, battery, and rape. Without attention to these unchanging experiences of women, MacKinnon argues, there can be no accurate analysis of sex and power, and indeed no real history of sexuality.

A feminist theory of sexuality, according to MacKinnon, "locates sexuality within a theory of gender inequality."[12] That is, it addresses sexuality not as constructed by a diffuse multiplicity of powers (in Foucault's sense), but "as a social construct of male power: defined by men, forced on women, and constitutive of the meaning of gender."[13] As a result, gendered hierarchy has been at the core of the "sexual" in Western culture. This is the past that historians must expose. Without it, they are likely to promote (with continuing dire consequences for women) the stance that all sex can be good if only it is socially reconstructed with ideas of freedom, if only it is liberated from ideologies of what is allowed and not allowed. MacKinnon's proposal for a feminist history of sexuality looks very different from Foucault's history, even though it begins with some of the same assumptions regarding the social construction of sex.

Evolutionary Histories: Sexuality and Change

Foucault and MacKinnon represent interpretations of the history of sexuality and sexual ethics that deny the achievement, though not the possibility, of progress. They refuse to applaud advances in understandings of sexuality or to sanctify the present as enlightened and free. To some extent, they even reject notions of change in history—Foucault arguing for different, but not causally or ideationally connected, historical perspectives; and MacKinnon focusing on similarities across time that represent a failure to change. Others,

---

11. See Catherine A. MacKinnon, *A Feminist Theory of the State* (Cambridge, MA: Harvard University Press, 1989), 126–54; "Does Sexuality Have a History?" in *Discourses of Sexuality*, ed. Domna Stanton, 117–36.

12. MacKinnon, *A Feminist Theory of the State*, 127.

13. Ibid., 128.

however, have charted an evolutionary process across the Western history of ideas about sex and the moral norms that should govern it. Those who believe that contemporary sexual revolutions have liberated individuals and their sexual possibilities belong here. So do those who acknowledge the significance of advances in biology and psychology and find appropriate historical adjustments in philosophical and theological ethics. Others do not necessarily report what they judge to be real progress, but they nonetheless identify evolutionary changes. Key representatives of an evolutionary kind of interpretive history include Edward Shorter, John D'Emilio and Estelle Freedman, and Richard Posner.

The historical narratives produced by these and other scholars have in common two things: a strong interest in economic developments and a turn to sources other than traditional forms of philosophical and theological discourse. Population statistics, employment patterns, personal diaries and memoirs, physicians' journals, church and court records of marriages, births, infant mortality, and so forth, all yield trends that illuminate major changes in Western European and North American sexual practices and beliefs. In Shorter's *The Making of the Modern Family*, the story of the Western family since the seventeenth century is a story of broken ties.[14] Under the influence of modern capitalism, families lost interest in traditional kinship, generational, and wider community interaction. Preferring romantic love, intense mother-infant bonding, and the close intimacy of the nuclear family, a "shield of privacy" made the family its own isolated world.[15] The family was thus gradually transformed from a productive and reproductive unit into an emotional unit, chosen for the individual freedom and fulfillment it promised. In Shorter's telling, the story ends ironically with the destabilization of the bond between spouses and the "destruction of the nest" of the nuclear family, for soon women move out, and children move quickly away.[16]

---

14. Edward Shorter, *The Making of the Modern Family* (New York: Basic Books, 1977). There are multiple studies available on the history of marriage and family. See chapter 7 below for a fuller consideration of these.

15. Shorter, *The Making of the Modern Family*, 5.

16. Ibid., 277–79.

In D'Emilio and Freedman's *Intimate Matters*, the more specific focus is on sexuality in United States history.[17] Attempting to combine their own research with the findings of highly specialized studies done by others, their goal is a "synthetic, interpretive narrative."[18] What they provide, then, is an account of a change from colonial family-centered reproductive systems, to "romantic, intimate, yet conflicted," marriages in the nineteenth century, and then to contemporary "commercialized" sexuality in which "sexual relations are expected to provide personal identity and individual happiness, apart from reproduction."[19] The story ends with political crisis: The apparent freeing of sex from institutional constraints fails to gain a stable consensus, and contemporary political controversy shows just how vulnerable the sexual sphere is to conflict, confusion, and manipulation.

In *Sex and Reason*, Richard Posner constructs a narrative of change in Western views of sexuality based on what he calls an "economic theory of sexuality."[20] Posner relies heavily on economic analysis both to describe the practice of sex and to evaluate legal and ethical norms in its regard. There are, he argues, three stages in the evolution of sexual morality, and they correlate with the status of women in a given society. In the first stage, women's occupation is that of a "simple breeder." When this is the case, companionate marriage is an unlikely possibility, and practices that are considered "immoral" are likely to flourish (for example, prostitution, adultery, homosexual liaisons). The second stage begins when women's occupation expands to include "child rearer and husband's companion." Here, companionate marriage becomes a possibility, and because of this, "immoral" practices that endanger it are vehemently condemned. When companionate marriage is idealized as the preferred and perhaps only model for everyone, societies become puritanical in their efforts to promote and protect it. In stage three, women's roles are further

---

17. John D'Emilio and Estelle B. Freedman, *Intimate Matters: A History of Sexuality in America* (New York: Harper & Row, 1988).

18. Ibid., xiv.

19. Ibid., xi–xii.

20. Richard A. Posner, *Sex and Reason* (Cambridge, MA: Harvard University Press, 1992), 3, 173–80. For a critical review of Posner's perspective, see Martha M. Nussbaum, *Sex and Social Justice* (New York: Oxford University Press, 1999), chapter 14.

enlarged to include "market employment." Marriages are fewer, but where they exist they are companionate. Other forms of sexual relationship, previously considered "immoral," no longer appear either immoral or abnormal.

There have, of course, been critics of all of these evolutionary theories. Opposition is based on disagreements regarding empirical data, its selection and interpretation, and controversies regarding the importance of theoretical discourse (as opposed to or in addition to empirical data) in historical analysis of the meaning and practice of sexuality.[21] Given the interest, however, in this kind of social history, studies like these have multiplied in the last two decades, frequently combining social-scientific resources with an examination of historical discourses about sex. They are as likely to draw on literature and the graphic arts as they are on population statistics or philosophical treatises. Many of these studies contribute to large narrative schemes, but that is not their purpose. Their focus is frequently limited to local historical periods and places, or to one aspect of human sexual experience such as homosexual relations, prostitution, or adolescent sexual activity.

Keeping in mind the difficulties and the possibilities of historical research for gaining perspective on sexual practice and ethical norms, we still need some overview of Western ideas about sex and morality. History in this regard offers not only a background, and not only a genealogy or archaeology of ideas, but a potential dialogue partner in the search for a contemporary sexual ethic.

Sexual Ethics in the West:
Historical Perspective

Given the limited aims of this volume, my focus here is on Western philosophical, religious, and to some extent medical, traditions of sexual ethics. The central strands of this history can be traced

---

21. See, for example, Louise A. Tilly, Joan W. Scott, and Miriam Cohen, "Women's Work and European Fertility Patterns," *Journal of Interdisciplinary History* 6 (Winter 1976): 447–76; Laqueur, "Sexual Desire and the Market Economy During the Industrial Revolution," in *Discourses of Sexuality*, ed. Domna Stanton, 185–215.

to classical Greece and Rome, Judaism, and early and later developments in Christianity. This by no means signals a view that other religious and cultural traditions are not important to the history of the West. Islam, for example, has not only existed in Western culture at significant points in history; it has contributed to developments in Western thought (as when Islamic scholars influenced the interpretation of Aristotle in the Middle Ages). Native American beliefs and practices obviously count as important traditions in the West, as do traditions retrieved by African Americans and, more recently, Asian Americans. Still, in developing a sexual ethic for Western culture, there can be no doubt that there is a dominant history to be dealt with, a history for the most part resistant to modification by coexisting subcultures. "Cross-cultural" considerations will, however, ultimately be important to our reflections, not only as they relate to cultures far away but to cultures that dwell in the West itself.[22]

Sexuality in Antiquity: The Legacy of Greece and Rome

The Ethos: General Attitudes and Practice[23]

Ancient Greece and Rome shared a general acceptance of sex as a natural part of life. Both were permissive regarding the sexual behavior

---

22. See chapter 3 below.

23. I draw here on a variety of historical studies, significant among which are: David Cohen, *Law, Sexuality, and Society: The Enforcement of Morality in Classical Athens* (New York: Cambridge University Press, 1991); Kenneth J. Dover, *Greek Popular Morality in the Time of Plato and Aristotle* (Berkeley: University of California Press, 1974); Dover, *Greek Homosexuality* (Cambridge, MA: Harvard University Press, 1978); Foucault, *The History of Sexuality*, vols. 2 and 3; John Boswell, *Christianity, Social Tolerance, and Homosexuality: Gay People in Western Europe from the Beginning of the Christian Era to the Fourteenth Century* (Chicago: University of Chicago Press, 1980); John T. Noonan, *Contraception: A History of Its Treatment by the Catholic Theologians and Canonists*, enlarged ed. (Cambridge, MA: Belknap Press of Harvard University Press, 1986); Roger Just, *Women in Athenian Law and Life* (New York: Routledge, 1989); Otto Kiefer, *Sexual Life in Ancient Rome* (New York: AMS Press, 1975; reprint of 1934 ed.); R. MacMullen, *Roman Social Relations 50 B.C. to A.D. 284* (New Haven, CT: Yale University Press, 1974); Sarah Pomeroy, *Goddesses, Whores, Wives, and Slaves: Women in Classical Antiquity* (New York: Schocken Books, 1975); John J. Winkler, *The Constraints of Desire: The Anthropology of Sex and Gender in Ancient Greece* (New York: Routledge, 1990); Rosemary Radford Ruether, *Christianity and the Making of the Modern Family: Ruling Ideologies, Diverse Realities* (Boston: Beacon, 2000), chapter 1; Ross Shepard Kraemer and Mary Rose D'Angelo, eds., *Women and Christian Origins* (New York: Oxford University Press, 1999), Part I. These sources are important sometimes for their disagreements as well as their agreements.

of men. In Athens, for example, the only clear proscriptions applicable to citizen-class men were against incest, bigamy, and adultery insofar as it violated the property of another man. One focus of concern in the two sexual cultures was significantly different, however. For the Greeks, adult male love of adolescent boys occupied a great deal of public attention, while the Romans focused public concern on heterosexual marriage as the foundation of social life (although both Greeks and Romans knew same-sex relations, and heterosexual marriage was important also for the survival of the family among the Greeks). Unfortunately, almost any generalizations about either ancient Greece or Rome are questionable given the diversity of contexts and historical periods that are part of the separate as well as the shared histories of both.[24]

Marriage for both Greeks and Romans was monogamous. In neither Greece or Rome, however, was sex confined to marriage. Male human nature was generally assumed to be bisexual, and the poly-erotic needs of men were taken for granted. Concubinage, both male and female prostitution, and the sexual use of slaves by citizen-class men were all commonly accepted. In Rome, women as well as men of the elite classes "sought erotic satisfaction from partners other than legitimate spouses."[25] Nonetheless, Roman culture is sometimes today described as "polygynous," since by far more men than women established enduring liaisons with individuals other than their marriage partners.

Greece and Rome were male-dominated societies, and for citizens a gendered double standard prevailed in sexual morality. Both Greek and Roman brides but not bridegrooms were expected to be virgins. Generally women were considered intellectually inferior to men. In

---

24. See Judith P. Hallett, "Women's Lives in the Ancient Mediterranean," in *Women and Christian Origins*, ed. R. S. Kraemer and M. R. D'Angelo, 19. Hallett differentiates what we know more readily about Athens, for example, from what we know about other Greek societies and city-states, and what we know about Alexander the Great's Hellenistic empire from what we know about both Greece and Rome after the Roman Empire became the context for both. I point my readers to this essay, since it is not possible to take account of all levels of diversity in my own brief consideration here.

25. Ibid., 31. This does not mean, however, that no marriages were marked by romantic love, but at least in ancient Greece these seem to be the exception rather than the rule.

addition, husbands and wives were often unequal in age (wives were much younger) and in education. Nonetheless, gender differences were mitigated by a blurring of typical male and female role assignments for the deities and for some members of the elite classes.[26] In other words, male/female similarities as well as dissimilarities were acknowledged. Female goddesses in both Greece and Rome were quite capable of warrior activity as well as dispensing wisdom. Roman girls from elite families, with elite male blood relatives, were sometimes educated along with their brothers, and they exercised some political influence after marriage. Lower class women could be gainfully employed (for example, as tailors). By and large, however, these construals of gender roles did not add up to gender equality. Women were still dependent on men and on their relationships with men for their status in society. A Roman woman could inherit property, but only if she had a legal guardian for the administration of the property.[27]

Gender dissimilarities outweighed similarities overall. Greek wives had little or no public life, though they were given the power and responsibility of managing the home. In Rome the ideal of the *pater familias* (and *patria potestas*) reached fulfillment. Women were still largely under the control of men. And although by the first century C.E. women in Rome achieved some economic and political freedom, they could not assume the sexual freedom traditionally granted to men.

Male homosexuality was accepted in both Greek and Roman antiquity. Especially for the Greeks, however, it was less a matter of some men being sexually attracted only to men (or more likely, boys) than of men generally being attracted to beautiful individuals, whether male or female (though most often among the citizen class, males were considered the more beautiful). Men were expected to marry, in order to produce an heir. Yet love and friendship, and sometimes sex, between men were considered to be of a higher order than anything possible within marriage — for between men there existed

---

26. Ibid., 17–32.
27. Ibid., 18. Hallett notes that the emperor Augustus, hoping to provide an incentive to women to bear children, introduced legislation that allowed freeborn women to be exempted from the requirements of legal guardianship after they had three children (and freed women to achieve this same exemption after giving birth to four). Hallett adds, "but most women did not qualify for this distinction."

gender equality despite differences in age. Same-sex relations were not, however, wholly unproblematic, as cultural cautions against male passivity attested.[28] Sexual relations between men and boys, if both belonged to the citizen class, were preferably restricted to certain physical positions, ones that would not represent total passivity or submission on the part of the boys (and certainly not on the part of adult men); and these relations were to cease when a boy reached a certain age. Moreover, the prevailing ethos tended not to support a positive evaluation of sexual relationships between women.[29] Lesbian relationships were often judged negatively because they counted as adultery (since women belonged to their husbands) or because a cultural preoccupation with male sexual desire made sex between women appear unnatural.

In both Greece and Rome abortion and infanticide were common forms of contraception. At various times concerns to limit population influenced Greek sexual practices, while efforts to improve a low birth rate in later Imperial Rome, as I have noted, led to legal incentives to marry and to procreate. Divorce was readily available in ancient Greece and (eventually) in Rome, and both cultures attempted to provide for the resulting economic needs of divorced women.

Historians today tend to dispute the belief that the last years of the Roman Empire saw a greater weakening of sexual norms, a sexual dissipation at the heart of a general moral and political decline. The favored historical reading is now just the opposite, that general suspicion of sexuality grew as the Empire aged, and normative restrictions of sexual activity increased. In part, this was the result of the gradual influence of philosophical theories that questioned the value of sexual activity and emphasized the dangers of its consequences.

---

28. See, for example, Foucault, *The History of Sexuality*, 2:193–97; Boswell, *Christianity, Social Tolerance, and Homosexuality*, 74–82.

29. There is a great deal of ambiguity on this issue, however. See Boswell, *Christianity, Social Tolerance, and Homosexuality*, 82–84; Pomeroy, *Goddesses, Whores, Wives, and Slaves*, passim; Martti Nissinen, *Homoeroticism in the Biblical World: A Historical Perspective*, trans. Kirsi Stjerna (Minneapolis: Fortress, 1998), 74–79; Bernadette Brooten, *Love Between Women: Early Christian Responses to Female Homoeroticism* (Chicago: University of Chicago Press, 1996).

Greek and Roman Philosophical Appraisals of Sexuality

Foucault and others have identified two problems regarding sexuality that preoccupied philosophers in antiquity: the natural force of sexual desire with its consequent tendency to excess, and the power relations involved in the seemingly necessary active/passive roles viewed as intrinsic to sexual activity.[30] The first problem contributed to the formulation of an ideal of self-mastery within a broad-gauge aesthetics of existence. Self-mastery could be achieved, it was thought, through a regimen of life that included diet, exercise, and various practices of self-discipline. The second problem yielded criteria for love and sex between men and boys. Active and passive roles were not a problem in adult male relations with women or with slaves, for the inferior passive role was considered natural to women, including wives, and to servants or slaves. As I have already suggested, however, these roles could be a problem for citizen-class boys who must eventually come to be equal with adult men. The solution, according to some philosophers (for example, Demosthenes[31]), was to regulate the age of boy lovers and the circumstances and goals of their liaisons with men. Others (for example, Plato[32]) preferred the transcendence and ultimate elimination of physical sex in erotic relations between men and boys.

Aspects of Greek and Roman philosophical thought about sex that were to have great influence on subsequent Western speculation included a distrust of sexual desire and a judgment of the inferior status of sexual pleasure among other human pleasures, in line with the inferior status accorded to the body in relation to the soul. Sex was not considered evil in itself, but it was thought to be potentially dangerous: not only in its excess but in its natural violence (orgasm was

---

30. Foucault, *The History of Sexuality*, vols. 1 and 2. See also references in note 22 above.

31. Demosthenes, *The Erotic Essay*, trans. N. W. Dewitt and N. J. Dewitt (Cambridge, MA: Harvard University Press, 1949).

32. Plato's preference for transcendence beyond sexual desire is to be found most explicitly in Socrates's rendition of Diotima's teaching in the *Symposium*, 201d–212c; also in the general theme of the *Phaedo;* and in the *Laws* VIII. Alternate views held more or less by Plato can be found in Alcibiades's speech in the *Symposium*, 215b–222c, and in the *Phaedrus.*

sometimes described as a form of epileptic seizure), and in its ex-
penditure of virile energy (it was thought to have a weakening effect
on men in particular — hence the prohibition of sexual relations for
soldiers before battle). Lastly there was its association with death (nature's provision for immortality through procreation made sex also a
reminder of mortality).[33]

The Pythagoreans in the sixth century B.C.E. advocated purity of
the body for the sake of the culture of the soul. The force of their position was felt in the later thinking of Socrates and Plato. Although
Plato moved away from a general hostility to bodily pleasure, he made
a careful distinction between lower and higher pleasures, identifying
sexual pleasure among the lower.[34] While this meant that the desire
for sexual pleasure required self-mastery over it, Plato nonetheless
advocated unleashing, not finally restraining, the power of eros (in
its highest manifestations) for the sake of uniting the human spirit
with the highest realms of good, beauty, and truth. Insofar as bodily
pleasures can be taken up into this pursuit, there was no objection
to them. But Plato thought that sexual intercourse diminished the
power of eros for the contemplation and love of higher realities; it ultimately even compromised the possibility of tenderness and respect
in individual relationships of love.

Aristotle, too, distinguished lower and higher pleasures, placing
pleasures of touch at the bottom of the scale, shared as they are in
common with animals.[35] Less world-denying than Plato, Aristotle
advocated moderation in sex rather than transcendence. However,
the highest forms of friendship and love, and of happiness in the
contemplation of the life of one's friend, seemed no longer to need
the incorporation of sexual activity or even of Platonic eros.[36] Aristotle never conceived of the possibility of equality or mutuality in
relationships between women and men, and he opposed the utopian
design for this that Plato had offered in the *Republic* and *Laws*.

---

33. See Foucault, *The History of Sexuality*, 2:126–39. Foucault draws these generalizations from a number of texts, e.g., Hippocrates, *The Seed*; Plato, *Philebus*,
Symposium, *Timaeus*, and *Laws*; Aristotle, *De Anima* II.4.415a-b.
34. See *Republic* IX, as well as references given in note 32.
35. See Aristotle, *Nicomachean Ethics*, III.1118a.
36. Aristotle, *Nicomachean Ethics*, VIII-X.

Of all Greco-Roman philosophies, Stoicism probably had the great-est explicit impact on later developments in Western thought about sex. Musonius Rufus, Epictetus, Seneca, and Marcus Aurelius, for example, held strong views on the power of the human will to regu-late emotion and on the desirability of such regulation for the sake of inner peace. Sexual desire, like the passions of fear and anger, was by itself considered to be irrational, disruptive, liable to excess. There-fore it needed, they said, to be moderated and taken up into a larger whole of human experience and intention. It ought never to be in-dulged in for its own sake, but only insofar as it served a rational purpose, thereby aiming toward its real end. Procreation of offspring was that purpose, that end. Hence, even in marriage sexual inter-course was morally good only when it was engaged in for the sake of procreation.[37] Thus came to be formulated what others later named the "procreative norm" for sex.

With the later Stoics there emerged, according to Foucault, the "conjugalization" of sexual relations.[38] That is, sexual desire repre-sented a fundamental natural drive not only to procreation but to the companionship of spouses. The norm governing sexual activity must therefore be "no sex outside of marriage." Marriage became the context for self-control and the fashioning of the virtuous life. It was considered a natural duty, excused only in special circumstances, such as when an individual undertook the responsibilities of life as a philosopher. Plutarch took the position, then, that marriage, not homosexual relationships, was the primary locus for erotic love and for friendship.[39]

Overall, however, the Greco-Roman legacy to Western sexual ethics held little of the freedom for sexuality that had characterized ancient Greece. The dominant themes carried through to later tra-ditions were ones of skepticism and control. Sexuality was seldom integrated into the fullest insights of Greek and Roman thinkers

---

37. See, e.g., Musonius Rufus, *Reliquiae*; Seneca, *Fragments*, no. 84; Epictetus, *En-ciridion*. For a still useful study of the influence of Stoic authors on early Christian writers who addressed these matters, see John T. Noonan, *Contraception*, pp. 46–49.

38. Foucault, *The History of Sexuality*, 3:166.

39. See Plutarch, *Dialogue on Love* and *Marriage Precepts*.

regarding human relationships. Whether such an integration is possible in principle has been a tacit question for other traditions
as well.

Judaism: Sexuality, Morality, and Religion

Like most religious and cultural traditions, the history of Jewish
thought regarding sexuality is complex and marked by profound tensions.[40] Many of these tensions were present from the beginning in
Judaism's foundational document, the Hebrew Bible. Narratives (like
the story of Ruth) stand in tension with strict legal codes; sexual
transgressions (such as David's adultery) are taken up into God's plan
for the future of Israel; erotic desire is subordinated to communal
concerns (though not in the Song of Songs); purity laws coexist with
indifference to women's perspectives on rape (as in Deut. 22:28–
29).[41] Tensions did not disappear in the Talmudic writings of the
rabbis or in any of the historical periods of Jewish history, though
some strands of the tradition were emphasized and conflicts were
submerged. Hence, while in all the branches of Judaism the attitude
toward sex has been an enduringly positive one, it has never been
without ambivalence. The sexual instinct is considered a gift from
God, a natural part of human life, essential to the demographic survival of a frequently beleaguered people. Yet this instinct holds danger,
both because it is close to the divine and it is liable to loss of control.

In contrast to many neighboring religions, the Jews believed in
a god who is beyond sexuality but whose plan for creation makes

---

40. I draw here on such key (though not always univocal in their assessments) studies as: David Biale, *Eros and the Jews: From Biblical Israel to Contemporary America*
(New York: Basic Books, 1992); Elliot N. Dorff and Louis E. Newman, eds., *Contempo-*
rary Jewish Ethics and Morality: A Reader (New York: Oxford University Press, 1995),
271–327; Louis M. Epstein, *Sex Laws and Customs in Judaism* (New York: Block,
1948); David M. Feldman, *Marital Relations, Birth Control, and Abortion in Jewish*
Law (New York: Schocken Books, 1974); Michael Kaufman, *Love, Marriage, and Fam-*
ily in Jewish Law and Tradition (Northvale, NJ: Jason Aronson, 1992); Maurice Lamm,
The Jewish Way in Love and Marriage (San Francisco: Harper & Row, 1980); David Novak, *Jewish Social Ethics*, chap. 4 (New York: Oxford University Press, 1992), 84–103;
Judith Plaskow, *Standing Again at Sinai: Judaism from a Feminist Perspective*, chap. 5
(San Francisco: Harper & Row, 1990), 170–210; Plaskow, "Embodiment and Ambiva-
lence: A Jewish Feminist Perspective," in *Embodiment, Morality, and Medicine*, ed. Lisa
Sowle Cahill and Margaret A. Farley (Dordrecht: Kluwer Academic, 1995), 23–36.

41. See Biale, *Eros and the Jews*, chap. 1, 11–32; Plaskow, *Standing Again at Sinai*,
178–85.

marriage and fertility holy and the subject of religious duty. At the heart of Judaism's historical tradition of sexual morality is a religious injunction to marry. The command to marry holds within it a command to procreate, and it assumes a patriarchal model for marriage and family. These two elements in the tradition, the duty to procreate and its patriarchal context, account for many of its specific sexual regulations and the ethical commentaries that have surrounded them.

While at the core of the imperative to marry is the command to procreate, marriage has been considered a duty also because it conduces to the holiness of the partners. Holiness includes more than the channeling of sexual desire, although it means this as well; but it includes the companionship and mutual fulfillment of spouses. Monogamous lifelong marriage was valued from the beginning (though other structured relationships were long taken for granted); in time it became the custom as well as an ideal. In some historical periods, however, the command to procreate stood in tension with the value given to the marriage relationship as such. The laws of *onah*, of marital rights and duties, aimed to make sex a nurturant of love. But polygyny, concubinage, and divorce and remarriage were accepted for a long time as solutions to a childless marriage. In the eleventh century polygyny was finally banned by Rabbenu Gershom of Mainz, and in the twelfth century Maimonides explicitly banned concubinage.[42]

Throughout the Jewish tradition there has been a marked difference in the treatment of women's and men's sexuality.[43] In part, this was because of women's subordinate role in the family and in society. Ross Kraemer cautions, however, against painting too gloomy a picture of the lives of Jewish women, especially in the first century C.E.[44] The actual stories of some Jewish women indicate women's influence in shaping their communities and their frequent appearance

---

42. See Novak, *Jewish Social Ethics*, 93.

43. Plaskow, 171–77.

44. See Ross Shepard Kraemer, "Jewish Women and Christian Origins," and "Women's Judaism(s) at the Beginning of Christianity," in *Women and Christian Origins*, ed. R. S. Kraemer and M. R. D'Angelo, 35–79. Kraemer critiques many standard historical presentations of Jewish women in this era as serving a hidden agenda, one that will make the attitudes and actions of Jesus (and early Christianity) look liberating.

in the public sphere. Still, in the sexual sphere, some key differences
in the social control of women and men are apparent. The regulation
of women's sexuality was considered necessary to the stability and
the continuity of the family. Premarital and extramarital sex, even
rape, were legally different for women and for men. In the biblical
period, husbands but not wives could initiate divorce (Deut. 24:1–
4), and though the rabbis later tried to find ways to allow a wife to
initiate divorce (and hence to force a husband to divorce his wife),
the fundamental imbalance of power between husband and wife on
this issue was not changed. Adultery was understood as violating the
property rights of a husband, and it could be punished by the death
of both parties. Women's actions and dress were regulated in order
to restrict their potential for luring men into illicit sex. The laws
of *onah* required men to respect the sexual needs of their wives, but
the laws of *niddah* (menstrual purity) had the symbolic consequence,
however unintended, of associating women with defilement.

The laws of *onah*, in regulating a man's sexual obligations to his
wife, revealed some of the most affirmative attitudes of Judaism toward sexuality. Although formulated in a patriarchal context (hence,
they were male-defined), they aimed to take account of women's
needs and to protect women's interests. Since it was believed that
women, being more passive than men, would not initiate sex with
the same freedom as men, husbands were admonished to consider
and respond to not only their own desires and impulses, but those of
their wives. Thus they might together, with appropriate moderation
on a husband's part and with observance of the laws of menstrual
purity, celebrate sexuality with tenderness and pleasure.

The Jewish sexual ethic, then, is traditionally an ethic that affirms sexuality within heterosexual marriage. Sex outside of marriage
(or recognized alternative heterosexual structures) has generally been
forbidden or at least discouraged (there is no explicit legislation
against premarital sex or against a married man having sexual relations with a single woman, but ethical norms have been against
these). Masturbation, incest, adultery, male homosexuality, have all
been considered serious transgressions. Lesbian relations were not
regulated by biblical law, and in rabbinic literature they were treated

far less seriously than male homosexuality (in part because they involve no "improper emission of seed").

The tensions in the Jewish tradition from the beginning, especially between its overall affirmative attitude toward sex and its concern for the dangers of the sexual impulse, grew sharply when Jewish thinkers were influenced by Hellenistic philosophers. In the first and second centuries C.E., rabbinic Judaism was not immune to the suspicion of sex that, with the rise of Stoic philosophies and the advent of certain religious movements from the East, permeated Middle Eastern cultures. Jewish writers had considered the sexual instinct to be a gift from God, but they also named it the "evil impulse" (*yetzer ha-ra*). That is, they believed that it was an impulse in particular need of control; and without careful, even ascetic, discipline it could triumph over an individual's possibilities of faithfulness to God and to the community. This fit well with the Stoic pessimism regarding sexual desire, and it moved Judaism of the time toward a more negative view of sex than had been central to its tradition. Correspondingly, it exacerbated the tendency to control the female body (in order to limit temptation for men) and to cast suspicion on sex — certainly beyond, but even within, marriage.

Judaism comprehends multiple rich traditions regarding sexuality through the ages. Yet tensions within the Jewish tradition remain as issues for contemporary Judaism. The Jewish community, like other religious communities, faces a growing pluralism regarding questions of premarital sex, gender equality, and same-sex relations. Current conflicts involve the interpretation of traditional values, analysis of contemporary situations, and the incorporation of hitherto unrepresented perspectives — in particular, those of women and of gay men and lesbians.

Christian Traditions

Like other religious and cultural traditions, including Judaism, the teachings of the Christian tradition regarding sex are complex and subject to multiple influences; and they have changed and developed through succeeding generations. Christianity does not begin with a systematic code of ethics. The teachings of Jesus and his followers, as recorded in the New Testament, provide a central focus for the moral life of Christians in the command to love God and neighbor. Beyond this, the Christian Testament (or Second Testament) offers grounds for a sexual ethic that (1) values marriage and procreation on the one hand and singleness and celibacy on the other; (2) gives as much or more importance to internal attitudes and thoughts as to external actions; and (3) affirms a sacred symbolic meaning for sexual intercourse, yet both subordinates it as a value to other human values and finds in it a possibility for evil. As for unanimity on more specific sexual rules, this is difficult to find in the beginnings of a religion whose founder taught as an itinerant prophet and whose sacred texts are formulated in "the more tense world" of particular disciples, a group of wandering preachers.[45]

Early Influences on Christian Understandings of Sex

Christianity emerged in the late Hellenistic Age, when even Judaism was influenced by the dualistic anthropologies of Stoic philosophy and Gnostic religions. Unlike the Greek and Roman philosophers of the time, Christianity's main concern was not the art of self-mastery and not the preservation of the city or the Empire. Unlike major strands of Judaism at the time, its focus was less on the solidity and continuity of life in this world than on the continuity between this world and a life to come. Yet early Christian writers were profoundly influenced both by Judaism and by Greco-Roman philosophy. With Judaism they shared a theistic approach to morality, an affirmation of creation as the context of marriage and procreation, and an ideal of single-hearted love. With the Stoics they shared a suspicion of bodily passion and a respect for reason as a guide to the moral life. With the Greeks, Romans, and Jews, Christian thinkers assumed

---

45. Peter Brown, *The Body and Society: Men, Women, and Sexual Renunciation in Early Christianity* (New York: Columbia University Press, 1988), 42–43. See also Wayne A. Meeks, *The Moral World of the First Christians* (Philadelphia: Westminster, 1986); Meeks, *The Origins of Christian Morality: The First Two Centuries* (New Haven, CT: Yale University Press, 1993), especially chaps. 3, 4, 7, 8; Constance F. Parvey, "The Theology and Leadership of Women in the New Testament," in Rosemary Radford Ruether, ed., *Religion and Sexism: Images of Women in the Jewish and Christian Traditions* (New York: Simon & Schuster, 1974), 117–49; Elisabeth Schüssler Fiorenza, "Discipleship and Patriarchy: Early Christian Ethos and Christian Ethics in a Feminist Perspective," *Annual of the Society of Christian Ethics* (Missoula, MT: Scholars, 1982), 131–72.

and reinforced views of women as inferior to men — despite some signs of commitment to gender equality in the beginnings of Christianity as a movement. As Christianity struggled for its own identity, issues of sexual conduct were important, but there was no immediate agreement on how all of these issues would be resolved.

Gnosticism was a recurrent religious movement that influenced formulations of Christian sexual ethics for the first three centuries C.E.[46] Some Fathers of the church taught that there were two extreme positions among gnostics — one in opposition to all sexual intercourse and the other permitting any form of sexual intercourse so long as it was not procreative. The ascription of this kind of ascetic/libertine dichotomy seems not to be accurate, but in any case, Christian thinkers tried to avoid it.

What did prevail in Christian moral teaching was a doctrine that incorporated an affirmation that sex is good (because part of creation) but seriously flawed (because, as a result of a human cataclysmic "Fall," the force of sexual passion can no longer be controlled by reason). The Stoic position that sexual intercourse can be brought back under the rule of reason not by completely subduing it but by giving it a rational purpose (that is, procreation) made great sense to early Christian thinkers. The connection made between sexual intercourse and procreation was not the same as the Jewish affirmation of the importance of fecundity, but it was in harmony with it. Christian teaching could thus both affirm procreation as the central rationale for sexual union and advocate virginity as a praiseworthy option (indeed, the ideal option) for Christians who could choose it.

With the adoption of the Stoic norm for sexual intercourse, the direction of Christian sexual ethics was set for centuries to come. A sexual ethic that concerned itself primarily with affirming the good of procreation and thereby the good use of otherwise evil tendencies was, moreover, reinforced by the continued appearance of antagonists who played the same role the Gnostics had played. No sooner had Gnosticism begun to wane than, in

---

46. Noonan, *Contraception*, chap. 3. But see also Karen L. King, *What Is Gnosticism?* (Cambridge, MA: Belknap Press of Harvard University Press, 2003), esp. 123–24 and 201–8.

the fourth century, Manichaeanism emerged. It was largely in response to Manichaeanism that Augustine formulated his sexual
ethic, an ethic that continued and went beyond the Stoic elements already incorporated by Clement of Alexandria, Origen, Ambrose, and
Jerome.

St. Augustine: Legacy for Sexual Ethics[47]

Augustine argued against the Manichaeans in favor of the goodness
of marriage and procreation, though he shared with them a negative
view of sexual desire as in itself an evil passion (that is, distorted by
original sin). Because evil was for him, however, a "privation" of right
order (that is, something missing that should be there, or something
out of order in what is otherwise basically good[48]), he thought at first
that it was possible to reorder sexual desire according to reason, to integrate its meaning into a right and whole love of God and neighbor.
This, he maintained, could be done only when sexual intercourse is
within heterosexual marriage and for the purpose of procreation.[49]
Intercourse within marriage but without a procreative purpose is,
according to Augustine, sinful, though not necessarily mortally so.
Marriage, on the other hand, serves three "goods:" not only the good
of children, but also the goods of fidelity between spouses (as opposed
to adultery) and the indissolubility of their union (as opposed to divorce).[50] Augustine and many who followed him could wax eloquent

---

47. Key primary texts for Augustine's view of sexuality and ethics include: *On the
Goodness of Marriage* (401 C.E.); *On Holy Virginity* (401 C.E.); *A Literal Commentary
on Genesis* (401–14); *On Marriage and Concupiscence* (419–21 C.E.). Useful studies
relevant to Augustine's sexual ethics and to other early Church writers include: Brown,
The Body and Society; Rowan A. Greer, *Broken Lights and Mended Lives: Theology
and Common Life in the Early Church* (University Park: Pennsylvania State University Press, 1986), especially chap. 4; John Mahoney, *The Making of Moral Theology: A
Study of the Roman Catholic Tradition* (Oxford: Clarendon Press, 1987), chaps. 1–2;
Margaret R. Miles, *Augustine on the Body* (Missoula, MT: Scholars, 1979); Noonan,
Contraception, chaps. 1–6; Elaine Pagels, *Adam, Eve, and the Serpent* (New York: Random House, 1988); Paul Ramsey, "Human Sexuality in the History of Redemption,"
Journal of Religious Ethics 16 (Spring 1988): 56–86.
48. See, for example, Augustine, *On Free Choice of the Will* 1.1–8, 2.20; *Confessions*
5.10, 7.3–13. Augustine's position was developed as a refutation of the Manichaean
belief that evil can exist in itself, and that there is an ultimate principle of evil just as
there is an ultimate principle of good.
49. Augustine, *On the Goodness of Marriage* 6.
50. Augustine, *On the Goodness of Marriage* 32.

on the real and symbolic meanings of Christian marriage, but the valuation of sex was a different matter.

In his later writings against the Pelagians,[51] Augustine tried to clarify the place of disordered sexual desire in a theology of original sin. Although for Augustine Adam and Eve's original sin was a sin of the spirit (a sin of prideful disobedience), its consequences were most acutely present in the conflict between sexual desire and reasoned love of higher goods. Moreover, this loss of integrity in affectivity was passed on from one generation to another precisely through the mode of procreation — that is, sexual intercourse. In this debate Augustine argued that there is some evil in all sexual intercourse, even when it is within marriage and for the sake of procreation. Most of those who followed Augustine disagreed with this, but his basic formulation of a procreative ethic held sway in Christian moral teaching for centuries.

Some early Christian writers (for example, Augustine and John Chrysostom) also emphasized the Pauline purpose of marriage — that is, marriage as a remedy for lust (1 Corinthians 7:1–6). Such a position hardly served to foster a more optimistic view of sex, but it did offer a possibility for moral goodness in sexual intercourse without a direct relation to procreation. From the sixth to the eleventh century, however, Augustine's rationale was codified in Penitentials (that is, manuals for the guidance of confessors, providing lists of sins and their prescribed penances) with detailed prohibitions against adultery, fornication, oral and anal sex, masturbation, and even certain positions for sexual intercourse if they were thought to be departures from the procreative norm.[52] Gratian's great collection of canon law in the twelfth century contained rigorous regulations based on the persistently held principle that all sexual activity is evil unless it is between husband and wife and for the sake of procreation. A few voices (for example, Abelard and John Damascene) maintained that concupiscence (disordered desire) does not make sexual pleasure

---

51. See, for example, Augustine, *Marriage and Concupiscence; City of God* XIV.11–24; *Against Julian.*

52. See Pierre J. Payer, *Sex and the Penitentials: The Development of a Sexual Code 550–1150* (Toronto: University of Toronto Press, 1983), for a careful analysis of the context and content of the penitential tradition in its Irish, Frankish, and Anglo-Saxon expressions.

evil in itself, and that intercourse in marriage can be justified by the simple intention to avoid fornication.[53]

Early Christian writers easily combined negative judgments regarding sexual desire with negative judgments regarding women. Though the Eve of the canonical scriptures does not bear the same weight of responsibility for the Fall as the Eve of some apocryphal literature, her role was nonetheless frequently interpreted as that of a seducer of Adam. And whether or not women were consciously thought to be a threatening force, the great temptresses of men, they nonetheless appeared throughout Christian writings as a special agent of evil. Instead of losing an identification with pollution and defilement through the development of Christian thought, the notion of "woman" became theoretically entrenched as the dangerous "other" in theologies of original sin, of higher and lower nature, mind and body, rationality and desire. Even without attributions of evil, women were considered intellectually inferior to men, naturally more passive, less important in the movements of history, only derivatively and partially participants in the *imago dei*, the image of God. Sexuality was therefore essentially lodged in gendered hierarchical relations that prevented it from being integrated into the major theologies of grace.[54]

---

53. For an interesting overview of these centuries, with a focus on the prohibition of contraception, see Noonan, *Contraception*, chaps. 5–6. Karl Rahner offers a more nuanced view of "concupiscence" in *Theological Investigations*, vol. 1 (Baltimore: Helicon Press, 1961), 347–82.

54. Ironically, theology exalted women at the same time that it relegated them to inferior status. As symbols of virtue, however, women were more vulnerable than ever. Failing in the ideal reinforced an association with evil and confirmed a belief in their weakness and inferiority. Countless studies have explored the writings of Justin Martyr, Irenaeus, Tertullian, Origen, Jerome, Augustine, and others, with few examples to offset the negative conclusions about women. Greek fathers of the church, for example, found the *imago dei* in what they thought to be the nonsexual soul of both men and women, but they determined that it resided more fully in men in history since men, not women, were like God in their role of leadership. The Latin fathers pointed to the image of God in the combination of spirit and body; but while both men and women partook of the *imago dei* by reason of their spirit, only the male body was (in its activity and power) in the image of God. Hence, women shared in the image fully only insofar as they were corporally joined to men or virginally free from their bodies. It was left to Thomas Aquinas to establish the inferiority of women even in soul (*Summa Theologiae* I.91–92; II-II.149.4). See Rosemary Radford Ruether, "Misogynism and Virginal Feminism in the Fathers of the Church," in *Religion and Sexism*, ed. R. Ruether, 150–83; Kari

Overall, then, the Christian tradition in its early centuries developed a consistently negative and pessimistic view of sex, and a view of women as not equal to men despite the fact that Augustine and most of those who followed him were neither anti-body nor anti-marriage. To say that the view of sex was negative must be a qualified claim, of course, for the early tradition was frequently silent or vacillating on many questions of sexuality (for example, on the question of homosexuality); and there is little evidence that Christians in general were influenced by the more severe sexual attitudes of their leaders.[55] To say that the view of women was deprecating may also be qualified, for the earliest insight that "in Christ there is neither . . . male nor female" (Gal. 3:28) emerged from time to time. The direction and tone that the early centuries gave to the tradition's future, however, were unmistakable. What these writers were concerned about was freedom from bondage to desires that seemingly could not lead to God. In a quest for transformation of the body along with the spirit, even procreation did not appear very important. Hence, regulation of sexual activity, gender complementarity, and even the importance of the family were often overshadowed by the ideal of celibacy. As Peter Brown's massive study has shown, sexual renunciation served both eros and unselfish love, and it suited a worldview that broke boundaries with this world without rejecting it as evil.[56]

Thomas Aquinas: Sustaining the Tradition[57]

Thomas Aquinas wrote in the thirteenth century when rigorism regarding sex already prevailed in Christian teaching and church discipline. His remarkable synthesis of Christian theology did not

---

Børreson, *Subordination and Equivalence: The Nature and Role of Women in Augustine and Thomas Aquinas* (Washington, D.C.: University Press of America, 1981).

55. See John Boswell, *Christianity, Social Tolerance, and Homosexuality*, 206 and passim.

56. Brown, *The Body and Society*.

57. Key primary texts for Aquinas's teaching on sexuality include: *Summa Theologiae* I-II.22–48; I-II.81.1; II-II.151–56; *Summa Contra Gentiles* III.122.4 and 5. Useful secondary sources include Eleanor McLaughlin, "Equality of Souls, Inequality of Sexes: Women in Medieval Theology," in *Religion and Sexism*, ed. R. Ruether, 213–66; John G. Milhaven, "Thomas Aquinas on Sexual Pleasure," *Journal of Religious Ethics* 5 (1977): 157–81. See also Jean Porter, "Chastity as a Virtue," *Scottish Journal of Theology* 3 (2005): 285–301.

offer much that was innovative in the area of sexual ethics. Yet the
clarity of what he brought forward made his contribution significant
for the generations that followed. He taught that sexual desire is not
intrinsically evil, since no spontaneous bodily or emotional inclina-
tion is evil in itself; only when there is an evil moral choice is an
action morally evil. Consequent upon original sin, however, there is
in human nature a certain loss of order among natural human in-
clinations. Sexual passion is damaged by this disorder, but it is not
morally evil except insofar as its disorder is freely chosen.

Aquinas offered two rationales for the procreative norm which the
tradition had so far affirmed. One was the Augustinian argument that
sexual pleasure, in the "fallen" human person (as the result of original sin), hinders the best working of the mind. It must be brought
into some accord with reason by having an overriding value as its
goal. No less an end than procreation can justify it.[58] But secondly,
reason does not merely provide a good purpose for sexual pleasure. It
discovers this purpose through the anatomy and biological function
of sexual organs.[59] Hence, the norm of reason in sexual behavior requires not only the conscious intention to procreate but the accurate
and unimpeded (that is, noncontraceptive) physical process whereby
procreation is possible.

From the procreative norm followed other specific moral rules,
many of them aimed at the well-being of offspring that could result
from sexual intercourse. For example, Aquinas argued against fornication, adultery, and divorce on the grounds that children would
be deprived of a good context for their rearing. He considered sexual
acts that do not meet the requirements of heterosexual intercourse
immoral because they could not be procreative. Aquinas's treatment
of marriage contained only hints of new insight regarding the relation of sexual intercourse to marital love. He offered a theory of love
that had room for a positive incorporation of sexual union,[60] and he
suggested that marriage might be the basis of a maximum form of
friendship.[61]

---

58. Thomas Aquinas, *Summa Theologiae* I-II.34.1 ad 1.
59. Aquinas, *Summa Theologiae* II-II.154.11; *Summa Contra Gentiles* III.122.4–5.
60. Aquinas, *Summa Theologiae* II-II.26.11.
61. Aquinas, *Summa Contra Gentiles* III.123.

Though what had crystallized in the Middle Ages canonically and theologically would continue to influence Christian moral teaching into the indefinite future, the fifteenth century marked the beginning of significant change. Finding some grounds for opposing the prevailing Augustinian sexual ethic in the thirteenth century work of Albert the Great and in the general (if not specifically sexual) ethics of Aquinas, writers (for example, Denis the Carthusian and Martin LeMaistre) began to talk of the integration of spiritual love and sexual pleasure and of the intrinsic good of sexual pleasure as the opposite of the pain of its lack. This did not reverse the Augustinian tradition, but it weakened it. The effects of these new theories were felt in the controversies of the sixteenth century Reformation.

The Protestant Reformation: New Perspectives on Sexuality

Questions of sexual behavior played an important role in the Protestant Reformation. Clerical celibacy, for example, was challenged not just in its scandalous nonobservance but as a Christian ideal. Marriage and family replaced it among the reformers as the center of sexual gravity in the Christian life. Martin Luther and John Calvin were both deeply influenced by the Augustinian tradition regarding original sin and its consequences for human sexuality. Yet both developed a position on marriage that was not dependent on a procreative ethic. Like most of the Christian tradition, they affirmed marriage and human sexuality as part of the divine plan for creation and therefore good. But they shared Augustine's pessimistic view of fallen human nature and its disordered sex drive. Luther was convinced, however, that the necessary remedy for disordered desire is marriage.[62] And so the issue was joined over a key element in Christian sexual ethics. Luther, of course, was not the first to advocate marriage as the cure for unruly sexual desire, but he took on the

---

62. See Martin Luther, *On the Estate of Marriage* (1522). Other important primary texts of Luther relevant to his sexual ethics include *The Large Catechism* (1529) and *A Sermon on the Estate of Marriage* (1519). Useful secondary sources include Paul Althaus, *The Ethics of Martin Luther*, trans. Robert C. Schultz (Philadelphia: Fortress, 1972), chap. 5; E. W. Cocke, "Luther's View of Marriage and Family," *Religious Life* 42 (1973), 103–16; William Lazareth, *Luther on the Christian Home* (1960); Lazareth, "Luther on Sex, Marriage, and Family," in *Crisis in Marriage*, ed. George Forell and William H. Lazareth (Philadelphia: Fortress, 1978).

whole of the tradition in a way that no one else had. He challenged theory and practice, offering not only an alternative justification for marriage but a view of the human person that demanded marriage for almost all Christians.

According to Luther, sexual pleasure itself in one sense needs no justification. The desire for it is simply a fact of life. It remains, like all the givens in creation, a good so long as it is channeled through marriage into the meaningful whole of life, which includes the good of offspring. What there is in sex that detracts from the knowledge and worship of God is sinful, and it has to be forgiven (not simply given a special justification such as the aim of procreation), as do the sinful elements that Luther believed are inevitable in all human activity. After 1523 Luther shifted his emphasis from marriage as a "hospital for incurables" to marriage as a school for character. It is, he taught, within the secular, nonsacramental institution of marriage and family (part of the order of creation) that individuals learn obedience to God and develop important human virtues. The very structure of the family serves this, for it is essentially hierarchical and obediential, with the husband having authority over his wife, and parents exercising authority over their children.

Calvin, too, saw marriage as a corrective to otherwise disordered desires. He expanded the notion of marriage as the context for human flourishing by maintaining that the greatest good of marriage and sex is the mutual society that is formed between husband and wife.[63] Calvin was more optimistic than Luther about the possibility of controlling sexual desire, though he, too, believed that whatever guilt remains in sexual desire and activity is "covered over" by marriage and forgiven by God.[64] Like earlier writers, he worried that marriage as a remedy for incontinence could nonetheless itself offer provocation to uncontrolled passion.

---

63. See John Calvin, *Commentary on Genesis* 2:28; *Commentary on Deuteronomy* 24:5. Other significant texts in Calvin's writings on these questions include *Institutes of the Christian Religion* 2.8.41–44; *Commentary on 1 Corinthians* 7:6–9. Secondary sources include Georgia Harkness, *John Calvin: The Man and His Ethics* (New York: Abingdon, Apex Books, 1958); Jane Dempsey Douglass, *Women, Freedom, and Calvin* (Philadelphia: Westminster, 1985).

64. Calvin, *Institutes of the Christian Religion* 2.8.44.

As part of their teaching on marriage, Luther and Calvin opposed premarital and extramarital sex and homosexual relations. So concerned was Luther to provide some institutionally tempering form for sexual desire that he once voiced an opinion (in response to a particular case) favoring bigamy over adultery. Both Luther and Calvin were opposed to divorce, although its possibility was admitted in a situation of adultery or impotence, or in a case where one spouse refused to have sex with the other.[65]

Modern Roman Catholic Developments

During and after the Roman Catholic Reformation (or "Counter Reformation"), from the late sixteenth century on, new developments alternated with the reassertion of the Augustinian ethic. The Council of Trent (1545–63) was the first ecumenical council to address the role of love in marriage, but it also reaffirmed the primacy of procreation and reemphasized the superiority of celibacy. In the seventeenth century, the morally austere and ultimately heretical movement known as Jansenism reacted against what it considered a dangerous lowering of sexual standards and brought back the Augustinian connection between sex, concupiscence, and original sin. Alphonsus Liguori in the eighteenth century gave impetus to a manualist tradition (the development and proliferation of moral manuals designed primarily, like the Penitentials, to assist confessors) that attempted to integrate the Pauline purpose of marriage (marriage as a remedy for lust) with the procreative purpose. Nineteenth-century moral manuals focused on "sins of impurity," choices of any sexual pleasure, in mind or in action, apart from procreative marital intercourse. The twentieth century witnessed the rise of Catholic theological interest in personalism and the tendency on the part of the Protestant churches to accept birth control.

In 1930, Pope Pius XI responded to the Anglican approval of contraception by reaffirming for Roman Catholics the procreative ethic. But he also gave approval to marital intercourse at times or under physical conditions when conception cannot occur.[66] Sufficient

---

65. See, for example, Luther, *On the Estate of Marriage* (1522).

66. See Pius XI, *Casti Connubii* (1930) 53–56, 59. This latter is not a new position in Catholic sexual ethics, since Augustine himself was clear that marital intercourse

knowledge of human reproductive processes was not yet available to consider intentional use of infertile times in a woman's cycle, but the reiteration by Pius XI of the traditional allowance of marital intercourse when conception was not possible paved the way for Pius XII's later approval of the "rhythm method."[67] Moral theologians began to move cautiously in the direction of allowing sexual intercourse in marriage without a procreative intent, but for the purpose of fostering marital union. The change in Roman Catholic moral theology from the 1950s to the 1970s was dramatic. The separation of procreation and sexual intercourse by the acceptance of the rhythm method, and the new understandings of the totality of the human person brought about a radically new vision of sex as an expression and cause of married love. The effects of this theological change were striking in the 1965 Second Vatican Council teaching that the love essential to marriage is uniquely expressed and perfected in the act of sexual intercourse.[68] Although the Council still held that marriage is by its very nature ordered to the procreation of children, it no longer ranked what the tradition considered the basic ends of marriage, offspring and spousal union, as primary and secondary.

In 1968 Pope Paul VI insisted that contraception is immoral.[69] Rather than settling the issue for Roman Catholics, however, this occasioned intense conflict. A world-wide majority of moral theologians disagreed with the papal teaching, even though a distinction between *non*procreative and *anti*procreative behavior mediated the

---

between sterile couples (whether because of age or some defect) was allowed. In this encyclical, Pius XI is strongly Augustinian in his overall view of sexuality.

67. The "rhythm method" employs "fertility awareness" in the sense that sexual intercourse is restricted to the infertile period in a woman's monthly ovulation cycle. Pius XII taught that this method could be used even on a permanent basis when serious medical, economic, or social reasons obtained. See Pius XII, "Address to the Italian Catholic Society of Midwives," *Acta Apostolicae Sedis* (October 29, 1951), 43:845–46. For some overview of the theological context of this development, see Noonan, *Contraception*, 438–47; John Gallagher, "Magisterial Teaching from 1918 to the Present," in *Readings in Moral Theology No. 8: Dialogue About Catholic Social Teaching*, ed. Charles E. Curran and Richard A. McCormick (New York: Paulist, 1993), 71–92. For a general description of developments in "fertility awareness" (or "natural") methods of birth control, see Michael Policar, "Fertility Control: Medical Aspects," in *Encyclopedia of Bioethics*, ed. Warren T. Reich, rev. ed., 2:825.

68. Second Vatican Council, *Gaudium et Spes* (1965) 49.

69. Paul VI, *Humanae Vitae* (1968).

dispute for some.[70] Since then many of the specific moral rules governing sexuality in the Catholic tradition have come under serious question. Official teachings have sustained past injunctions, though some modifications have been made in order to accommodate pastoral responses to divorce and remarriage, homosexual orientation (but not sexual activity), and individual conscience decisions regarding contraception. Among moral theologians there is serious debate (and by the 1990s, marked pluralism) regarding issues of premarital sex, homosexual acts, remarriage after divorce, infertility therapies, gender roles, and clerical celibacy.[71]

Post-Reformation Protestantism

In the meantime, twentieth-century Protestant sexual ethics developed even more dramatically than Roman Catholic. After the Reformation, Protestant theologians and church leaders continued to affirm heterosexual marriage as the only acceptable context for sexual activity. Except for the differences regarding celibacy and divorce, sexual norms in the Protestant churches looked much the same as those in the Catholic tradition; nineteenth-century Protestantism shared and contributed to the cultural pressures of Victorianism. But in the twentieth century, Protestant thinking was deeply affected by biblical and historical studies that questioned the foundations of Christian sexual

---

70. See, on the one hand, in disagreement with *Humanae Vitae*, Charles E. Curran, ed., *Contraception, Authority, and Dissent* (New York: Herder & Herder, 1969); and on the other hand, Germain Grisez, Joseph Boyle, John Finnis, and William E. May, "NFP: Not Contralife," in *The Teaching of Humanae Vitae: A Defense* (San Francisco: Ignatius, 1988), 81–92.

71. See Curran and McCormick, *Readings in Moral Theology No. 8*, for key church documents as well as a collection of writings that represent important developments in regard to these sorts of issues. This volume does not, however, include some views of either the far right or the far left. For an overview of developments in U.S. Catholic sexual ethics, see Leslie Griffin, "American Catholic Sexual Ethics, 1789–1989," in *Perspectives on the American Catholic Church*, ed. Stephen J. Vicchio and Virginia Geiger (Westminster, Md: Christian Classics, 1989), 231–52, reprinted in *Readings in Moral Theology No. 8*, ed. C. Curran and R. McCormick, 453–84. See also Philip S. Keane, *Sexual Morality: A Catholic Perspective* (New York: Paulist, 1977); André Guindon, *The Sexual Creators* (Lanham, MD: University of America, 1986); Lisa Sowle Cahill, "Catholic Sexual Teaching: Context, Function, and Authority," in *Vatican Authority and American Catholic Dissent*, ed. William W. May (New York: Crossroad, 1987), 187–205; Christine E. Gudorf, *Body, Sex, and Pleasure* (Cleveland: Pilgrim, 1994); Cahill, *Sex, Gender, and Christian Ethics* (Cambridge: Cambridge University Press, 1996).

ethics, by psychological theories that challenged traditional views, and by the voiced experience of church members. Major Protestant theologians, such as Paul Tillich, Karl Barth, and Helmut Thielicke, incorporated questions of sexuality and gender into their constructive theologies, anchoring their varying perspectives in the tradition while attempting to incorporate new information and insights.[72]

It is difficult to trace one clear line of development in twentieth-century Protestant sexual ethics, or even as clear a dialectic as may be found in Roman Catholicism. The fact that Protestantism in general was from the beginning less dependent on a procreative ethic allowed it eventually and almost unanimously to accept contraception as a means to responsible parenting. Overall, Protestant sexual ethics has moved to integrate an understanding of the human person, male and female, into a theology of marriage that no longer deprecates sexual desire as self-centered and dangerous. It continues to struggle with issues of gendered hierarchy in the family, and with what are often called "alternate lifestyles," such as the cohabitation of unmarried heterosexuals and the sexual partnerships of gays and lesbians. For the most part, the ideal context for sexual intercourse is still considered to be heterosexual marriage, but many theologians are accepting of premarital sex and of homosexual partnerships, including gay marriage. Every mainline Protestant church has had since the 1990s task forces working particularly on questions of homosexuality, professional (including clergy) sexual ethics, and sex education.

Secular Paths: Philosophical Developments, Medical Influences

The long arms of Greek and Roman antiquity reached down not only through theological construals of sexuality and its meanings,

---

72. See, for example, Paul Tillich, *Systematic Theology* 2.44–59 (Chicago: University of Chicago Press, 1967); Tillich, *Love, Power, and Justice* (New York: Oxford University Press, 1954); Helmut Thielicke, *The Ethics of Sex*, trans. John W. Doberstein (Grand Rapids, MI: Baker Book House, 1964); Karl Barth, *Church Dogmatics* III/2, 325–436, and III/4, 116–240 (Edinburgh: T. & T. Clark, 1960, 1961). What is important in these writings is the effort at a fuller theological framework for sexual ethics. With the exception of acceptance of the moral justification of contraception, the positions taken on specific moral questions are frequently quite traditional. See, e.g., Barth's concern for "protest, warning, and conversion" regarding the "malady called homosexuality," *Church Dogmatics* III/4, 166.

but through philosophical ones as well. And all the while, medical experts were both influenced by prevailing ideas about sex and moral behavior, and in turn, influenced them. Even a tentative exploration of historical perspectives on questions of human sexuality has at least to take note of these disciplines and of others as well. Intellectual histories do not take place in a vacuum; so that to make sense of ideas about sex one must also study literature, music, painting, economic developments, migrations, political struggles, and the many other elements of Western society that have served to sustain or to change view of sexuality and gender. The rise of the courtly love tradition in the Middle Ages was probably more important for shaping ideas about sex than any single theologian's writings at that time; shifts in economic structures under capitalism were massively influential in changing familial roles and the rationales that accompanied them. Here, unfortunately, I can only look to developments in philosophy and medicine, but simply nod to the importance of all the other factors in Western sexual history.

Philosophy and the Understanding of Sex

As surveys of the history of philosophy note, philosophers in most periods have not paid much attention to sex. They have written a great deal about love but have left sexual behavior largely to religion, poetry, medicine, and the law.[73] After the Greeks and Romans, and medieval thinkers like Thomas Aquinas whose work is philosophical as well as theological, there is not much to be found regarding sexuality until the twentieth century. Exceptions to this are the sparse eighteenth-century writings on sex and gender by David Hume, Jean-Jacques Rousseau, Immanuel Kant, Mary Wollstonecraft, and Johann Gottlieb Fichte, and the nineteenth-century writings of Arthur Schopenhauer, Karl Marx, Friedrich Engels, John Stuart Mill, and Friedrich Nietzsche. Most of these writers reinforced

---

73. See Robert Baker and Frederick Ellison, eds., *Philosophy and Sex* (Buffalo: Prometheus Books, 1975), 1; Alan Soble, ed., *The Philosophy of Sex*, 2nd ed. (Savage, MD: Littlefield Adams Quality Paperbacks, 1991), 3. For a useful historical study of philosophical treatments of love and to some extent sex, see Irving Singer, *The Nature of Love*, 3 vols., 2nd ed. (Chicago: University of Chicago Press, 1984–87).

the norm of heterosexual procreative sex within marriage. Hume in his "Of Polygamy and Divorce" insisted that all arguments about sexual behavior finally lead to a recommendation of "our present European practices with regard to marriage."[74] Rousseau's *La Nouvelle Héloïse* deplored the faults of conventional marriage but strongly opposed marital infidelity and divorce. Kant defended traditional sexual mores, although in his *Lectures on Ethics* he introduced a justification for marriage not in terms of procreation but of altruistic love, arguing that only a mutual commitment in marriage can save sexual desire from making a sexual partner into a mere means to one's own pleasure.[75] Schopenhauer, in *The Metaphysics of Sexual Love*, viewed sexual love as subjectively for pleasure, though objectively for procreation; his strong naturalism paved the way for a more radical theory of sex as an instinct without ethical norms.[76]

Philosophers in these centuries represented both sides of the question of gender equality. Fichte asserted an essentially passive nature in women, who, if they are to be equal to men, will have to renounce their femininity.[77] But Mary Wollstonecraft in her *A Vindication of the Rights of Women*, and Mill in his *On the Subjection of Women*, offered strong challenges to the traditional inequality of gender roles in society.[78] Marx and Engels critiqued bourgeois marriage as a relationship of economic domination.[79] Schopenhauer, reacting to feminist agendas, advocated polygyny on the basis of a theory of male needs

---

74. David Hume, "On Polygamy and Divorce," *Essays Moral, Political, and Literary*, vol. 1, ed. T. H. Green and T. H. Grose (London: Longmans, Green, 1875), 231–39. For a relevant and valuable feminist interpretation of Hume's general work, see Annette C. Baier, "Hume, the Women's Moral Theorist?" in Eva Feder Kittay and Diana T. Meyers, eds., *Women and Moral Theory* (Totowa, NJ: Rowman & Littlefield, 1987), 37–55.

75. Immanuel Kant, "Duties Towards the Body in Respect of the Sexual Impulse," *Lectures on Ethics*, trans. Louis Infield (New York: Harper Torchbooks, 1963), 162–68.

76. Arthur Schopenhauer, "The Metaphysics of Sexual Love," in *The World as Will and Representation*, vol. 2 (New York: Dover Publications, 1958).

77. Johann Gottlieb Fichte, "Fundamental Principles of the Rights of the Family," in *The Science of Rights*, trans. A. Eger Kreger (Philadelphia: J. B. Lippincott, 1869), Appendix, Book 1.

78. Mary Wollstonecraft, *A Vindication of the Rights of Women* (New York: W. W. Norton, 1967, original publication 1792); John Stuart Mill, *On the Subjection of Women* (New York: Fawcett Books, 1973, original publication 1869).

79. See Friedrich Engels, *The Origin of the Family, Private Property, and the State* (New York: International, 1942).

and female instrumental response.[80] Nietzsche, like Schopenhauer, moved away from traditional ethical norms but at the same time dramatically reinforced a view of the solely procreative value of women.[81]

The relative silence of philosophers on sex was broken in the twentieth century. As noted in chapter 1, European and North American philosophers — both women and men — have taken up questions of sex and freedom, paradigms of sexuality, gender bias, sexual abuse, and many other questions about the sexual sphere of human activity.[82] These writings consider very seriously the findings of biological and social-scientific studies, and they take account of philosophical perspectives of the past while constructing proposals for the present. Like the publications of contemporary theologians, theirs remain important works in progress.

Medicine as Historical Agent

Historically, medicine has interacted with philosophy and religion in shaping and rationalizing the sexual ethical norms of a given culture.[83] Medical opinion has often simply reflected and conserved the accepted beliefs and mores of a society, but sometimes it has also been a force for change. In either case, its influence has been powerful. For example, from the Hippocratic corpus of writings in ancient Greece to the writings of the physician Galen in the second century C.E., medical recommendations regarding sexual discipline

---

80. Schopenhauer, "Essay on Women," in *The Works of Schopenhauer,* ed. William Durant (New York: Simon & Schuster, 1928).

81. See Friedrich Nietzsche, *Thus Spake Zarathustra,* Part 1, in *The Portable Nietzsche,* trans. Walter Kaufman (New York: Viking, 1954).

82. In addition to the philosophical writings cited earlier in this present chapter, and writings listed in notes 6–9 and passim in chapter 1, we should note such works as: Robert J. Stoller, *Observing the Erotic Imagination* (New Haven, CT: Yale University Press, 1985); Robert M. Stewart, ed., *Philosophical Perspectives on Sex and Love* (New York: Oxford University Press, 1995); Robert C. Solomon, ed., *Wicked Pleasures* (Lanham, MD: Rowman & Littlefield, 1998); John Corvino, ed., *Same Sex: Debating the Ethics, Science, and Culture of Homosexuality* (Lanham, MD: Rowman & Littlefield, 1998); Alan Soble, ed., *Sex, Love, and Friendship: Studies of the Society for the Philosophy of Sex and Love 1977–1992* (Atlanta: Rodopi, 1997).

83. For connections between medicine and sexual ethics, see Earl E. Shelp, ed., *Sexuality and Medicine,* 2 vols. (Dordrecht: D. Reidel, 1987); Ronald M. Green, ed., *Religion and Sexual Health: Ethical, Theological, and Clinical Perspectives* (Dordrecht: Kluwer Academic, 1992).

echoed and reinforced the ambivalence of Greek and Roman philoso-phers regarding human sexual activity.[84] Galen's theories retained considerable power all the way into the European Renaissance. The interpretation of syphilis as a disease rather than a divine punish-ment came only in the fifteenth century as the result of medical writings responding to a high incidence of the disease among the so-cial elite. In nineteenth-century western Europe and North America, medical writers were enormously influential in shaping norms re-garding such matters as masturbation (physicians believed it would lead to insanity), homosexuality (newly identified with perversions that medicine must diagnose and treat), contraception (considered unhealthy because it fostered sexual excess and loss of physical power), and gender roles (promoted on the basis of medical assess-ment of physical and psychological health). In the twentieth century, of course, most of these particular medical opinions changed (per-haps less so regarding an interpretation of gender and implications for gender roles).

The emergence of psychoanalytic theory at the turn of the century brought with it new perceptions of the meaning and role of sexual-ity in the life of individuals. It also gave new direction to much of medicine's approach to sex. Whatever the final validity of Sigmund Freud's insights, they burst upon the world with a force that all but swept away the foundations of traditional sexual morality. Au-gustine's and Luther's assertions about the indomitability of sexual desire found support in Freud's theory, but now the power of sexual need was not the result of sin but a natural drive, centrally con-stitutive of the human personality.[85] Past efforts to order sexuality

---

84. Foucault draws on this material to a great extent in *The History of Sexuality*, vol. 2. For an alternative reading of the Hippocratic Corpus that takes more account of the gynecological works of the Corpus, see Lesley Dean-Jones, "The Politics of Pleasure: Female Sexual Appetite in the Hippocratic Corpus," in *Discourses of Sexuality*, ed. Domna Stanton, 48–77.

85. See in particular, Sigmund Freud, *Three Essays on the Theory of Sexuality*, in *The Standard Edition of the Complete Psychological Works of Sigmund Freud*, 24 vols. (London: Hogarth, 1953–74), 7:130–243; *Civilization and Its Discontents*, SE 21:64–145. Valuable contemporary interpretations of Freud's theories of sexuality, especially as they relate to ethics, can be found in Ernest Wallwork, *Psychoanalysis and Ethics* (New Haven, CT: Yale University Press, 1991); and in Teresa de Lauretis, "Freud, Sexuality, and Perversion," in *Discourses of Sexuality*, ed. D. Stanton, 216–34.

according to rational purposes could now be interpreted as repression. After Freud, when sex went awry, it was a matter of psychological illness, not moral evil.[86] Taboos needed demythologizing, it was widely thought, and freedom might be attained not through repentance and forgiveness but through medical treatment.

Yet psychoanalytic theory raised as many questions as it answered. Freud argued for liberation from sexual taboos and from the hypocrisy and sickness they cause, but he nonetheless maintained the need for sexual restraint. His theory of sublimation called for discipline and a channeling of the sexual instinct if individuals and society were to progress. The concern for sexual norms therefore remained, and Freud's own recommendations were in many ways quite traditional. But new work had clearly been cut out for those in both secular and religious traditions.

With the medicalization of human sexuality, sex became less an ethical or even aesthetic problem than a health problem. Ironically, however, experts of all kinds — physicians, counselors, therapists, social workers, teachers — offered guidance; and the guidance carried moral weight. Examples of this abound in the long efforts to define and identify sexual deviance or perversion, the new pressures on individuals toward sexual activity as a part of human flourishing, the intertwining of medicine and law in the punishment or rehabilitation of perpetrators of sex crimes. Women in particular have appeared vulnerable to moral restrictions and judgments based on prevalent medical assessments of their sexual capabilities, "feminine" characteristics, and compliance with the rules for mothering.[87] Similarly, gay men and lesbians have been stigmatized as much by the medical profession as by religious traditions. Accused of immorality or diagnosed with a pathology, they have been marginalized,

---

86. In the late twentieth century, however, there has been an important shift to consider physiological, not only psychological, causes for sexual dysfunction.

87. Feminist studies have multiplied in which these phenomena have been detailed and documented in women's experience. See, for example, Adrienne Rich, *Of Women Born: Motherhood as Experience and Institution* (Buffalo: Prometheus, 1976); J. B. Donegan, *Women and Men Midwives: Medicine, Morality, and Misogyny in Early America* (Westport, CT: Greenwood, 1978); Mary O'Brien, *The Politics of Reproduction* (London: Routledge and Kegan Paul, 1981); Susan M. Wolf, *Feminism and Bioethics: Beyond Reproduction* (New York: Oxford University Press, 1996).

sometimes even jailed, and subjected to strategies of behavioral and character reform. Whatever the politics behind the American Psychiatric Association's removal of homosexuality from the official list of pathologies in 1973, the social consequences of this decision were significant.[88]

From the Past to the Present

We have long recognized, especially in regard to human experience, that the meaning of the past is somehow in the present, and the meaning of the present is at least in part in the future. Whether there are or should be any grand narratives; whether unbiased tales can be told or human events neutrally recorded; the history of questions and convictions about human sexuality is useful for the tasks that remain. What we have traced in this chapter is incomplete, subject to interpretation, in need of ongoing revision. One glaring omission is the same one MacKinnon observed in Foucault's historical accounts: that is, history of violence toward women. This is largely because it has not been the subject of much historical attention, although awareness of it surely lurks in the prevailing gender inequality through each tradition and era.

This chapter, then, offers only the proverbial "tip of the iceberg." Still, it provides both resources and historical context, relevant and I hope useful for discernment of a contemporary sexual ethic. Today's questions are not completely new, though they are not just old, either, and they are surely at least as complex as they were at most points in the past. We turn again, then, to some of the larger questions that fascinated antiquity, troubled faithful believers in religious traditions, and that have preoccupied modern professionals. The reasons for caution remain; if anything they are intensified by a look at history. But historical perspectives may free us as well as enrich us, for the conversation they help to keep open.

---

88. There is a plethora of literature — medical, psychiatric, and sociological — on these developments. For useful contextualization of it all, see, for example, David F. Greenberg, *The Construction of Homosexuality* (Chicago: University of Chicago Press, 1988), especially chaps. 9–11; Andrew Sullivan, *Love Undetectable: Notes on Friendship, Sex, and Survival* (New York: Alfred A. Knopf, 1998), especially chap. 2

Chapter 3

DIFFICULT CROSSINGS
Diverse Traditions

═══ ❖ ═══

T HE ETHICAL QUESTIONS that remain open and troubling regarding human sexuality include not only those regarding specific
moral rules or categories of acceptable sexual behaviors. They include
larger and in some respects more basic questions, such as what are
the aims of sexual desire, the value of sexual pleasure, the purposes of
sexual activity, the place of gender in public and private lives, the role
of personal and familial affiliations in the forming of identity and the
structuring of societies. Some of these questions have been opened
in chapter 1, and they have been explored historically in chapter 2.
When questions are difficult there is always hope that history will
shed the light we need for discerning the answers. When a turn to
history does not suffice, there is strong motivation to look for insight
beyond our own Western traditions. Knowledge of other traditions at
the very least helps us to clarify an understanding of our own tradition, but it may also open up new possibilities for an overall approach
to the issues at hand.

Ever since studies of culturally diverse sexual practices have become available, Western readers interested in sexual ethics have
largely used them, on the one hand, to critique our own cultural
assumptions and rules, suggesting that we can be freed from rigid restrictions because we now know they are not universally recognized;
in other words, there must not be a naturally "human" moral requirement to believe and act as Westerners have traditionally done. On the
other hand, we have used cross-cultural studies to reinforce our own
traditional ethical perspectives, by identifying some commonalities
across cultures or by attributing differences to the fact that the sexual

practices of other cultures are simply more primitive than ours. In recent years, however, both of these options have become problematic.
For example, the supposed sexual freedom in some cultures has now
been relativized by the discovery of more complex patterns of relationship internal to the cultures themselves (as we shall see below).
And it is no longer generally acceptable to rank cultures in terms
of some theory of progress. This does not mean that cross-cultural
studies are no longer important for the understanding of sexuality,
but their contribution is now as problematized as is the retrieval of
a usable past from the Western tradition.

Cross-Cultural Perspectives: Importance for Sexual Ethics

Possibilities of Cross-Cultural and Interreligious Awareness

There are significant theoretical and practical reasons to engage in
cross-cultural studies of sexual beliefs and practices. The simple need
for a broader perspective is one of them. But so is the growing acknowledgment of the importance of respecting differences in cultural
backgrounds, of moderating the tendency to universalize Western
cultural experience as if it represented the essentially human, and of
correcting the often naive assumptions of Western Christianity when
it comes to judging the sexual mores of other societies and cultures.
Moreover, Christianity itself, insofar as it is a world religion, exists
in cultures other than those of Western Europe and North America;
and challenges to a monolithic sexual ethic have been part of the
agenda for a Christian sexual ethic for a long time.[1] Finally, it is almost impossible for one culture to ignore others in the twenty-first
century when communication and transportation bring the practices

---

1. An obvious example is the troubling question of polygyny (or polygamy) as
it has been met over the years by newly baptized Christians in African nations. See
Eugene Hillman, *Polygamy Reconsidered: African Plural Marriage and the Christian
Churches* (Maryknoll, NY: Orbis, 1975); Musimbi R. A. Kanyoro, "Interpreting Old
Testament Polygamy through African Eyes," in *The Will to Arise: Women, Tradition,
and the Church in Africa*, ed. Mercy Amba Oduyoye and Musimbi R. A. Kanyoro
(Maryknoll, NY: Orbis, 1992), 87–100; Anne Nasimiyu-Wasike, "Polygamy: A Feminist
Critique," in *Will to Arise*, 101–18. I will return to this question in chapter 7.

of almost all cultures into close interaction with one another. The issue of female circumcision, for example, confronts not only world organizations operating in many countries, but it comes across borders as the migration of peoples increases for a variety of political and economic reasons.[2]

Obstacles to the Search for Alternative Perspectives

Resources

If there are reasons for engaging in and with cross-cultural and inter-religious studies regarding sexual beliefs and practices, there are also significant practical and theoretical reasons against it. First among these is the nature of the resources available for Western readers, particularly for ethicists.[3] Disciplines engaged in studies of sexual practices in diverse cultures are themselves facing internal professional criticisms, conflicts, and questions of direction and purpose. For example, the field of "folklore studies" has become radically self-critical, no longer collecting traditions but questioning the very meanings of "folk" and "tradition."[4] Anthropology in the twentieth century produced an explosion of studies focused on sexuality in a variety of cultures. But the anthropological (and within it, ethnographic) study of sexuality produces sometimes confusing results, for a variety of reasons. The field of study remains difficult to define, perhaps primarily because there is not a univocal meaning for "sexuality" across all cultures. The scope of empirical studies is extremely broad, covering sexual behavior, identity, institutions, structures,

---

2. The literature on this particular issue is growing. As an example of the power of the issue to fuel the controversy over cross-cultural ethics, see Sandra D. Lane and Robert A. Rubinstein, "Judging the Other: Responding to Traditional Female Genital Surgeries," *The Hastings Center Report* 26 (May–June 1996): 31–40.

3. See the difficulties noted by Rita Nakashima Brock and Susan Brooks Thistlethwaite regarding their work on issues of prostitution in *Casting Stones: Prostitution and Liberation in Asia and the United States* (Minneapolis: Fortress, 1996), 24. In the last ten years, resources on these and other issues have multiplied considerably, but they continue to be difficult to use in ways I describe further in this chapter.

4. See Arjun Appadurai, Frank J. Korom, and Margaret A. Mills, eds., *Gender, Genre, and Power in Southeast Asian Expressive Traditions* (Philadelphia: University of Pennsylvania Press, 1991), 3–5. There is attention paid here to the fact that women scholars have moved to the fore in these efforts, bringing together folkloristics, anthropology, history of religions, and a study of geographical areas in dramatic new ways.

orientation, passion and desire, health and disease, sex education, and so forth.[5] Despite the breadth of scope, traditional research has tended to focus (with some exceptions[6]) on rites of initiation, and on kinship systems and marriage — in other words, on sexuality as a mode of social organization. Within this, there has been a tendency on the part of researchers to emphasize the "exotic," which is basically whatever is different from the scientist's own culture.[7]

Not only the focus but the actual investigation of anything like a stable subject matter has become more problematic. As the world in a sense grows smaller, interaction between and among cultures brings about change.[8] Simple passage of time accounts for internal change within cultures as they adapt to new situations. The study of cultures, especially when they are distant from our own, becomes, therefore, an attempt to grasp "an ever-receding point of social reference."[9] Personal and cultural biases of researchers,[10] as well as their frequent need to align with political authorities, yield sometimes conflicting results as one researcher challenges the findings of another. Perhaps the greatest difficulty of all has been the influence of colonialism on cross-cultural research, particularly research on the sexuality of colonized peoples. This issue must be examined in its own right, and I return to it shortly.

---

5. See Lenore Manderson, Linda Rae Bennett, and Michelle Sheldrake, "Sex, Social Institutions, and Social Structure: Anthropological Contributions to the Study of Sexuality," *Annual Review of Sex Research* 10 (1999): 184–210.

6. This refers to the work of a few scholars such as Bronislaw Malinowski and Margaret Mead, which I take up below.

7. It must be noted, however, that some of this has changed in the last twenty years, as empirical research on sexual practices has been more and more driven by public health concerns.

8. In the twenty-first century there are some still-isolated peoples, but not many, and probably not for long. In 1999 Diana Jean Schemo reported that the Brazilian Amazon valley shelters "approximately 15 tribes of the rain forest that have never been studied or, in some instances, even named by scholars." See Schemo, "The Last Tribal Battle," *New York Times Magazine* 148 (October 31, 1999): 72.

9. Eric Hobsbaum and Terence Ranges, *The Invention of Tradition* (New York: Cambridge University Press, 1983), 22.

10. The problem of bias in anthropological studies is dramatically underlined in regard to interpretations of male/female inequalities, as noted by Marilyn Strathern in her "Conclusion" to *Dealing with Inequality: Analyzing Gender Relations in Melanesia and Beyond*, ed. Marilyn Strathern (New York: Cambridge University Press, 1987), 278–302.

Comparative Sexual Ethics

Even the best of social scientific research on sexual beliefs and practices across cultures is not generally matched by comparable studies of the religious and cultural underpinnings of attitudes and practices.[11] Moreover, what resources there are regarding sexual mores in diverse cultures and religious traditions remain largely untapped for dialogue regarding sexual *ethics*, whether because of language barriers or because sexuality tends not to be high on the agenda of interreligious or inter-cultural dialogue. An exception may be the new work of feminist scholars in ethics.[12] Until recently, comparative religious ethics has, for its part, focused largely on issues of theory and method. Even now, when specific normative ethical issues are addressed, the tendency is to concentrate on questions such as nonviolence, genocide, the environment, distributive justice, and general human rights.[13] While this is changing, especially in regard

11. An early effort to bridge the gap between anthropology and the study of religious traditions can be found in Geoffrey Parrinder, *Sex in the World's Religions* (New York: Oxford University Press, 1980); and in Ping-Cheung Lo, "Zhu Xi and Confucian Sexual Ethics," *Journal of Chinese Philosophy* 20 (1993): 465–77.

12. See, e.g., Patricia Beattie Jung, Mary E. Hunt, and Radhika Balakrishnan, eds., *Good Sex: Feminist Perspectives from the World's Religions* (New Brunswick, NJ: Rutgers University Press, 2001); Laura E. Donaldson and Kwok Pui-lan, eds., *Postcolonialism, Feminism, and Religious Discourse* (New York: Routledge, 2002).

13. The essays in Sumner B. Twiss and Bruce Grelle, eds., *Explorations in Global Ethics: Comparative Religious Ethics and Interreligious Dialogue* (Boulder, CO: Westview, 1998), represent a significant contribution in this regard. See also John Kelsay, "Islam and Comparative Ethics: Review of Selected Materials, 1985–95," *Religious Studies Review* 23 (January 1997): 3–9; and the focus issue of the *Journal of Religious Ethics* 26 (Fall 1998): "The 50th Anniversary of the Universal Declaration of Human Rights." A growing number of cross-cultural studies in medical ethics can also be found, though these are not necessarily taken up into comparative religious ethics. See, for example, A. S. Berger and J. Berger, eds., *To Die or Not to Die? Cross-disciplinary, Cultural, and Legal Perspectives on the Right to Choose Death* (New York: Praeger, 1990); Robert Baker, "A Theory of International Bioethics: Multiculturalism, Postmodernism, and the Bankruptcy of Fundamentalism," and "A Theory of International Ethics: The Negotiable and the Non-Negotiable," *Kennedy Institute of Ethics Journal* 8 (September 1998): 201–31 and 233–73. For more general considerations of theory and method, see Sumner B. Twiss and Bruce Grelle, "Human Rights and Comparative Religious Ethics: A New Venue," in *Annual of the Society of Christian Ethics*, ed. Harlan Beckley (Washington, DC: Georgetown University Press, 1995), 21–48. See also David Little and Sumner B. Twiss, *Comparative Religious Ethics: A New Method* (New York: Harper & Row, 1978); and for a substantive comparative study of virtue, see Lee H. Yearley, *Mencius and Aquinas: Theories of Virtue and Conceptions of Courage* (Albany: State University of New York Press, 1990).

to questions of gender and its relevance to human rights, the sexual ethical conversation is still in its beginning stages.[14]

Cultural Constructionism and Common Morality

More seriously, cross-cultural and interreligious studies can challenge the very enterprise of ethics as a discipline insofar as they reinforce questions of ethical relativism and of the overwhelming determination of moral norms by historical and cultural contingencies. If moral rules and principles are in every respect specific to and conditioned by particular cultural contexts (including particular religious traditions); if they have no basis whatsoever in a shared humanity or a universally intended command of God; then no amount of ethical reflection will yield anything like an objective moral assessment of human sexual behavior (one capable of transcending a particular culture), or anything of a common sexual morality that would apply to human persons as such.[15] These questions, not new to comparative religious and ethical studies in general, are especially significant for sexual ethics. The social construction of moral rules is hardly anywhere more evident than in the historical-cultural shaping of sexual roles, duties, prohibitions, even desires. Insofar as knowledge of cross-cultural differences threatens all strong claims to universality for sexual norms, perhaps all that ethicists can do is describe attitudes and practices as they appear in diverse cultures, acknowledge their validity within the context of each culture (or even subculture), and critique them internally but judge them as a whole to be of equal ethical merit. If this is accurate, cross-cultural studies remain important, but primarily for the sake of fostering tolerance of diversity in sexual behaviors and respect for differences in interpretations of the meaning of sexual desire.

---

14. For important moral philosophical work that crosses cultures in regard to gender issues, see Martha Nussbaum, *Sex and Social Justice* (New York: Oxford University Press, 1999); and the many relevant essays in Martha Nussbaum and Jonathan Glover, eds., *Women, Culture and Development: A Study of Human Capabilities* (Oxford: Clarendon Press, 1995).

15. For a spectrum of views on the question of a common morality, see Gene Outka and John P. Reeder, eds., *Prospects for a Common Morality* (Princeton, NJ: Princeton University Press, 1993).

However, cross-cultural work on sexual ethics may be not only less useful but less benign than this. Critical assessments of the cultural bias involved in all of these studies (biased precisely because of the Western lenses through which non-Western cultures are viewed) make one less than confident that what is produced through research on non-Western cultures is accurate or adequate. The problem is no doubt less serious as more and more research is done by persons indigenous to the cultures and standing within the religious traditions being studied. Yet even here, older stereotypes as well as new biases make it an uphill climb for ethicists who wish to take cultural and religious traditions other than their own into account.

Colonialist Research and Its Postcolonial Critics

Massive problems have emerged in the late twentieth and early twenty-first centuries regarding Western interpretations of non-Western cultures, and perhaps especially regarding sexual practices within these cultures. As we have already seen, studies of sexual beliefs and practices in non-Western cultures have not been undertaken in a kind of historically "pure" world, where peoples form communities and live out traditions autonomously, without a mixing with outside traditions. Past studies that continue to influence our understanding of cultures other than our own were done mainly in a world already divided into colonizers and colonized. Scholars among the former studied peoples among the latter. Even when a particular people had not yet been colonized, the ways upon which they were looked by scholars were the ways of a colonizing power, ways that rationalized the colonization of "backward" people by those who considered themselves to be "progressive," more fully evolved, and therefore rightful leaders among nations. Colonies were established under ancient regimes, but it is the four hundred years of post-Renaissance Western colonialism that blanketed the world into which anthropologists (particularly ethnographers) entered in the nineteenth and twentieth centuries. It is into a largely postcolonial world that they now go, but a world no less already inscripted by a history of powerful outside influences.

The Lessons of "Orientalism"

Edward Said's 1978 publication of *Orientalism* provided a sobering perspective on Western approaches to non-Western cultures.[16] This by now classic work offered new lenses for the interpretation of social scientific research as well as literary depictions regarding formerly colonized Asian, Latin American, and African lands. *Orientalism* has served as a model for postcolonialist critique that now calls so much of that research into question. Said's own focus was on the historical development of concepts and attitudes regarding the so-called Orient. "Orientalism" for him meant (1) an academic field of studies (crossing disciplines of anthropology, sociology, languages, history, philology, and more) that addresses things Oriental; (2) a way of thinking about or imagining differences between the "Orient" and the "Occident"; and (3) a discourse (in Foucault's sense of language and knowledge shaped by power, and in this case, by powerful Western systems of thought) that produces and circumscribes the meaning of the Orient politically, ideologically, socially, militarily, scientifically, and artistically. As such, "Orientalism" (or Said's analysis of it) provides a tool for the interpretation of all colonizing efforts: It represents colonization as a restructuring of people's experience and an exercising of authority over an "Other" — a hitherto unknown other who must be understood according to the colonizer's categories. With the emergence of Orientalism out of the eighteenth century, European (mainly French and British) culture created an understanding of the cultures of the East (particularly India, China, Japan, the East Indies), an understanding whose content was shaped by Western attitudes of superiority, racism, and imperialism.[17] This understanding constituted a stage on which the whole of the East was to be confined.[18] Orientalism "is fundamentally a political doctrine willed over the Orient, because the Orient was weaker than the West, which elided the Orient's difference with its weakness."[19]

---

16. Edward W. Said, *Orientalism* (New York: Vintage Books, 1979; originally published in 1978 by Pantheon Books).

17. Ibid., 3–4.

18. Ibid., 63.

19. Ibid., 204.

Said's claim is not that there is no correspondence at all between Orientalism and what is to be found in the East; nor does he claim that only those who are indigenous to a culture can truly understand it.[20] It is, rather, that however much the West wants to define it, there is no stable, essential reality that is "the East." The imaginative meanings of the people of the Orient, their customs and destiny, can be produced from within but also from without. Said's analysis leads him to the broader observation that "the notion that there are geographical spaces with indigenous, radically 'different' inhabitants who can be defined on the basis of some religious, cultural, or racial essence proper to that geographical space is . . . a highly debatable idea."[21] In the case of the colonization of the East, its meaning was predominantly shaped from without — so that Easterners as well as Westerners internalized the meaning established through the eyes of the colonizers. Scholars who studied the East looked at it through these same eyes; and the results of their research must now be interpreted in that light.

Since Said denies that Orientalism is *simply* a systematic weaving of fictions and lies by outside powerful observers and rulers, his plea is not that no one study or interact with another culture, but that outsiders become cautious and critical in their interpretation of the aims, discourse, and power relations involved.[22] Colonizer and colonized are changed by their historical encounter; images of the "West" depend in part on the West's images of the "East" (and vice versa); researcher and subject are both changed as well. Every effort to understand ourselves and others, therefore, requires that we challenge the legacies of previous interpreters, probe our own biases, critique our place in the historical dynamics of power and knowledge, and identify the categories that lead to error and to harm.

Lessons for Sexual Ethics

Said's perspective may be nowhere more helpful than in efforts to understand the *sexual* beliefs and practices of cultural and religious

---

20. Ibid., 4–6, 272–73, 322.
21. Ibid., 322.
22. Ibid., 272–73.

traditions that are alien. It is, in fact, astonishing how central sexuality appears in the programs of colonization everywhere (and the influence of colonial views on subsequent Western interpretations of non-Western expressions of sexuality). The more distant and different peoples appeared to their visitors and colonizers, the more were their "native" bodies sexualized, eroticized, in racially charged fields.[23] Postcolonial (particularly feminist) scholarship today has begun to shed light on the epistemic violence[24] visited upon non-Western cultures by their Western conquerors or settlers — a violence that indeed aimed to restructure the experience and the self-understanding of peoples through the imposition of Western ideas. In the early twentieth century, Carl Jung popularized a view of the peoples of India and China as reflective of the archetypal "anima," complementary to a Western "animus."[25] Consonant with this view, Eastern sexuality was understood as lyrical, childlike, innocently free, and radically different from sexuality in the West. Early visitors and colonizers of the South Seas, Africa, and Latin America interpreted indigenous sexual practices as permissive, licentious, "savage," an affront to Western sensibilities.[26] Such practices were measured against longstanding Western religious and cultural beliefs that sex is a powerful and instinctive drive, requiring discipline and

---

23. The language of the "eroticized body" of dominated peoples has become quite common in postcolonial studies, but see in particular, Ann Stoler, "Educating Desire in Colonial Southeast Asia: Foucault, Freud, and Imperial Sexualities," in *Sites of Desire/Economies of Pleasure: Sexualities in Asia and the Pacific*, ed. Lenore Manderson and Margaret Jolly (Chicago: University of Chicago Press, 1997), 27–47.

24. See Laura A. Donaldson, "The Breasts of Columbus: A Political Anatomy of Postcolonialism and Feminist Religious Discourse," in *Postcolonialism, Feminism, and Religious Discourse*, 51.

25. Kwok Pui-lan, "Gender, Colonialism, and the Study of Religion," in *Postcolonialism, Feminism, and Religious Discourse*, 19–23. See also the critique of oppositional and complementary interpretations of East/West in Sherry Ortner, "East Brain, West Brain: Do Ways of Thinking Cleave Along Lines of Geography?" *New York Times Book Review* (April 2003). Ortner is reviewing Richard E. Nisbett's *The Geography of Thought: How Asians and Westerners Think Differently . . . and Why* (New York: Free Press, 2003).

26. See Stephen O. Murray and Will Roscoe, eds., *Boy-Wives and Female Husbands* (New York: Palgrave, 1998), xi; Adam Reed, "Contested Images and Common Strategies: Early Colonial Sexual Politics in the Massim," in *Sites of Desire/Economies of Pleasure*, 49.

control. Hence, indigenous peoples were informed that their sexualized bodies were in need of restraint, and their sexual practices must
be limited in purpose.

Ironically, white male colonizers who liked the sexual freedom they
themselves could exercise apart from what they considered to be the
bourgeois norms of their own countries, took local women in the
colonies as concubines.[27] This was particularly true of white men,
often soldiers, who could easily hire native women as both domestic
and sexual servants. When white women arrived, they were segregated in order to "protect" them from the supposed licentiousness of
the local inhabitants. Whether married or single, white women became models of European domesticity and restrained sexuality, and
helped to set the standard for civilization in the colonies.

It was not only visitors, conquerors, settlers, and researchers who
shaped Western (and ultimately non-Western) beliefs about sexuality among the inhabitants of far away lands. On the contrary, it is
hardly possible to overestimate the influence of religious missionaries in this regard. While some colonizers and researchers were
interested in the sexual mores of "native" peoples insofar as they
provided a basis for critique of Western practices, many Christian
missionaries directed their zeal toward changing indigenous behaviors and beliefs. They judged inhabitants of mission countries to be
unrestrained and sexually dangerous to themselves and to their colonizers. If these as yet "uncivilized" peoples were to be redeemed, they
must be educated to a radically more disciplined practice of sexuality.
This became a criterion for receiving the good news of the Christian gospel. What many missionaries did, therefore, was to focus on
the sexual bodies of indigenous persons and groups, making these a
"target of intervention."[28]

The goals of missionary activity reinforced the goals of colonization — that is, to "civilize" peoples. Civilization, of course, was
equated with judgments of progress according to Western ways. As
Sophia Chen observes, "missionaries who came to China were not
prepared to meet a culture that could rival the one they had been

27. See Stoler, "Educating Desire in Southeast Asia," 32–38.
28. Reed, "Contested Images and Common Strategies," 48.

used to."[29] Although China was no doubt a special case in this regard, something of the same could be said of missionaries in parts of Africa and Latin America as well.

Despite the fact that most colonies have by now achieved political independence, colonialism continues. Colonial ideologies continue to shape the interaction between West and East, and between the West and the world's South. The emergent leaders of newly independent countries were, after all, largely trained in the schools and seminaries of the colonizers. Western notions of modernity, industrial progress, and sexuality continue, therefore, to shape the self-understandings of formerly colonized peoples. Moreover, many economic and political forms of contemporary globalization sustain power relations whereby the West continues to control the ordinary lives of peoples around the world.

Postcolonialist critiques of colonialist interpretations of non-Western sexual mores aim not only to deconstruct the processes that led to these interpretations but to offer remedies. That is, they aim not only to avoid what are considered mistakes or at least confusions of the past, but to propose necessary new ways of interacting with diverse cultures in the present. For example, Lenore Manderson and Margaret Jolly indicate their "desire to view sexuality not just as an autonomous realm of the senses, but as embedded in a social world structured and saturated with relations of power,"[30] a world in which gender, sexual orientation, race, and class must be taken into account. And African theologian Musa Dube insists that postcolonialist analysis must include "a search for answers and change in the face of entrenched global structures of oppression and exploitation."[31] To this end, postcolonialist theories must highlight not only

---

29. Sophia H. Chen, "A Non-Christian Estimate," *Chinese Recorder* 65 (1934): 114, as cited in Kwok Pui-lan, "Unbinding Our Feet: Saving Brown Women and Feminist Religious Discourse," in *Postcolonialism, Feminism, and Religious Discourse*, 62.

30. Manderson and Jolly, *Sites of Desire/Economies of Pleasure*, 26. See also Gayatri Chakravorty Spivak, *In Other Worlds: Essays in Cultural Politics* (New York: Methuen, 1987); Spivak, "Can the Subaltern Speak?" in *Marxism and the Interpretation of Culture*, ed. G. Nelson and L. Grossberg (Urbana: University of Illinois Press, 1988).

31. Musa W. Dube, "Postcoloniality, Feminist Spaces, and Religion," in *Postcolonialism, Feminism, and Religious Discourse*, 102.

oppression and exploitation, but the ways in which colonized nations developed strategies "to resist domination, to decolonize their own lands, minds, and to charter their own liberation as well as to propose better, more just forms of international relations."[32]

To avoid here an overly abstract theoretical consideration of these issues, one that remains two or more levels removed from actual sexual practices, it is useful to look at some particular studies, reports, and analyses of cultural and religious traditions. Given the general critiques we have just seen of such studies, we must proceed with all due caution, but nonetheless proceed. After all, the argument I made at the beginning of this chapter regarding the importance of taking diverse traditions into account, still holds. Our access to the traditions is necessarily mediated by more or less helpful interpretations, with all of their inevitable biases. But it may not be completely blocked. We may learn from studies and representations of diverse traditions, even if a major part of what we learn is through the critiques they have provoked. Moreover, the caution with which we approach this material may serve, to some extent, to mitigate the problems of ideological overlay. If we do not count on an adequate and stable view of diverse traditions, we may nonetheless come to understand why there is conflict and confusion regarding sexual ethics not only in the West but elsewhere as well.

It is neither possible nor appropriate to attempt here a comprehensive survey of cross-cultural and interreligious studies of sexuality. A small sampling of reports on indigenous traditions in the South Pacific and Africa,[33] a new study of a classical text from India (the *Kamasutra*), and a critical rendering of Muslim sexual beliefs and norms, can serve to particularize questions at stake. I am aware that my "samples" do not fit a common category (for example, all of them fitting into cultural *or* religious traditions); yet as such they provide

---

32. Ibid.

33. In *Explorations in Global Ethics*, 167–71, Twiss provides a succinct overview of "indigenous traditions" as a contemporary class of traditions representing more than 300 million people in Asia, Africa, the Americas, and the Pacific Islands. His attention to indigenous people differs from what follows in this chapter in that it addresses general questions of human rights, and it does not go back in history to select examples. My identification of one tradition in the nineteenth century, while less satisfactory in some respects, makes the point about sexual mores that is important here.

a broader sweep of possibilities, which I hope will be instructive in
the end.

Pre-modern Islands of the South Seas

Some of the most important ethnographic studies done in the early
1920s, focusing on people in the South Sea Islands, continue to be
influential in our thinking about sexuality and "other" cultures today. Bronislaw Malinowski, for example, studied the sexual lives of
the natives of the Trobriand Islands (located off the coast of what is
now Papua New Guinea, in the Solomon Sea).[34] Though his work is
in many ways outdated, it remains significant as an early study focusing precisely on sexual mores. The perspective he brought to his
studies and articulated as a result of them still pervades the Western
anthropological interpretation of indigenous sexuality among similar
peoples.[35] Influenced by early missionary reports of sexual permissiveness on these islands, Malinowski began his work with a hope
of ultimately critiquing, by contrast, what he considered to be European moral rigidity regarding sexuality. He came to agree with
missionary impressions of other-world permissiveness, but unlike
the missionaries, Malinowski by and large refrained from judging unfettered "savage" sexuality as morally inferior to repressive Western
practices and attitudes.

When Malinowski arrived to study the sexual lives of the Trobriand Islanders, he found what appeared to him to be a truly
different world.[36] Sex was more than a physiological transaction
between two individuals, and more than a mode of reproducing a
people; it permeated almost every aspect of the Islanders' lives. In its

---

34. See Bronislaw Malinowski, *The Sexual Life of Savages in North-Western
Melanesia* (New York: Halcyon House, 1929).

35. See, for example, Reed, "Contested Images and Common Strategies," 48.

36. For a partial history of anthropological studies regarding sexuality in Melanesia,
see Gilbert H. Herdt, "Introduction," in *Ritualized Homosexuality in Melanesia*, ed.
Gilbert J. Herdt (Berkeley: University of California Press, 1984), 1–6; and Bruce M.
Knauft, *South Coast New Guinea Cultures: History, Comparison, Dialectic* (New York:
Cambridge University Press, 1993), 16–24. For an overview of the island cultures of
Melanesia, see Matthew Spriggs, *The Island Melanesians* (Cambridge, MA: Blackwell,
1997), especially chaps. 1–7.

widest meaning it constituted a "sociological and cultural force."[37] Sex among the islanders, as Malinowski interpreted it, implied love and love-making; it was at the heart of marriage and family; it motivated art and was incorporated into magic and spells. But precisely because sex was woven into the fabric of life, both desire and activity were formed and colored by the details of that life. It looked different from what Malinowski and other researchers were used to in Europe, yet in some respects, at least, it appeared to be the same — not parallel, but analogous.[38]

For example, among the Trobrianders, some occupations were strictly gender assigned. Men were expected to carry loads on their shoulders, while women carried them on their heads. Women were responsible for the water supply, and it would be unthinkable for them not to spend time every day filling jars at water holes. Household tasks were divided along gender lines. Should there be a crossing of gender roles on these matters, however small they might seem, the result was shame for the whole of a family.

As for gender equality, nineteenth- and early-twentieth-century Western visitors and researchers found it difficult to understand. Here was a matrilinear society where legal relations of kinship and descent were determined through the mother.[39] Trobrianders believed that a child's body was solely and exclusively formed from the mother.[40] A child, therefore, is of the same substance as its mother; between father and child there is "no bond of physical union whatsoever.[41] (Indeed, there was — according to Malinowski — no understanding of reproduction as the joining of two entities through intercourse; all that was essential was the "simple dilation of the vagina."[42]) Yet strong emotional ties could be forged between father and child, and (something Malinowski considered "odd") the male child was considered to resemble the father, not the mother or her brothers.[43]

---

37. Malinowski, *The Sexual Life of Savages*, xxiii.
38. Ibid., xxv.
39. Ibid, chaps. 1, 5, and 8.
40. Ibid., 3.
41. Ibid., 4.
42. Ibid., 182.
43. Ibid., 206.

While the society was matrilineal, marriage was patrilocal, meaning that a wife moved to her husband's village and the married couple lived in the husband's house. Here the wife was the legal head of the family, and she could have her own separate possessions (though she could not own land). Yet in effect, the husband was master of the house, since the house was in his village, and it belonged to him. Moreover, regarding children, a wife was actually second in command, next to her own eldest brother. Gradually a male child learned that he was not from the same clan as his father, and that his property rights and rights of citizenship were lodged in the village where his maternal uncle lived, an uncle who assumed increasing authority over him. In other words, social position was handed on in the mother-line, but from a man to his sister's children. Social privileges were passed down through women, but they were exercised by men. As Malinowski put it, in every generation women continued their line, and men represented it. Power and functions in the family and clan were vested in men, though they had to be transmitted by women.[44]

Another area of sexual behavior of great interest to researchers like Malinowski was the sexual experience of the young. Early years of sexual experience for Trobrianders were marked by great freedom.[45] Since there was little privacy in the home, children knew a lot about the sexual activities of their elders. As children, their own sexual activity "in the bush" was not regulated. When they became adolescents, however, it was usual for personal preferences to develop, based on passion or "affinity of characters."[46] Gradually, mutual ties strengthened and stabilized, leading ultimately to marriage. Marriage was preceded by a period of active sexual life during which two individuals could live together as publicly recognized lovers, but without legal obligations. For economic and social reasons, these relationships usually moved eventually into marriage. Malinowski's observation was that after marriage, the passionate stage of sex was left behind, and much more rigid expectations of propriety came into

44. Ibid., 28.
45. Ibid., especially chaps. 3, 4, and 10.
46. Ibid., 67.

place. Privacy was lost, as the couple moved into the husband's parents' house; and in public, intimacy was not to be expressed (there could be no holding of hands, nor even walking side by side).

Interestingly, although sexual activity among the young and as yet unmarried was frequent, illegitimate children were rare and considered reprehensible. Out of family interest, they were concealed and ultimately adopted by a male relative. What they needed was a "social father," since, as noted above, physical fatherhood was not understood.

Malinowski reported observable sexual behavior that was very different from what he and other researchers were familiar with: for example, they seldom saw kissing, but they did see rubbing of noses, cheeks, and mouths, and biting and scratching as signs of love and affection.[47] When it came to particular sexual rules, however, these Malinowski interpreted as at least analogous to European norms.[48] Incest taboos were absolute, not only between parent and child but between brother and sister (something required in the matrilineal structure of the society where brother-sister relations had to be carefully restricted). Marriage was monogamous (except for tribal chiefs, who had the privilege of more than one wife). Adultery was prohibited. If a marriage did not work out, it could easily be dissolved (sometimes simply by one party leaving). Divorce was frequent, and when it took place, children followed the mother, not the father. Sex and marriage were not allowed between members of the same clan. There were limits (as suggested above regarding married couples) to what was acceptable in public regarding touching or the showing of tenderness. Modesty was required in dress.

Bestiality, exhibitionism, oral and anal sex, were all prohibited, though not necessarily unpracticed. Masturbation was judged undignified for a man, though it was considered more amusing than repulsive. Homosexuality, as Malinowski reported it, was held in contempt, except in the form of nonsexual friendship.[49]

Malinowski looked for a strange new world, and he found one; but in the end, it was not so strange. The Trobrianders had as many

---

47. Ibid., 331.
48. Ibid., 120–42, 201, 438–39, 455–56.
49. Ibid., 448, 453, 468, 471–76.

rules as they had liberties. Their society was stabilized by norms of decency and decorum as well as rigid restrictions. Sexual indulgences had their place, but the place was circumscribed. Malinowski's findings seem clear, and his reports straightforward. Yet his research and publications have been problematized in ways that both justify the caution with which we began and sustain the interest (and labor) needed to understand better any traditions that are not our own.

Malinowski's research has been challenged in several respects. Subsequent claims made by other anthropologists regarding Melanesian attitudes toward homosexuality offer an interesting case in point. Gilbert Herdt, for example, is critical of Malinowski (and other researchers) for what Herdt considers to be a biased interpretation of male same-sex relations in island cultures.[50] He argues that homosexuality is denied, left out, or treated as a perversion in these cultures (as in Malinowski's report of contempt for it) primarily because of researchers' prejudice. Herdt's own study distinguishes ritualized homosexuality from homosexual "identity" and finds the former to be common in island cultures. By "ritualized" Herdt usually means that it is incorporated into male initiation rites, so that it involves sex between males of different ages. He later came to refer to it as "boy-insemination." What this means is that there is not contempt for outward homosexual behavior (as Malinowski alleged); there just is no concept of feelings, goals, or an internal sense of self that yields an accepted homosexual identity.

In response to Herdt, Bruce Knauft tends to support Malinowski, though he acknowledges a postmodern skepticism regarding the possibility of any real objectivity in ethnographic research.[51] Critical of Herdt's own bias, Knauft insists that it is "highly questionable" whether ritualized homosexuality was in fact prevalent in west or lowland south New Guinea, though there is some documentation of it along the southern coast.[52] Knauft argues that a search for accurate data is and can be driven by confidence in some degree of possible objectivity. Ethnographic research need not, therefore, simply produce an artefact, a projection of the researchers' own cultural biases.

---

50. See Herdt, *Ritualized Homosexuality in Melanesia.*
51. Knauft, *South Coast New Guinea Cultures,* 3–9, 45–48.
52. Ibid., 47–48.

As for Malinowski's report of gender relations, subsequent scholars have quarreled about whether or not matrilineal societies as he described them brought anything like gender equality. Male dominance seems to hold sway, no matter what importance is given to women's biological role in inheritance. In response to this dispute, Marilyn Strathern suggests that questions of equality simply cannot be adjudicated by Western scholars attempting to interpret a non-Western culture. Their contemporary categories of power do not allow them to understand quite different categories and experiences of power as it was and is divided between men and women in other cultures. Her claim is that peoples in pre-modern indigenous cultures simply did not have conceptual tools for understanding notions of common humanity or individual agency.[53] Distinctions between active and passive roles were not recognized. Relationships were sufficiently complex that it is almost impossible for us to sort out what various descriptive terms like "complementarity," "dominance," "separation" really meant in contexts far removed from our own. Western ideas about equality have legal and political, as well as philosophical, roots. Nonetheless, Strathern observes that in many cases it is men who appear to be the principal public "transactors of value" and women the "transacted."[54] Men everywhere have authoritative responsibility for public and cultural activity, while women remain associated with powers in the spheres of reproduction.

In addition to challenges regarding the usefulness of Malinowski's findings on same-sex relations and on gender parity, there are critics of his and others' work on the sexual behavior of indigenous young people. The most direct attack on this kind of work was mounted in

---

53. Strathern, ed., *Dealing with Inequality*, 1–14. For a skeptical view about women's achievement of autonomy in matrilineal societies, see also Ann Chowning, " 'Women are our Business': Women Exchange and Prestige in Kove," in *Dealing with Inequality*, 131. Martha MacIntyre is more optimistic in her essay in this same volume: "Flying Witches and Leaping Warriors: Supernatural Origins of Power and Matrilineal Authority in Tubetube Society," in *Dealing with Inequality*, 207–8. Matthew Spriggs observes that matrilineal societies are definitely not matriarchies, but in them women are held in higher esteem than in patrilineal or patriarchal societies; see Spriggs, *The Island Melanesians*, 279–81.

54. Strathern, "Conclusion," *Dealing with Inequality*, 278, 298–99. For reports of variations on distribution of power between women and men, see Knauft, *South Coast New Guinea Cultures*, 86–116.

response not to Malinowski but to another ethnographer, Margaret Mead. The questions raised, however, are applicable to Malinowski's research as well.

Mead, like Malinowski, contributed to the view of the indigenous individual as an "innocent savage," unrepressed by civilization and its constraints. Beginning her work as a graduate student in the 1920s, Mead first sought to determine whether the experience of adolescents is as difficult in non-Western cultures as in Western.[55] Also like Malinowski, she went to the South Seas, in particular to Samoa, an island group east-northeast of Fiji. The subjects of her research were 68 young women. From them, she heard and reported that Samoan young people deferred marriage but not sex for many years. After considerable experience with what Westerners would call "casual sex," they later married, reared children, and helped to build and sustain their families. The society appeared completely stable; there was no adolescent angst; and all members were incorporated into Samoan society in patterned ways that were not threatened by multiple early sexual encounters.

Unfortunately, Mead's work came under a cloud after her death in 1978. The anthropologist, Derek Freeman, claimed that his own field work in Samoa fifty years later revealed that Mead's subjects had lied to her about their sexual experiences.[56] Indeed, he reported that one of Mead's primary informants confessed that she and a friend had played a joke on Mead; that, in fact, what they had told her was completely untrue. Far from young Samoans being sexually promiscuous, they adhered to a very strict sexual code wherein female virginity prior to marriage was valued and required. The controversy about this research raged for several years among anthropologists, with Mead not alive to respond. Freeman had a larger thesis he wanted

---

55. See Margaret Mead, *Coming of Age in Samoa* (New York: William Morrow, 1928).

56. Derek Freeman, *Margaret Mead and Samoa: The Making and Unmaking of an Anthropological Myth* (Cambridge, MA: Harvard University Press, 1983). Freeman reiterated his claims in an article he wrote in 1992 and in a second book in 1999. See Freeman, "Paradigms in Collision: The Far-reaching Controversy Over the Samoan Researches of Margaret Mead," *Academic Questions* 5 (Summer 1992): 23–44. See also Freeman, *The Fateful Hoaxing of Margaret Mead: A Historical Analysis of Her Samoan Research* (Boulder, CO: Westview, 1999).

to promote: that is, not only was Mead's research invalid, but the assumptions about Polynesian sexuality with which she began, and the conclusions that she drew about the social construction of sexuality, were also both wrong. The heart of the controversy was, then, really over whether there are some biological universals for human sexual activity, or whether each culture completely shapes the sexual paradigms that operate within it.

The issue here is not whether Mead or Freeman were right (many anthropologists today think it is impossible to settle this definitively), but whether cross-cultural social-scientific studies can help in the development of a sexual ethic. For one thing (as I have noted above), no culture remains static over time, and what were thought to be "primitive" cultures have not remained so, by and large. Mead's research subjects, for example, are now great-grandparents in a culture that has endured, but changed. As Mead herself said in a later edition of her work: "The young Samoans in universities throughout the United States often find this account of how their ancestresses lived as embarrassing as all of us find the clothes our mothers wore when we were young."[57] Yet many Western thinkers continue to reify "primitive" cultures, holding them in seemingly timeless images that are convenient when comparisons are made to more "progressive" cultures.

African Cultures

What is true of Western perspectives on sexuality among the peoples of the South Sea Islands is to some extent mirrored when it comes to Western perspectives on African peoples. Yet the African continent is in a much more complicated historical relationship with the West, and it presents a much more complicated subject—whether for colonizers and former colonizers, missionaries, visitors, or researchers. In fact, it is probably foolhardy to try to represent anything about sexuality as it is experienced, understood, and lived, in Africa as a whole. For one thing, Africa is a continent with hundreds of different peoples in every country, each with its own cultural histories, kinship

---

57. Mead, "Preface 1973 Edition," *Coming of Age in Samoa*, vi.

structures, rituals, and morality codes. The difficulty of generalizing from one African people to another is rendered even more complex by today's growing movement of individuals and families from rural to urban settings and by the forced migration of workers and of political refugees.

Moreover, throughout Africa there are at least three layers of historical experience that continue to shape sexual mores. These are the layers of (1) indigenous traditional experience, (2) the experience of colonialism, and (3) "modern" and contemporary experience. These historical periods did not simply succeed one another; they remain as elements of belief and practice within Africa today. Traditional systems that were once integral wholes may have broken down, yet they endure in significant measure and influence. Even the legal systems in most parts of Africa are a mixture of customary, colonial, and postcolonial law.[58] Moreover, each of these layers of experience is permeated and shaped by religious traditions — African traditional religions, the religions of colonizers and conquerors (primarily Christian and Muslim), and the mixture of these traditions as they coexist in the contemporary world of change. Custom, law, and religious belief all have significant impact on sexual meanings and practice.

An additional complication in approaching African ways of living out human sexuality is that we have today not only co-mingled elements from different historical periods but significant retrospective and prospective critiques of beliefs and practices. There are feminist postcolonialist critiques, Christian theological ethical critiques, and the existential critical questions raised by the dire situation regarding HIV and AIDS across vast regions of the continent. Critiques are revelatory of traditions, but they focus on what is problematic and tend only to presume whatever constitutes the strength and richness in traditions they critique. This works well as internal critique, though it can be misleading for Westerners who stand outside the traditions themselves. Despite these complications, it is important to attend to

---

58. See Ifi Amadiume, *Male Daughters, Female Husbands: Gender and Sex in an African Society* (London: Zed Books, 1987), 185–86; Jeanne Maddox Toungra, "Changing the Meaning of Marriage: Women and Family Law in Côte d'Ivoire," in *African Feminism: the Politics of Survival in Sub-Saharan Africa*, ed. Gwendolyn Mikell (Philadelphia: University of Pennsylvania Press, 1997), 54–56.

African experiences of culture, religion, and sexuality. Whatever the diversity within Africa, there are some generalizations with which we can begin, as long as we identify them provisionally. Without denying the problems raised from within by a tradition's adherents, it may be possible to glimpse something of the fabric of life that has served peoples well, at least until now.

Sexuality and Community

If there is a shared central element in African understandings of sex, it is that sexuality is primarily for the sake of the community. This cardinal belief shapes many sexual norms in ways that make them difficult for Westerners to interpret. Marriage, for example, is generally expected of everyone. And despite hundreds of years of colonial and missionary efforts to promote and even enforce a principle of individual choice, the arrangement or at least approval of marriages remains to a significant extent in the hands of families, each extending to multiple generations in the present and in the past. The communitarian character of marriage is represented by the tendency of traditional marriage (unlike either civil or ecclesiastical marriage) to take place in stages, allowing for family covenanting.[59] This characteristic also explains other aspects of a sexual ethic — such as the importance of blood lineages (over the relatively unimportant status of the nuclear family); the power of male elders both in life and in death (as revered ancestors) over processes of discernment regarding sexual arrangements; practices such as bridewealth (or brideprice) which signal that a woman is married not only to her husband but to his family; strict gender role differentiation; widespread fostering of children by relatives; incest taboos whose boundaries are much broader than those of Western mores (in Africa extending to all degrees of relationship in a family tree).

---

59. I am indebted here to such works as: Bénézet Bujo, *Foundations of an African Ethic: Beyond the Universal Claims of Western Morality* (New York: Crossroad, 2001); John C. Caldwell and Pat Caldwell, "Sexual Intercourse in Pre-literate Societies," in *The Evolution the of Meaning of Sexual Intercourse in the Human*, ed. Giuseppe Benagiano, Gian Carlo Di Renzo, Ermelando V. Cosmi (Cortona, Italy: International Institute for the Study of Marriage, 1996), 57–65; Mercy Amba Oduyoye, *Daughters of Anowa: African Women and Patriarchy* (Maryknoll, NY: Orbis, 1995); Oduyoye and Kanyoro, eds., *The Will to Arise*; Adrian Hastings, *Christian Marriage in Africa* (London: SPCK, 1973).

Above all, the subordination of sexuality to the well-being and perpetuation of family and community explains the focus on fertility, rather than sex, at the heart of traditional African sexual ethics. The worst death for most Africans is to die childless. Yet sexuality from an African perspective aims at more than mere procreation, as is evidenced in some parts of Africa by the ceremonial practice of intercourse at events such as the marriage of one's children, the appearance of a child's first tooth, initiation rites, and funeral rites. Whether increasing or sustaining family and tribe, sexuality is for the sake of the good of the whole.

Gender, Marriage, and Family

Both patrilineal and matrilineal families can be found in Africa, though the large majority are patrilineal. Just as in Melanesia, these represent the line of descent in terms of family membership. In matrilineal societies neither the wife nor children are members of the husband's family, although husbands are expected to house and maintain their children (in exchange for their help with the father's work). In patrilineal societies, male offspring (brothers and their offspring) of the same patriarch constitute a family; female offspring (sisters) are also members of the patrilineal family, but their children are not (the latter attaining their family membership through their own father's lineage).[60] Inheritance rights of women and girls, as well as their prerogatives in family decision-making, are generally weaker than those of men and boys. Female rights are determined by a variety of factors (such as whether or not the living accommodations of a family are gender segregated; how much women and girls contribute to family resources; how economically autonomous — in either a matrilineal or patrilineal society — wives actually are; how colonial ordinances support or undermine customary law).

Sex is considered to be beneficial, not enervating, and attitudes toward sexual activity are generally not pessimistic or suspicious in ways reminiscent of Western cultures. Yet sexual rules vary along gender lines. Male but not female extramarital sex is condoned in

---

60. See Takyiwaa Manuh, "Wives, Children, and Intestate Succession in Ghana," in *African Feminism*, 79–83.

most traditional codes of behavior, though in some parts of Africa women, too, can engage in extramarital sex as long as they are discreet.[61] There has been a general assumption, however, that men need sex more than women, and that they therefore require more than one sexual partner (an assumption not effectively modified by the Christian missionary work of a hundred years). Despite this, men are not usually considered "macho" in traditional African societies.[62]

Girls and boys are brought up traditionally with gendered sex education. Mutuality is ultimately prized between women and men, and both gain their identity in roles of importance. Yet Isabel Apawo Phiri notes: "Girls learn from their mothers that they are created to serve their brothers. Boys also grow up believing that they were born to be served by girls and women."[63] Gender roles are reinforced through traditional puberty rites, and the traditional and religious education that precedes them. Initiation includes an introduction into the secrets of sexuality, shaped to accord with the responsibilities, rights, and expectations of womanhood and manhood. Boys and young men are taught that they both need and have a right to sexual intercourse with girls and women. Sexual experience for them most likely begins after initiation and before marriage. Girls and young women are taught that they are to satisfy the sexual needs of their husbands. For most of them, sexual experience traditionally begins with marriage. As they are prepared for marriage, young women must also learn the strict and precise regulations that govern not only their relationship with their husbands but with the whole of the husband's family.

Husbands hold exclusive sexual rights over their wives, but wives can ordinarily not expect to have exclusive sexual rights in regard to their husbands.[64] Moreover, given the emphasis on fertility, childlessness in a marriage is often remedied by the addition of a second wife or a concubine. These two factors — the belief in male sexual needs and an overwhelming concern for children — account in large part for

---

61. Caldwell and Caldwell, "Sexual Intercourse in Pre-literate Societies," 61–62.

62. Ibid., 63.

63. Isabel Apawo Phiri, "African Women of Faith Speak Out in an HIV/AIDS Era," in *African Women, HIV/AIDS, and Faith Communities*, ed. Isabel Apawo Phiri and Beverly Haddad (Pietersburg: Cluster Publications, 2004), 9.

64. Anne Nasimiyu Wasike, Unpublished manuscript and personal correspondence (April 2004).

the institution of polygyny.[65] The traditional rationale, therefore, for polygyny is that it can serve the goal of both sexuality and marriage, which is to keep the community together. It secures offspring, helps in the accumulation of wealth, prevents widespread prostitution and adultery, stabilizes the home by providing help for a first wife, and allows sexual activity to the husband in the long periods when access to any given wife is forbidden (according to taboos prohibiting sexual intercourse with a wife during menstruation, pregnancy, and a stipulated lengthy post partum period after each child is born).[66]

Divorce is not common in most African communities, at least until recent times. Marriage is intended to be lifelong, though it is not indissoluble.[67] Traditional structures are designed to serve stability and provide for contingencies. Reconciliation processes are available within a larger social organization — the clan or tribe.

One can imagine a time when a seamless order prevailed, not challenged or disturbed by the uprooting of peoples from their lands, or the destruction of traditional economies, or the imposition of alien cultures on long-surviving social systems. Yet further exploration of all historical periods now coexisting in Africa gives warning that what may have worked in the past cannot by itself solve the problems of the present.

New Interpreters and Critics: Sustainable African Sexualities

Interesting and important constructive critiques have been made of some elements in African sexualities by African Christian theological ethicists such as Bénézet Bujo.[68] Strongly affirming the value of an African emphasis on community, he nonetheless cautions against

---

65. Though, as is suggested in chapter 2, the term most often used by Westerners to describe this form of marriage is "polygamy," "polygyny" is the more accurate term for the simultaneous marriage of one man to more than one woman. "Polyandry" refers to the marriage of one woman to more than one man. Since the experience in Africa is overwhelmingly of one man married to more than one woman, the better term here is "polygyny."

66. For both traditional rationales for polygyny and arguments that it can be consistent with Christian belief, see Hillman, *Polygamy Reconsidered*; Hastings, *Christian Marriage in Africa*, 6–22.

67. See Hastings, *Christian Marriage in Africa*, 35; Oduyoye, *Daughters of Anowa*, 147–51.

68. Bujo, *Foundations of an African Ethic*.

too "romantic" an idealization of traditional African culture, including an "exaggerated understanding of community."[69] While arguing that polygyny, for example, is not "automatically unjust" (since it once served to protect women and to assure stability in marriages where childlessness might have led to adultery), Bujo observes that today it no longer serves these functions. Rather, in his view, second and third marriages are now frequently entered into on hollow pretexts, and the result is often damaging to first wives who are deceived (their husbands concealing a second marriage in another locality) or ignored (simply set aside sexually and emotionally in favor of a younger second wife).

Contemporary anthropologists and historians are also shedding new light on traditional as well as twenty-first century African sexual practices. Notable in this regard are studies of homosexuality in African societies.[70] Challenging what they consider to be the unfounded myth that same-sex relationships are absent or extremely marginal in these societies, researchers document forms of homosexual relations in every region of the continent. The results of these studies are interesting and significant, even though their meaning remains controversial.[71]

By far the strongest new voices — both affirmative and critical of African sexual systems — are those of a rapidly growing number of African feminist writers, including theologians.[72] While they, like

---

69. Ibid., 162–69.

70. See Murray and Roscoe, eds., *Boy-Wives and Female Husbands*.

71. See Amadiume's contention that naming some institutionalized relationships between women "lesbian" in a Western sense is a false interpretation of these relationships. It would be, she says, "shocking and offensive" to the African women involved. Amadiume, *Male Daughters, Female Husbands*, 7.

72. I am indebted here especially to the work of Mercy Amba Oduyoye, Anne Nasimiyu Wasike, Musimbi R. A. Kanyoro, Isabel Apawo Phiri, Beverly Haddad, Madipoane Masenya, and Ifi Amadiume, some of whose writings are cited earlier in this chapter. I am grateful to all the members of the Circle of Concerned African Women Theologians whose conferences and increasing numbers of publications have enabled me to hear (with my own limitations) the voices of African women. I am similarly grateful to all the participants in the All-Africa Conference: Sister to Sister, who have allowed me to share in their deliberations regarding African culture and responses to HIV and AIDS. Finally, I have learned a great deal from the African "faith fellows" who have come to Yale University, 2002–5: Sylvia Amisi, Fulata Moyo, Vuadi Vibila, Anne Nasimiyu-Wasike, Dorothy Ucheaga, Constance Shisanya, Therese Tinkasiimire, Isabel Phiri, Dorcas Akintude, and Hazel Ayanga. My rendering of what I have learned from all of

Bujo, affirm the African communitarian character of sex, marriage, and family, they believe it can be sustained only in ways that do not threaten the inherent dignity of women or ignore women's need for some degree of economic and social control over their own lives. The well-being of children, they argue, as well as that of women and men, requires some modification in traditional marriage structures and in the possibilities accorded women and girls. Without this, not only will the basic structures of African societies fail to survive contemporary social, economic, and political challenges, but Africa as a whole will be devastated by the HIV and AIDS pandemic of the twentieth and twenty-first centuries.

In order to understand what changes are needed, African feminists' task has been to identify what is problematic in African sexual systems. What they focused on first was the problem of gender disparity — endemic, it seemed, to African traditional social arrangements. That is, African sexual practices are lodged in gendered patterns of relationship that currently put women at risk (and harm men and children as well). When cultural practices jeopardize the well-being of women, they are almost always part of a sexual system that subordinates women to men and that takes away their choice regarding their own sexuality. Traditional patterns of relationship that provided security and dignity to women in the past were perhaps always also vulnerable to abuse as long as these patterns (not unlike Western patterns) accorded honor to mothers, queens, and goddesses, but at the same time assigned female images for moral evil (whores, polluters, witches) and treated women as minors.[73] Prior to colonization, gender ideologies in a few parts of Africa (for example, among the Igbo in what is now Nigeria) were flexible, with roles not so rigidly circumscribed.[74] In some instances, then, colonization and the influence

---

these African women may still be inaccurate and inadequate in many respects, failings that are in spite of, and not because of, their efforts to help me to understand. For further information on these organizations and programs, see Margaret A. Farley, "Partnership in Hope: Gender, Faith, and Responses to HIV/AIDS in Africa," *Journal of Feminist Studies in Religion* 20 (Spring 2004): 133–48.

73. See Mutombo Nkulu-N'Sengha, "Bumuntu Paradigm and Gender Justice," in *What Men Owe to Women: Men's Voices for World Religions,* ed. John C. Raines and Daniel C. Maguire (Albany: State University of New York Press, 2001), 70–71.

74. See Amadiume, *Male Daughters, Female Husbands,* 16.

of Western religions may have tipped the balance so that women's roles became more severely limited and monitored. Yet patriarchy (whether in patrilineal or matrilineal systems) seems embedded in much, perhaps most, of traditional, colonial, and postcolonial Africa.

With a general critique of gender-differentiated roles and identities has come an identification of particular practices that appear harmful to women and girls. Here, the focus is on domestic institutions and on specific cultural practices that are either supported or tolerated by these institutions. Thus, for example, while family-arranged marriages have served communities and societies, they have also sometimes fostered extreme forms of coercion with regard to girls and young women. "Child marriage" is one of these. In order to assure continuation of the family line when there is only one son, a little boy's father might propose marriage (for his son) to a girl's family. If the proposal is accepted, the girl is given to a relative of the boy's family for "marital" sexual relations until the boy is old enough, at which time she is required to join him.[75] It is, of course, still not infrequent that teen-age girls are married to elderly men as second or third wives.[76] Moreover, sometimes girls continue to be "kidnapped" (*thwala*) for marriage from their schools, without their own prior knowledge but with the knowledge and approval of their families.[77]

Traditional customs (sometimes reinforced by Christian and Muslim teachings) still promote the belief that women's bodies and their sexualities are not their own. Once married, women's bodies belong to their husbands. Women are expected to respond to their husbands' needs and wishes, often without regard for their own. But at the same time, as we have seen, husbands' bodies can be shared with other women.[78] Among some African tribes with which feminist writers are familiar, this belief undergirds practices not only of polygyny, but

---

75. Judith Mbula Bahemuka, "Social Changes and Women's Attitudes Toward Marriage in East Africa," in *Will to Arise*, 122.

76. Nasimiyu-Wasike, unpublished manuscript, 2004.

77. See P. Whooley, "Marriage in Africa: A Study in the Ciskei," in *Church and Marriage in Modern Africa: 1975 Supplement to Report to Catholic Bishops of East and Central Africa*, ed. Trevor David Verryn (Johannesburg: Zenith Printers, 2001), 295–98.

78. Phiri, "African Women of Faith Speak Out in an HIV/AIDS Era," 116.

of "wife sharing," wherein the giving of one's wife to a guest for sex constitutes a form of hospitality. And there are communities in Africa where, when a man dies, his wife's sexuality still belongs to his family (a function of the practice of bridewealth).[79] Hence, she can be required to undergo "ritual sexual cleansing" (by means of sexual intercourse with a man designated or self-identified for this purpose), and to abide by the custom of "wife inheritance" (or "levirite marriage") whereby she is thought to continue her conjugal relationship with her husband by marrying a relative of his.[80]

It is perhaps not surprising that feminists have found polygyny troubling. We have already seen the significance of polygyny in traditional and contemporary Africa (as well as Bujo's critique of it, not from the perspective of a standard Christian preference for monogamy but from the perspective of its present loss of past benign rationales). Polygyny remains extremely important in Africa, constituting approximately 40 percent of marriages in West Africa and 20–30 percent in Eastern and Southern Africa.[81] It is still not only accepted but promoted by many women and men, for all the reasons I have already noted. Many Western male scholars, in an effort to counter longstanding Christian opposition to polygynous marriages, have unfortunately waxed eloquent about its value for African society. Eugene Hillman, for example, argues that it is the context out of which African virtues of unity, harmony, solidarity, and hospitality are developed.[82]

---

79. See Oduyoye, *Daughters of Anoah*, 133–34, for an alternate view of what gifts given by one family to another might mean if they are reciprocal and if they do not involve one family "buying" a woman from another family who "gives" her (a human being) away.

80. Nasimiyu-Wasike, unpublished manuscript, 2004. The biblical parallels to some of these practices are notable.

81. These percentages are unstable and reported differently in a variety of sources. Obviously, preferred forms of marriage are in flux. Nonetheless, these numbers give some sense of the continuing prevalence of polygyny throughout Africa.

82. This is the whole thesis of Hillman in his *Polygamy Reconsidered*. Adrian Hastings offers a useful historical overview of responses to polygyny by the Christian churches in Africa, and concludes that twentieth century marriage, especially in South Africa, changed in ways that suffered from the too negative appraisals of traditional "domestic institutions" by missionaries. See Hastings, *Christian Marriage in Africa*, 20.

For African feminist critics, polygyny has become a more and more controversial form of marriage, even though there are many women who continue to accept and support it. Feminists appear of one mind in at least challenging, and often directly opposing, it. Anne Nasimiyu-Wasike, for example, argues that even traditional rationales for polygyny show it to be an arrangement for the sake of men and harmful to women.[83] It represents men's search for progeny and immortality; it sees women as dependent on men, yet made for the sexual and economic service of men; it identifies women's worth with childbearing; it yields not harmony but conflict between women as co-wives; it subordinates some women to other women. Women are, Nasimiyu-Wasike maintains, culturally conditioned to project their dislike of polygyny not on the institution itself but on their co-wives. "The tongue of co-wives is bitter."[84] Her conclusion is that polygynous relationships have crippled both women and men, and that this domestic institution is a sign of human brokenness.[85]

The problems that African feminists identify in African sexual systems become, in their view, even more dire in the context of HIV and AIDS, especially when the major transmitter of the AIDS virus is (as it is in sub-Saharan Africa) heterosexual sex. Most of the patterns and practices described above — that is, little power on the part of women over their own sexuality, multiple sexual partners through polygynous marriages, wife-sharing as a mode of hospitality, and the treatment of widows (with ritual cleansing and wife inheritance) — put populations at risk for HIV. Even if these patterns and practices were beneficial in their original contexts, they become extremely problematic when people die from them.

Two other problems are often cited by African feminist writers when it comes to sexuality and the spread of HIV and AIDS in Africa. One is the problem of gender violence. As in many other parts of the world, rape, domestic violence, and the abuse of women in settings of political instability and warfare, are all too common.[86] Feminist

---

83. Nasimiyu-Wasike, "Polygamy: A Feminist Critique," 101–18.

84. Ibid., 112. Nasimiyu-Wasike is here citing a traditional African proverb, drawing on the tremendously important role of proverbs for understanding African cultures.

85. Ibid., 107 and 116.

86. *United Nations Special Session on AIDS Fact Sheet* (June 2001), 21.

analysts point to a link between unequal power relations between women and men, toleration of domestic violence, and HIV.[87]

The other problem is that of female circumcision in regions of Africa. Its prevalence varies from country to country, with no practice of it in some countries and practice in others that includes nearly 80 percent of the female population. As I have noted at the beginning of this chapter, female circumcision is a practice that has received a great deal of attention in recent years — by feminists and others. Sometimes called "female genital cutting" or even "female genital mutilation," it has proven not to be a simple cultural or ethical question. On the face of it, it looks like it harms girls and women terribly. It can take various forms: the least extensive form involves the removal of only the cliteral hood and some (or sometimes all) of the clitoris; the most common form entails the removal of all or part of the labia minora (in addition to the clitoris and clitoral hood); the most radical form (known as "infibulation") involves the removal of all external genitalia and a portion of the labia majora (which is then stitched together, leaving a small opening for passage of urine and menstrual blood). There are other permutations on these forms, but in the majority of practices, these predominate.[88] In all of its forms, female circumcision is thought to add to the risk of HIV, since it is often not carried out with hygienic precautions (the use of the same knife for a whole group being circumcised may signify a blood bond between the subjects, but it also transmits infection). In its most severe forms, it makes sexual intercourse and childbirth so difficult that open lesions are generated, and infection has its chance.

Usual explanatory concepts, such as patriarchy, tradition, religion, are not the ones given by participants in the practice.[89] Clearly for women who value this practice, it is a source of personal and social identity, and it ultimately allows them the possibility of marriage which is their entry into the most important gender roles of wife and

---

87. See, e.g., Beverley Haddad, "Choosing to Remain Silent: Links Between Gender Violence, HIV/AIDS and the South African Church," in *African Women, HIV/AIDS and Faith Communities*, 149–67.

88. See Lori Leonard, "Interpreting Female Genital Cutting: Moving Beyond the Impasse," *Annual Review of Sex Research* 11 (2000): 158–90.

89. Ibid.

mother. As part of a rite of initiation, it stands also as a test of a girl's capacity to withstand suffering; it is a sign that she is ready for adult life. African feminist critics observe (and often decry) that all of this symbolic meaning is embedded in traditions of female subservience, fear of women's sexual desire or pleasure, and concern to prevent women's engaging in premarital sex and later adultery. What remains to be explained is why some African subgroups "have only recently adopted female genital cutting"[90] in situations where adolescent girls themselves demand it, over the opposition of their parents and traditional leaders.

Some African feminists have been loathe to criticize female circumcision, especially if it is not practiced among their own people. Yet when they come face to face with it, it is difficult to support it.[91] One obvious problem is that Western scientists and others (including Western feminists) have focused on the issue of female circumcision in ways that are perceived by African feminists as showing disrespect, even contempt, for Africa. All of this is perhaps why there is so little comparative ethics or even interreligious discussion of this most delicate of matters. Some African feminists, as feminists elsewhere, decide to take a stand against female circumcision — especially in its most radical forms — only when they see women opposing it and speaking out of the regions where female circumcision is practiced. The response becomes, then, not one of criticism from another cultural context, but of standing in solidarity with those whose experience it is.

The overall concerns of African feminists include breaking the silence on cultural practices that injure women. The point of listening to them here is not simply to gain another perspective on African sexual beliefs and practices, although this is important. It is, rather, to consider whether a more adequate understanding of African sexual systems and practices can be achieved when the anguish of women becomes a vantage point of interpretation, when it has its own hermeneutical function.

---

90. Ibid., 158.
91. See Amadiume, *Male Daughters, Female Husbands*, 87 n. 6; Lloyda Fanusie, "Sexuality and Women in African Culture," in *Will to Arise*, 148–49.

Kamasutra: Hindu Textbook on Erotic Love

Hinduism is not a single unified religion but a family name that covers a variety of religious teachings, philosophical perspectives, and practices. It has no single founder or predominant teacher, and no central institution or spokesperson. It is sustained by a wide array of oral and written sacred sources, including hymns and mantras, manuals for rituals and prayers, instructions for religious hermits, philosophical treatises, and mystical discourses. Among its traditional writings are also texts (or more accurately, textbooks) on erotic love and techniques for achieving sexual union and pleasure. The oldest and best known of the erotic texts is *Kamasutra.*

As one might imagine, *Kamasutra* has had a mixed past in terms of its acceptance both in the East and in the West. Written in the third century C.E. by Vatsyayana Mallanaga, a scholar from northern India, it incorporates texts by earlier authors whose works are no longer extant. It is cited as a foundational text by authors of numerous erotic textbooks that followed. Scholars today claim that "no other single work has influenced more the treatment of love themes in Indian sculptures, paintings, and literature."[92] This is despite the fact that *Kamasutra* was not widely read by Hindus until the publication of an English translation by Richard Francis Burton and Forster Fitzgerald Arbuthnot in the late nineteenth century, which made it popular among tourists to India.[93]

Kamasutra means a "treatise on pleasure," coming from *sutra* (treatise or guide) and *kama* (erotic desire and sexual pleasure). It has been thought of primarily as a guide to positions for sex, even a form of pornography, but its purpose and substance — and hence its historical importance — extend much farther. Divided into seven books, each with multiple chapters, the *Kamasutra* covers a broad statement regarding human life (Book I), a typology of forms of loving and minutely detailed and categorized accounts of acts of love (Book II), guidance for men who want to woo women who are still

---

92. Moni Nag, "Paradox of Eroticism and Sexual Abstinence in Hindu Culture," in *Evolution of the Meaning of Sexual Intercourse,* 171. Nag offers here, in addition to an analysis of the *Kamasutra,* a brief but telling overview of erotic sculptures in and on Indian temples.

93. Ibid., 171.

virgins (Book III), descriptions of the roles of wives, co-wives, and members of a harem (Book IV), analyses of ways to seduce other men's wives (Book V), a discussion of courtesans, their aims and strategies (Book VI), and "exotic esoteria" regarding such things as becoming "lucky in love" (Book VII). It is Book II — notably only one book of the seven — that has been the object of prurient interest, satire, and a certain amount of infamy; indeed, the *Kamasutra* is frequently equated with the sorts of material in this one book. It is within Book II that we get primarily descriptions of heterosexual foreplay and intercourse, but also some considerations of male homosexuality and lesbian relations (the latter are treated as something that happens only when there are no men available).

Scholarship regarding *Kamasutra* has taken on surprising new life since the publication in 2002 of a contemporary English translation by Wendy Doniger (American scholar in the history of religions and an expert in Sanskrit, the original language of the text) and Sudhir Kakar (Indian psychoanalyst and Hindu scholar).[94] New readings of the purpose and predominant themes of the text are strongly suggested by the presentation, translation, and interpretation that Doniger and Kakar provide. Like other scholars today, they are highly critical of the 1883 Burton-Arbuthnot English translation, claiming that it is filled with mistranslations and skewed by the translators' fear of Victorian censorship.[95] The bias of Burton and Arbuthnot was twofold. That is, they were all too happy to translate and publish a text that would serve as an antidote to the European Christian subordination of sexual pleasure to the goal of reproduction and to what they considered nineteenth-century prudishness about sex. But at the same time they were concerned to avoid the kind of backlash that would undermine the distribution of the text and harm their

---

94. Vatsyayana Mallanaga, *Kamasutra: A New, Complete English Translation of the Sanskrit Text with Excerpts from the Sanskrit Jayamangala Commentary of Yashodhara Indrapada, the Hindi Jaya Commentary of Devadatta Shastri, and Explanatory Notes by the Translators*, trans. Wendy Doniger and Sudhir Kakar (New York: Oxford University Press, 2002). The extracts that follow on pp. 93 and 94 are used by permission of Oxford University Press.

95. For more detailed information about the translators who worked with Burton, see Doniger and Kakar, "Introduction" to *Kamasutra*, li–lxii. I am indebted primarily to Doniger and Kakar's work for my rendering of the nature and consequences of Burton's edition.

own careers. To remedy this fear, they did things with their translation to make the most salacious passages appear "Oriental," hence
more of a curiosity than something that might be read as relevant to
Western experience. They used Hindu terms for words they thought
might be offensive to a Western readership, and they modified texts
to mitigate the force of some of the *Kamasutra's* instructions.

Doniger and Kakar also had particular aims in producing their new
translation. In the contemporary Western world, there is no longer
the fear of scandalizing the potential readership for *Kamasutra*. Even
Book II is hardly shocking in the twenty-first century. What might be
appalling to current readers is the apparent gender bias of the text.
It is, for example, fairly clear (though not without minor dispute)
that Vatsyayana Mallanaga was writing for men, especially for men-
about-town or urbane playboys. Yet, Doniger and Kakar point out
that women's voices are heard in the text, and their roles are not
totally passive (whether in sex or in social relations).[96] So Doniger
and Kakar in some respects have opposite aims from Burton and
Arbuthnot. They want *Kamasutra* to speak to the experience of their
readers across the world, both West and East. Even more importantly,
they want the full breadth of the text to be more visible. A more
accurate translation (of both text and some commentaries), can show
how this ancient textbook is situated in Hindu culture as a whole. A
further result of this will be to reveal the parallels and analogies with
other cultures and world religions.

In this new translation, then, the explicitness of sexual description
is not watered down, but it is integrated into the larger aims of the
treatise. The text as a whole is made more accessible by the accuracy
and the gracefulness of the translation itself, as well as by the selection of commentaries that go with the text. Moreover, the translators'
introduction and clarifying notes point the reader to the structure of
the text and the passages that identify the aims and caveats of the
author. In Book I, for example, Vatsyayana Mallanaga sets the stage
by announcing that the subjects of the text are threefold: religion,
power, and pleasure. These correspond to Hinduism's three aims
of human life: *dharma* (religion, morality, law, duty, justice), *artha*

---

96. Ibid., xxviii–xxxii.

(wealth, political power, success), and *kama* (sensual and sexual desire and pleasure).[97] These are not ultimately to be separated, says Vatsyayana, since the achievement of power depends on religion, and the attainment of pleasure depends on some form of power.

> Undertake any project that might achieve
> the three aims of life, or two, or even just one,
> but not one that achieves one
> at the cost of the other two.[98]

Doniger and Kakar conclude that *Kamasutra* is about the art of living, not just about sex.[99] But, of course, it is about sex and the interpersonal and physiological methods that are related to sex. "Because a man and a woman depend upon one another in sex, it requires a method, and this method is learned from the *Kamasutra.*"[100]

Kamasutra sits in the middle of what some scholars call a paradox in the complex beliefs and practices of Hinduism.[101] On the one hand, Hindu culture includes the astonishing display of eroticism in literature and sculpture and even religion (for example, the salvific use of sexual intercourse in religious rituals in Tantrism and Sahajiya Vaishnavism[102]). On the other hand is the powerful strain of asceticism in Hindu religion, the tradition of the yogis, of Gandhi, and of some of the Hindu epics. On the one hand, a concerted search for every form of pleasure; on the other hand, sexual abstinence as a route to spirituality through sublimation. *Kamasutra* seems to be clearly on the side of eroticism and the search for pleasure. Yet within it there are hints of the traditions of renunciation; at least there are brief and paradoxical reminders that asceticism ought not be forgotten.

Both religion and pleasure require restraint. Both require techniques of control of the body. *Kamasutra* is interested in pleasure,

---

97. There is what is sometimes called a fourth aim, *moksha*, which implies spiritual release.

98. Vatsyayana, *Kamasutra*, trans. Doniger and Kakar, 1.2.41.

99. Doniger and Kakar, "Introduction," *Kamasutra*, xi.

100. Vatsyayana, *Kamasutra*, trans. Doniger and Kakar, 1.2.18.

101. See Nag, "Paradox of Eroticism and Sexual Abstinence in Hindu Culture," 183–85; also Doniger and Kakar, "Introduction," xiii-xiv.

102. Nag, "Paradox of Eroticism and Sexual Abstinence in Hindu Culture," 177–79.

but the texts of restraint are not missing. Vatsyayana insists that
in a "scientific" text like the *Kamasutra*, it is necessary to describe
everything, but not recommend everything. Hence, some practices
are presented that the reader is ultimately warned against. Every
form of lovemaking is described, but some are finally judged to be
"base."[103] "Pleasures are a means of sustaining the body, just like
food, and they are rewards for religion and power. But people must
be aware of the flaws in pleasures, flaws that are like diseases."[104]

A man who knows [*Kamasutra's*] real meaning
sees religion, power, and pleasure,
his own convictions, and the ways of the world
for what they are, and he is not driven by passion.
The unusual techniques employed to increase passion,
which have been described as this particular book required,
are strongly restricted right here in this verse,
right after it.
For the statement that 'There is a text for this'
Does not justify a practice. People should realize
that the contents of the texts apply in general,
but each actual practice is for one particular region.
... [Vatsyayana] made this work in chastity and in the highest
     meditation,
for the sake of worldly life;
he did not compose it
for the sake of passion.[105]

Of what use is this text in our search for wisdom about sexual
ethics? For one thing, the history of its translations tells us that
classics are read and understood with eyes and minds shaped by particular cultural experience. In part, we learn from them according
to what we seek. In part, we learn something new which can illuminate our own experience and sometimes teach us what we ought
to seek. If the bridge between one era and another, one culture and

---

103. This, at least, is the judgment of some of Vatsyayana's commentators. See
Doniger and Kakar, "Introduction," xx-xi.
104. Vatsyayana, *Kamasutra*, trans. Doniger and Kakar, 1.2.37–38.
105. Ibid., 7.2.53–55, 57.

another, is crossed even part way, our eyes turned forward and backward may be sharpened, and our thoughts may be both concentrated and provoked.

The World of Islam

In the early twenty-first century it is all too easy to reduce Islamic understandings of sexuality to dramatic stereotypes drawn from right-wing fringe groups such as the Taliban in Afghanistan. To do so is to add to a "clash of ignorance," as Said called efforts to pit "the West" and "Islam" against each other without taking account of the "internal dynamics and plurality of every civilization."[106] Islam had its beginnings nearly 1500 years ago, and its history of spiritual devotion, political struggle, community and empire building, intellectual pursuits, aesthethics, and profound humanism provides a basis for the deep commitments of its now more than a billion adherents worldwide. Like the other major religions that we have considered both in the previous chapter and this one, Islam represents a tradition of great complexity. It is rich with multiple sacred texts, diverse in the cultures of its many nations, and profoundly varied in its great schools of thought.

Muhammed ibn Abdallah (560–632 C.E), the Prophet and founder of Islam, believed he was bringing to the Arabs the same faith that Abraham had given to the Jews and Jesus to the Christians. In a fullness of time, Allah gave to Muhammed a revelation for his people, calling them to repentance and to surrender (*"islam"*) to the one true God (in whom many had already come to believe through the cult of Kabah).[107] The ethics of Islam is ultimately based on the Qur'an, the

---

106. Said, "The Clash of Ignorance," *The Nation* 276 (October 22, 2001): 11–13. In this essay Said is responding to Samuel Huntington's theory of the "clash of civilizations," excoriating it for its simplistic and ultimately false characterization of international cultural struggles today. For an earlier critique of Western perceptions of and attitudes toward Islam, see also Said, *Orientalism*, 48–49, 60–63, 151–52, and passim.

107. I am drawing here on Karen Armstrong, *Islam: A Short History* (New York: Modern Library, 2000); Maurice Gaudefroy-Demombynes, *Muslim Institutions*, trans. John P. MacGregor (London: Allen & Unwin, 1961); George Hourani, *Reason and Tradition in Islamic Ethics* (Cambridge: Cambridge University Press, 1985); A. Kevin

Book of Revelation that is Muhammed's record of what the Archangel Gabriel transmitted to him over twenty years, directly from God. After Muhammed's death, other texts were needed to compensate for the community's no longer receiving new revelations (in response to problems and crises) through Muhammed. Hence, those who had known Muhammed well — members of his family and close companions — recorded the sayings and actions of Muhammed in what are now called *ahadith* (*hadith*, in the singular). After several centuries scholars considered these reports of the Prophet's words and actions to be a second binding source for Islamic ethics and law. Laws, of course, had to be discerned and tested for authenticity by tracing them to the sacred sources, ultimately to the Qur'an. The body of laws, discerned and tested, was and is the *shariah*.

Laws and ethical norms could not, however, simply be read out of the Qur'an or the *ahadith*. Their meaning had to be interpreted and applied as well as authenticated. There are, for example, inconsistencies in the Qur'an itself and in the *ahadith*. And there is actually very little legislation in the Qur'an that deals with moral matters, with the exception of prescriptions regarding family law, sexual relations, and women. Yet Islamic laws can be very detailed, covering ways of praying, eating, washing, sleeping, even whether to use the right or left hand. Hence the development of detailed prescriptions regarding the behavior of women or the suitability of sexual relations is not surprising. New insights were needed as the Muslim communities encountered new situations and challenges. Religious understanding of laws, therefore, had to be achieved through a process called *fiqh*, wherein scholars and mystics pondered the sacred texts, disagreed over the usefulness of philosophical reasoning, formed strong but sometimes opposing traditions of scholarship and teaching, sought consensus wherever possible, brought to bear a kind of "common sense" on specific matters of communal life.

The first duty of every Muslim is to build community. In a sense, the summary of all law has to do with solidarity in community.

Reinhart, "Islamic Law as Islamic Ethics," *Journal of Religious Ethics* 11 (1983): 186–203; Elizabeth Ann Meyer, *Islam and Human Rights: Tradition and Politics*, 3rd ed. (Boulder, CO: Westview, 1999); Akbar Ahmed, *Living Islam: From Samarkand to Stornoway* (London: BBC Books, 1993).

Throughout Arab nomadic history, the lesson was learned that one cannot survive alone in the desert. Everything depends on the clan or the tribe. If an individual does anything that contradicts or undermines the solidarity of the group, it cannot be tolerated. Even when tribes became economically successful and more sedentary (as in Mecca), there was the danger (to the community) of a gap between rich and poor. A traditional tribal ethic called for some form of equitable sharing in the goods that everyone needed. Muhammed saw the failures in this regard, and reinforced the moral requirement of caring for and being responsible to one's neighbor (within the tribe). So in some sense, from the beginning, the central moral virtue of Islam had to do with social justice and compassion among believers.[108] Our concern here, of course, is with Islamic sexual ethics. As in any other religious and cultural tradition, however, it is difficult if not impossible to understand the overall sexual system of Muslims without trying to see it against both the spiritual and ethical framework of Islam.[109] What I have offered above is all too brief, but at least it takes note of complexities in moral discernment as well as the importance of historical perspective when it comes to considering specific sexual moral rules. Despite ongoing controversies and the need for discernment, as well as variations in customs in different parts of the world where Muslims live, there are commonalities to be identified in the overall tradition of Islamic beliefs and practices in the sexual sphere.[110]

When contrasted with Christianity, Islam is often considered a "sex-positive" tradition, one that eschews mind/body dualism, and

---

108. See Hourani, *Reason and Tradition in Islamic Ethics*, 31; Armstrong, *Islam*, 6.

109. I am quite aware that I am doing nothing here with crucial ethical questions regarding, for example, war and peace, forms of government, etc. I refer readers to the excellent work of, for example, John Kelsey and others. See note 13 above.

110. I will be drawing here on such sources as Parrinder, *Sex in the World's Religions*, chap. 8; B. F. Musallam, *Sex and Society in Islam* (London: Cambridge University Press, 1983); Gamal I. Serour, "Traditional Sexual Practices in the Islamic World and Their Evolution," in *Evolution of the Meaning of Sexual Intercourse*, 101–10; Ayesha M. Imam, "The Muslim Religious Right ('Fundamentalists') and Sexuality," in *Good Sex*, 15–30; Valerie J. Hoffman-Ladd, "Mysticism and Sexuality in Sufi Thought and Life," *Mystics Quarterly* 18 (1992), 82–93; and above all, Valerie J. Hoffman, "Islamic Perspectives on the Human Body: Legal, Social, and Spiritual Considerations," in *Embodiment, Morality, and Medicine*, ed. Lisa Sowle Cahill and Margaret A. Farley (Dordrecht: Kluwer Academic, 1995), 37–55.

that makes room for the attainment of mystical union with God through — and not in spite of — sexual passion. Sexual desire is not tainted by sin; in fact, strictly speaking, there is no "fall" and no doctrine of original sin in Islamic literature.[111] The physical delights of sex belong not only to this world but also to Paradise. The emotionally overwhelming characteristics of the sexual drive are not evil, but a part of nature, and able to be incorporated into Muslim spirituality and life. Muhammed himself offers a model of sexual prowess, and an example of the importance of marriage.

"Natural sexuality" is not solely for the sake of reproduction, but it is always heterosexual. This means that — at least in the dominant Islamic sexual discourse — masturbation, homosexuality, and bestiality are all condemned as unnatural. (Male homosexuality is prohibited in the Qur'an, though sex between Islamic men and their male slaves has been acceptable in some historical instances, as have erotic relationships between eunuchs.) The assumption regarding a natural desire and need for heterosexual sex also means that celibacy has been generally denounced by Muslims, although Islamic mystical traditions (such as Sufism) have affirmed the value of celibacy for liberating the spirit to begin its ascent to God. Muhammed is reported to have said, "I fast and eat, sleep and pray and practice my marital relation. These are my traditions. Those who don't follow my traditions are disobedient."[112]

In Islam as in other traditions, sexuality is perceived as good, natural, but in need of boundaries and controls. For all of its importance to human flourishing, sex also has a destructive potential. Relevant to this is the belief among Muslims that women's sexuality is naturally greater and more powerful than men's, even though it is more passive. As Ayesha Imam puts it, "women are thought to have nine

---

111. Though there is no doctrine of a "Fall" in Islam, or of Eve as the cause of Adam's disobedience, Islamic theologians have been much influenced by Jewish and Christian interpretations of Genesis in this regard. While none of these theological traditions, for example, actually holds Eve responsible for human sin, popular impressions within them tend to do so. See Riffat Hassan, "Muslim Women and Post-Patriarchal Islam," in *After Patriarchy: Feminist Transformations of the World Religions*, ed. Paula M. Cooey, William R. Eakin, and Jay B. McDaniel (Maryknoll, NY: Orbis, 1991), 47–51.

112. Hadith Shareef, as quoted in Serour, "Traditional Sexual Practices in the Islamic World and Their Evolution," in *Evolution of the Meaning of Sexual Intercourse*, 103.

times the potential for sexual desire and pleasure" than that of men, but it is "women's passive exuding of sexuality"[113] that makes men vulnerable and constitutes a threat to the order of the community. From this perspective, nothing will succeed as sufficient restraint of the destructive potential of sex unless there is important control of women.

Not unlike some strands of Christianity, Islam affirms that marriage is the primary remedy for the destructive potential of sex; without marriage, the indomitability of sexual desire leads to discord and corruption. Yet protection against unruly desire is not the only or the primary goal of marriage. Abu Hamid al-Ghazali, a revered religious authority at the end of the eleventh and beginning of the twelfth century (d. 1111), cites "five advantages to marriage: procreation, satisfying sexual desire, ordering the household, providing companionship, and disciplining the self in striving to sustain them."[114] Procreation, he goes on to say, is the prime advantage and the main reason for the institution of marriage. But the other advantages are also extremely important. Sexual desire "bridled by piety" becomes a harbinger of the pleasure to be enjoyed in Paradise. Sex between husband and wife is a form of giving alms, one to the other, and both husband and wife have a right to be sexually satisfied. Writing to men, al-Ghazali observes that "the companionship of women provides relaxation which relieves distress and soothes the heart."[115] Moreover, a virtuous woman who takes care of the house leaves her husband free from the concerns of household duties, thereby abetting his spiritual devotions.[116] And finally, both husbands and wives achieve self-discipline and moral reform through their family duties and burdens.

---

113. Imam, "The Muslim Religious Right ('Fundamentalists') and Sexuality," in *Good Sex*, 18.

114. Abu Hamid al-Ghazali, *Marriage and Sexuality in Islam: A Translation of al-Ghazali's Book on the Etiquette of Marriage from the Ihya*, trans. M. Farah (Salt Lake City: University of Utah Press, 1983), 53.

115. Ibid., 65.

116. Though Armstrong notes that Muhammed himself "scrupulously helped with the chores, mended his own clothes and sought out the companionship of his wives." Armstrong, *Islam*, 16.

These "advantages" notwithstanding, marriage in traditional Islamic societies did not generally involve much interpersonal partnership (though it must be admitted that we know little about what really went on between husbands and wives). Marriage was for sexual satisfaction and children. Beyond this a kind of gender apartheid prevailed. The architecture of houses was such that women and men lived in different rooms or quarters. Marriages were negotiated and arranged by families. (Most of Muhammed's marriages, for example, were entered into for the sake of forging alliances with important tribal families.)

Traditionally, men have been allowed more than one wife, but only as many wives as they can support and treat equally and fairly (this was usually limited to four, though Muhammed, when he became a great chief, was expected to have a large harem). The Qur'an itself permitted polygyny, though the reasons for this frequently included protecting women whose husbands had been killed in war. There have always been some Muslim guidelines for sex in marriage — such as a requirement of privacy, preference for vaginal (not oral) intercourse, prohibition of anal intercourse, and avoidance of sexual intercourse (though not other forms of sexual relating) with a wife when she is menstruating.[117]

Today, while medically assisted reproduction is acceptable for Islamic couples, the use of third party genetic or conceptual contributions is not.[118] Incest is prohibited; adultery is forbidden and subject to punishment for both men and women (though severe punishments such as stoning were not meted out early on in the tradition; they have, however, emerged in frightening ways in countries where right-wing Islamic forces now hold sway). Divorce has at times been relatively easy for men, but also available to women; contemporary restrictions on women have tended to make divorce a more difficult option for them.

As Ziba Mir-Hosseini has noted, "Women's issues and gender relations have been central to religious and political discourses in the

---

117. See Serour, "Traditional Practices in the Islamic World and Their Evolution," 104.
118. Ibid., 104.

Muslim world since early in this century."[119] As she notes, too, there is now a "vast literature" on women and gender in Islam.[120] For almost a century there have been Muslim modernist and feminist movements that promote the education of women and their greater participation in national life. The issue of women's rights appears at the heart of today's struggles for Islamic cultural identity. Yet (as in other traditions) it was not always so. Armstrong argues that the Prophet Muhammed favored the emancipation of women.[121] The Qur'an gave women rights of inheritance and divorce (long before women were granted these in most Western societies). It prescribes "some degree" of segregation and veiling for the Prophet's own wives (as a protection from customs that made women vulnerable to abuse), but the Qur'an does not require these for all women.[122] In the early years of the Islamic movement women were important participants in the public life of the community; some even fought as warriors along with Muslim men. And while Muslim societies have never regarded women and men as equal before one another, the Qur'an offers texts in which they stand as absolutely equal creatures before God. In time, these did not prevent Islam from incorporating into its social and political structures the patriarchy that was all around it. These structures remain reinforced by Qur'anic verses and *ahadith* literature calling on women to be obedient to men, acquiescent to a male management of their lives.

While Muhammed may have introduced restrictions on women's activities, dress, and participation in public life in order to protect them, the tradition came to require these restrictions as a means of protecting men and society from the passive allure of women's sexuality that we have identified above. To solve this problem, Muslim women in many localities are secluded in the home, forbidden to go

---

119. Ziba Mir-Hosseini, *Islam and Gender: The Religious Debate in Contemporary Iran* (Princeton, NJ: Princeton University Press, 1999), 3.

120. For some useful examples, see Hassan, "Muslim Women and Post-Patriarchal Islam," 39–64; Fatima Mernissi, *The Veil and the Male Elite*, trans. M. J. Lakeland (Reading, PA: Addison-Wesley, 1991); Mernissi, *Beyond the Veil: Male-Female Dynamics in Modern Muslim Society*, rev. ed. (Bloomington: Indiana University Press, 1987).

121. See Armstrong, *Islam*, 16.

122. Ibid., 16. The notable discrepancy between this report and the reports I have heard from African women regarding polygyny are puzzling.

out in public without the permission and accompaniment of a male, and required to cover themselves if they do leave the home. Women's beauty must be visible only to their husbands (and sons and sometimes other close relatives); in relation to all other men, they must be invisible. There is a *hadith* that says, "When you see a woman approaching you, she comes in the form of Satan."[123]

Today's stories of forced marriages of young girls with old men; women unable to survive economically because they cannot leave home to find work; women accused of adultery and sentenced to be stoned; women attacked if they do not wear required veils and appropriate clothing; women and girls forced to accept practices (although not Islamic in origin) such as female circumcision; women without any say in political decisions that affect their everyday lives: these are stories of Islam where it is in the hands of conservative leaders who make women the line of battle in thwarting the perceived threat of non-Islamic sexual mores. Some women have other stories, however, wherein they refuse to let a veil determine their identity, yet they wear it gladly because it allows them safe space in the public world; or they embrace the wearing of headscarves because it does acknowledge their identity in ways they affirm; or they refuse to accept certain interpretations of the Qur'an, *ahadith*, and customary practices, choosing instead to challenge the tradition to be truer to itself and to the capabilities and rights of its women.

Sexual ethical and gender justice struggles are not unique to Islam. Even the role of extremists within Islam (or "fundamentalists" — a term first coined proudly by Protestants in the United States, and not completely apt for the situation of contemporary Islam) has parallels with conservative movements in other religious and secular traditions. Yet the particular history of Islam makes its challenge its own. The evolution of its sexual system bears the marks not only of the original vision of its Prophet and its acknowledged duties to build and sustain community, but also the marks of the cultures in which it has been embedded and the scars of an era of colonization. Its current battle involves devising a way to live on its own terms in a modern and postmodern world. Its desire is to sustain its own

---

123. Quoted in Hoffman, "Islamic Perspectives on the Human Body," 48.

identity. Its challenge is to do this in the face of modern individual-ism on the one hand, and on the other hand with genuine concern for the role of women as well as men in a just and compassionate sexual system.

Diversity Unlimited?

But where shall we go from here? Of what use in developing a frame-work for contemporary human and Christian sexual ethics is the kind of material I have presented above? Perhaps we just need to know more. We need to move from here to countless other cultures and traditions, finding worlds upon end in which sexuality gains its meaning in profoundly different ways of living and believing. Or we need to explore more deeply the traditions I have already sketched so briefly. If we go more carefully, for example, to traditional African cultures, we can focus more directly on the intricacies of marriage structures in which for centuries polygyny has served social, eco-nomic, and religious ends. If we travel to India, we can see better the multiple paths which have led to intersections between religious rationales for sexual asceticism and sex manuals for flamboyant and creative sexual practices. We can also study the complex image of the Hindu goddess Kali, learning to appreciate the combination of benevolence and malevolence, sorting out the possibilities of sexual creativity and destruction. In Japan we might try to understand the juxtaposition of extreme sexual reserve in marriage and toleration of sex outside of marriage, even to the point of a vast sex industry for pornography and access to prostitution. We could enter into strands of Buddhism where mortality is not the whole story, and where both sexual asceticism and domesticity serve concerns for transcendence. If we go to China, we may learn how a relatively sexually free Taoism is muted from one Chinese dynasty to another by the rational plausi-bility of Confucianism. We might also observe the tensions between the deep-seated sexual austerity of a Confucian past and a culture now influenced by notions of liberated sex.

We may come to observe not only diversity but similarity among the many cultures and religious traditions. After all, everywhere there is the effort to make sense of sexuality as a positive force in human life that is also potentially destructive. All cultures have moral and political concerns for the procreation and rearing of children. They all try to provide for some stability in familial and communal relations. Incest taboos appear everywhere, despite differences in what relationships count as incest. All traditions find it necessary to understand, restrict, or provide for sexual desires aimed otherwise than at reproduction. Every tradition, at least to some degree, offers gendered structures, differentiating identities and roles for men and women. There are tensions everywhere between recurring themes of asceticism and valuations of sexual pleasure, between communal concerns and individual preferences, and between past practices and new circumstances and demands.

The closer we come to each of these contexts, the most important factor that emerges may not be either difference or similarity. It may be the very plasticity of human sexuality, its susceptibility to different meanings and expressive forms. Not that it is infinitely malleable; nor that it matters very little how its meaning and practices are constructed; and not that it simply varies, despite similarities, from culture to culture. Rather, along with variety among traditions, what is striking is that any particular tradition's internal understanding of sexuality and gender might have developed differently had there been some variation in particular circumstances. It may be that such an observation is possible only in a critical age such as our own, when reformers emerge in almost every major tradition — reformers who do not reject their traditions, but who advocate change, transformation that is grounded in lost (silenced or contradicted) elements in the tradition itself.

Thus, just as Judith Plaskow argues for a new perspective on human sexuality within Judaism, and Christine Gudorf for a new Christian sexual ethic, so Lina Gupta maintains that in Hindu images of Kali there are resources for new interpretations of the tradition that will be more conducive to the liberation of women, and Ziba Mir-Hosseini attempts to retrieve an Islamic tradition that is capable of addressing the questions of the present age.[124] African novelists

---

124. See Judith Plaskow, *Standing Again at Sinai: Judaism from a Feminist Perspective* (San Francisco: Harper & Row, 1990); Christine E. Gudorf, *Body, Sex, and Pleasure:*

like Tsitsi Dangarembga and Mariama Bâ provide tales of anguished individuals and conflicted tribes in search of change yet continuity in the sexual systems of their African home countries.[125]

Having barely glimpsed the multiple tracks of cross-cultural and interreligious experience and values, we nonetheless cannot here pursue them further. Neither can we forget them. They belong to the map of human sexual meanings. To assure our remembrance, we can identify what we have learned that may help us in the next stages of our exploration. Three questions will yield some brief and provisional conclusions: (1) How much do we really know at this point? (2) What procedural clues may we have gained for developing a sexual ethic? (3) What substantive insights may be useful in our ongoing explorations?

(1) In response to the first question, it can be said that overviews such as the ones I have offered above do give us some information about various traditions. Yet we still know so little. This makes our use of this information highly vulnerable to oversimplification and distortion. We know so little because, as I suggested earlier, it is one thing for those standing outside a tradition to glimpse a general outline of its sexual practices and norms; it is quite another to know what really goes on in the human relations involved. This latter depends on genuine experience, even if vicarious experience, of the tradition itself. It requires long listening not only as researcher but as friend. It requires access and attention to hearts and voices within a tradition and to texts that are literary, symbolic, practical, mystical, sacred, of every available genre.[126]

Reconstructing Christian Sexual Ethics (Cleveland: Pilgrim, 1994); Lina Gupta, "Kali, the Savior," in *After Patriarchy*, 15–38; Mir-Hosseini, *Islam and Gender*.

125. See Tsitsi Dangarembga, *Nervous Conditions* (New York: Seal Press, 1989); Mariama Bâ, *So Long A Letter*, trans. Modupé Bodé-Thomas (Oxford: Heinemann Educational, 1981). In the first of these, Dangarembga tells the story of a young girl in Rhodesia in the 1960s, struggling to find herself in the tribal trauma of a colonized nation. In the second, Bâ recounts a new kind of emotional trauma in a Muslim Senegalese woman whose husband takes a second wife and whose eventual widowhood makes her struggle one of survival.

126. For sexual ethicists, it may be that a nuanced case study approach, within an inter-traditional dialogue, is a remarkably helpful way to come to some understanding. This is exemplified in Regina Wentzel Wolfe and Christine E. Gudorf, eds., *Ethics and World Religions: Cross-Cultural Case Studies* (Maryknoll, NY: Orbis, 1999).

Having said this, we can temper our fears of never being able to understand another tradition, especially regarding not only the policies but the intimacies of its sexual life, by noting that those who are within a tradition often do not understand it well, either. We need only take ourselves as examples. Whatever the sexual experience of an individual or a group, it is seldom marked by great reflection. Adherents of a tradition are themselves often unaware of the roots of their practices. Only when the practices become problematic is there the need to understand them and to assess them. Hence, as sexual ethicists pursue our own tasks, the questions we ask may generate insights both for those within a tradition and without. But this leads directly to the second question I have posed above.

(2) What procedural clues may we have gained through the exercise of a chapter such as this one? My response is that we have four clues. First, *it is impossible simply to transplant the beliefs and practices from one tradition to another*, nor should we want to do so. "Multiculturalism," embraced by many North American thinkers, represents a critique of any one tradition's cultural superiority in relation to the practices and values of any other.[127] Multiculturalism grew in the late twentieth century as a response to the kind of Western liberal hegemony assumed in relation to other cultures and exhibited in, for example, the colonizing and evangelizing of non-Western sexualities. Efforts to change other traditional sexual systems to accord with ours have not succeeded well; in fact, they have all too often left confusion and injury, as well as anger, in their wake. Nor will it work to try simply to import sexual mores from other cultures into our own.

Any sympathy with multiculturalism entails a correlative clue. That is, not only should we not attempt to impose our sexual beliefs and practices on peoples of another culture, *we should also not stand in general judgment of other cultures* (whether we act to change them or not). It is not a priori obvious that our sexual practices are more

---

127. See Joshua Cohen, Matthew Howard, and Martha Nussbaum, eds., *Is Multiculturalism Bad for Women?* (Princeton, NJ: Princeton University Press, 1999), 4. The formulation assumed in this volume is of multiculturalism as the "radical idea that people in other cultures, foreign and domestic, are human beings, too — moral equals, entitled to equal respect and concern."

conducive to human flourishing and human happiness than are those of others.

But a third clue goes along with the first and second and may qualify them in a way. If "multiculturalism" as an ethical and political stance means that no assessments can be made, culture to culture, this too is problematic. *We cannot respect every cultural practice, whether our own or others', unconditionally.*[128] If, for example, respecting other cultures' gender arrangements means that we must never again think in terms of human rights (including women's rights), then this is unacceptable. If it means that we can draw no conclusions regarding a practice like female circumcision, then it yields not pluralism but relativism. Deception, coercion, enslavement, manipulation, oppression: We need not extend moral respect to all. Hence, each culture must make some judgment on other cultures, mindful (one hopes, whether at home or abroad) of the temptation to judge only because some cultural practices are different from our own. If judgments are grounded in basic respect for other peoples, they will be made in ways that are not harmful to cultures or to their adherents.

The fourth clue is that what we learn from the sexual beliefs and practices of cultures other than our own may be *useful in critiquing our own culture and traditions.* In seeing the vulnerability of all traditions to extremes, to forgetfulness of their more salutary roots, to internal contradictions through time, we may understand better the problems in every tradition, including our own.

(3) In response to my third and last question, what substantive insights may be useful in our ongoing explorations into a contemporary sexual ethic, let me say that we surely do not — from this brief entry into cross-cultural studies of sexual systems — have sufficient knowledge to propose policies for cross-cultural interactions. We do, however, have insights into (or at least impressions of) flaws in every system, not excluding our own. These insights should serve us well in proposing a framework for contemporary Christian sexual ethics. We surely have learned something about the genuine tensions between

---

128. Ibid. This is the position of Susan Moller Okin, vigorously debated in the whole of *Is Multiculturalism Bad for Women?*

the goods of individual and community. We may have learned that ongoing transformation of sexual systems can profit from (and not only be injured by) respectful dialogue, extended learning, between one tradition and another.

We turn again, therefore, to general questions about the sexual sphere of human life, influenced by our own cultural commitments and vantage points; but we do so with an eye on practices and beliefs of cultures and times other than this one. We turn again to the "large questions" that precede normative considerations of a sexual ethic.

Chapter 4

SEXUALITY
AND ITS MEANINGS

═══ ❖ ═══

I SAID IN PREVIOUS CHAPTERS that ethical issues which remain open and difficult regarding human sexuality include large questions, questions that are in some respects more basic than those of specific moral rules. Of course, the most basic questions of all are those that underlie all ethical discernment: inquiries into the nature and goals of humanity, the relation of human persons to God and to the rest of creation, the sources and methods of ethical discernment, the meaning of good and evil, and many more questions that have kept philosophers, theologians, scientists, and poets busy from generation to generation. In this chapter, however, my concern is with questions that are more particular to ethical discernment regarding human sexuality.

Of what I have been calling the "large questions" about sexuality, at least three are central to the intelligibility of any framework for sexual ethics. The first has to do with the moral status of the human body — its meaning, its interest and value vis-à-vis the whole person, its givenness and contingencies. The second is the increasingly complex question of gender — the social construction (or not) of its meaning and its role in personal identity and human relationships of every kind. A third question focuses on the sources and aims of sexual desire — perhaps the heart of the question of the meaning of sexuality in human lives. In terms of their relevance to sexual ethics, these three questions are inseparable, though they can be distinguished. Their interconnectedness is finally part of each question, and it holds them all together.

Each of these questions points to a part of whatever meaning we give to sexuality. The complexity of the questions and the variety of

answers put forward for them today tell us that there is surely more
than one meaning for sexuality. The question then becomes how we
discern and assess multiple meanings, and how these meanings may
fit within a worldview that makes sense to us. Ultimately for Christians, the question is whether and how these meanings fit within a
Christian framework of faith; and how they can be shared, or not,
with others whose frameworks are significantly different.

In this chapter, then, I explore questions related to the human
body, gender differentiation, and human experiences of sexuality. I
return here to a primary focus on Western and Christian thought,
though I try not to ignore or leave behind the significance of
cross-cultural and interreligious approaches. To pursue questions of
embodiment, sex, and gender, it seems logical to start with questions
about the body, since our understandings of it seem more basic than
either sex or gender. We begin here with some risks — of skewing
our subsequent explorations of gender and sexuality, of choosing a
logic whose presuppositions are themselves in question, and most
of all of getting caught in and delayed by conflicting metaphysical
analyses of human embodiment. My aim, however, will not be to
settle the meaning of human embodiment (an effort bound to be
disappointing in any case) but to suggest ways of thinking about
it that may shed light on the further questions of sexuality and
gender.

How the Body Matters

It does not take acute powers of observation to note that in contemporary Western culture we are preoccupied with the "body," even
though we frequently describe ourselves as "body-alienated." This
does not mean only that we are obsessive about health and beauty,
or that we are concerned about the control of some persons' bodies
by others — though both of these are true. It means, in addition,
that the body is of great interest to theorists who are trying to figure
out what we are as human beings — bodied, sexed, gendered, in the
world. Shedding an Enlightenment focus on the "mind," they have
tried to understand what it means to be "embodied." At stake in all of
this for sexual ethics is the question of whether, or to what extent, our

bodies provide a basis, or even small clues, for determining acceptable practices of human sexuality.

Theories of the Body

There are two sets of issues around which swirl most of the controversial questions regarding the meaning of the human body. The first is the centuries old, yet still alive and well, set of issues about the relation between soul (or mind or spirit[1]) and body. These are the issues of dualism (we are made up of two distinct parts, perhaps even two distinct entities) and monism (we are really only one entity, either soul or body; or we are one entity, but it has distinguishable aspects). These issues have sometimes proven critical in moral assessments of the body and moral understandings of sexuality.

The second set of issues is much newer, and it usually includes a rejection of the first set as misguided or irrelevant. These are the issues of social constructionism; that is, whether and how the meaning of the body is culturally and socially formed, influenced, constructed. While I do not want to become mired in the seemingly endless debates about these two sets of issues, it is not possible to explore human embodiment without taking them into account. Both of them, for example, are key to understanding the human self, or to discerning whether or not there even is a human self. Both can be important, then, to understanding what gender means for identity, what sex means to being "human," and what society has to do with our conceptions and images of our bodies.

---

1. For some theorists, the binary division is between mind and body, for others, between soul or spirit and body. I am not addressing any of these theories in detail; hence, I will use the terms "mind," "soul," "spirit" interchangeably. However, there are differences among them that are important to many. "Mind," for example, most often connotes the thinking, knowing, reasoning, and directing "part" and capabilities of the person; "soul" often connotes the "part" that forms the body and gives life to the person; "spirit" can mean the same as "soul," though it tends to connote not only the life principle but the capacities of mind and heart, as well as an openness to other beings. In dualistic theories — those that emphasize the distinction between these terms, on the one hand, and the body, on the other — "mind/soul/spirit" all tend to refer to the "immaterial" part of the human person, while "body" refers to the "material" part.

Body and Spirit: One, Two, or Two-in-One?

Major philosophical traditions of Western culture have tended to explain the human body by distinguishing it from, and often opposing it to, the soul (or spirit or mind). The boundary between body and soul, in such views, constitutes a fissure within the human individual, and it prevents full union between persons. As I have indicated above, some theorists (notably in Platonic traditions[2]) hold that the distinction between body and soul is that of two separate entities temporarily held together in the human person. In this binary division, the soul is frequently the truly "human," while the body constitutes an unfortunate and temporary limitation on the human spirit (signified by famous metaphors like container and contained, prison and imprisoned).

For other theorists (for example, St. Augustine[3]), the mind and body are separate entities yet inseparable as parts of human nature. Both are part of what it means to be human, but they are held together in a kind of fragile "political" unity. The soul needs the body for knowledge (which is dependent in the beginning on sense perception), but the soul is ideally to rule the body, ordering its feelings and desires and providing for its needs. Soul and body are thus essentially related, each dependent on the other and mutually determined in some ways. Centuries later, René Descartes also coupled two substances — mind and body — in the person, but weakened their relationship to the point where mind is the center of the self, and the body — although close to and interacting with the mind — is rather like a complex machine.[4]

Aristotle and Thomas Aquinas, on the other hand, thought that soul and body are not two entities but two metaphysical principles,

---

2. See, for example, Plato, *Laws* 896 a 1–2; *Phaedo* 85 e 3–86 d 4, 93 c 3–95. See also Philo, *Allegorical Interpretation of the Laws* 3.69.

3. Augustine, *City of God* XXII.26; *De Genesi ad litteram* XII.35.68; *Sermones* CLV.15.

4. René Descartes, *Meditations* (1641), cited by Richard M. Zaner in "Embodiment: the Phenomenological Tradition," *Encyclopedia of Bioethics*, ed. Warren Thomas Reich, rev. ed. (New York: Simon & Schuster Macmillan, 1995), 1:291. Scholars like Zaner caution that Descartes appears in his later writings to have modified this view, observing a more intimate mind/body relation based on a more complex understanding of the body.

"form" and "matter," together making up a human essence that exists as one entity or substance.[5] The soul makes the body to be a human body, while the body individualizes the soul so that a particular, unique human being can exist. Although the soul is in an important sense "immaterial" and hence (at least according to Aquinas) can exist apart from its body (which makes immortality plausible), it could not have existed in the first place without being individualized (limited to this particular share of humanity) by a material principle; and it cannot exist after death without some ongoing relationship to matter (which makes resurrection of the body plausible).

For still other theorists, body and mind are not finally distinguishable. They are in fact reducible one to the other. Either the body is reducible to mind (as in extreme forms of philosophical idealism or some forms of linguistic constructionism), or the mind is reducible to the body (the majority view among contemporary scientists). From the latter perspective, the mind is a function of a highly developed organism. This is a perspective frequently represented in behavioral psychology, sociobiology, and neuroscience. Philosophical appropriations of these scientific theories are more and more on the increase.

Religious traditions, too, have worried about such matters.[6] Themes of embodiment have been inevitably intertwined with beliefs about creation, good and evil, the order of the cosmos, individual human immortality, and on and on. Some religions have emphasized the distinction between body and soul, some the unity. Philosophical perspectives have been incorporated into theologies of the body, often with the same diversity noted above. Practical religious concerns have led to interpretations of the moral status of the body and evaluations of bodily practices in relation to human wholeness and to relationships with the divine.

The trouble with theories and beliefs that emphasize a distinction between soul and body is that dualisms breed hierarchies. Hence,

---

5. Aristotle, *De Anima* 412 a; Thomas Aquinas, *Summa Theologiae* I.75–76, I-II.22.

6. For interesting and significant collections of essays on diverse religious traditions and their approaches to the body, see Sarah Coakley, ed., *Religion and the Body* (Cambridge: Cambridge University Press, 1997); Jane Marie Law, *Religious Reflections on the Human Body* (Bloomington: Indiana University Press, 1995).

in Western intellectual history, the soul has been persistently valued over the body, the intellect over emotions, the will over bodily needs and desires. It is easy to see how such dualisms have influenced the moral evaluation of sex. On the other hand, the trouble with theories that eliminate any mind/body distinction is that the dramas of human freedom, and the experiences of personal dividedness, diminishment, and death, can be underestimated or ignored.

Constructing the Body

Contemporary feminist theories have addressed problems about the body in significant ways, to some extent changing the very landscape of our thought on the human body.[7] Feminist philosophical debates have become not so much about whether to be human is to be a body or to be a soul, or even how body and soul are related (though these questions remain implicit in most of the views set forth).[8] The goal of feminist theorists is primarily to remedy the deficiencies of the past, particularly theories that have had bad consequences for women.

Some feminists explore the possibilities of de-emphasizing gender, of focusing, rather, on universal understandings of human bodily capabilities and needs.[9] Others want to revalue women's bodies as gendered and different, looking to women's experience for new insights into the varieties of human embodiment.[10] Still others offer powerful postmodern proposals regarding the social construction of

---

7. For selective and critical overviews, see Caroline Bynum, "Why All the Fuss about the Body? A Medievalist's Perspective," *Critical Inquiry* 22 (Autumn 1995): 1–31; Amy Hollywood, "Transcending Bodies," *Religious Studies Review* 25 (January 1999): 13–18. For a helpful treatment of theories in the context of biomedical ethics, see Rosalyn Diprose, *The Bodies of Women: Ethics, Embodiment and Sexual Difference* (London: Routledge, 1994).

8. It is arguable, for example, that postmodern social constructionist views of the body finally leave out materiality, opting only for language as the reality of the body. I am not sure I agree with this charge, though it is tempting. See Martha C. Nussbaum, "The Professor of Parody," *The New Republic* (February 22, 1999): 37–45.

9. See, for example, Nussbaum, "Human Capabilities, Female Human Beings," in *Women, Culture, and Development: A Study of Human Capabilities*, ed. Martha Nussbaum and Jonathan Glover (Oxford: Clarendon Press, 1995); Lisa Sowle Cahill, *Sex, Gender and Christian Ethics* (Cambridge: Cambridge University Press, 1996).

10. See, for example, Luce Irigaray, *This Sex Which is Not One*, trans. Catherine Porter, with Carolyn Burke (Ithaca, NY: Cornell University Press, 1977); Irigaray, *An Ethics of Sexual Difference*, trans. Carolyn Burke and Gillian C. Gill (London: Athlone, 1993).

bodies, whereby all of our understandings of the human body are the result of, on the one hand, powerful social forces shaping our experiences and perceptions of our bodies; and, on the other hand, our own activities and practices that accord with the social content of what is shaping us.[11] Ideas and practices of the past are not irrelevant, for these beliefs and practices have played key roles in the construction of the meaning of the human body at any given point in time. Hence, theorists debate historical interpretations, challenging biased readings and offering new texts for our consideration.[12] The aim of all of these feminist approaches, however diverse, is not only to enhance understandings of the human body but to correct the exclusionary results of past theories wherein some bodies have counted in importance, and some have not.

I cannot here take on either all of these theories and perspectives (feminist or otherwise) or the histories on which they build. We recognize how theories of the past have yielded dualisms with which we still live. We know that views of the human person as a soul imprisoned in or temporarily dependent upon the body continue to operate in our cultural interpretations of who we are. We realize that neither Augustinian theories of a political relation between soul and body, nor Aristotelian/Thomistic theories of an ontological relation between soul and body, have succeeded in preventing gendered privileging of some bodies over others. We know that, despite our efforts to dislodge it, Descartes' split of mind from body has become our split. We also know that contemporary scientific default theories which see the human as only body have not remedied (and in some ways may have reinforced) tendencies to torture or instrumentalize human bodies.

---

11. See especially Judith Butler, *Bodies That Matter: On the Discursive Limits of Sex* (London: Routledge, 1993).

12. Bynum, "Why All the Fuss About the Body?"; Margaret R. Miles, *Augustine on the Body* (Missoula, MT: Scholars, 1979); Miles, "Sex and the City (of God): Is Sex Forfeited or Fulfilled in Auguisine's Resurrection of the Body?" *Journal of the American Academy of Religion* 73 (June 2005): 302–28. See also the massive project undertaken by a multi-cultural group of scholars from multiple disciplines (some feminists, some not) whose work has opened up new vistas in terms of the history of the body's "modes of construction" in relation to God, society, bodily techniques, religious and philosophical ideologies and so forth: Michael Feher, ed., with Ramona Naddaf and Nadia Tazi, *Fragments for a History of the Human Body*, 3 vols., Zone Series (New York: Urzone, 1989).

Nonetheless, I have found myself impressed by the kernels of truth in each of the theories and each of the historical accounts. We may be at a point where we need not settle for either/or interpretations of the human body (for example, either we completely transcend our bodies, or when our brain is damaged our spirit shrinks as well; either there is a solid material reality intimate to ourselves, or constructions of its meaning give us an unsettled, sedimented but always shifting and elusive reality).[13] I agree with those who express dismay that understandings of the body might today dissolve into nothing but language disputes, and that we might thereby forget the needs of real women and men. I therefore agree with those who observe that as bodies we still need to eat and sleep and deal with pain and pleasure. Yet I also agree that if anything has been culturally and socially constructed, surely it is our understandings and hence our experiences of the human body especially as gendered.

If this chapter, as it presses questions of human embodiment, is not primarily about grappling with historical and contemporary theories, it *is* about finding new ways to understand ourselves as embodied. My attention is focused on experience (though I know there is no such thing as "raw" or "pure" experience). I want to ask all over again how it is that humans are complex beings who experience themselves as bodies but not only as bodies, as spirits but not only as spirits. As I examine experiences of human embodiment I assume a basic background of Christian perspectives, but I consider the questions I raise to be genuine questions — for Christians no less than for everyone else. That is, they are questions for which we all still search for understandings.

Transcendent Embodiment

Our task is to explore what it means to be "embodied spirits" and "inspirited bodies."[14] I use these terms interchangeably, though I am

---

13. I am not alone in this provisional conclusion. See Bynum, "Shape and Story: Metamorphosis in the Western Tradition," Jefferson Lecture in Humanities, Kennedy Center for the Performing Arts (Washington, DC, March 22, 1999). Bynum, however, would not include quite so much in her conclusion as I do; she refers only to certain dichotomies in understanding the self.

14. Although the concept "embodied spirit" is now fairly common currency among many theologians and some philosophers, my own first appreciation of it came in

aware that others may use them to emphasize either body or spirit. The fact that humans are embodied spirits, inspirited bodies, is the glory of our species and the basis of its vulnerability. We live incarnated in a world that is revelatory of the sacred. We are gifted in body and spirit by all creation's speaking to us God's word and providing for us a home where we may find sustenance and joy. We embody ourselves in intimate relationships with one another, and in less intimate though still bodily relationships with many others in societies where our dwellings extend our skins and we learn to thirst not only in body but in spirit. We are the ones who ask questions of ourselves as embodied and who can encounter God in whatever searches we undertake and whatever answers we find.

Yet, our inspirited embodiment renders us vulnerable to the world, ourselves, and even to God. We are misfits among other creatures in our world because we are the ones who worry about who we are and what we are doing. We are, within our species, one another's enemies not because the conflicts among us are like conflicts among other embodied living beings; ours are conflicts in which we harm one another *as embodied spirits, inspirited bodies.* And we are the ones who challenge God as we contradict our own incarnation or violate the rest of divinely created beings.

I will ultimately propose a view of ourselves as human persons whereby our bodies and our spirits are one — distinguishable as aspects of our personhood, but unified in a way that they are neither mere parts of one whole nor reducible one to the other. I will also propose that the self-transcendence that Christians associate with what it means to be a human person pertains to ourselves not just as spirits but as bodies. At stake in this view is the basis for a comprehensive

---

reading Gabriel Marcel, who along with Maurice Merleau-Ponty, Jean-Paul Sartre, and others in the early twentieth century began raising the sorts of questions I raise here. See, for example, Gabriel Marcel, *Being and Having: An Existentialist Diary* (New York: Harper Torchbooks, 1965); Marcel, *Creative Fidelity*, trans. Robert Rosenthal (New York: Noonday, 1964), especially 17–20, 22–26, 94–95, 101–2; Marcel, *The Mystery of Being*, vol. 2 (Chicago: Gateway edition, 1960); Maurice Merleau-Ponty, *Phenomenology of Perception*, trans. Colin Smith (New York: Humanities, 1962), part 1, chap. 6; Jean-Paul Sartre, *Being and Nothingness*, trans. Hazel E. Barnes (New York: Washington Square, 1966), part 3, chap. 2. My exploration of the concept does not depend on these earlier writings, though their place in the history of thought has no doubt prompted some of my own questions.

approach to human flourishing, an approach that is necessary — if not sufficient — for an understanding of human sexuality. At stake also is the claim that some human suffering is imposed by us on one another not just by and in our bodies, not just by and in our souls, but by and in ourselves as embodied spirits, inspirited bodies.

Although it might make sense to proceed by examining our most obvious experiences of body/spirit unity, I shall do the opposite. The more interesting and significant challenge is to find clues for this unity by reflecting on our experiences of *disunity*. First I will try to set the problem, and then turn to some of our more troubling experiences of the lack of internal unity between body and spirit.

The Problem

The problem I am looking at arises out of our diverse experiences of body and spirit. On the one hand, we experience our bodies as burdens, limits, adversaries of ourselves in our efforts to labor and to love. On the other hand, we experience something of the unity of body and spirit when, for example, we reflect on our body memories — of pain, joy, striving — as memories of ourselves, our coming to be who we are. Sometimes we experience a kind of total unity of body and spirit, as when our skill in dancing and our immersion in music bring our whole being together in one glorious activity; or when our experience of bodily union with another person transcends our divided self and our divided selves in loving gesture and joy of mind and body.

Despite our experiences of both disunity and unity of body and spirit, we tend to be, as some theorists have observed, "natural dualists."[15] No matter what our theory, it is easy to think of ourselves as made up of two parts, parts that we value differently on diverse occasions and from within diverse traditions. We are often unaware of our bodies until we experience pain or a particular pleasure, and these experiences are quickly interpreted in dualistic ways. For example, we may be intently reading a book, our body and spirit one in

---

15. Paul Bloom, *Descartes' Baby: How the Science of Child Development Explains What Makes Us Human* (New York: Basic Books, 2004), xii.

the effort, until our eyes begin to hurt.[16] Our body appears as an inter-ference with what we are so intent on doing. Or, we may be walking along blithely on a lovely spring morning, thinking not at all of our feet on which we walk — until they begin to ache and call attention to themselves as limit to our plans and our discoveries. Our body can become our "project," as we attempt to improve its fitness, or to enhance it through chemicals or genetic engineering. It can be for us a kind of machine, which we must tune up as best we may as long as we may, replacing parts if necessary or finding the right lubricant for our faltering systems. We experience our body as something we have, must care for, something whose tissues and organs we may give to another. We question the "ownership" of our bodies and their parts: Do they belong to God, to ourselves, or to society?[17]

Sometimes in one another we see no spirit, but only bodies to be liked or disliked, manipulated, enslaved, ignored, and abandoned. Sometimes we see only spirit in one another, with no thought for the spirit's need for food for the body.

No wonder we have had trouble understanding who we are, and who the other person is. No wonder we have had difficulty figuring out these two aspects of our experience, these two aspects of our-selves. Just when we think we have an adequate understanding, we come across new experiences, or old ones for which our previous interpretations seem no longer tenable or tolerable. With all of our theories, it is not superfluous to explore again the unity between soul and body and their mutual transcendence. Whether this is a task of discovery or of reconstruction, it seems necessary for it to continue.

Body/Spirit Disunity Revisited

I begin my exploration with a search for unity in the unlikely places of our experiences of *disunity*. I therefore look for clues in experiences that seem to challenge the very possibility of genuine spirit-embodiment. I consider four such experiences: (1) profound suffering, (2) objectification, (3) aging and dying, and (4) experiences

---

16. The example is Sartre's. See his *Being and Nothingness*, 436–37.
17. See Henk A. M. J. ten Have and Joseph V. M. Welie, eds., *Ownership of the Human Body: Philosophical Considerations of the Use of the Human Body and its Parts in Healthcare* (Boston: Kluwer Academic, 1998).

of what we often call a "divided self." Although this exploration appears as a digression from our examination of sexuality and the body, I intend it to come full circle with insights that are central to this main concern.

(1) There are paradigmatic experiences of human *suffering* in which spirit and body appear to be wrenched apart. The dimension of spirit, insofar as it continues at all, becomes almost an abstraction, so that it fades out of our conscious awareness. Alternatively, if spirit is the location of our agony, we come to have no use for embodiment; we no longer care for our body or attend to its needs. What we thought was unified is cut asunder, or it collapses into only body or only spirit. These are the kinds of sufferings that some have called "tales of terror" and "whirlpools of torment,"[18] where bodies are destroyed, minds ravaged, and spirits broken.[19] These are the sufferings that go on in human history, generation after generation — a "voice heard in Ramah weeping" (Jer. 31:15), peoples subjugated by peoples, women violated in their very persons, families rent asunder, stories of abandonment, starvation, and death. This is the sort of human pain that Simone Weil named "affliction," differentiating it from "suffering" in the ordinary sense.[20] But at its heart, as Weil says, affliction is always both physical and spiritual; it is never only of the body (like a toothache that is soon over and gone), and it is also never only of the spirit. With this kind of suffering the person suffers *as a unified whole;* there is no competition between miseries of the body and miseries of the soul. Affliction when it is of the spirit also afflicts, leaves wounds in, the body; and when it is bodily, if it goes on long enough, it always also afflicts the spirit. This is the kind of suffering that has the potential to attack the self, making thoughts become a state of mind that persons can live with for twenty, thirty,

---

18. See Phyllis Trible, *Texts of Terror: Literary-Feminist Readings of Biblical Narratives* (Philadelphia: Fortress, 1984), and James Crenshaw, *A Whirlpool of Torment: Israelite Traditions of God as an Oppressive Presence* (Philadelphia: Fortress, 1984).

19. I have written of this kind of suffering many times; as, for example, in my "How Shall We Love in a Postmodern World?" *Annual of the Society of Christian Ethics* (1994), 12–13.

20. Simone Weil, *Waiting for God*, trans. Emma Crauford (New York: Harper & Row, 1973), 117–25.

fifty years, a lifetime; so that the soul and body become its accomplices, pulling to inertia and despair. But *only inspirited bodies, only embodied spirits*, can experience such suffering. In the very threat to the whole self, on the brink of ultimate disunity, comes a glimpse of a unity in the possibility of its destruction.

(2) We commonly consider *objectification* of a person as a failure to apprehend and respect the person in her or his whole reality. This can happen when one is valued only for one's skills, mental or physical. It can happen when one is reduced, in the eyes of the beholder, only to one's bodily beauty or disability or racial difference. It can happen when an individual is looked upon only as a source of another's pleasure. Objectification of an other is especially onerous when it is accompanied by efforts to make the other into what she is judged to be, constrain the other into roles and actions that are judged for her to be appropriate, subject the other in ways that allow no identity beyond the judgment imposed. At the heart of the experience of objectification is an experience of being put in a box, one's meaning and value determined without appeal, one's supposed self-unity canceled.

No more dramatic depiction of objectification can be found than in Jean-Paul Sartre's description of the conflict inherent in human relations. His telling example is the by now classic one of the "keyhole peeper."[21] I am outside a door, listening and peering through a keyhole. I hear footsteps behind me. I feel the eyes of another on me. In whatever way I have previously understood my own action (however justified I considered my reasons for being outside this door and looking in), the other who approaches will give it (and me) a different meaning. I begin to feel profoundly threatened, my justification taken away by the suspicious stare of the other who comes up behind me. I am prevented from determining my own meaning for my action; the judgment of the other imprisons me in a category of meaning ("keyhole peeper") that is not mine. I am made into, frozen into,

21. I repeat here my rendering of this example in my article, "A Feminist Version of Respect for Persons," *Journal of Feminist Studies in Religion* 9 (Spring/Fall 1993): 192–93. The source is Sartre, *Being and Nothingness*, 348–49. It should be noted that Sartre's concern with this example was not the same as mine. Influenced by Hegel's "master/slave" analysis, he was building a large theory of human relations — not, as I am here, simply instancing "objectification" of one individual by another or others.

what my body appears to be. This, according to Sartre, is the basis of the ordinary forms of conflict between human persons — judgment, suspicion, categorization, shame — and an ultimate threat to peace and unity within. So potentially devastating is the block to my freedom, my spirit, from every suspicious stare, that I feel compelled to respond. The threat of objectification is unbearable. I have two options, says Sartre. I can either overpower the gaze of the other ("knock out his eyes" literally or figuratively), or I can submit to the gaze so fully, absorb the other's judgment so completely, that I no longer feel it or see it; I lose my own eyes and become what the other is judging me to be. In the first case, my freedom prevails, but only by taking away the other's freedom and judgment in my regard. I reduce the other to his body. In the second case, I reduce myself to my body. I use my freedom to submit, to let my meaning be determined by the other. I do what is expected of me, limit myself to the role prescribed. The power of the other's gaze and freedom prevails.

In Sartre's theory, all of this not surprisingly is played out most clearly in the sexual sphere. For Sartre, sexuality represents the most basically structured attempt to overcome or to submit to the subjectivity, freedom, and judgment of the other. The fundamental responses become sadism or masochism. I can try to manipulate the other's gaze by seduction, attempting to shape it, to change it, to elicit it as a gaze I will accept. Failing this, I can turn upon the gaze, making the other my object, subduing the other through physical or emotional violence and pain. These are the sadistic responses. Alternatively, I can let myself be so lost in my desire to be judged well by the other that I am lost to myself, masochistically absorbed by the other's gaze, so completely submissive to it that I no longer recognize or feel it.

We need not think as Sartre did that all human relations or all sexual relations are dramatically conflictual in this way. Yet we recognize an accurate description of the experience endemic to some human relationships, or at least to some moments in human relationship. These are experiences, so it seems, of the ultimate disuniting of body and spirit, or the ultimate collapse of spirit into body. And yet, at the heart of such experiences there lies a clue to body/spirit unity. For to conquer another's body in this way, or be conquered, is precisely to conquer the other's spirit, or be conquered. If we were not embodied spirits, inspirited bodies; if we could eclipse either body or spirit in a significant way, we would not have such experiences. Objectification of one by the other is, finally, not a reduction of the other to body or spirit, but an effort to dominate an *embodied spirit*.

A similar illustration of objectification is to be found in the work of Elaine Scarry on the torture of human persons.[22] One would think that torture would have as its goal simply to destroy humans, with the goal only of extracting information or whatever else serves the purpose of the torturer. As Scarry analyzes it, however, torture has as its goal the destruction of persons; but it is the destruction of *persons as persons* that is at stake. Torture is aimed at making people "disappear" as people, the deconstruction of their humanness. It is not the same as human torture of animals might be — achieving a bizarre pleasure in causing pain to another living being. The intention in torture of humans is, rather, to silence the other's voice by wrecking his or her body; it is to make the tortured speak the torturer's words instead of his own. Hence, torture is unsuccessful if it does not gain the other's spirit as well as body. Such an aim would make no sense unless there are beings who are *embodied spirits, inspirited bodies*. Once again, in experiences of greatest disunity, we can find a presupposition of unity between body and spirit.[23]

(3) It may be instructive to turn now to more ordinary experiences of *aging and dying*. Here, if anywhere, are experiences of the body as limit and burden, and of the soul as gradually and finally being disunited from its embodiment, even as the body is in process of disunification from soul. All of our discovered or socially constructed meanings for the human body are challenged at this point. Embodiment is no longer opportunity, but loss of opportunity in the life of the person. The experience of aging, in particular, gives powerful evidence that we are more than our bodies, unless we want diminishment of

---

22. Elaine Scarry, *The Body in Pain: The Making and Unmaking of the World* (New York: Oxford University Press, 1985), 27–59.

23. I grant that the unity might only be the kind of mutual influence of body and spirit that Augustine and others envisaged. Still, the whole process of torture is aimed, it seems to me, at overpowering a person as embodied *spirit*.

body to entail diminishment of self. But aging is more complicated than this.

The realities of aging include diminishment, fear, pain, loneliness; they also can include courage, graciousness, patience, and trust. There is loss, insecurity, one part of the body after another breaking down, and the menace of injury. There is the necessity to relinquish freedom — certainly freedom of movement, but also of self-disposition in countless ways. Constant adjustments are required as identity is threatened and as relationships change. For some, indomitable spirits may rage against the inevitable, but for others, gradual and gracious acceptance may also prevail.

Two important observations can be made about these experiences of human aging. One is that although body and spirit do appear to be diverging (in an experience of disunity), they are nonetheless one in the process. Not all individuals experience diminishment of mental acuity as their bodies break down. Some do. In either case, both body and spirit are profoundly affected by aging; aging is both biological and spiritual. Whether experiences are of diminishment or enhancement (in wisdom and grace), they are tied to the body and spirit in the process of aging.

A second observation is that the experience of aging, like other experiences of embodied spirits, is to an important extent socially constructed. It can be shaped and transformed as it is thought about differently — within given cultures or religious traditions, and within significant interpersonal relationships. In other words, it makes a difference to our actual experience how we come to *think* about aging. Take, for example, a Christian view of aging like the one Karl Rahner articulated. "Old age is a grace (both a mission and a risk) not given to everyone, just as, in the Christian understanding, there are possibilities and situations [thought of] as graces which are granted to some and withheld from others."[24] In other words, not everyone gets to live into old age; but for anyone who does, it is a part of her or his vocation. Old age is not merely an external situation, "like a costume in which a person plays a role in the theatre of

---

24. Karl Rahner, "Growing Old," *Prayers and Meditations: An Anthology of Spiritual Writings*, ed. J. Griffiths (New York: Crossroad, 1981), 91.

life which remains extraneous to himself, which he simply drops at death."[25] On the contrary, the period of life that is old age is, like every other period in life, potentially definitive of the meaning of a given life. Other religious and cultural traditions have offered analogous interpretations of the experience of aging and its significance for both individual and community. The point is that although aging and biological diminishment offer experiences of body/spirit disunity, they are nonetheless for human beings a signal of body/spirit unity.

Death, of course, is another matter. It is not in us, as some say, all our lives — at least not in the same way that life is in us. It is on our horizon throughout our lives, however, and it comes closer as our circumstances change. In contemporary Western culture, we lean toward understanding death as simply part of the life span. Death is natural, we say, even though we find ourselves pleading, along with Dylan Thomas, "Do not go gentle into that good night... [but] rage, rage against the dying of the light."[26] However we "naturalize" death, it remains a problem for us — in a way that it is not for other biological beings. We are the ones who anticipate it, worry about it, struggle against it, try to understand it. In this sense, we transcend it. We stand outside of it and ponder it, fear it, attempt to come to peace with it. We are the ones who rebel against it or accept it — though no matter what, we die.

We may conclude that in death the natural resources of the biological life of the individual simply exhaust themselves. Death therefore stands as an inevitable limiting condition for our possibilities in this life, the ultimate "given" in relation to which our freedom will have its last stand. We can think of it as a necessary limit, one that allows us to focus our lives and to finalize our choices in relation to God, one another, our own selves. But, as either biological limit or psychological horizon and existential moment of personal self-integration, death defies our interpretation of it as only a natural process. In fact, it seems unnatural to us that our very selves diminish and die, that

---

25. Ibid.
26. Dylan Thomas, "Do Not Go Gentle into that Good Night," in *Collected Poems of Dylan Thomas 1934–52* (New York: New Directions, 1971), 128.

our relationships are torn asunder, that the wrenching that occurs at the heart of our beings is possible despite all of our efforts against it.

It is not only our spirit that rages against our death; it is our bodies. We try our best to control death in all circumstances; and if we cannot control it, even our bodies weep. Why? Because the body struggles to live, just as does the spirit. The forces within body and spirit are, from each perspective, each dimension, both for and against death. It is not accurate to think that only our bodies die. Death is an event for us as spiritual persons, not only as biological persons. We as embodied spirits, inspirited bodies, die. In a Christian context, our understandings of death and life are shaped by the promises of God offered in Jesus Christ. This transforms the meaning of death as we anticipate it and prepare for it. It may harbinger a new unity of spirit and body in an unlimited future. But it does not erase the clues of body/spirit unity in every experience of dying.

(4) A final clue for body/soul unity in experiences that appear to signify only disunity may be found in those experiences that make us speak of a *"divided self."* Philosophical and religious traditions have tried seemingly forever to understand such experiences. A common interpretation is that the soul is divided from the body. The desires and needs of the body are often at odds with the desires and needs of the spirit. Experiences of precisely this division have yielded beliefs about the adversarial relation of spirit and body. The moral life is explained as a struggle by the soul against the body and the body against the soul. Whatever was originally intended by God in creating human persons, some kind of general human moral "Fall," terrible moral failure, has had as its chief consequence the disordering of body and soul, a disorder between intellect and emotions, between will and the dynamics of the body.[27] The soul's task is to deal with this, to manage it, to bring back a reasoned order, and to continue to hold control over a disciplined body.

---

27. There are theologies of "original sin" that do not today hark back to an original "Fall." They interpret the human condition, rather, as a social phenomenon that infects individuals; or they consider the struggles endemic to human existence not to be the result of moral evil as such but as a part of an evolutionary process in which the human race is engaged. Whatever interpretation is made, the same kind of experience of a "divided self" is possible and common, and the same misinterpretation of spirit/body unity is also possible and common.

But is this accurate? It is true that in our experience, as the saying goes, "the spirit is willing but the flesh is weak." Yet our interpretations of this experience are not without dispute. The history of theological, philosophical, psychological, scientific analyses of the body's need for governance by the spirit is a contested history. At the heart of the controversy is the question of just where the source of conflict and hence the remedy lies. Writers of Christian classics, including St. Augustine, have consistently maintained that the real division within us is within the spirit, not between spirit and body.

But we need to say more. We do indeed experience ourselves as divided. A probing of the experience, however, tells us that the divide is not so much "body" versus "spirit," as it is the body divided against itself — sometimes desiring this, sometimes that — and the spirit divided against itself — sometimes desiring this, sometimes that. These divisions *within* body, *within* spirit — can be more acute than anything that could be described as division *between* body and spirit. These divisions — within body, within spirit — are deep within the self, that self which is an embodied spirit, an inspirited body. The "divided self" gives us clues, not contradictions, for the unity of spirit and body. It points to an underlying unity that calls more for integration than control.

In the end, then, among the most dramatic experiences of disunity within the human person are experiences that nonetheless tell us of the unity of the person. They are experiences of disunity that are only possible in unified inspirited bodies, embodied spirits. It is as such that we are self-constituted. Our language falters here, for it is *we* who are embodied, inspirited. If you touch my arm, you touch *me*. If you minister to my diseased body, you minister to *me*. If our bodies come together in tenderness and love, it is *we* who come together. The bodies that we "have" are also the bodies that we "are." Despite our incompleteness, our limitations, our experiences of fragmentation and lack of wholeness, we are in an important sense whole in ourselves.[28]

---

28. Having articulated this position, I believe that it is possible to look back on the theories I noted earlier (the "one, two, or two-in-one" theories as well as social constructionist theories) and argue that they do not have to be in opposition to what I have been saying. Aristotelian and Thomistic theories do offer an ontological basis

Unity and Transcendence

I said at the start of this section that human embodiment is a "transcendent" embodiment. Unity and destiny must be combined. Hence, to say that spirit and body are united in one personal whole is not yet to say enough about either body or spirit. The transcendence that characterizes embodied spirits is self-transcendence. For anything to be self-transcendent is for it to be at least potentially more than it is at any one point in time. I suppose everything in a dynamic universe, at least every living thing, is transcendent in some sense; it grows and is transformed according to its potential. But human persons are self-transcendent in ways beyond mere growth and simple change. We commonly consider humans transcendent in at least two particular ways: first, through free choice, and second, through active and inspired relationships to others.[29]

Freedom is a capacity to determine oneself in a way that is not totally explainable in terms of the past, of what has already come to be, what one already is. The capacity for free choice is the capacity to introduce something new into what one is — as when we ratify

---

for a theory of body/spirit unity whereby each human being is constituted by two "principles," not two parts. Whatever change takes place in a human individual is of the person as a whole. The body is not a passive object, not even a passive principle. For there is no existing human body, from this perspective, that is not already ensouled; there is no existing human spirit that is not already embodied. Moreover, theories according to which the human person is only a body or only a spirit may miss the reality of spirit/body unity, but they need not do so. If there is a "wisdom" inherent in the body, and if embodiment evokes reflexive wonder and awe, then the consciousness of the body is not far from the embodiment of consciousness. See Sherwin B. Nuland, *The Wisdom of the Body* (New York: Alfred A. Knopf, 1997), 369; see also Teilhard de Chardin, who was by no means a monist, but whose theory of consciousness in matter comes to mind. See *The Phenomenon of Man*, rev. ed. (London: Collins & Harper, 1965). See also the impressive theory worked out by Lynn Rudder Baker in *Persons and Bodies: A Constitution View* (Cambridge: University of Cambridge Press, 2000). And finally, unless social constructionism takes a form whereby the concrete body is lost in language, or the interpretation of the body is fated by social forces without the possibility of critical distance and change, it also need not rule out spirit/body unity.

29. I am not making a statement here about what possibilities other higher animals may or may not have in these regards. I simply do not know these possibilities. I am also obviously not using the term "transcendent" in the same way that Judith Butler uses it. For Butler, transcendence of the body and transcendence of gender means only (though this is significant) that we are not trapped in given meanings for body and gender. See Butler, *Bodies That Matter*.

love in a new way, nurture an attitude that is only partially formed, develop talents in this way or that, attempt to gain possessions or to let them go, respond to a call that still beckons, or choose against all calls and all loves and hence end up alone. We usually think of freedom as a capacity of the spirit, and free choice as an act of the spirit, with the body being simply the object or the instrument of our choice in some way. Yet choice is always of an action, and although action may sometimes seem to be wholly interior (as when we choose to accept a situation about which we can do nothing), it is always action that rises from and is realized by ourselves as embodied spirits, inspirited bodies. As I have been trying to show, our bodies are not purely passive, not appendages, not merely instruments for our selves; they are intrinsic to our selves. The body, inspirited, is therefore intrinsic to ourselves as subjects; we "live" our bodies even when we are using them.[30] Our motivations for choice, actions of choice, and choice itself are embodied and inspirited. Hence, it is as embodied spirits, inspirited bodies, that we are self-transcendent through our freedom.

Moreover, when we open to relationship through knowledge and love, we transcend what we already are. To step into relation with another is to step out of a center that holds only ourselves. We open ourselves radically, whether minimally or maximally, to come into union by knowing and loving and sometimes also by being known and being loved. Our center is now both beyond ourselves and within ourselves.[31] Here, too, we enter into relation not only as spirits but

---

30. For a fuller description of what I mean by free choice, see my *Personal Commitments: Beginning, Keeping, Changing* (San Francisco: Harper & Row, 1986), 23–29. See also chapter 6 below. I am in some sense going beyond this description in emphasizing the subjectivity of the body — a topic that needs much fuller exploration. I am drawing partially on insights generated by writers like Sartre and Merleau-Ponty, but also Paul Ricoeur, *Freedom and Nature: the Voluntary and the Involuntary*, trans. Erazim V. Kohák (Evanston, IL: Northwestern University Press, 1966), chap. 2; Henri Bergson, *Matter and Memory*, trans. Nancy M. Paul and W. Scott Palmer (London: Allen & Unwin, 1970); Richard Zaner, *The Problem of Embodiment* (The Hague: Martinus Nijhoff, 1971). I am also affirming here some of (though not all, and in many ways much more than) the insights and arguments of Judith Butler, *Bodies That Matter*, especially chap. 1.

31. See Margaret A. Farley, "A Feminist Version of Respect for Persons," *Journal of Feminist Studies in Religion 9* (Spring/Fall 1993): 183–98.

as embodied spirits, inspirited bodies — whether or not our relationships are "physical" in the ordinary sense of the word. It is *we* who know and love and are known and loved. Our subjectivity is embodied consciousness, conscious embodiment; and hence as bodies we are transcendent of ourselves in relation to others.[32]

Whatever transcendence is ascribed to spirit, then, must also be ascribed to body — for they are intimately one. There are boundaries to transcendence; there *are* "givens" that we cannot transcend — whether biological, ontological, or socially constructed — and we remain human throughout. Yet we not only yearn to become what we imagine we can yet be; we choose to become what we want to be. Our memories and hopes, our strivings for survival and for a future, our affirmation of life-plans, are the memories, hopes, strivings, choices of beings that are embodied and inspirited. The human body gets its meaning only in the context of who we are.

Finally, but of utmost significance, these explorations would be incomplete if we did not acknowledge that religious traditions have a great deal to say about human embodiment in relation to human self-transcendence.[33] Given the Christian framework that I am presupposing, I must integrate a Christian perspective on the ultimate

---

32. Insofar as the experience of our bodies is socially constructed, it might appear that free choice is an illusion and that relationships are causally determined solely by forces outside of ourselves. In this view, the practices that are the result of these social forces shape our eating or fasting, our sexual practices, the way we clothe ourselves; they produce economic, juridical, and religious institutions that provide us with beliefs that we internalize in our bodies. Yet social construction does not have to be reduced to this, any more than a metaphysic of the body has to be reduced to this. Even social constructionists like Butler argue that human bodies are not passive slates on which society imprints meaning. There are enough gaps in socialization that questions can arise and we can shape our bodies anew. See M. Therese Lysaught, "Body: II. Social Theories," in *Encyclopedia of Bioethics*, rev. ed., I:300–5; Bryan Turner, *The Body and Society: Explorations in Social Theory* (New York: Blackwell, 1986); Mary Douglas, *Purity and Danger: An Analysis of the Concept of Pollution and Taboo* (London: Routledge & Kegan Paul, 1966). See also such studies as Caroline Walker Bynum, *Holy Feast and Holy Fast: The Religious Significance of Food to Medieval Women* (Berkeley: University of California Press, 1987); Valerie Steele, *The Corset: A Cultural History* (New Haven, CT: Yale University Press, 2001); Harold Koda, *Extreme Beauty: The Body Transformed* (New Haven, CT: Yale University Press, 2001); Anne L. Hollander, *Seeing Through Clothes* (New York: Viking, 1978). See also Butler, *Bodies That Matter*, 10.

33. See Coakley, *Religion and the Body*; Law, *Religious Reflections on the Human Body*; Lisa Sowle Cahill and Margaret A. Farley, eds., *Embodiment, Morality, and Medicine* (Dordrecht: Kluwer Academic, 1995).

telos, goal or end of the body. Not everyone in the Christian tradition has interpreted the body, its past and its future, in the same way. If this were a book on a theology of the body, we would need to examine the multiple thinkers and traditions within Christianity in this regard, assessing their coherence, intelligibility, and persuasiveness as interpreters of the Bible, and as illuminators of our own experience. I simply lift up here one major pattern of Christian theologizing about the body because it seems to me to make most sense of the clues of embodied unity and transcendence glimpsed in our explorations in this chapter thus far.

Despite the many historical and contemporary permutations in a Christian theology of the human person, at the heart of Christian belief is the affirmation that not only is the human body good, but it is intrinsic to being human. Created by God, sustained in being by God, offered an unlimited future by the promises of God in Jesus Christ, each human person — embodied and inspirited — has the possibility of and the call to a destiny of relation and wholeness as embodied spirit, inspirited body. The inclusion of the body in this destiny is by no means an afterthought on the part of a God who became embodied and whose own body now lives still in this world and in the reign of God.

There are two major frameworks in which Christian theologians have tried to think about the human body: the framework of creation, fall, and redemption, and the framework of creation and consummation. If Augustine adopts the first of these, Thomas Aquinas adopts the second. David Kelsey explores the second in his careful comparative study of Aquinas and Karl Barth.[34] Bodily creation and consummation are located within a context of belief that all things come forth from God with the destiny to return to God. Aquinas's rendering of this belief is in metaphysical and cosmic terms; Barth's is in relational, covenant terms. For both, however, the body is one with the soul in the human person, and the *body* as well as the soul is engaged by God's grace.

---

34. David H. Kelsey, "Aquinas and Barth on the Human Body," *The Thomist* 50 (October 1986): 643–89.

Aquinas's account of the human person is in terms of "rationally empowered bodily life"[35] which is concretely related to God as creator and consummator. God destines the human person for ultimate and utter union with God and with other human persons in God. God's action in this regard (grace) engages us "precisely *in* our bodiliness," "as a terminal individual [an end in herself, with the responsibility of freedom] to which bodiliness is intrinsically necessary."[36] Barth follows an overall plot line similar to that of Aquinas: the human being comes forth from and returns to God. The human person is "bodily soul, as he is also besouled body."[37] God's "primal intention" in creating humans is to enter into covenant communion with them, in and through the *incarnation* of and redemption by God in Jesus Christ. There are important differences in the theologies of Aquinas and Barth — overall systematic differences in arguments for body/soul unity and differences in the ultimate sacramental view of the body that Aquinas provides, on one hand, and the relational view that Barth offers on the other. Despite these differences, the view of the human body as self-transcendent in its path from creation to consummation is shared.

From this Christian perspective, then, the human person is unified and transcendent. St. Paul wrote that all creation groans for its promised future, and "we ourselves . . . wait for . . . the redemption of our bodies" (Rom. 8:23). What is promised to human persons in and through Jesus Christ is an ultimate bodily, inspirited, resurrection of those who have died, and as Barth says, "from this manifestation of redemption no hair of our head can be excluded."[38] Both *in via*, on the way, and in the end, this is the framework in which human sexuality must somehow also be understood.

---

35. I am using Kelsey's framework, although if there were space here, I would want to expand upon his rendering of the theological anthropology of Thomas Aquinas. See Kelsey, "Aquinas and Barth on the Human Body," 646, 655.

36. Ibid., 651, 660.

37. Karl Barth, *Church Dogmatics*, ed. G. W. Bromiley and T. F. Torrance, trans. H. Knight et al. (Edinburgh: T. & T. Clark, 1960), III/2, 350. Here, too, my thinking has been focused and stimulated by Kelsey's essay, although I am working directly with Barth's own text.

38. Barth, *The Epistle to the Romans*, trans. Edwyn C. Hoskyns (London: Oxford University Press, 1933), 313.

Whether Gender Matters

There is a story to be told about what many people consider the most basic characteristic of inspirited *bodies*. It is narrated as a romantic story, a glorious and inspiring story, and in many of its chapters, a tragic story. It is the story of gender. It starts with a shared belief that sex, male or female, characterizes every human being and is central to everyone's identity, for it qualifies not only bodies but embodied *spirits*. Sex serves, therefore, to divide the human species in utterly important ways. Building on sex, all people grow into a gender identity; they become not only male and female but boy or girl, man or woman. Gender is influenced by cultural and social factors, but it is nonetheless universally recognizable across cultures. It yields images of women as representatives of an "eternal feminine" and sometimes also images of men as representatives of an "eternal masculine."

In this story, cosmic rhythms are interpreted in masculine/feminine terms, and these provide background and context for the story of human sexual and gender dualities. Societies are universally ordered along gender lines; particular roles and tasks are assigned either to women or men but not to both. Traditional kinship structures, religious associations, and social arrangements of all kinds are famously gendered throughout the centuries. Scientific evidence for the importance and inevitability of this division is presented within this story. Philosophical and theological anthropologies take gender dualities for granted, and dramatic renderings of the gender story can be found not only in the past but in the present. "In the whole reach of human life," wrote Karl Barth, "there is no abstractly human, but only concretely masculine or feminine being, feeling, willing, thinking, speaking, conduct and action, and only concretely masculine and feminine co-existence and cooperation in all these things."[39] "The polarity of man and woman can stand as the paradigmatic instance of the thoroughgoing communal character of humanity," echoed Hans Urs von Balthasar.[40] And this was reiterated time and again by Pope John Paul II: "In the 'unity of the two,' man and

---

39. Barth, *Church Dogmatics* III/2, 286.
40. Hans Urs von Balthasar, *The Von Balthasar Reader*, ed. Medard Kehl and Werner Löser, trans. Robert J. Daly and Fred Lawrence (New York: Crossroad, 1982), 72.

woman are called from the beginning not only to exist 'side by side' or 'together,' but they are also called to exist mutually 'one for the other.' "[41]

This story, this rendering of embodied persons, inspirited bodies, is questioned today—not because the history of the story is completely false, but because the message of the story is problematic. No one doubts that human persons are in some sense gendered, but what this means and whether or why it is important are disputed questions. Equally contested are the assumptions that there are only two genders and the question of whether and why gender should control social roles within human communities. Sexologists and feminist writers in the 1960s and 1970s distinguished "sex" from "gender," accepting sex as a biological and anatomical category, but challenging gender as a socially constructed category. This distinction has been blurred since then, however, with the implication that our understandings of sex are socially and culturally constructed as well. This means that both sex and gender have become unstable, debatable, categories.

Challenges to the meanings and the importance of gender arose first out of the recognition that role differentiations disadvantage women. Masculine/feminine dualism is as likely as spirit/body dualism to breed hierarchy. Hence, as feminists have noted,[42] throughout

---

41. John Paul II, *On the Dignity and Vocation of Women*, Apostolic Letter issued August 15, 1988, *Origins* 18 (October 6, 1988): 266.

42. I have been referring to the writings of feminists in each chapter, assuming some general understanding of what it means to be a feminist. Here, however, it seems finally important and appropriate to indicate what I understand "feminism" to be. It is clearly a contested term in the twenty-first century, and it is not well understood by its opponents. The theory that can be called "feminist theory" now takes multiple forms (so that it would be better to refer to "feminisms" in the plural). Nonetheless, feminism in its most fundamental sense means a position (a belief and a movement) that is opposed to discrimination on the basis of gender. Feminism as such is not anti-male or anti-family; its central concern includes taking account of women's experience as a way to understand what well-being means for women and men and children. Another way of putting this is: Feminism is the "belief that women should not be disadvantaged by their sex, that they should be recognized as having human dignity equal to that of men, and that they should have the opportunity to live as fulfilling and as freely chosen lives as men." Susan Moller Okin, *Is Multiculturalism Bad for Women?*, ed. Joshua Cohen, Matthew Howard, and Martha C. Nussbaum (Princeton, NJ: Princeton University Press, 1999), 10. For a fuller rendering of my own view on this see Margaret A. Farley, "Feminist ethics," in *The Westminster Dictionary of Christian*

Western history the male has been more valued than the female; men have been considered more appropriate for roles of leadership; men have been identified with mind and women with body; women have been considered intellectually inferior to men; women are thought to be passive, while men are active; and on and on. Moreover, women came to recognize a profound disparity between their own experience of themselves on the one hand, and on the other hand, the ways in which their gender identity had been construed. The conclusion drawn by many women in response to blatantly inaccurate interpretations of female gender identity and role capabilities was that indeed gender is a constructed concept. Questions quickly became how to counter the injustices spawned by inaccurate views of gender and of women.

Feminist theorists have argued variously (and not infrequently against one another) for the equality of persons, with gender as only a secondary attribute of human beings; for the revaluation of women's embodiment whereby gender becomes even more important; for a general denaturalization of notions of gender; and for a kind of social constructionism that destabilizes not only gender but sex and that can accommodate more forms of gender than the binary gender systems of the past could imagine. None of these theories has to date appeared either to settle all questions about gender or to change the world so that gender injustices no longer occur. Yet all of the theories have helped in some way to focus questions, provide insights helpful to many people, and show some ways to justice. Still, liberal theories of equality often appear to submerge gender too quickly, underestimating the importance of difference and covering over without healing the scars of gender differentiation.[43] But revaluation of women's (and men's) bodies tends to reinforce traditional gender stereotypes, however much its aim is against this.[44]

Ethics, ed. James F. Childress and John Macquarrie (Philadelphia: Westminster, 1986), 229–31.

43. Although it may be argued that this version of feminism, in the hands of someone like Martha Nussbaum, has found a way to incorporate gender and still to advocate for the concrete needs of gendered persons.

44. The highlighting of gender difference in the form of women's reclaiming their bodies, as well as difference in the way women's minds and hearts work, has yielded

Postmodern cultural and social constructionism probes these matters more deeply than all of its forerunners, perhaps, but it leaves
little leverage for the kind of political action most forms of feminism
consider important.[45]

So acute and far-reaching have these questions become that Susan
Parsons asks whether, on account of them, ethics itself has come to
some kind of end.[46] Postmodern ways of thinking have so subverted
and destabilized notions of the human body and of gender that there
is no longer any room for a moral "law." Or in other words, our very
understandings of the "good" are called into question when we discover how intertwined they are with assumptions especially about
gender. Whether or not the situation is as dire (or as filled with possibility) as Parsons suggests, we can all articulate deep concerns for
the injuries that have been perpetrated both against groups who carry
the burdens of gender role differentiation and against individuals who
are judged not to be gendered in acceptable ways. This means, however, that considerations of sex and gender do not begin as neutral
examinations of "interesting" aspects of what it means to be human,
embodied and inspirited. They begin as efforts to correct or reinforce
previous understandings and to challenge or to deny imbalances of
power based on gender. They continue as investigations into "the political stakes in designating as an *origin* and a *cause* those identity
categories that are in fact the *effects* of institutions, practices, and
discourses with multiple and diffuse points of origin."[47] They yield
personal and political challenges, and they may both heighten and
diminish the importance of gender for the human community of the
future.

---

powerful insights for many women. What began in an important way with the work of
Carol Gilligan rang bells for women. Yet it left the community with "difference" and
no clear way to bridge the gap to equality.

45. Judith Butler, for one, does offer some leverage for political action, but it takes
the strange form of parody. For many women, the theory is insightful, and the reasons
for this form of action are understandable, but the questions remain regarding what to
think and what to do.

46. Susan Frank Parsons, *The Ethics of Gender* (Malden, MA: Blackwell, 2002).

47. Butler, *Gender Trouble: Feminism and the Subversion of Identity* (New York:
Routledge, 1990), ix.

Gender Theory and Practice

I once heard the Kenyan linguist and feminist theologian, Musimbi Kanyoro, ask of a group of Southeastern African women, "In your tribes, who milks the cows? women or men?" When the hands went up, they were about evenly divided between those who said that in their tribes women milk the cows and those who said men do. Dr. Kanyoro's point was clearly made — that is, that gender-assigned roles can seem quite arbitrary as we view them across cultures (in this case, across African tribes). So serious are these gender-assignments, however, that if a wife from a tribe in which women are expected to milk the cows actually milks the cows belonging to the tribe of her husband — who is from a tribe where this task belongs to men — she can be cursed, shunned, and exiled. This is not just an isolated example from traditional and contemporary African life. It is analogous to situations in Western cultures where wives of civic leaders, for instance, are still excoriated for attempting their own leadership roles in the public sphere or even for expressing their opinions in public. It is also analogous to the plight of widows in parts of India whose caste determines that they may not work outside the home — even if their survival depends on it.[48] Countless other examples can be found in multiple contexts, from the continued gendered division of labor into low and high paying employment to the gender restrictions on roles of leadership still sustained in many religious traditions today.

When no one questions sexual arrangements, they are assumed to be based in nature — in the givenness of anatomy, physiology, and the directions of sexual desire.[49] When no one questions gendered divisions of labor, they look neutral (what is needed for efficient life in family and society) and benign (everyone has their assigned roles,

---

48. See this case and others in Martha Chen, "A Matter of Survival: Women's Right to Employment in India and Bangladesh," in *Women, Culture, and Development*, ed. M. Nussbaum and J. Glover, 37–57. See also Nussbaum, *Sex and Social Justice* (Oxford: Oxford University Press, 1999), 29 and passim.

49. As will become clear, I do not here include considerations of gender and sexual orientation. Obviously, to heterosexuals and to gays and lesbians the gender of a sexual partner matters. What I am treating here in this chapter, however, is not *which* gender matters but more deeply, what gender is. See my discussion of same-sex relations in chapter 7 below.

and no roles are better than others). Pain in body and spirit, however, makes us *think* about sexual arrangements and gender roles. We think first about the rationales for sexual arrangements and gender division; we think next about the effort it takes to sustain these rationales. In recent years such thinking has involved major historical, philosophical, and theological explorations of the foundations for beliefs about sex and gender, and major sociological, anthropological, and psychological explorations of the patterns of practice undergirded by these beliefs. The overwhelming results have been theoretical challenges to rationales and political challenges to social practices. Whether these results are in every way helpful remains to be seen. There is no doubt, however, that the story of gender has begun to change. In order to understand this change, we need not and cannot here survey the multitude of important studies and analyses, but it is helpful to look at some of them.

Christian Theologies

Historical studies of gender identity and roles have multiplied in Christian theology in the last half century.[50] Christian misogynism is now well documented in the texts of patristic and medieval writers such as Justin Martyr, Tertullian, Origen, Augustine, Thomas Aquinas, Bonaventure; and of sixteenth-century Reformers like Martin Luther and John Knox.[51] Notions of "woman" were from the beginning theoretically entrenched in sophisticated theologies of original sin and in anthropological theories of higher and lower nature. Women were considered to be (like Eve) a source of temptation to men; hence they were symbolically identified with evil and

---

50. See, for example, such studies as George Tavard, *Woman and the Christian Tradition* (Notre Dame, IN: University of Notre Dame Press, 1973; Rosemary Radford Ruether, ed., *Religion and Sexism* (New York: Simon & Schuster, 1974); Mary Daly, *The Church and the Second Sex* (New York: Harper & Row, 1975); Margaret A. Farley, "Sources of Sexual Inequality in the History of Christian Thought," *Journal of Religion* 56 (April 1976): 162–76); Barbara Hilkert Andolsen, "Whose Sexuality? Whose Tradition? Women, Experience, and Roman Catholic Sexual Ethics," in *Readings in Moral Theology No. 9: Feminist Ethics and the Catholic Moral Tradition*, ed. Charles E. Curran, Margaret A. Farley, and Richard A. McCormick (Mahwah, NJ: Paulist, 1996), 207–39; Sarah Coakley, *Powers and Submissions: Spirituality, Philosophy, and Gender* (Oxford: Blackwell, 2002). See also chap. 2 above.

51. It would be superfluous to note the best known texts in this regard. They have all been well documented in such studies as those cited in n. 50 above.

disorder. They had to be controlled, relegated to ordered spheres (marriage and family or cloister). Women's bodies needed redemption either through childbearing or through alienation from the body by virginity.

Paradoxically, Christian theologies of the past exalted "woman" and her role at the same time that they considered her to be inferior in body and mind. She was at once the symbol of sin and the symbol of all virtue. The latter, unfortunately, reinforced the former. If a woman is on a pedestal, there is presumably no cause for appeal for better status or more accurate rendering of her reality as a human person. Moreover, what is perceived too easily as sacred is also perceived too easily as profaned.

As noted earlier, the Greek fathers maintained that the *imago dei*, the image of God, is in the nonsexual soul, but not body, of both women and men, although it resided more fully in men's souls — since they were judged to be more like God in their roles of leadership. Augustine and the Latin fathers pointed to the image of God in both spirit and body; but they thought that only the male body (in its characteristics of activity and power) is in the image of God. For Thomas Aquinas, both men and women (in body and in spirit) participate in the image of God, but in different degrees. In agreement with Aristotle, Aquinas considered women deficient as human beings, and hence deficient in their status as images of God.

Although through the centuries there were other perspectives — those of medieval women, for example, whose gender identity, leadership roles, and relationships to God were radically different from what the fathers and doctors of the church thought possible for women — these other perspectives were marginal to the church's central traditions. Today, however, with the persistent and dramatic critique (feminist and otherwise) of mainstream traditional notions of gender and the status of women, alternative theologies have appeared that not only critique but retrieve and reconstruct central Christian teachings regarding God, human persons, the *imago dei*, and all other Christian doctrines that have contributed to the oppression of people by reason of their gender. Key examples of these new theologies are to be found in Elizabeth Johnson's *She Who Is* and *Friends of God and Prophets*, which together take seriously, yet transform in terms of gendered concepts and conclusions, the central Christian beliefs about a Triune god, redemptive incarnation, and an eschatological future.[52] Serene Jones, in her *Feminist Theory and Christian Theology*, also transforms, in regard to gender, major Christian beliefs as articulated primarily in Reform theology.[53]

Biblical Challenge

The majority of contemporary theologies eschew the kinds of gendered hierarchies of the Christian past. Few if any theologians today argue that women are intellectually inferior to men. Not many argue that a binary division of gender characteristics (men are strong, women weak; men are active, women passive; men appeal to requirements of justice, women to compassion; men prefer principles, women focus on relationships) applies absolutely. So theological claims for gender hierarchy are to some extent removed or moderated; the most contestable attributions of gender characteristics have faded; and in some theologies gender plays a completely new and transforming role. There is, however, no serious or widespread move to eliminate the binary construction of gender as such. Yet within Christianity there is some basis for doing just this, at least in the context of relationships among Christians.

Christian scripture itself records: "There is no longer Jew or Greek, there is no longer slave or free, there is no longer male and female; for all of you are one in Christ Jesus" (Gal. 3:28). When Paul's "no longer male and female" is juxtaposed to high theological claims about the centrality of gender such as we have seen in the writings of Barth and John Paul II, what are we to think? Even when these words are compared with the kind of transformed use of gender that can be seen in Johnson and Jones, what are we to think?

Barth thought that Paul never meant to say that the male/female distinction should be canceled, but only that there should be equality

---

52. Elizabeth A Johnson, *She Who Is: The Mystery of God in Feminist Theological Discourse* (New York: Crossroad, 1992); and Johnson, *Friends of God and Prophets: A Feminist Theological Reading of the Communion of Saints* (New York: Continuum, 1998).

53. Serene Jones, *Feminist Theory and Christian Theology: Cartographies of Grace* (Minneapolis: Fortress, 2000).

and mutuality between men and women.[54] Equality for Barth does not, however, rule out super- and subordination, since both are in Jesus Christ (who is above all humans, but who also subordinated himself to God and humans). What is revealed in the command of God regarding gender does not include culturally shaped specific masculine and feminine traits, but it does include a "sequential" ordering where men are "A" and women are "B," and where women must cover their heads (or do something analogous), but men need not do so (1 Cor. 11:1–16).[55] So for Barth, Paul's "no longer male and female" meant that the "male is male in the Lord only, but precisely, to the extent that he is with the female, and the female likewise. That they are one in the Lord holds them together,"[56] each "in their proper place."[57] Gender distinction remains sacrosanct, and despite Barth's disclaimers, it is still haunted by the shadows of hierarchy.[58]

John Paul II certainly did not think that Paul intended to eliminate gender difference. In a theology of gender based on the accounts of creation in Genesis, John Paul understands the very substance of the human, the *imago dei*, to incorporate the transformation of Adam's solitude into the communion of persons made possible only by sexual difference.[59] Reminiscent of Plato's *Symposium* in which Aristophanes tells the mythical tale of humans being only halves of the whole they once were, longing and searching always in love for their other half, John Paul presents man and woman as incomplete until they come into union with one another.[60] Human life, then,

---

54. Barth, *Church Dogmatics* III/2, 310–12; III/4, 153–56, 164, 174.

55. Barth, *Church Dogmatics* III/2, 310; III/4, 169–72.

56. Barth, *Church Dogmatics* III/4, 164.

57. Ibid., 174.

58. Ibid., 169–76. Barth introduces this sequential order after he has insisted that men and women are equal before God. He here acknowledges that "every word is dangerous and liable to be misunderstood when we characterize this order. But it exists. . . . A precedes B, and B follows A. Order means succession. It means preceding and following. It means super- and sub-ordination." Ibid., 169.

59. John Paul II, *Original Unity of Man and Woman* (Boston: Pauline Books and Media, 1981), 56.

60. Plato, *Symposium*, 189e–194 e. There are some obvious differences between Plato's tale of Aristophanes and the appropriation of the Genesis story by John Paul II. In the *Symposium* the history of the human race does not begin with a single human who is solitary but with three kinds of humans: male, female, and androgynous. To control the unruliness of these beings, the gods cut them in half. Forever after each one roams the world looking for its other half (each male for a male, each female for a

would not be human were the distinction between man and woman erased. For John Paul, the reason why women and men seek one another is because they are complementary. They need their "other half" who is different from them but who will complete them. Binary gender characteristics remain, and the importance of gender escalates.

Biblical scholars have other things to say about Galatians 3:28, however, observing that the brief formula, "no male and female," involves major problems of interpretation. Situated in a pre-Pauline tradition regarding baptism, and in the associated belief in a "new creation" for the baptized, the words "no male and female" offer an interpretation — perhaps an abrogation — of Genesis 1:27. To abrogate Genesis 1:27 would be to abrogate: "So God created humankind [*adam*] in his image, in the image of God he created them [him]; male and female he created them." For Paul and the Galatians, "new creation" may transform or leave behind some things given in the first creation.[61]

It is not immediately clear, however, which of the many meanings attached to "male and female" in Genesis 1:27 might be abrogated by the baptismal formula in Galatians 3:28. Mary Rose D'Angelo identifies four functions of the phrase, all of which can be found in texts of the first to third century C.E. or at least supported by similar usages during this period:[62] (1) "Male and female" is here a figure of speech (used frequently in antiquity) which names a whole reality by naming its opposite poles. Hence, "male and female" in Genesis 1:27 means "all human beings," as does, in a negative form, "no male and female" in Galatians. In Genesis, gender division applies

---

female, and each male for a female [and vice versa] when they were originally part of the androgyne).

61. For this description I draw on Mary Rose D'Angelo, "Gender Refusers in the Early Christian Mission: Gal 3:28 as an Interpretation of Gen 1:27b," in *Reading in Christian Communities: Essays on Interpretation in the Early Church*, ed. Charles A. Bobertz and David Brakke (Notre Dame, IN.: University of Notre Dame Press, 2002), 149–73. D'Angelo expands on Paul's notion of "new creation" by turning to other texts, such as 2 Corinthians 5:17–18 ("So if anyone is in Christ, there is a new creation; everything old has passed away; see, everything has become new!"). She also adds the observation that this need not mean that all of Genesis 1–3 is negated. More likely, what Paul thinks has passed away are certain aspects of human life in community, particularly those that for him were considered "fleshly."

62. D'Angelo provides detailed documentation of these texts and usages.

to all; in Galatians all, regardless of gender, are included in Christ through baptism. (2) "Male and female" in Genesis refers to a "relation of disadvantage." "No male and female" in Galatians would then mean an abrogation of disadvantage in the relation of male and female. (3) The Genesis "male and female" can mean "sex and marriage," so that "no male and female" in Galatians means no more sex and marriage. This corresponds to 1 Corinthians 7:1 and 7:17–24, and to the belief among early Christians that everything "fleshly" of this world would soon pass away. (4) Finally, "male and female" in Genesis 1:27 refers to the original Adam, the image of God, as androgynous. That is, Adam was both male and female until the creation of Eve, which in some traditions was interpreted to mean (like Aristophanes's myth) that Adam was split into two (Eve taken from Adam's side), so that only then did human gender come into the picture. In this case, "no male and female" in Galatians could mean a return to the androgyne — for all the baptized.[63] With this, the new creation would transcend sexual and gender division.

D'Angelo considers that of the four interpretations of "male and female" in Genesis 1:27, the second (disadvantage to one pole of the relationship) is the most likely to be negated by Galatians. This negation fits with the other pairs in the text; it is consonant with the vision of equality in the early church; and it is visible in the early church practice of both male and female leadership. The third meaning (sex and marriage), according to D'Angelo, is the easiest to demonstrate from the first century tradition of interpretation. The fourth (the image of the adrogyne) has been deduced from a wide variety of texts that refer in some way to sexual duality. Various mythic images are absorbed in the idea of the image of the adrogyne, each of which might have explained or reinforced any of the other three functions of Galatians 3:28.[64]

---

63. See D'Angelo, "Gender in the Origins of Christianity," in *Equal at the Creation: Sexism, Society, and Christian Thought* (Toronto: University of Toronto Press, 1998), 25–48.

64. For a helpful study on the androgyne in antiquity, see D'Angelo, "Transcribing Sexual Politics: Images of the Androgyne in Discourses of Antique Religion," in *Descrizioni e iscrizioni: politiche del discorso* (Trento: Dipartimento di Scienze Filologiche e Storiche, 1998), 115–46; see also Wayne A. Meeks, "The Image of the Androgyne: Some Uses of a Symbol in Earliest Christianity," in *In Search of the Early Christians:*

What seems clear is that the second and fourth options, in particular, offer a radical challenge to later theological traditions in which gender distinction becomes central to an understanding of the human (as it does in Barth, von Balthasar, and John Paul II, for example). These options would not mean that gender differences disappear in terms of bodily anatomy but in terms of the irrelevance of gender distinctions between people. These options challenge most especially theologies in which gender hierarchy is neither eliminated nor transformed in a "new creation." Feminists have appealed to Galatians 3:28 primarily as an argument for equality among women and men — in the church, the family, and even society. More can be said about its contemporary relevance, however, and I return to this below.

Biology, Culture, and Experience

It is tempting to think that we might be able to solve all of our gender questions through advanced scientific studies. We know that inadequate scientific methods have contributed to the problems we have had in understanding sexual and gender difference in the past. Is it possible that the behavioral and biological sciences are now finally "adequate" to the task of discerning these differences and/or similarities? This is a question not only for the sciences but for other disciplines as well. Philosophers and theologians, for example, have based many of their theories about gender on their perception of the biological and medical information of their times — or more likely, they have used this information to bolster their own culturally formed presuppositions about gender.

The problem with expecting all of our answers to come from science is that the "facts" of sexual and gender difference have been looked for and seen through the lenses of context and culture.[65] As the historian Thomas Laqueur concluded from his lengthy study of

Selected Essays, ed. Allen R. Hilton and H. Gregory Snyder (New Haven, CT: Yale University Press, 2002), 3–54. For an interpretation of Genesis 1:27 that runs counter to the idea of an androgynous creation of Adam, see Phyllis Trible, God and the Rhetoric of Sexuality (Philadelphia: Fortress, 1978), 12–23.

65. For a fascinating study of the role of culture in relation to scientific studies of gender, see Cynthia Eagle Russett, Sexual Science: The Victorian Construction of Womanhood (Cambridge, MA: Harvard University Press, 1989).

the meanings of sex and gender from the Greeks to Freud, "destiny is anatomy," rather than, as Freud thought, the other way around.[66] This sort of insight is what has led many of those who think about gender and sex to elide sexual and gender difference into culturally constructed meanings and behaviors — rejecting a presumed "givenness" for sex, and a presumed "construction" only of gender.

The most striking example of Laqueur's phrase appears in what he calls one-sex and two-sex models of human bodies. In the one-sex model which prevailed from the Greeks to the eighteenth century, there is only one kind of human body. The difference between male and female is a difference of incompleteness on the part of the female. The male is unquestionably human; the female is an inverted male, the vagina is an inverted penis, and so forth. As such, the female body is a lesser, deficient, version of the male body. In the eighteenth century, the two-sex model emerged as a result of concern for the "otherness" of the female and the "opposition" of the sexes. Difference then was between two incommensurably different bodies, one male and one female. The female was still the anomaly, however, the one that needed to be explained, and the one who was ultimately disadvantaged. The challenge was to decipher what about her accounts for *her* difference, *her* otherness, *in relation to the male.* The meanings already given to gender had to be secured by a foundation in women's bodies — "in the very nature of their bones, nerves, and, most important, reproductive organs."[67] Hence, for example, an explanation of women's supposed lack of passion (or women's greater than men's ability to control passion) had to be found in the female body.

---

66. Thomas Laqueur, *Making Sex: Body and Gender from the Greeks to Freud* (Cambridge, MA: Harvard University Press, 1990), 25 and passim. One form of scientific theory that goes completely against arguments for the cultural construction of gender is sociobiology. It proposes, on the contrary, a view of evolution that insists that in human as in nonhuman animals there is an insatiable drive in genes to reproduce, an urgency in male genes to find multiple partners, and a settled tendency in female genes not to have many partners but to settle down and nurture. When it comes to humans, however, this set of assumptions needs testing. Even if we accepted these assumptions, it is still possible that humans can intervene in their genetic determinism and change its course.

67. Ibid., 150.

Of course, from the eighteenth century on, there has been definite
gain in knowledge about sexual embodiment. According to Laqueur,
however, this new knowledge was not what changed ways of viewing
women and men. On the contrary, it was shifts in cultural meanings
of gender that changed the scientific questions about sex and influenced the answers that were found. It is not certain that the same
dynamic does not exist today. When the equality of women and men,
for example, is challenged, we see a flurry of scientific studies claiming to explain why boys are better at some things (say, mathematics)
and girls are better at others (say, literature). It is hard not to be skeptical about the unstudied variables in studies such as these especially
when other studies show, for example, that girls in Iceland are ahead
of boys in their mathematical prowess.

But what do we know today? We know that, biologically speaking,
women and men have different chromosomal make-ups, different
hormones (or more accurately, different amounts of the same gender-
related hormones), as well as the different anatomies (particularly
reproductive organs) and secondary sex characteristics that chromosomes and hormones produce. We also know that major illnesses
such as lung cancer, osteoporosis, and heart disease require different
medical treatments for women and for men.[68] We know that brain-
imaging technologies show differences in the responses of women
and men to external stimulations of all sorts, even though brain responses along gender lines frequently do not seem to represent gender
differences in behavior.[69]

Much of what science tells us about gender difference is confusing,
however. Currently significant brain studies tell us that on average

---

68. Recent criticism of the medical professions for providing the same treatments
for men and women (assuming that only reproductive problems require differential
treatment), and the correlative criticism of the neglect of medical research on women,
have led to more focused studies of sexual and gender differences and to insistence on
deeper gender analysis. Much of this is still in beginning stages.

69. See, for example, Deborah Blum, *Sex on the Brain: The Biological Differences
Between Men and Women* (New York: Viking, 1997). Examples of the two sides on
the issue of the significance of biology for understanding gender, human freedom, and
so forth, see (on the pro biology side) Patricia Smith Churchland, *Neurophilosophy:
Toward a United Science of the Mind/Brain* (Cambridge, MA: MIT Press, 1986), especially 88–97; and (pro limits on what the sciences can offer) John Dupré, *Human
Nature and the Limits of Science* (Oxford: Clarendon Press, 2001), especially chaps. 3
and 7.

men's brains are 9 to 10 percent larger than women's, but we also know that gender-related brain size is not a predictor of intellectual performance (men and women perform similarly on IQ tests). We know that the *parts* of the brain related to intelligence appear to be different for women and men, although the net results appear to be similar on average. We know that the connector between the brain's two hemispheres is larger in women than in men, and that this lessens the damage of some strokes. The speculation that this is the source of "women's intuition" seems more dubious, more a matter of the lens being used than the object being seen. We know that brain size for girls peaks at eleven and a half years, and for boys three years later. We also know that some areas (sources for certain capabilities) mature faster in boys, and that some mature faster in girls; but that as they age, these capabilities even out. We do not know whether developmental differences may be due less to the brain itself than to sensory capacities, or for that matter, to the ways boys and girls are stimulated differently from birth by their parents and others.

As noted above, brain-imaging technologies make it possible to see differences in the responses of women and men to external influences, but not necessarily to see gendered correlations with behavior. The brain changes constantly in reaction to hormones, personal encouragement, the development of behavioral habits, what we eat, the medications we take. We do not know for sure whether the brain is hardwired for gender difference, or whether it accrues software through social and cultural influences from birth. And we do not know whether the brain "lights up" (on the brain-imaging screen) because it is causing some action, directing some emotion; or whether the person (whose embodiment includes a brain) is acting, directing, responding, in a way that simply requires the brain for support and completion. Without returning to questions of mind/body, almost everyone nonetheless remains confused as to what a gendered brain does to determine what *we* do. If the claims of biology (or biologists) rise too high, so that they render moot our thinking about gender and its problems, or make futile our efforts to change gendered attitudes and behavior, we can hope for caution lights to go on in our brains and in our selves. We need biological studies; we just should not expect more from them than they can deliver.[70]

If biology is vulnerable to cultural bias, how much more so are the behavioral sciences of anthropology, sociology, and psychology. Still, as we saw in chapter 3, anthropological and sociological studies are important to cross-cultural perspectives and to the understanding of ourselves. Psychologists still give us multiple, often contradictory, explanations of why people act in certain ways, as we shall see below, but the interpretations of even descriptive studies come under scrutiny for their cultural biases.[71] Ongoing work by scholars like Carol Gilligan and Lyn Mikel Brown never fail to illuminate human experience of the development of young girls in a process of growing insecurity, yet questions remain about the causes of such development and about the importance of such gender differences in adults.[72]

We cannot avoid, then, the scientific as well as cultural challenges to our assumptions about gender difference when it comes to females and males, women and men. But there are also scientific and cultural challenges that go beyond this, that ask whether there are

---

70. Interesting animal studies are available to us as well as studies of humans. Studies of chimpanzees and bonobos, close to us on the evolutionary tree, are especially interesting. Most female primates, it is reported, are caring, while males are competitive; males are promiscuous, and females are less so (although in some species both males and females have multiple mates). Bonobos (a species of great apes), unlike chimpanzees, are ruled by females, not males; they settle disputes by forming alliances rather than fighting with competitors. Most scholars are aware of the cautions that are needed when comparisons are made between nonhuman primates and human. See, for example, Meredith E. Small, *Female Choices: Sexual Behavior of Female Primates* (Ithaca, NY: Cornell University Press, 1993); Richard Wrangham and Dale Peterson, *Demonic Males* (New York: Houghton Mifflin, 1996).

71. See, for example, Eleanor E. Maccoby, *The Two Sexes: Growing Apart, Coming Together* (Cambridge, MA: Harvard University Press, 1998). This is a book about evidence that when boys and girls are very young, they prefer to play in gender identified groups, but that in time, they come together. One reviewer of this book notes that this evidence is interesting and in some ways very useful, but there are many questions the author does not ask — for example, what about those children who do not fit this pattern? And what about adult influences that may be shaping children's behavior? See Carla Golden, "Separate and Unequal," *The Women's Review of Books* 16 (December 1998): 24–25.

72. Lyn Mikel Brown and Carol Gilligan, *Meeting at the Crossroads: Women's Psychology and Girls' Development* (Cambridge, MA: Harvard University Press, 1992).

more genders than two; and that ask whether gender assignment at birth settles the basic gender issues for all human persons.

Biology, Culture, and More Experience

We can always return to the few things we seem sure of, bolstered by scientific research: Males and females are, baseline, sexually differentiated by chromosomes, hormones, and anatomy. Gender may be constructed out of a myriad of influences, but it has to relate somehow to biological difference. And yet even here our surety becomes unstable. We have learned, mainly from people's experience but also from scientific exploration, that these clearly defined male or female configurations are not universal among humans. To attend to differences in this regard is no longer a marginal or minor concern.

There are human bodies that are neither entirely female nor entirely male; they do not fall neatly into a binary sexual division. Some persons are born with alternative chromosomal sexual constitutions — that is, alternative to the statistically standard XX for females and XY for males. Moreover, some persons have a mixture of male and female reproductive organs; others have secondary sex characteristics that appear to be out of harmony with their chromosomal sexual identity. Hence, in the human community there are not only unambiguously identifiable males and females but intersexuals.[73]

---

73. Estimates of the incidence of intersex in the population are difficult to make, but some have offered 1.7 percent; others 1 in 2000. This makes it relatively rare, but as Anne Fausto-Sterling notes, "Even if we've overestimated by a factor of 2 [her estimate is 1.7 percent], that still means a lot of intersexual children are born each year. At the rate of 1.7 percent, for example, a city of 300,000 would have 5,100 people with vary⁺ng degrees of intersexual development." Anne Fausto-Sterling, *Sexing the Body: Gender Politics and the Construction of Sexuality* (New York: Basic Books, 2000), 51. Other important resources on intersexuality include: Alice Domurat Dreger, " 'Ambiguous Sex' — or Ambivalent Medicine? Ethical Issues in the Treatment of Intersexuality," *Hastings Center Report* 28 (May–June 1998): 25–35; Dreger, *Hermaphrodites and the Medical Invention of Sex* (Cambridge, MA: Harvard University Press, 1998); Suzanne J. Kessler, *Lessons from the Intersexed* (New Brunswick, NJ: Rutgers University Press, 1998); Kessler and W. McKenna, *Gender: An Ethnomethodological Approach* (New York: Wiley, 1978); Stephanie S. Turner, "Intersex Identities: Locating New Intersections of Sex and Gender," *Gender and Society* 13 (August 1999): 457–79. There is also the novel by Jeffrey Eugenides, *Middlesex* (New York: Farrar, Straus & Giroux, 2002).

Once called hermaphrodites and still so called in some scientific circles, they are not new to the human community.[74] Aristotle thought they were a kind of twin; Galen believed they represented an intermediate sex. Physicians in the middle ages thought they were in the middle of a sexual continuum. By the nineteenth century science and medicine took over, determining that intersexuality is pathological and requires a medical remedy — surgery, hormone treatments, and social programming. With this remedy, intersexuals largely disappeared from the public eye, for they were medically and surgically melded into the standard binary sexual model.

Today, however, the heretofore hidden stories of intersexed persons are being told. They are stories of individuals whose sex is deemed "ambiguous" at birth (neither "purely" male or female). In Western cultures a child with mixed sex is deemed so anomalous that physicians and parents consider themselves faced with a "medical emergency." So important is gender difference that a baby must be assigned one gender or the other, and this must be done immediately. Criteria are in place to determine male or female assignment, and standard medical practice has until recently favored not chromosomes but the possibility of a penis of acceptable length for males and interior reproductive organs for females. The use of these criteria is based on the medical opinion that gender identity is changeable until approximately eighteen months of age, after which it can be wholly determined by the way in which a child is reared. This view usually includes the corollary that healthy psychosexual adjustment

---

74. According to Myra J. Hird and Jenz Germon, the term "intersexuality" was first introduced in 1920, and before that time, "hermaphroditism" was the common term. See Myra J. Hird and Jenz Germon, "The Intersexual Body and the Medical Regulation of Gender," in Constructing Gendered Bodies, ed. Kathryn Backett-Milburn and Linda McKie (New York: Palgrave, 2001), 175, n. 1. For a succinct history of intersexuals, see Fausto-Sterling, Sexing the Body, 32–36. My brief historical comments here are dependent upon Fausto-Sterling and the historians she cites. Note also that since the mid-nineteenth century physicians have sometimes made a distinction between "true" hermaphrodites and "pseudo" hermaphrodites. The distinction is based on the particular configuration of sexual organs — the pseudo-hermaphrodite having mixed sexuality because of the development of one set organs into an intersex configuration or having only ovaries or only testes; the "true" hermaphrodite having two genuinely different sets of organs or at least having testes and ovaries. See Fausto-Sterling, ibid., 37–38.

is related to the appearances of the genitals.[75] The experiences of persons whose intersex has been resolved according to these criteria are, however, often fraught with confusion and pain.[76] Debate rages, therefore, between physicians who hold to this gender theory and medical practice, and those who critique it as false and harmful.[77] An organization of persons whose intersex was managed according to this theory was formed in 1993 to oppose the theory and practice, and to advocate not only for consideration of other criteria for treatment but for the delay of any treatment until the intersexed child is old enough to choose a gender assignment or to choose simply to be a person of mixed sex.

The question for all of us is not only what treatment should be given for a condition considered to be pathological, but whether the condition is pathological or not. In other words, if a culture were less preoccupied with male/female sexual division and with boy/girl, man/woman gender differentiation, would the medical imperative regarding intersexed persons remain as it is? Or more fundamentally, is gender assignment as a "pure" male or female, man or woman, essential to human flourishing?

There is another form of human social gendering that is relevant to these questions. Cross-cultural anthropological studies have led

75. See Susanne J. Kessler, "The Medical Management of Gender: Case Management of Intersexed Infants," *Signs: Journal of Women in Culture and Society* 16 (1990): 3–26; Milton Diamond and H. Keith Sigmundson, "Sex Reassignment at Birth: Long-term Review and Clinical Implications," *Archives of Pediatric Adolescent Medicine* 151 (May 1997): 298–304. For interreligious perspectives on these issues, see Christine E. Gudorf, "The Erosion of Sexual Dimorphism," *Journal of the American Academy of Religion* 69 (December 2001): 863–91.

76. See, for example, John Colapinto, *As Nature Made Him: The Boy Who Was Raised as a Girl* (New York: HarperCollins 2000). This is actually a story of a boy who was not born with mixed sex at birth, but whose penis was accidentally severed during a circumcision procedure. It has, however, shed what appears to be a great deal of light for critiquing the criteria for sex assignment at birth. See also Daphne Scholinski, *The Last Time I Wore a Dress* (New York: Riverhead Books, 1997).

77. The theory was first articulated by John Money and his colleagues at Johns Hopkins University. See John Money, J. G. Hampson, and J. L. Hampson, "Hermaphroditism: Recommendations Concerning Assignment of Sex, Change of Sex, and Pschologic Management," *Bulletin of the Johns Hopkins Hospital* 97 (1955): 284–300. The major critics of Money's theory and recommendations are Milton Diamond and H. Keith Sigmundson. See Diamond and Sigmundson, "Sex Reassignment at Birth." Many believe now that Money's approach has been discredited. See also Hird and Germon, "The Intersexual Body and the Medical Regulation of Gender," 179–203.

some scholars, not without controversy, to identify what they call a "third sex."[78] This differs, at least in some cases, from intersex in that it does not refer necessarily to a sexually formed body but more specifically to a social role. Gender for a third sex is not one (man or woman), and not always two (intersexed man and woman), but more often neither woman nor man. Examples include *hijras* in India,[79] *berdaches*[80] in traditional Native American societies, and the *guevedoce* in the Dominican Republic.[81] A *hijra* is a male according to chromosomal make-up and anatomy, who is impotent and who is thought to receive a call from a mother goddess to dress and act like a woman, as well as to undergo removal of male genitals. Some *hijras* can be chromosomally and anatomically females who do not menstruate. In either case, *hijras* are considered to be vehicles of divine power who live and act as such in the community.[82]

Berdaches, male or female, are not only accepted members of their communities; they enjoy special respect. The honor attributed to their social role is not measured in standard ways by gender. The productive specializations of *berdaches* tend in traditional Native American communities to involve domestic work and crafts for both male and female *berdaches*, though females may be hunters and warriors. They are renowned for their spiritual powers — whether as visionaries or wise spiritual guides within the community. There is a great deal of gender variation in the behavior of individual *berdaches*. Cross-dressing at least used to be common though not universal; sexual partnerships were generally same-sex but they could also be bisexual and heterosexual. The prestige of the *berdaches*, however, is based more on the religious dimension of their role, along with

78. See Gilbert Herdt, ed., *Third Sex, Third Gender: Beyond Sexual Dimorphism in Culture and History* (New York: Zone Books, 1994); Carl Elliott, "Why Can't We Go On as Three?" *Hastings Center Report* 28 (May–June 1998): 36–39.

79. See Serena Nanda, "Hijras: An Alternative Sex and Gender Role in India," in Herdt, *Third Sex, Third Gender*, 373–417.

80. See Will Roscoe, "How to Become a Berdache: Toward a Unified Analysis of Gender Diversity," in Herdt, *Third Sex, Third Gender*, 329–72.

81. Juliame Imperato-McGinley et al., "Androgens and the Evolution of Male-Gender Identity among Male Pseudohermaphrodites with 5-alpha Reductase Deficiency," *New England Journal of Medicine* 300 (1979): 1235–36, as cited in Elliott, "Why Can't We Go On as Three?" 36.

82. Nanda, "Hijras: An Alternative Sex and Gender Role in India," 379–80.

their economic success, than it is on their assumed gender identities.[83] This means, however, that their gender identities are accepted as part of who they are in the community.

Guevedoce are children whose physical sexual ambiguity at birth leads them to be identified and reared as girls but who at puberty develop less ambiguous male sex organs and secondary sexual characteristics. As scientists in the 1970s determined, these children have a rare deficiency of testosterone metabolism called 5-alpha-reductase deficiency syndrome. They are genetically XY, but at birth they present as sexually ambiguous. When it becomes visible at puberty that they are "really" boys, they appear to change their gender identity without much difficulty, which provides support for the much debated position that it is biology that matters, not rearing.[84] Gilbert Herdt has argued, to the contrary, that the change is easier for these adolescents than it might be for their counterparts in other cultures precisely because they live in a culture which, despite a strong emphasis on the binary male/female physical and social gender model, have nonetheless developed a concept of a "third sex."[85] Hence, the *guevedoce* move from a stigmatized identity that is ambiguously female, to a preferred one which is male, but they remain something else, something that represents an alternative to the two genders, male and female. This may indeed be a "third gender," but it may also mean that here are individuals whose gender simply does not matter.

There are also persons who may be unambiguously male or female in terms of chromosomes, hormones, and anatomy, but who are certain that their gender identity is at odds with their biological sex, at odds with their bodies. Hence, in the human community there are transsexuals; or better, there are transgendered persons, which is a broader designation that can include cross-dressing and other

---

83. Roscoe, "How to Become a Berdache," passim. I use the present tense in speaking of *berdaches*, since their tradition did not stop with the move of Native Americans to the reservation stage of their history.

84. Elliott, "Why Can't We Go On as Three?" 36.

85. Herdt, "Mistaken Sex: Culture, Biology and the Third Sex in New Guinea," in Herdt, ed., *Third Sex, Third Gender*, 419–45. Herdt draws comparisons between the Dominican Republic experience and that of the Sambia of Papua New Guinea.

forms of gender identity change[86]. The goal for transsexuals is not a
new kind of gender but only a change from the sexual body of their
birth, whether male or female, to the sexual body needed by their
psyche, whether male or female. Transsexuality does not necessarily,
therefore, call into question the male/female binary, but in fact can
reinforce it, even though the alignment of transsexuals with cross-
dressers and others has brought with it greater interest in flexibility
of categories of gender. Here are persons whose experience tells them
that gender identity is fixed, unchangeable, and so important that if
it does not correspond with anatomy, then anatomy must change.[87]

Transsexuals may have been around a long time, too, but the
possibilities of actually transforming bodies from one biological sex
to another depended on developments in contemporary medicine.
While intersexed persons are beginning to resist surgery as a remedy
for anything that has to do with them, transsexuals have become
more assertive in demanding the surgery they believe is appropriate for them. In the 1950s the first sex reassignment surgery was
performed in the United States, and it brought resistance from the
medical community — resistance to the idea of removing tissue or organs that are perfectly healthy.[88] The availability of this surgery grew
in the 1960s, however, and increased after that.[89] At the same time,
the broader category of transgender includes transsexuals — some
who want surgery, some who do not — but also individuals who are
not looking for change between sexes. They want something other

---

86. For a sociological description of the meanings that can be included in the
term "transgender," see Richard Ekins and Dave King, "Telling Body Transgendering
Stories," in *Constructing Gendered Bodies*, ed. Milburn and McKie," 180.

87. For a very useful resource on transsexuality, see Joanne Meyerowitz, *How Sex
Changed: A History of Transsexuality in the United States* (Cambridge, MA: Harvard
University Press, 2002).

88. There have been some analogies drawn between sex reassignment surgery and
the kind of surgery requested by individuals with "body integrity identity disorder" —
that is, individuals who are psychologically driven to have arms or legs or fingers, etc.,
amputated. One objection to the analogy is that transsexuals want a change from one
"normal state" to another (that is, from one set of sexual organs to another), whereas
those who want to be amputees go from a normal state to an abnormal state.

89. At first, it was only John Money and colleagues, again at Johns Hopkins, who
could provide this surgery in new and more sophisticated ways, along with criteria,
requirements for candidates, and pre- and post-operative hormonal treatments. The
surgical techniques are now more broadly represented in the United States.

than these, or in the middle of these, and in fact reject the either/or of Western gender systems. Once again, the stories of persons' lives are more complex than labels can accommodate.[90] Even when transsexuals want to change bodily identity, surgically and otherwise, they do so in a way that their deepest personal identity does not change; they understand themselves, after all, as seeking to become more wholly themselves. I am reminded of the deeply poignant scene in the film, *Normal*, when the husband (who is in the process of changing his body to a woman's body) says to his wife, "It's me. I'm still here"; and she still loves him, for "he is my heart, he is my heart, he is my heart," she tells an uncomprehending minister.[91]

No one ought here pass judgment on any configurations of gender. In fact, this is my point. Once we see other possibilities for gendering, gender is itself rendered at once more important and less. It is more important for those who must struggle to discover their gender identity and come to be at home in it. It is less important as a way to exclude some identities from the circle of our common humanity. The same can be said when we examine the supposed differences between women and men — differences other than chromosomal, hormonal, and anatomical — gender remains important,

---

90. Even the description "gender queer," which is claimed by many today as a way of communicating a rejection of all culturally imposed identities, does not work for everyone. Concrete stories of persons' lives are perhaps, once again, the best way to come to insights into human experiences. We have had the well known stories of Christine Jorgensen, Renee Richards, and more recently of Jennifer Finney Boylan, as well as descriptions of individual and family struggles to deal with sex change or gender identity change. See the poignant and graceful story of formerly James Boylan, a novelist, who became Jenny Boylan: Jennifer Finney Boylan, *She's Not There: A Life in Two Genders* (New York: Broadway Books, 2003). See also the stories of others (the less common female to male transsexuals) told by the novelist and psychotherapist, Amy Bloom, in *Normal: Transsexual CEO's, Crossdressing Cops, and Hermaphrodites With Attitude* (New York: Random House, 2002). And see the very useful set of stories as well as interpretation of the stories overall in Ekins and King, "Telling Body Transgendering Stories," 183–99. Here the story of the transsexual is seen as an instance of the archetypal story that begins with suffering, moves through epiphany and new understanding, includes a desire for action, and leads to transformation.

91. I am reminded also of Caroline Walker Bynum's study of tales of "metamorphosis," from Ovid to the medievals to a contemporary writer. Bynum is trying to understand what it means for our bodies to change, even drastically. She argues finally that while change is a staggering fact, there is no story if there is only change without continuity. Bynum, *Metamorphosis and Identity* (New York: Zone Books, 2001).

but it becomes less important — certainly for the social roles we aspire to play.

Whether Gender Matters

I return to the question with which I began our exploration of gender: whether and how much gender should matter. I hope my own answer is at least somewhat clear. Gender matters, indeed; yet gender also does not matter. Let me try to say, in summary, what I mean by these apparently paradoxical (but not contradictory) statements. I begin with the negative: gender does not matter, ought not to matter, in certain respects.

There are three ways in which I want to argue, finally, that gender ought not to matter, or at least ought not to matter so much. (1) Gender ought not to divide us, one from another. When we look across creation, and across unfortunate gender divides, we are after all more alike than different. Gender wars would cease if we saw that we are not "opposite" sexes but persons with somewhat different (but, in fact, very similar) bodies. This is a significant reason why we are members of the human community. Moreover, gender gives us no reason to judge other embodied humans as "abject bodies" (to use Judith Butler's term[92]); it provides no justification for dominance over one another, or for exclusion, shaming, or doing violence to other human bodies. Whatever the forces and powers of culture and society, they must be disarmed insofar as they make us lose sight of what we share.

(2) The solution to the gender divide, however, does not lie in an uncritical notion of "complementarity." No one of us is complete as a person, and maybe not even as a gendered person. Yet when all determinations of, for example, masculine and feminine "traits" prove nonuniversal; when these characterizations of what is normatively a woman or a man prove deeply culturally constructed; when women, for example, do not find themselves in the descriptions of the traits they are supposed to represent; then we must see these characterizations as what they are: social and cultural stereotypes that promote hierarchical relations, and that do not, in the end, succeed in making

---

92. Butler, *Bodies That Matter*, chapter 6.

us complements across a gender divide. To say that we are incomplete in ourselves does not mean that we are "halves" of persons who will be "whole" only when we find our gendered complement. We may indeed long for union with another, for a kind of wholeness that comes from both a profound love and a sharing of our lives. Gender by itself has never guaranteed we will find what we seek. Rather, as the poet Rainer Marie Rilke once wrote, we must move toward a time when "there will be girls and women whose name will no longer signify merely an opposite of the masculine, but something in itself, something that makes one think not of any complement and limit, but only of life and existence."[93]

(3) Gender may have importance, but it is not in the differentiation of roles. This is an argument that is easier to make in the twenty-first century than in the past. There are still many, however, who do not understand it and are not persuaded by it. Opposition to it comes generally from those who are still convinced of gender complementarity: what applies to persons in terms of gender applies, they believe, to roles. In response, it must be said that there are indeed differences among us, but they cannot be reduced to gender. What differences there are between women and men are not differences that justify gender-specific variations in a right to education, to work, to participation in political life, to just wages, to a share in the burdens and responsibilities of family, society, and church. What is at stake, then, is the structure of institutions — from the family to the state, from business corporations to universities and churches. The removal of restrictions to roles that are based solely on gender requires and has to some extent brought about a political as well as a moral revolution.

There are also three ways in which gender certainly does matter. (1) Attention must be paid to the struggles of individuals and societies to address precisely the problems of gender. This is why "gender analysis" is necessary for all of our social structures, situations, and patterns of relating. We cannot simply cover over the

---

93. Rainer Marie Rilke, *Letters to a Young Poet*, trans. M. D. H. Norton (New York: 1962), 59. I am not sure Rilke's view would fit completely a feminist view of today, but it is a poetic rendering of the need for every gender to be considered whole in itself; so that insofar as gender signals potential relation, it will be of two wholes, not two halves.

wounds that have been inflicted or the vulnerabilities that continue to exist, whether in man/woman gender conflicts or in the lack of interest, understanding, and acceptance of those who deal with alternative gender identities. This means that we must work toward societies that will understand the importance of biology and the importance of culture, but that will not yield every question about gender either to biological or cultural determinism.

(2) Gender matters in human relationships, especially in ones of intimate love. I do not refer here only to gender and genitals, but to the whole bodies of persons who come together in the gestures of love. When women-persons and men-persons, or persons of the same sex, or persons of unspecified sex, come together in respect, love, passion, or tenderness, it matters to each of them who the other is — in respect to gender and in every other respect. Gender identity in this context can be cause for celebration.[94] Gender also matters in nonsexual human relationships and human endeavors, if for no other reason than that women and men are still socialized very differently. They thus sometimes do bring different experiences to relation and action, experiences that enrich or correct one another's contribution.

(3) Finally, we do not know fully what it means that in this world and the next "there is no longer male and female." We do not know, in other words, what transcendence will finally mean for gender. Gender still matters in this world, so we can expect that it will matter in the next. If so, it will not be burdened by this world's stereotypes nor this world's judgments of what we ought to welcome or exclude, celebrate or mourn. In a new world we will not mistake limited possibility for unlimited; we will not make strangers out of our differences; we will not expect either too much or too little from our identities as women or men. For now, we have eyes that do not yet see as far as a world with gender transformed, and ears that do not yet hear of what is prepared for us. Yet also for now, some things are demanded of us in terms of our justice and our care for one another in what can be a better gendered world.

---

94. I do not here mean to preclude situations in which respect, love, passion, or tenderness are either missing, misjudged, or distorted. Clearly when this is the case, gender may be cause for destruction. I postpone considerations of this to the next chapters.

Sexuality and Its Meanings

If our historical and cross-cultural considerations of sexual ethics in previous chapters and our explorations of embodiment and gender in this chapter have served us well, we do not start from zero in our thinking about the meanings of sexuality. The term itself is relatively new (appearing in English dictionaries only since the early nineteenth century). Its meaning in the abstract remains difficult to identify, despite the dictionaries. I take it here to include everything that pertains to the sexual — in the sense of sexual desires and loves, feelings, emotions, activities, relationships. As such, sexuality can have physical, psychological, emotional, intellectual, spiritual, personal, and social dimensions. When we ask about its meanings, we can include individual, relational, species, and cosmic meanings, private and public meanings, biological and cultural meanings. Sex can refer to genital and non-genital sex, sex with or without desire, sex with or without pleasure. The aims and goals of sex and sexuality include, but do not necessarily reduce to, the aims and goals commonly thought to be intrinsic to sexual desire or sexual activity.

When we come to ask about the meanings of sexuality, it is hard not to recall Foucault's questions in its regard. That is, how did contemporary Western culture come to believe that sexuality is the key to individual identity? How did sex become more important than love, and almost more important than life? Given the sexualization of our societies, the desire for sex is matched by the desire to understand it, to find or to produce the truth about it. "What is peculiar to modern societies ... [is that] they dedicated themselves to speaking of it [sex] *ad infinitum*, while exploiting it as *the* secret."[95]

One would think that after Foucault's own search into the history of sexual desire, and the massive literature it generated in response, we would finally now understand sexuality; we would have uncovered its secrets. But historical studies still proliferate, and scientific research turns in the direction of sex more often than ever before.[96]

95. Foucault, *The History of Sexuality*, vol. 1: *An Introduction* (New York: Pantheon Books, 1978), 35 and passim. See my identification of these questions above in chapter 2.

96. Important historical works not previously cited include: Philippe Ariès and André Béjin, eds., *Western Sexuality: Practice and Precept in Past and Present Times*,

Philosophies and theologies of sex are as numerous as those of the body or of gender.[97] The fact that we still do not understand the "sexual" fits well with our contemporary recognition that so much of the meaning of body, gender, sex, and sexuality is socially and historically constructed. Hence, experiences of sexuality will vary not only from individual to individual but in significant ways from culture to culture and across time.[98] This is why I do not here attempt a definition of human sexuality. Yet descriptions of varied experiences have enough in common to be generally recognized (at least today) as "sexual." Perhaps the only way to understand this is to mull over the multiple elements that may be integral even if not distinctively essential to sexual experiences.

---

trans. Anthony Forster (Oxford: Blackwell, 1982); Jeffrey Weeks, *Sexuality and Its Discontents: Meanings, Myths and Modern Sexualities* (London: Routledge & Kegan Paul, 1985); Lesley Dean-Jones, "The Politics of Pleasure: Female Sexual Appetite in the Hippocratic Corpus," in *Discourses of Sexuality: From Aristotle to AIDS*, ed. Domna C. Stanton (Ann Arbor: University of Michigan Press, 1995); David Allyn, *Make Love, Not War: The Sexual Revolution: An Unfettered History* (Boston: Little, Brown, 2000); Lawrence Stone, "Sex in the West: The Strange History of Human Sexuality," *The New Republic* 193 (July 8, 1985): 25–37; Timothy Taylor, *The Prehistory of Sex* (New York: Bantam Books, 1996); Giuseppe Benagiano, Gian Carlo Di Renzo, Ermelando V. Cosmi, eds., *The Evolution of the Meaning of Sexual Intercourse in the Human* (Rome: International Institute for the Study of Man, 1996); Roy Porter and Lesley Hall, *The Facts of Life: The Creation of Sexual Knowledge in Britain, 1650–1950* (New Haven, CT: Yale University Press, 1995). Interesting scientific studies not previously cited: Sharon K. Turnbull, "Sex Therapy and Sex Research: Scientific and Clinical Perspectives," in *Encyclopedia of Bioethics*, rev. ed., 5: 2348–51; Tim Birkhead, *Promiscuity: An Evolutionary History of Sperm Competition* (Cambridge, MA: Harvard University Press, 2000); Geoffrey Miller, *The Mating Mind: How Sexual Choice Shaped the Evolution of Human Nature* (New York: Doubleday, 1999); Marlene Zuk, *Sexual Selections: What We Can and Can't Learn About Sex from Animals* (Berkeley: University of California Press, 2001); Helen Fisher, *Why We Love: The Nature and Chemistry of Romantic Love* (New York: Henry Holt, 2003); Niles Eldredge, *Why We Do It: Rethinking Sex and the Selfish Gene* (New York: W. W. Norton, 2003).

97. As evidence of this, see the many useful anthologies, such as: Alan Soble, ed., *The Philosophy of Sex: Contemporary Readings*, 4th ed. (New York: Rowman & Littlefield, 2002); Soble, ed., *Sex, Love, and Friendship: Studies of the Society for the Philosophy of Sex and Love 1977–1992* (Amsterdam: Editions Rodopi, 1997); James B. Nelson and Sandra P. Longfellow, eds., *Sexuality and the Sacred: Sources for Theological Reflection* (Louisville: Westminster John Knox, 1994); Earl E. Shelp, ed., *Sexuality and Medicine*, 2 vols. (Dordrecht: D. Reidel, 1987).

98. This accounts for the valuing of personal stories such as the ones recorded of nineteen African American women in Tricia Rose, *Longing to Tell: Black Women Talk about Sexuality and Intimacy* (New York: Farrar, Straus & Giroux, 2003).

Elements in Sexual Experience

If sexuality involves anything at all, it involves *embodiment;* even
phone sex involves the body if it really is experienced as sexual. Yet
sexuality is embodied in multiple ways. Sometimes only genitals and
erogenous zones — which vary according to culture[99] — are involved,
sometimes the whole body. Sometimes the body as a whole is involved but either with or without special attention to genitals or other
erogenous parts of the body. Sometimes the role of the body is very
different — as in sex experienced between sexual partners and, for
example, maternal feelings of some mothers as they nurse their infants. Sometimes inexplicit sexuality permeates relationships — both
private and public — simply because powerful embodied, gendered
personalities awaken wholeness of engagement and response.

Emotions also seem intrinsic to sexuality, whether emotions of
love, desire for pleasure, or desire for union with another person. Yet
loves and desires can be extremely diverse in sexual experiences —
selfish or unselfish, angry or jealous, romantic or without romance,
passionate or steady, mature or immature, promised or uncommitted. Primary emotions may reflect experiences of empowerment and
freedom on the one hand, or vulnerability on the other. They may
be more closely tied to the perceived consequences of sexual activity
than to the activity itself (consequences ranging from a desired ex-
pansion of one's own personality, future bonding with one's lover, the
possibility of creating new life, or feared consequences such as unwanted pregnancy or disease). Diverse feelings and emotions related
to sex can include pleasure and pain, joy and sadness, peacefulness
and anger, a sense of well-being and a sense of shame. Experiences of
a totally indifferent partner, or of prostitutes, or of victims of sexual
assault may be largely emotionless, or marked by emotions radically different from those commonly associated with the meaning
of sex.[100]

---

99. In some societies breasts, for example, are erotic, but in other cultures they are
not; hence in the latter there is no wish or need to hide them; they are simply taken
for granted in communal living situations.

100. At least one of these examples, sexual assault, leads to the conclusion that the
experience is *not* a sexual experience; it is an experience of violent attack, and the
emotions of the one attacked will not be "sexual" but those emotions that characterize
being violated. This conclusion is significant, since it disallows all sorts of judgements

Despite all of this diversity, sex is somehow embodied, and it has a range of recognizable constitutive emotions. Moreover, in most sexual experiences (though not all) *pleasure* is a key component. This is one reason sexual activity can be desired for its own sake; pleasure is a good in itself (though not all traditions have thought this, and it remains for us to consider whether sexual pleasure is in every context and circumstance an overall, or moral, good). Following the focus of researchers such as Masters and Johnson, it has been commonly thought (and promoted by popular media) that "successful" sex and sexual pleasure are to be measured in terms of orgasms.[101] Indeed, overwhelmingly passionate sexual activity that produces orgasms certainly represents one of life's most acute and treasured forms of pleasure; yet it is not the whole of the pleasurable possibilities of sexuality, nor even necessarily their height. Sex and the sexual involve, or can involve, multiple forms and dimensions of pleasure — or in a broader sense, enjoyment. Physiological pleasure (and the zest for life that can come from this), psychological pleasure, spiritual pleasure, the pleasures of mutuality, bonding, transcendence: All of these kinds of pleasure can be part of sexual experience — either constitutive of the experience or an accompaniment to it.

Sex has also been considered a form of *language and social communication.*[102] Pleasure and communication are not mutually exclusive; the one need not be an obstacle to the other. For what sex communicates can be pleasure itself, as well as passionate love, desire, trust, compassion, poignant sweetness in relation, gratitude, joy, hope and promise for future relation. (It can also express and communicate conflict — as Sartre thought — or anger, embarrassment, possessiveness, submission.) The language of sex can articulate many things, including a desire for fruitfulness in a shared love.

---

such as "she was asking for it," or the perpetrator "was simply driven to have sex." On the other hand, even this experience involves in some sense the "sexual," which is why the trauma involved is so radical.

101. See William H. Masters and Virginia E. Johnson, *Human Sexual Response* (Boston: Little, Brown, 1966).

102. See the interesting conversation between Robert Solomon and Janice Moulton on this aspect of sexuality. Robert Solomon, "Sexual Paradigms," in *The Philosophy of Sex*, ed. Alan Soble, 3rd ed. (Boston: Rowman & Littlefield, 1997), 21–30; Janice Moulton, "Sexual Behavior: Another Position," ibid., 31–38.

The meanings of sex and sexuality in the past emphasized its *procreative aim* along with the aim of *union* between two persons. Today when we focus on the significance of sex in itself, almost for its own sake — depending on whether some of its aims are considered intrinsic to it — the procreative dimension of its action and its goals is often relegated to something almost extrinsic to sexual love and activity. It is true that sexuality has multiple possibilities beyond its reproductive capabilities and design, and even when it is procreative, the focus of attention in the immediate experience of sexual activity is, as Lisa Sowle Cahill has said, "much more likely to be one's own sexual experience and that of one's partner, and the physical and affective relation of the couple, rather than the likelihood of conception."[103] Nonetheless, as Cahill goes on to argue, if we are to take account of all of the meanings of sex, we must include its capability for procreation. This is obvious when we consider the meaning of sex for the human species as well as for individuals who want to parent children. Although, like the other aspects of sexuality, procreation need not and cannot, given considerations of actual fertility, be part of every sexual experience, it is an utterly significant part of some. And in these experiences it is possible that meanings of sexuality come together — in passion, tenderness, and a love so full that sexuality mediates new being.

As I have already suggested, the *motivations and aims* of sex are as multiple as are its forms of embodiment and pleasure. For different individuals and on different occasions these can include a desire to enhance self-esteem, drive out depression and despair, express love and faithfulness, sustain a relationship or a marriage that is without mutual love, repay favors, escape into recreation and play, reveal one's intimate self and attain access to the intimate self of another, earn a living, and on and on. We shall have to assess these aims, but for now the goal is descriptive not normative.

Power is often associated with sexuality — with its aims, forms, and motivations. Sex offers the possibility for individuals to exercise power over one another, and for society to garner its forces for

---

103. Lisa Sowle Cahill, "On the Connection of Sex to Reproduction," in *Sexuality and Medicine*, ed. Earl E. Shelp, 2: 39–50.

or against individuals and groups. The kind of power *over* sexuality that Foucault and others have found most significant, however, is the power to "normalize" sex according to social and cultural interests and expectations, the power to make sex conform to certain values. This, as we have seen, is the power of largely hidden social and cultural forces to produce sexuality and sex (to awaken it and shape the directions it takes). "In a sense power works on sex more deeply than we can know, not only as an external constraint or repression but as the formative principle of its intelligibility."[104] This is a power (or powers) to determine the meaning of sexuality in our lives, to make it central or marginal to our identities. Socially constructed meanings are not unimportant just because they are constructed and not embedded in our beings from the beginning.

Simply to name diverse sexual meanings and their probable sources and grounds can leave us without much to go on when it comes to a sexual ethic. Hence, as a preliminary step toward more normative considerations, we need to probe more deeply one of the central elements in sexuality and sexual experience. We need to look more carefully at the meanings for sexual desire and love.

Love, Desire, and Sexuality

Just about everyone today thinks that sex has something to do with love — somewhere, somehow, for some persons; or at least that this is possible. Sex and sexual desire, of course, cannot be reduced to or equated with sexual love. Moreover, it is always a risk to focus on love in relation to sexuality since it tends to escalate the rhetoric about love in ways that imply that sex, no matter what, is always about love — and about certain forms of love.

Despite these caveats, it is important to focus at some point on the meanings of sexuality in relation to love. At least in a Christian context, this is reasonable, since commandments and calls to love are arguably at the heart of any Christian ethic. From this perspective, it is important to offer a reminder of the significance of love. I do this, initially, not by examining psychological, theologi-

---

104. Teresa de Lauretis, "Freud, Sexuality, and Perversion," in *Discourses of Sexuality*, ed. D. Stanton, 349.

cal, philosophical, biblical analyses of love. I begin only with some reminders of experiences of human interpersonal love — sexual and nonsexual. We need here to remember an array of such experiences: tender love as when a longtime friend touches one's arm to express sympathetic understanding; sweetly memorable love as when parents taking a drive with their children begin to sing the love songs of their youth; endearing love as when a child offers a wild flower to her grandmother; love as shared excitement and relief when colleagues working intensely together on a treasured project collapse united in satisfaction and fatigue. We need also to remember experiences (vicarious or our own) of fierce love, when separation between lovers is like an arm being torn off; or "first love," when the whole world becomes patterned with the color of love. We must remember troubled loves, when feelings are disparate, or love becomes war, or insecurity threatens to destroy the future of love. Insofar as we can, we must remember, too, the love that dawns between persons from vastly different cultures as they grow in mutual knowledge and respect. We remember courageous love, when parents struggle against those who would be unjust to their child, or when co-believers challenge what they consider distorted practices of faith. We remember love's experience of peace and of turmoil, of gentleness and of passion, of wisdom and confusion, bitterness and respect, companionship and death, endurance and transcendent hope.

These experiences and many others like them characterize the fabric of our lives. All life is not love, but life's significance surely depends on what we love. Like love in general, love conjoined with sexuality can take many forms. Consider the experiences described in these two poems by American authors in the twentieth century. The first is an excerpt, entitled "Aria," from Delmore Schwartz's *Kilroy's Carnival.* I originally saw this text on a page opposite a photograph of a magnificent glass sculpture of two figures: a woman and a man, as beautiful as Greek gods, glorious and shining in naked strength and splendor, standing in mutual embrace. The lines of the poem are not gender assigned, and it does not really matter which figure speaks which lines (or for that matter, whether the figures are male and female):

" — Kiss me there where pride is glittering
Kiss me where I am ripened and round fruit
Kiss me wherever, however I am supple, bare and flare
(Let the bell be rung as long as I am young:
      let ring and fly like a great bronze wing!)
Until I am shaken from blossom to root."

" — I'll kiss you wherever you think you are poor,
Wherever you shudder, feeling striped or barred,
Because you think you are bloodless, skinny or marred:
   Until, until
    your gaze has been stilled —
Until you are shamed again no more!
I'll kiss you until your body and soul
     the mind in the body being fulfilled —
Suspend their dread and civil war!"[105]

Taken on its own (without attempting to interpret it in the context of the author's life and writings but only in the context of the meaning offered by the sculpture that reflects it), the poem speaks of embodied and inspirited love, expressing profound vulnerability and acceptance, affirmation of the sort that allows a loved one to be whole. Together with the sculpture it inspired, it is a poem about one aspect of sexual love.

    The second poem, by Sybil P. Estess, is entitled "The Woman who Married Her Brother-in-law." It tells a story which, like "Aria," is about sexual love of a sort — though the storyteller denies that it is about romantic or erotic sexual love.

I was living happily in Boston when he called:
"Will you fly on a crow's back back to Houston?"

"I don't love you — romantically," I replied.
I am not pretty and do not speak well.

---

105. "Aria [from Kilroy's Carnival]" by Delmore Schwartz, from *Last and Lost Poems*, copyright © 1962 The New Republic. Reprinted by permission of New Directions Publishing Corp.

"No matter," he argued. "That will come."
I returned, and we had a lovely courtship, then

wedding. When people ask me, "Do you love
him?" I am honest: I say, "No, but he is

the best of good husbands so I can't complain."
Forty years together and I never loved

my first husband, either. My background, I suppose;
it's my background: undemonstrative.

I don't remember my mother kissing or
hugging my brother, my sister, or me.

She was sort of . . . Victorian. But my sister
and I were close anyway. Since I married

her husband, I moved into her old house, wear her
old clothes he never removed.

Last week was her birthday. I saw myself
buried with her, felt her in my bones. But I,

who don't know about feelings, am content.
It hardly matters at all.[106]

As I interpret it, the woman who speaks in this poem is not denying love for her second husband, only romantic love. Still, her affirmation of him, and perhaps her sex with him, represent a kind of affection, approval, and gratitude that go beyond her words. We may wish more for her, but she herself does not complain, and she is not unhappy; she is, she says, content.

It would be good to add other stories or poems of sexual love here — steamier perhaps, newer and younger perhaps, less happy perhaps. But my only point is to show that there are varieties of sexual loves. No doubt some are romantic, and some are not. No doubt all romantic loves are in some way sexual, though they need not all express themselves, or even desire to express themselves, in sexual

---

106. Sybil P. Estess, "The Woman Who Married Her Brother-in-law," *The New Republic* (February 29, 1988).

(especially genitally sexual) ways. But all sexual love need not be romantic in the ordinary sense of the term, as the poem above shows, or as persons' lives show when they stabilize in a love deeper than romance. With these complexities in mind, we can look more closely at love, romantic love, sexual love, and the forms of desire that may flow from each.

Love, as I understand it, is simultaneously an affective response, an affective way of being in union, and an affective affirmation of what is loved.[107] This applies to love of many different kinds of objects — whether personal or nonpersonal. It applies to love of nature, of food and drink, of soft materials and great drama and lilting melodies. It applies to our loves of neighbors near and far, and to our love of God. It may not be the only way to define love, or even to describe it — as we know from those who argue that "real" love is a duty, or is reducible to the deeds of love, or is a power that is not ours but that simply flows through us from God to objects whether they are lovable or not. Although I do think that love as affective response to, union with, and affirmation of what is loved is central to the meaning of every love, I need not insist on this here. I will, however, presume that this description of love fits well the kind of love that I am focusing on in this context — that is, love that is somehow sexual love. It certainly fits love that is romantic love.

First, then, sexual love and romantic love do indeed involve an affective ("emotional," if you will)[108] response because love is awakened by a beloved. The beloved, whether knowingly or not, reaches inside of us, figuratively speaking, and touches our capacity to love. The positive affective powers or capabilities that we have within us are, in other words, specified and activated when we behold a lovable object, or when we at least perceive lovable qualities, characteristics, in the one we love. It makes little sense to think of romantic love,

---

107. See Farley, *Personal Commitments*, especially chapter 3. See also Jules J. Toner, *The Experience of Love* (Washington, DC: Corpus Books, 1968).

108. Emotions can be equated with affective responses. They occur on more than one level — that is, on a sensory level, where they are more likely to be experienced as "feelings" (affective responses that come and go, with physiological connections); but also at the level of rational response, where they have a clear cognitive content, and where they can endure despite the coming and going of feelings that accompany them.

and one can hope also sexual love, as love for what we perceive to be in every way "unlovable."[109]

There is some mystery, of course, in our experience of the possibility of romantic love for some persons and not others — even though we might perceive many, indeed all, other persons as in some way lovable. To love some persons, even intensely, does not mean that we love, or are able to love, them with a romantic love, or a sexual love. But when we do love in any of these ways, it is because the other somehow awakens in us a response. Love, therefore, is in the first instance receptive — of the lovableness of the other.

Second, love is itself a form of being united with who or what is loved. This is often obscured by a more strongly felt *desire* for union — to be with the beloved, to know the beloved better, to be closer, to share with the beloved more deeply. Yet we do not desire union with someone we do not already love. To love is already to be within the beloved in some way, and to have the beloved in one's heart. I may be working closely with someone, or sitting crunched up against someone in a crowded bus, but all the while my mind and heart are in union with the one I love who is far away. Loneliness can be a form of desire for union with those whom we love, but we are not lonely for those we do not love. This kind of loneliness arises from the love that is already a union, and it reveals to us the union that is love itself.[110]

---

109. There are theories of love, especially Christian love, that are built on the belief that love is not genuinely love unless it is so other-centered that it has no element whatsoever of response to what is lovable. In these theories the point is that response to what is lovable implies that the lover is rewarded by the beauty of the beloved, or that love is conditional on the "worth" of the beloved. While these insights are important, nonetheless there is a sense in which love of the "unlovable," the "not able to be loved," is a contradiction. If the concern is that human love go forth to all persons without regard for their obvious attractiveness (whether physical or moral), then it is an important concern. If it means that we do not care, or try to see, that all persons are indeed worthy of love (because God loves them, or because persons as persons are intrinsically lovable in some profound sense), then a contradiction remains. I stand by my description of love as a response to the lovableness of the other, a lovableness that I behold or at least a lovableness in which I believe. See Farley, *Personal Commitments*, 29–32.

110. I realize, of course, that there is also a form of loneliness that characterizes not yearning for some particular person whom we already love but, rather, the emptiness and yearning simply for someone *to* love.

Finally, love is an internal action that is at once response to and union with, but also affective affirmation of the beloved. It is this aspect of love that differentiates it from some other affective responses, such as hate. For hate is indeed also an affective response — not, of course, to lovableness and to beauty but to what we perceive in another as inimical to us (or to others whom we love). And hate may also give rise to a desire for greater union — all the better to harm or destroy the one we hate. But by love we affectively affirm, not negate, the other. Just as we affirm someone in knowledge ("you are," "you are this or that"), so we affirm someone in love. *Affective* affirmation, however, goes beyond the affirmation of knowing, for affectivity, at least when it is in the form of love, engages more of ourselves than does knowledge alone. By love we pick up our own being, so to speak, and put it down in affirmation of the beloved, though there are obviously degrees of loving. The sign and test of this is that we do the deeds of love insofar as they are possible and called for. In and by love I do not say simply "you are," but "I want you to be, and to be firm and full in being."

The kind of love we are most concerned with here is primarily the kind we find in romantic love or in the friendship that can come as romantic love matures. Despite my earlier qualifications, and for the sake of simplicity, I am going to use the term "sexual love" to encompass these insofar as they have a sexual dimension — whether only felt or acted upon. These are loves that involve our whole affective self in some way, that engage us deeply, often intensely, sometimes passionately. As I have said before, there are loves like this that do not have as a primary ingredient sexual attraction or an orientation to physical sexual union. But they do involve embodiment in some way — our own bodily dimensions of affectivity and our delight in or desire for bodily connection with the one we love. Whether or not such a love attempts to touch the other; whether or not it speaks its desires; whether or not these desires are paramount in the experience of love; sexual love (especially when it is romantic, but even when it is not) involves some yearning to touch and be touched by the beloved. Touch can mean, though it need not, genital touching or lips meeting in a kiss; it may mean only touching, or wishing to touch, the hand of the other. Still, there is a relational bodily (in imagination if not in physical fact) dimension to sexual love.

Sexual love, like all love, gives rise to and is the ground of desire — for fuller union with, and greater affirmation of, the beloved. Neither sexuality as a whole nor sexual desire is to be explained solely in terms of an indomitable biological and psychological drive for which love and the object of love have no meaning. Despite the long history of Western ideas that focus on such a drive, and the remaining views that interpret sexuality still in this way (whether because it can be so disruptive in human lives or because sex industries seem to thrive on this view), sexual desire is or can be more than this. Even Freud, who has been so often blamed for modern mechanistic interpretations of sexuality, now has supporters who believe that in his later writings, he moved well beyond these views.[111] Sexuality in these later writings has greater plasticity in object and aim. It is shaped by experience — and, one must add, by culture, and by what happens in human relationships. Whatever the biological aims of sexuality, they can be redirected or transformed into genuine love for another person, as well as sublimated into the larger concerns of civilization.

Sexual desire rising from love may also be distinguished from "lust" in our ordinary use of this term. As we frequently understand it, lust is a craving for sexual pleasure without any real affective response to, union with, or affirmation of the other. If there is any love here, it is of oneself, for the sake of which something or someone else is "lusted after." The objects of lust in this sense are fungible, both interchangeable and substitutable; they are whatever entices one in sexually passionate ways. A lust for power is analogous to lust for sexual pleasure in that it can be satisfied by many forms of achievement of power, many "objects" that constitute situations of power.[112]

---

111. See, for example, Ernest Wallwork, *Psychoanalysis and Ethics* (New Haven, CT: Yale University Press, 1991); and Jonathan Lear, *Open Minded: Working Out the Logic of the Soul* (Cambridge, MA: Harvard University Press, 1998).

112. It goes without saying that the term "lust" may be used in less constrictive ways, as in "lust for life." If it means simply a strongly felt desire, even sexual desire, then it may be equatable with "sexual desire" as I am using it — presupposing sexual love. But if it is used to mean, for example, simply feeling sexually needy in a generalized sense; or if it means desire for sexual connection with an objectified (in no way cared for or loved) other, then it is not what I mean by sexual desire. Either way, I am not yet suggesting an ethically normative understanding of sexual desire or of lust.

Sexual and romantic desires and loves as I am describing them are more like Plato's *eros* than Freud's, even though the new interpretations of Freud bring them closer together. The love, erotic love, that is the substance of Diotima's speech in Plato's *Symposium* is personified as a combination of poverty and plenty. She — or he, in Plato's dialogue — experiences a lack of something until she encounters beauty. Then the lover's desire is a mixture of both pain and joy; for she is not yet full of beauty yet she is filled in part by beholding beauty. She can begin on a journey to happiness and wholeness by learning to love one beautiful material being, which can lead her to a love of all material beauty; and on to a love of one immaterial form of beauty, and to a love of all immaterial beauty. At each stage, love gives "birth" in beauty, so that beauty endures immortally even though love moves on. In Diotima's view, if the lover can climb this ladder of love all the way to the top — leaving behind sexuality and the material, leaving behind even the limited immaterial individual — he or she will finally come to the absolutely Beautiful.[113]

Sexual romantic love and desire as I have described them have a lot in common with the *eros* described by Diotima. Love gives rise to desire, and perhaps desire can also be transformed into love. Both love and desire are a combination of lack and fullness, poverty and plenty. Both are shaped by knowledge of what is loved. Both at least begin in embodied, sensual forms. Both can be transcendent of themselves, rising up the stairs (or, to change the metaphor, descending ever more into the depths) of love to what is always beyond.

Yet sexual romantic love and desire as I have been presenting them can also be quite different from Diotima's vision. They need not be for beloved beauties and unions that are mere stepping stones, or stairs, to something else — which, despite "birthing" in beauty, makes of the beloved a means to an end. Sexual love and desire, moreover, need not be primarily for the sake of the fulfillment of the lover, for they can take other-centered forms. They can also become part of a mutual love and desire, fruitful beyond what one person's love and desires could be by themselves. Finally, unlike Diotima's rendering of a ladder of love where the body is left behind, sexual

---

113. Plato, *Symposium* 203c–215a.

romantic love and desire, even when they are ultimately incorporated in a great love that affirms more than sexual union, need not discard sex or sexuality along the way.

In response to the questions pursued by Foucault, we may begin to see why sexuality is a key to identity, but not the only key; why sexuality, by itself, is not more important than love. Socially constructed, but not without the possibility of critique even in our cultural context, the meanings of sexuality are multiple — some creative, some destructive; some filled with love, some with the opposite of love. Although I have not yet offered an ethically normative view of any of these ways of loving and desiring, we may begin to suspect that only a sexuality formed and shaped with love has the possibility for integration into the whole of the human personality. At its most in- ✓ tense and most exhilarating heights, the experience of sex combines embodied love and desire, conversation and communication, openness to the other in the intimacy of embodied selves, transcendence into fuller selves, and even encounter with God. These human possibilities need not be limited by culturally constructed boundaries of gender; they can tell us something important about transcendent bodies; and they give clues to the kinds of loves that are stronger than death.

Chapter 5

JUST LOVE AND JUST SEX
Preliminary Considerations

═══ ❖ ═══

I SAID AT THE BEGINNING that this book is about the meaning of human sexuality and the ways in which it can be incorporated into a moral view of human and Christian life. We began by looking to the past of our own traditions and then to traditions and cultures that are different from our own. The insights from our own history and from other traditions are significant and necessary for framing a sexual ethic for today; but they are not by themselves sufficient. We turned, then, to contemporary understandings of human embodiment, gender, and sexuality, identifying more questions and also more insights without which we will not be able to frame a sexual ethics.

We come finally to major normative ethical questions. I have, of course, already pointed to some normative conclusions in previous chapters — offering guidelines for cross-cultural approaches as well as some preliminary proposals regarding the human body, gender, and sexuality. This chapter will move yet closer to the development of a framework for Christian sexual ethics, while leaving the actual framework to the following chapter. There are four important preliminary considerations still to be undertaken — some useful to our ultimate task and some not only useful but necessary. First, it is necessary to introduce a connection between *sexuality and justice*, and, in so doing, provide a perspective for what follows. Second, it is helpful to look briefly at *alternative ethical frameworks* — in particular, Jewish and Christian frameworks that are different in some respects from my own. Third, the classical *sources* for Christian ethics, including sexual ethics, require some delineation. Fourth, and essential to the framework I propose, is a consideration of the relationship between *justice and love.*

Sexuality and Justice

When I first began this project, I was struck by something that Paul Ricoeur wrote in his early work, *The Symbolism of Evil.* He was identifying three moments, or stages, in the ways in which Western civilization has symbolized the experience of moral evil.[1] He named the stages and their symbols: (1) defilement, (2) sin, and (3) guilt. Ricoeur's exploration of the moments, or stages, is focused largely on religious considerations, but it can be argued that these have their secular analogues as well. In Ricoeur's terms, "defilement" as a symbol refers to an experience of evil as pre-ethical, irrational, quasi-material, something that leaves a symbolic stain. One feels "dirty." Defilement resists reflection because it is the result of breaking a taboo. Taboos as such do not need (or even allow) reflective rationales; the point is simply that they are not to be broken — on pain of punishment. Symbolically infected when one violates a taboo, there is no recourse except in rituals of purification.[2]

---

1. Ricoeur, *The Symbolism of Evil*, trans. Emerson Buchanan (New York: Harper & Row, 1967), chap. 1 and passim. I see no reason to apply these stages necessarily and only to the development of cultures; for, insofar as they are applicable to cultures, they are also applicable to the moral development of individuals — all of us. It is in this latter sense that I appeal to them here. My rendering of the stages is without the full richness of Ricoeur's analysis, but I trust its relevance to the framework I develop will be clear. Also, because of my concern for this relevance, my rendering of the stages to some extent goes beyond what Ricoeur himself has written.

2. Ibid., chap. 1. There is not always an exact corollary between Ricoeur's notion of defilement and the work that has been done by scholars in a number of disciplines on shame, especially as distinguished from guilt. Nonetheless, these studies are relevant to the point that Ricoeur wants to make, and they offer resources for probing the phenomenon of defilement and the taboo morality that generates it. See, for example, Ruth Benedict, *Patterns of Culture* (Boston: Houghton Mifflin, 1934); Mary Douglas, *Purity and Danger: An Analysis of Concepts of Pollution and Taboo* (London: Routledge & Kegan Paul, 1966); Gerhart Piers and Milton B. Sincer, *Shame and Guilt: A Psychoanalytic and a Cultural Study* (New York: W. W. Norton, 1971); Nel Noddings, *Women and Evil* (Berkeley: University of California Press, 1982); Agnes Heller, *The Power of Shame: A Rational Perspective* (London: Routledge & Kegan Paul, 1985); Jean Delumeau, *Sin and Fear: The Emergence of a Western Guilt Culture, 13th–18th Centuries* (New York: St. Martin's Press, 1990); Andrew P. Morrison, *The Culture of Shame*

"Sin," on the other hand, is for Ricoeur the experience of evil not in the transgression of an abstract rule but in the rupture of a relationship, the violation of a personal bond. In religious terms, sin is the breaking of the covenant with God. It involves the violation of laws, but the laws have their meaning as part of the covenant. Because the covenant includes relationships with neighbors, sin is a rupture in relations between human persons as well as God. The remedy for sin is repentance on the part of the sinner and forgiveness from the one who has been sinned against; only so is a relationship healed.[3]

"Guilt," in Ricoeur's use of the term, is the subjective side of sin. It is my recognition, my consciousness, that a rupture in relationship is the result of my freedom. Set in the context of all three moments of fault, guilt involves what Ricoeur calls a "double movement";[4] beginning from the two other stages, it includes them yet goes beyond to a new understanding of one's own responsibility. At this stage there is a "veritable revolution in the experience of evil: that which is primary is no longer the reality of defilement . . . but the evil use of liberty."[5] Guilt is the subjective awareness that evil is in my heart. The cause of evil is not extrinsic to me; I am not caught in a cosmic web of taboos where my infraction may or may not be authored by me. Guilt is therefore different from either defilement or sin, though it nonetheless inherits their symbolism. In the experience and symbolism of guilt we recognize (accurately or inaccurately) sinfulness, and with this recognition may come also an experience of defilement, the result now of my misused freedom, not my ritual impurity. The conversion of heart required to remedy sin is now possible, and it requires a choice. Yet only the forgiveness and acceptance of God (and/or the neighbor who has been harmed) will "justify" me or heal me.[6]

(New York: Ballantine Books, 1996); Marilyn McCord Adams, "Hurricane Spirit, Toppling Taboos," in *Our Selves, Our Souls and Bodies: Sexuality and the Household of God*, ed. Charles Hefling (Boston: Cowley Publications, 1996), 129–41.

3. Ricoeur, *Symbolism of Evil*, chap. 2.

4. Ibid., 100–101.

5. Ibid., chap. 3, 102.

6. Ricoeur's view of sin and guilt, as I understand it, corresponds more closely to a Protestant, perhaps a classic Lutheran, view than a Roman Catholic. Still, the bare bones representation that I have given of it should find a resonance in Catholic readers as well as other Christians.

Now, we may ask, what does all of this have to do with sexuality? Although Ricoeur's comments on this question are minimal, they are telling: Our understandings of sexuality in particular remain immersed in the economy of defilement. One is struck, he says, "by the importance and the gravity attached to the violation of interdictions [based on taboos] of a sexual character in the economy of defilement."[7] Sexual prohibitions against incest, sodomy, relations at forbidden times, in forbidden places, and with forbidden actions are so fundamental that "the inflation of the sexual is characteristic of the whole system of defilement, so that an indissoluble complicity between sexuality and defilement seems to have been formed from time immemorial."[8]

However, belief in the defilement of sexuality is, in fact, pre-ethical and has nothing to do with the developed sense of evil that is symbolized in Ricoeur's terms by sin and guilt. But the sense of sexual defilement, unfortunately, is not easily left behind. An inarticulable but persistent tie between sexuality and evil remains in the implicit consciousness of persons, and in the symbolic structure of the West. So great is the resistance of conceptions of sexual defilement to correction that, as Ricoeur suggests, it is not from meditation on sexuality alone that we will come to an adequate sexual ethics. Despite our contemporary openness in displaying and deploying sex, we carry too much baggage regarding sex into our moral discernment and judgments. We must therefore turn away for a time from the sexual sphere to other spheres of human existence — such as labor, politics, and economics — and learn in these other spheres what justice means. It is here that "an ethics of relations to others will be formed, an ethics of justice and love, capable of turning back toward sexuality, of re-evaluating and transvaluating it."[9]

Advanced notions of justice in bonds between persons have not yet been fully translated into the sexual dimensions of personal relations. Thus, a necessary step in the formulation of a contemporary sexual ethic must be to move sexuality more completely from the realm of the pre-ethical (the realm of taboos) to the ethical. The blind sense

---

7. Ricoeur, *Symbolism of Evil*, 28.
8. Ibid.
9. Ibid, 29.

of defilement that still haunts sex and sexuality must be subjected to relentless criticism and responsible repudiation. One of the ways in which this can be done is to refine a justice ethic for sexuality. Ricoeur did not do this, and insofar as it requires long examinations of other spheres of human life or analyses of the multiple theories of justice currently on our tables in the West, I shall not be doing it here, either. Nonetheless, what I will do is to try to develop a justice ethic for sexual activities and relationships based simply on a general understanding of justice. To formulate a justice ethic in this regard is precisely not to ignore the fact that sex does, in fact, have a potential for evil and harm in our lives.

Before we move to a consideration of "just sex," however, it is useful to consider foci and frameworks for sexual ethics that are alternative to the one I will propose.

Alternative Frameworks

The alternative contemporary sexual ethical frameworks I have in mind are not those that are completely at odds with the one I propose. They are ones whose identification of specific foci and elements for sexual ethics I consider significant and useful. I might indeed attempt to incorporate them into the approach that I will take, or indicate how they may already be there, but from a different angle or with different language. I respect them sufficiently, however, to want them to stand on their own. Probably no one approach is adequate to the task of contemporary sexual ethics, but a continuing dialogue and a shared search for what is more adequate will be helpful to us all.

I think here, for example, of the emphasis placed on the erotic in many twentieth- and twenty-first-century feminist (largely Christian) approaches to sexuality and morality. From Audre Lorde to Carter Heyward to Marvin Ellison, the path has been opened for an ethic that not only affirms the value of *eros* but calls for its liberation.[10]

---

10. See Audre Lorde, "Uses of the Erotic: The Erotic as Power," in *Sister Outsider* (Trumansburg, NY: Crossing, 1984), 53–59; Carter Heyward, *Our Passion for Justice: Images of Power, Sexuality, and Liberation* (New York: Pilgrim, 1984); Marvin Ellison, *Erotic Justice: A Liberating Ethic of Sexuality* (Louisville: Westminster John Knox, 1996). In identifying these writings (and those that I subsequently cite) in terms of focal

I also think, on the other hand, of the thoughtful work of Barbara Blodgett, who in critical response to these approaches identifies a need for realism and for boundaries, and who proposes instead a sexual ethic based primarily on trust.[11] Beverly Wildung Harrison emphasizes "right relationship" and the need for new approaches to sexual boundaries that take important account of eros, justice, and power.[12] Among feminists, I also think of the writings of Lisa Sowle Cahill, with her profound and inspiring stress on community as a focus for sexual ethics; of Christine Gudorf's emphasis on the elements of pleasure, mutuality, embodiment, and spirituality; of Karen Lebacqz's attention to vulnerability at the heart of sexual ethics; and of Barbara Andolsen's opposition to violent or coercive sex and promotion of sexual enjoyment and intimacy.[13] To cite these approaches does not exhaust the contributions of Christian feminists to sexual ethics; it does, however, acknowledge the many possibilities for developing frameworks on the basis of feminist concerns.[14]

---

points or "frameworks," I am certainly not describing the fullness of the theories to be found in each of them. It would be fair for the authors to object that I have missed the most significant elements in their approaches, even though I have raised up something central to them.

11. Barbara J. Blodgett, *Constructing the Erotic: Sexual Ethics and Adolescent Girls* (Cleveland: Pilgrim, 2002). Feminist critical responses (even by "pro-eros" authors themselves) may cite the dangers of "eroticization" without boundaries, as when domination is eroticized, almost always to the detriment of women.

12. Beverly Wildung Harrison, *Justice in the Making: Feminist Social Ethics*, ed. Elizabeth M. Bounds et al. (Louisville: Westminster John Knox, 2005), especially Part I; *Making the Connections: Essays in Feminist Social Ethics*, ed. Carol S. Robb (Boston: Beacon, 1985).

13. See Lisa Sowle Cahill, *Sex, Gender, and Christian Ethics* (Cambridge: Cambridge University Press, 1996); Christine E. Gudorf, *Body, Sex, and Pleasure: Reconstructing Christian Sexual Ethics* (Cleveland: Pilgrim, 1994); Karen Lebacqz, "Appropriate Vulnerability: A Sexual Ethic for Singles," *Christian Century* (May 6, 1987): 435–38; Barbara H. Andolsen, "Whose Sexuality? Whose Tradition? Women, Experience, and Roman Catholic Sexual Ethics," in *Religion and Sexual Health*, ed. Ronald M. Green (Dordrecht: Kluwer Academic, 1992), 55–77.

14. I want to acknowledge here, too, the work of feminists such as bell hooks, Judith Plaskow, and Sarah Hoagland. It would be useful to pursue in more detail these and others' perspectives on sexual ethics — whether Christian, Jewish, or secular — even when what they propose is not a full framework. See bell hooks, *Feminist Theory: From Margin to Center* (Boston: South End, 1984); Judith Plaskow, *Standing Again at Sinai: Judaism from a Feminist Perspective* (San Francisco: Harper & Row, 1990); Sarah Lucia Hoagland, *Lesbian Ethics: Toward New Value* (Palo Alto, CA: Institute of Lesbian Studies, 1988).

There are also significant proposals from other Catholic, Protestant, and Jewish ethicists whose principles and frameworks have become in many ways complementary to one another, despite their different perspectives. I think here of the Jewish ethicist Eugene Borowitz, who offers an ethic of ascending degrees of commitment — from a safe-sex requirement of methods of *contraception* when the goal is simply "healthy orgasm"; to *mutual consent* when the rights of persons must be respected as much or more than their desires for pleasure; to *love* when the relationship itself is intrinsically important; to *marriage* which incorporates the other three levels but establishes them in covenant and permanent commitment.[15] What Borowitz provides is a nonjudgmental, yet powerfully persuasive, argument for some ethical norms in a variety of sexual relationships. The efforts of the Central Conference of American Rabbis to articulate values for incorporation into any sexual ethic are also significant. These values include: the image of God in all persons; truth and mercy; health; justice; family orientation; modesty; covenant relationship; joy; and love.[16]

James Gustafson, a Protestant ethicist, in 1981 proposed three fundamental "bases" for a Christian sexual ethic: human nature as both biological and personal; an acknowledgment of the reality of sin in the form of selfishness; and covenant as a reflection of human sociality and a framework for mutuality and accountability.[17] Stanley Hauerwas has argued for a particular focus in Christian sexual ethics on the mission of the church and the tasks of the Christian community — in other words, a sexual ethic where the issue is not so much the good of the individual but the good of the church.[18] And there are the multiple documents produced by the various Protestant denominations in recent years, focusing on specific questions,

---

15. Eugene B. Borowitz, *Choosing a Sex Ethic: A Jewish Inquiry* (New York: Schocken Books, 1979).

16. Central Conference of American Rabbis, Ad Hoc Committee on Human Sexuality, "Reform Jewish Sexual Values," *CCAR Journal* 43 (Fall 2001): 9–13.

17. James M. Gustafson, "Nature, Sin, and Covenant: Three Bases for Sexual Ethics," *Perspectives in Biology and Medicine* 68 (Spring 1981): 483–97.

18. Stanley Hauerwas, "The Politics of Sex: How Marriage is a Subversive Act," *After Christendom: How the Church is to Behave if Freedom, Justice, and a Christian Nation are Bad Ideas* (Nashville: Abingdon, 1991), 113–31.

often homosexuality, but in doing so, delineating frameworks fitting to denominational beliefs about sexuality.[19]

Among Roman Catholics, efforts at modifying the traditional framework for sexual ethics have been ongoing, certainly since the publication of *Human Sexuality: New Directions in American Catholic Thought* in 1977.[20] This volume proposed a framework based on particular values associated with human sexuality: self-liberation, other-enrichment, honesty, fidelity, service to life, social responsibility, and joy. The elements in the traditional framework that many Catholic thinkers consider problematic include procreation as a necessary justification of any sexual activity, and an assessment of each and every ethical infraction in the sexual sphere as gravely sinful. Efforts to develop new frameworks are visible in the writings of many contemporary Catholic ethicists, including Charles Curran, Richard McCormick, Andre Guindon, and James Keenan, as well as Gudorf, Cahill, and Andolsen whom I have noted above.[21]

My own proposal for a framework for a Christian sexual ethic looks like, yet unlike, many of these approaches. I am not sure that

---

19. See, for example, the report and recommendations of the Evangelical Lutheran Church in America (ELCA): *Journey Together Faithfully: A Call to Study and Dialogue*, *www.elca.org/faithfuljourney/tfreport.html*, downloaded February 16, 2005; *Presbyterians and Human Sexuality 1991* (203rd General Assembly Response to the Report of the Special Committee on Human Sexuality, 1991); *The Book of Resolutions of the United Methodist Church* (Nashville: United Methodist Publishing House, 2000). While these and others like them in all of the mainline Protestant churches may be "dated" in time, they signal a direction that deserves attention.

20. Anthony Kosnik, William Carroll, Agnes Cunningham, Ronald Modras, and James Schulte, *Human Sexuality: New Directions in American Catholic Thought* (Rahwah, NJ: Paulist, 1977). This was the result of a study commissioned by the Catholic Theological Society of America. It was welcomed by many Catholics, but also severely criticized by other Catholics (notably, leaders of the church). It should also be noted that dating new developments in Catholic sexual ethics from 1977 is somewhat misleading, even though this publication was a milestone. More accurately, however, discussions of sexual ethics changed significantly with Vatican II, and then in (largely critical) response to the papal encyclical on contraception, *Humanae Vitae*, published in 1968.

21. Many of these important writings are collected in *Readings in Moral Theology No. 8: Dialogue About Catholic Sexual Teaching*, ed. Charles E. Curran and Richard A. McCormick (New York: Paulist, 1993); *Readings in Moral Theology No. 9: Feminist Ethics and the Catholic Moral Tradition*, ed. Charles E. Curran, Margaret A. Farley, and Richard A. McCormick (New York: Paulist, 1996); and *Readings in Moral Theology No. 13: Change in Official Catholic Moral Teachings*, ed. Charles E. Curran (New York: Paulist, 2003).

the conclusions regarding specific sexual ethical questions would be so different within any of these frameworks — though they might be. To some extent, the frameworks I have so briefly identified above — especially those articulated by feminist ethicists — have recognized the importance of justice in regard to sexuality. Insofar as there is a focus on justice, the primary concern is with power inequities in gender relations or with more general considerations of social justice as it shapes sexual identity and activity. This focus is unquestionably significant — indeed, essential — as part of a justice framework for sexual ethics. But the task of articulating such a framework has barely begun.

All of these frameworks I have considered here pay serious attention to the standard sources for theological ethics: that is, *Scripture, tradition, secular disciplines*, and *contemporary experience*.[22] As a way of understanding any proposals it is helpful to consider these sources.

Sources for Christian Sexual Ethics

Despite past tendencies to emphasize one source or another — *sola scriptura*, for example, or church tradition identified with church authority — today there is general recognition among Christian ethicists that adequate moral discernment requires attention to all four of the sources. Moreover, it requires methods for correlating sources and for resolving apparent conflicts among them. In part, this recognition has come about as a result of developments in biblical studies (biblical scholars have made the texts more readily accessible for ethical discernment). In part, it has come through historical studies and the development of theories of interpretation not only for the Bible

---

22. I offer my own version of the essential sources for Christian ethics, though I acknowledge them as fairly "standard" for most Christian ethics. My version is one that parallels the original Methodist "quadrilateral." I began to develop it when co-teaching with my colleague Charles Powers, who had a similar rendering of this; but I have supplemented and revised the concepts a great deal through the years. My former students will recognize the "map" on which this appeared in nearly every course they took with me. For the Methodist "quadrilateral," see W. Stephen Gunter et al., *Wesley and the Quadrilateral: Renewing the Conversation* (Nashville: Abingdon, 1997).

but for traditions. In part, this recognition derives from the proliferation of scientific studies and the acknowledgment of differences in experiences of human sexuality.

A broadened use of sources for Christian ethics in general and sexual ethics in particular has come not only from their positive promise of moral insight, but from a recognition of the limits of each of the sources when appealed to by themselves. This recognition has served to relativize each in relation to the others and to look for their coalescence wherever possible. Hence, for example, Catholic ethicists, faced with the limits of past natural law perspectives (in terms of limited scientific information, a variety of philosophical analyses, and the weaknesses of mere reiteration of traditional church teachings), have opened more to the biblical witness and to contemporary experience as necessary complements when attending to new questions in sexual ethics. And although Protestant ethicists have not abandoned Scripture as a primary source, they attend also to critical studies of their traditions, to the sciences, and to the experiences of co-believers. All of the sources are necessary, then, but they are all in their own way problematic as well.

Scripture

The Bible is central to the received wisdom that Christians count on to illuminate their moral questions. Those for whom it counts as sacred writing reverence its authority. Although God seems not to have revealed everything we want to know, not in Scripture or through any other means, our assumption is that enough has been revealed for us to live on. Yet when we turn to Scripture, to the Bible, for guidance in our sexual lives, the message is spare and often confusing.

In the cultures of the Hebrew Bible, sexuality is situated in political and familial contexts, with a primary view to fertility. As David Biale has noted, "with the exception of the Song of Songs the Bible displays little interest in erotic desire as such,"[23] but only in its role in relation to the community. Central to the teachings of these foundational scriptures regarding sexuality (as noted in chapter 2) are two

---

23. David Biale, *Eros and the Jews: From Biblical Israel to Contemporary America* (New York: Basic Books, 1992), 13.

elements that account for the laws of marriage and for almost all other sexual regulations. The first of these is the command to procreate which is at the heart of the command to marry. The second is the presumption of a patriarchal model for all sexual relationships. In addition, however, the Hebrew Bible is replete with stories that have been and remain extremely important in our (both Jewish and Christian) attempts to understand the new sexual situations with which we are faced. Yet, conflicting conclusions are often drawn from the Bible, each assuming "that the biblical text and biblical culture [are] stable and monolithic."[24] This is a clue for us that the biblical legacy must be received as a whole, which includes patriarchal culture with its sometimes harsh strictures but also what Biale calls the "subversive texts" that counter these strictures — such as the stories of Ruth and Naomi, and the Song of Songs.[25] Finding in the Hebrew Bible the light we need for contemporary sexual ethics involves, therefore, a serious exegetical and interpretive task.

With the Christian Testament, there is no less a task for sexual ethics. Here we find no systematic code of sexual ethics (again, as noted in chapter 2), but only occasional responses to particular questions in particular situations. Yet moral guidelines for every sphere of human life, including the sexual, are to be gleaned from an overall command to love God and neighbor. Guidelines can also be drawn from instructions about the moral life that call for a radical re-orientation of each person toward God and a consequent transformation of all human relations. The depiction of human life provided in this Testament is essential to developing a Christian sexual ethic, but the challenge of exegesis, interpretation, and ethical discernment is considerable.[26]

---

24. Ibid., 11. We shall see a dramatic case in point for this when we come to a consideration of same-sex relations in chapter 7.

25. Ibid., 12, and the whole of chapter 1.

26. For an excellent exploration of the biblical witness in regard to human sexuality, especially that of the New Testament, see Cahill, *Sex, Gender, and Christian Ethics*, chap. 5. See also, among the many helpful works by biblical scholars, Raymond F. Collins, *Sexual Ethics and the New Testament: Behavior and Belief* (New York: Crossroad, 2000; Wayne A. Meeks, *The Origins of Christian Morality: The First Two Centuries* (New Haven, CT: Yale University Press, 1993); Dale B. Martin, *The Corinthian Body* (New Haven, CT: Yale University Press, 1995).

How considerations of justice in both Jewish and Christian scriptures relate to sexuality may be the most important question of all. Justice (or righteousness) is a central concept throughout the Bible. God alone is completely just and righteous, and God acts righteously and justly in relation to creation. God's justice — exceeding all human comprehension — is manifest both in judgment and in the forgiveness of God's people, again and again, from one generation to another. Humans are called to live righteously, by God's gift and God's command. They are called to believe and to hope in God who makes promises and whose mercy extends forever. They are called to an inward wholeness of love that both expresses the centrality of their God-relation and extends in action to their neighbors near and far. "Self-righteousness" is not an option that Scripture allows.

When it comes more specifically to justice in relation to human sexuality, however, the biblical witness is blurred — at least as we encounter it in today's world. In the Hebrew Bible, rules for justice in human sexual relationships have exceptions, sometimes approved, sometimes punished, by God. Moreover, both rules and exceptions appear culture-bound so that it is difficult to know what to make of them today. Injustice to Susanna is rectified (Dan. 13:1–64); but injustice to the daughter of Jeptha is counted as "justice" — even to her, within a grand scheme that looks to us more unjust than just (Judg. 11:29–40). Real sin and guilt are manifest in experiences of contagious "defilement," as when a whole household bears the consequences of David's adultery (2 Sam. 11:11–15). The God of righteousness and mercy is all too often depicted as the faithful and forgiving husband in relation to Israel, the unfaithful and adulteress wife — metaphors that reinforce patriarchal depreciation of women.

Nonetheless, the Bible remains a central source for discerning how to live our lives as sexual beings. At the very least it puts sexuality in perspective: it is not more important than love, not more important than life. The moral issues surrounding our sexual actions may be difficult for us all, so discernment in relation to revelatory texts as well as elsewhere must be careful, but judgment can be cautious. Self-righteousness may not be an option, though clearsightedness is a goal. To those who wanted "just punishment" for a woman caught in adultery, Jesus responds with silence. When he speaks, he makes only one point: we are all sinners whose stones are cast at our own great peril. To the woman he says, "Has no one condemned you? . . . Neither will I condemn you" (John 8:10–11). The whole of the biblical witness must be probed.

Tradition

Tradition adds to the received wisdom of which Scripture is a part.[27] As a source it refers to multiple elements that make up the ongoing life of a faith community through time. It includes, therefore, not only church teachings, laws, and practices but the history of theologies and the "sense of the faithful" as it has been formed and made manifest down through the years. As we saw in chapters 2 and 4, the tradition of Christianity is often as difficult to interpret as is Scripture. Not the least of its difficulties is that there are many strands, and strands within strands, in the whole tradition of Christianity. Hence, like Scripture, tradition and its strands require careful historical analysis, interpretation, and discernment about its usefulness for contemporary ethics.

Tradition in the sense of a "living" tradition certainly does not mean simply whatever has "always" been thought, taught, or practiced. As Joseph Ratzinger (later Pope Benedict XVI) once wrote: "Not everything that exists in the Church must for that reason be also a legitimate tradition; in other words, not every tradition that arises in the Church is a true celebration and keeping present of the mystery of Christ. There is a distorting, as well as legitimate, tradition. . . . Consequently, tradition must not be considered only affirmatively, but also critically."[28] If, in fact, tradition did mean only whatever has always, or for a long time, been taught or practiced,

---

27. I do not here detail the alternative ways of understanding the relation between Scripture and tradition that have marked developments in both Roman Catholicism and Protestantism. There are, however, concise and helpful descriptions of these available. See, for example, John E. Thiel, *Senses of Tradition: Continuity and Development in Catholic Faith* (Oxford: Oxford University Press, 2000), 3–5.

28. Joseph Ratzinger, "The Transmission of Divine Revelation," in *Commentary on the Documents of Vatican II*, vol. 3, ed. Herbert Vorgrimler (New York: Herder & Herder, 1969), 185.

then inequality between men and women would have to remain part of the ongoing tradition. Rather, if the *rationales* behind longstanding beliefs and practices are no longer persuasive in the context of the tradition as a whole, then the practices and beliefs will be challenged, and they may need to change.[29]

In a living tradition, beliefs and the theologies that interpret beliefs can be challenged by new experiences, cultural shifts, and new perspectives on the past. When this occurs, new and better rationales must be found to undergird ongoing beliefs, or beliefs themselves may evolve in their meaning and sometimes even be replaced. What is no longer "seriously imaginable" as a genuine part of the tradition gives way to what is coherent with the deepest held truths of the community.[30] That there is room for development of Christian beliefs and moral codes regarding sexuality is generally acknowledged by theologians and ethicists today. That some doctrines and some moral convictions are more central than others is also generally recognized.[31] The fact that all beliefs and convictions, perhaps especially those that are considered most central, can be understood from diverse perspectives, admit of new insights, are subject to more than one formulation, is what provides a task for theology and ethics. How to excavate historical layers of meaning, find lost treasures, take account of historical and cultural contexts for church life, hold on to gems of revelatory experience and shared faith: this is the question for those who go to tradition as a source of contemporary moral and theological insight. This, in part, is what is behind the question raised by many feminists: What is the "usable past" in the Christian

---

29. For a pertinent example of critique and proposal for reconstruction of something otherwise considered to be in the "tradition," see Catholic Theological Society of America, "Tradition and the Ordination of Women," *Proceedings* 52 (1997): 197–204.

30. The term was coined by David H. Kelsey in *The Uses of Scripture in Recent Theology* (Philadelphia: Fortress, 1975), 172; see also the whole of Kelsey's chap. 8 for a profound, incisive, and highly original discussion of the sources for Christian theology and their authority. I, of course, am concerned here about convictions and beliefs pertaining to sexual morality, not about more central beliefs such as those articulated in Christian creeds.

31. For an insightful exploration of patterns and possibilities of development of doctrine, see Thiel, *Senses of Tradition*. While this book focuses on the Roman Catholic tradition, its analyses are applicable to and illuminating for other traditions as well.

tradition as well as other traditions? And, one might add, how shall we find it?

Whatever the tasks involved in accessing tradition, there is no doubt that it is an important source for theology and ethics. The presupposition here is that a community's beliefs and moral insights through time not only are a fund of wisdom for each generation but are revelatory of God's presence and action in the life of the community. The fact that moral insights and even official church teachings have changed on some issues (for example, slavery, usury, marriage, religious liberty[32]) does not mean that tradition is less necessary for discerning moral questions that emerge in the church today. It does mean that we cannot expect simply to "read off" answers from history as if they were all obvious, or as if there were only a "literal" or "fundamentalist" meaning of tradition. What we have inherited by way of teachings and practices requires probing — in order to internalize or to modify or to find something new to which tradition has thus far only been able to point.

Turning to tradition with questions of justice and sexuality will mean asking new questions of traditional teachings and practices. Obligations of spouses in relation to one another for care, for love, for sexual intimacy, as well as responsibilities to families are embedded not only in theologies but in canonical regulations.[33] What these can mean for sexual ethics today has to be both winnowed for their ongoing validity and wisdom and contextualized in the present as they have been in the past.

Secular Disciplines of Knowledge

Some delineations of the sources of Christian theology and ethics identify the third source as "reason." This, however, is misleading. Reason, after all, is involved in addressing all of the sources. Of course, insofar as it is a distinctive source, "reason" means what we can know from the "light of human reason" as distinguished from

---

32. See John T. Noonan, *A Church That Can and Cannot Change* (Notre Dame, IN: University of Notre Dame Press, 2005); "Development in Moral Doctrine," *Theological Studies* 54 (1993); "Experience and the Development of Moral Doctrine," in Catholic Theological Society of America, *Proceedings* 54 (1999), 43–56.

33. See, for example, *The Code of Canon Law*, Can. 1135, 1136.

special revelation (as in Scripture). It is clearer and more useful, however, to consider this source as referring to every "secular discipline," every discipline not based in or dependent upon revelation, that offers the possibility of insight into the aspects of creation we seek to understand. Hence, in sexual ethics, the relevant disciplines will include not only philosophy but biology, medicine, psychology, sociology, anthropology, and even history, literature, and art. The achievements of these disciplines are not always lasting, of course, for they make mistakes, miss insights, and change in their conclusions. For example (one I have referred to before), biological understandings of human sexuality have expanded and improved — from beliefs that the whole of what constitutes a new human being is contained in a sperm to convictions about the contributions of both ovum and sperm. Psychological and sociological studies of sexual response, consequences of self-pleasuring, influences on sexual orientation, and on and on, have corrected past mistakes, generated new insights important to sexual ethics, or simply called into question as yet unverifiable conclusions long taken for granted.

Hence, the resources in secular disciplines for a sexual ethic require a kind of "exegesis," interpretation, and discernment of their usefulness, in ways not completely unlike what is needed in relation to the resources of the Bible or tradition. However, insofar as these disciplines give us a kind of "access" to reality — to the world and the universe, to human persons and the meanings of sexuality, to tragic or beneficial consequences of action — they are necessary for the doing of sexual ethics. Even if these disciplines do not give us actual access to "reality,"[34] but only a pragmatic way of dealing with the world and ourselves, they remain important to our moral discernment. We shall see how they assist us in discerning what is just in the sphere of sexuality.

---

34. Perhaps wherever I use the term "reality" (and I have and will continue to use it a lot) I should use quotation marks. I am mindful of David Tracy's appeal to Vladimir Nobokov's statement: "'Reality' is the one word that should always appear within quotation marks." See David Tracy, *Plurality and Ambiguity: Hermeneutics, Religion, and Hope* (San Francisco: Harper & Row, 1987), 47. The point is that we never have full access to reality; our knowledge is always partial, in some way provisional.

Contemporary Experience

Experience is also potentially misleading as a named source for Christian insight, for it is not just one source among many.[35] It is an important part of the content of each of the other sources, and it is always a factor in interpreting the others. Scripture, for example, is the record of some persons' experiences of God; tradition is the lived experience of a faith community through time; and secular disciplines, too, are shaped by the experience of those who engage in them. As a discrete source, however, I shall mean by "experience" the contemporary actual living of events and relationships, along with the sensations, feelings, emotions, insights, and understandings that are part of this lived reality. In this sense, experience is a given, providing data to be interpreted; but it is also something that is already interpreted, its content shaped by previous understandings in a context of multiple influences. Because experience is a more contested source than the other sources for Christian ethics — especially sexual ethics — we need to explore it at greater length.

As Foucault has helped to show, sex is probably the most "looked upon," most examined, human experience both in public discourse and in the minute self-examination which that public discourse determines in private. Experiences in the sexual sphere, perhaps more than in any other sphere of human life, are shaped by social norms, both religious and cultural, even to the point of determining what experiences are possible and what they will mean. This means that publicly provided norms, whether religious or secular, have shaped experiences so that, for example, sex is sometimes *experienced* as evil precisely because it has been socially interpreted as evil; sex has sometimes been *experienced* as deviant because it has been identified and treated as deviant; sex has been *experienced* as not open to communion with God because it has been interpreted as without this possibility. In other words, experience is constituted for us and interpreted by us within the limits and possibilities of the languages we already have, the social and cultural influences we absorb, and

---

35. I draw here on some of my earlier work. See Farley, "The Role of Experience in Moral Discernment," in *Christian Ethics: Problems and Prospects*, ed. Lisa Sowle Cahill and James F. Childress (Cleveland: Pilgrim, 1996), 134–51.

the worldview we already hold. Hence, it is never "pure" experience, unmediated by anyone or anything else.

Experience can belong both to the self and to the self together with others; that is, it can be both personal and communal. It is private, unique to the one who experiences; but there are shared experiences, communicated as well as formed within communities, cultures, and societies. Experiences are diverse, and we have learned the claims upon us to acknowledge diversity. Yet we take diversity seriously for the sake of community — not in order to separate ourselves finally and hopelessly from one another. What is learned uniquely from positions of experience gives privileged access to understanding, but what is learned from unique, privileged, perspectival experience can be rendered at least partially intelligible to others whose experience is nonetheless different.

Thus, for example, those who have not yet lost a parent through death have, in an important sense, no direct experience of this human event. And one might add, no two experiences of a parent dying are exactly the same. Yet if those whose parents are still living nonetheless share deeply in the experience of someone else who has previously lost a parent, they may already understand something of what this means. Later, when their own mother or father dies, they will experience something new, yet not wholly new; they will learn something they did not know before, but they will also recognize what has been shared with them from the experience of another. This is true also in the sexual sphere. A woman may not be a prostitute, or caught in the web of exploitation which characterizes the sex industry in many parts of the world, but she need not remain wholly outside of, a stranger to, such experiences if she attends to the narratives of others. One may not be a lesbian or a gay man, but she or he can grasp the integrity of what gays and lesbians say with their lives and what they tell of their loves and their hopes. One may not have borne a child, but he or she can hear the cries of women through the centuries and today in the situations where they have suffered violence in both child-conceiving and child-bearing; and one can share the burdens and the joy of parents in the welcoming and rearing of their children. Although it is true that our vicarious experiences and the analogies we draw from them remain different in important respects from the direct experiences of others, it is also true that we can to a significant extent not only understand the experiences of others but stand in solidarity with those whose experiences they most intimately are.

Not surprisingly, however, problems beset experience in terms of access, authority, and criteria for its use in ethical discernment. For example, what sort of evidence does experience actually offer? What sort of generalization from experience is possible? How is the authority of experience to be reconciled with the authority of the Bible, tradition, and systematized disciplines of reason? The first of these questions is closely related to what theologians and philosophers call the "hermeneutical circle," the circle of interpretation. As theories of language, social location, and power are developed, they threaten to make any appeal to experience vacuous. As an instance, what can an appeal to women's experience mean if that experience is shaped completely and ineluctably by normative expectations of a culture? What are we to make of an ethics of care based on women's experience of caring if we suspect that its construction is attributable to the social pressures on women to take care of men and children? As Catherine MacKinnon cautions, "Women are said to value care. Perhaps women value care because men have valued women according to the care they give. Women are said to think in relational terms. Perhaps women think in relational terms because women's social existence is defined in relation to men."[36] The supposed bedrock of evidence that experience provides disappears in the endless circles of social construction. Nonetheless, and perhaps ironically, it is experience itself that has taught us: the worldviews that shape experience can be challenged and in some respects modified and even overturned. The hermeneutical circle is not so tightly shut that we are denied a critical edge or opening.

The second question (about the aptitude of experience to generalization) I have already addressed in part. Everyone recognizes that experience is particular precisely because it is concrete, but is there sufficient overlap in the content of one person's experience

---

36. Catherine A. MacKinnon, *Toward a Feminist Theory of the State* (Cambridge, MA: Harvard University Press, 1989), 51.

and another's so that generalizations can be warranted? For example, women have learned to be cautious in generalizing for all women out of their own particular and hence limited experience and self-understanding. Just as women have argued that the experience of men cannot be universalized to stand for the experience of all humans, so they have had to acknowledge that diversity among women's experiences disallows uncritical generalizations based on the experience of only some women — in this case, white, middle-class, heterosexual, Western women. Yet some generalization from experience and insight is necessary to give power and inspiration to concerted action. As I have argued elsewhere, whatever the vast differences in human lives it is nonetheless possible for human persons to weep over commonly felt tragedies, laugh over commonly perceived incongruities, and yearn for common hopes. Human persons can and ought to experience moral claims in relation to one another, and some of these claims can and ought to cross (though not ignore or disrespect) the experiential boundaries of culture and history.[37]

The third question (on the authority of experience) is in a way particular to experience as a source, but it belongs also to all of the sources of moral insight. Whose experience counts, when experiences differ? How can experience — elusive, socially constructed, diverse — be authoritative in the process of moral discernment and decision-making? Should not experience be subject to the Bible and to faith traditions for its own interpretation and for its validity? We can identify some guiding criteria for appeals to experience in moral discernment, such as: coherence of the insights from experience with general moral norms; intelligibility of accounts of experience in relation to fundamental beliefs; mutual illumination when measured with other sources of moral insight; harmful or helpful consequences of interpretations of experience; confirmation in a community of

---

37. Farley, "The Role of Experience in Moral Discernment"; "Feminism and Universal Morality," in *Prospects for a Common Morality*, ed. Gene Outka and John P. Reader (Princeton, NJ: Princeton University Press, 1993), 170–91; "Feminist Consciousness and the Interpretation of Scripture," in *Feminist Interpretation of the Bible*, ed. Letty M. Russell (Philadelphia: Westminster, 1985), 41–54.

discernment; and integrity in the testimony of those who present their experiences. All of these may be tests for the validity and usefulness of given experiences in a process of moral discernment. Yet experience may challenge its own tests and assert an authority that modifies the prior norms that would order it. Something deeper is at stake.

Like the other sources for moral insight, experience is a necessary but not sufficient source for sexual ethics. There is here, as elsewhere, no incontestable, foundational, immediate, and direct "deposit" for insight in a fund of experience. Experience does not explain everything else without needing to be explained itself. Not only does it not automatically yield full-blown ethical universals, it also cannot be understood as an "anything goes" approach based on rival experiences of seemingly equal instructive value. Interpretations of some experiences can yield illusion and falsehood on a par with some interpretations of the Bible and of tradition. This is why actual or vicariously and analogously shared experience is necessary to sexual ethics, but also why in a Christian ethic at least, interpretations of sexual experience need to be rendered mutually coherent with interpretations of the whole of human and Christian life.

This question, as I said, belongs somehow to all of the sources. How can any of them be finally authoritative if they must cohere in some way with the others? If we ought not to adopt a fundamentalist view of experience, can we adopt one for the Bible, tradition, or what the sciences report? Underlying all of these considerations is an understanding of authority. It is impossible, however, to separate the question of authority from the question of the content or meaning of what is presented as authoritative. Hence, even if one accepts the authority of a source on some apparently extrinsic basis (for example, that it is God's word, or that the voice of the faith community is determinative), this very acceptance must have meaning, must "make sense" to the one who accepts it. The moral authority (that is, the power to "author" life) of any source is ultimately contingent on a "recognition" of the truth it offers and the justice of its aims. No source has real and living authority in relation to our moral attitudes and choices unless it can elicit from us a responding recognition.[38] When Christian ethicists consider Scripture, tradition, secular disciplines, and contemporary experience as authoritative sources, it is precisely because they find in and through these sources access to moral insight and motivation. This does not mean, of course, that their "recognitions" of truth never change, or that they are so adequate and full that they are never subject to critique and modification.

The biblical witness, in particular, claims to present truths that will heal us, make us whole; that will free us, not enslave us to what violates our very sense of truth and justice. Its appeal to us is, in the words of the philosopher Paul Ricoeur, a "nonviolent appeal."[39] As a revelation of truth, it asks for something less like a submission of will and more like an opening of the imagination — and hence the whole mind and heart. In its own terms, then, it cannot be believed unless it "rings true" to our deepest capacity for truth and goodness.

But is the Bible, or tradition for that matter, really required to answer the demands of reason and the cries of the human heart? Is this to reduce it to a measure that is outside of it? It depends, of course on what one means by the "demands of reason" and the "desires of the heart." But surely there is a sense in which every religious tradition has power only insofar as it offers just this — insofar as it helps to make sense of the whole of human life, to give meaning to human tragedy and horizons to human hope. "Hard sayings" can be liberating truths; and reason need not be opposed to presence and mystery, nor experiential insight inimical to a great-hearted love.

---

38. This does not mean that sources are completely subjectified, that there is — for example — no revelation in the Bible unless everyone perceives it. It does mean that not every interpretation of every verse or text of the Bible can be "authoritative" or normative by itself for every person. Nonetheless, a subjective "recognition" of a text (of whatever sort) as "making sense" is in some way inevitable. To take an extreme example: Whatever scholars make of the command of God to Abraham to sacrifice his son, Isaac, Abraham appears to have heard the command at some deep level as ultimately not contradicting the visage and promise of the God whom he had encountered. On the other hand, I am fully aware that one's worldview can be completely cohesive, so that every interpretation will cohere — and yet be mistaken.

39. Paul Ricoeur, *Essays in Biblical Interpretation*, ed. Lewis S. Mudge (Philadelphia: Fortress, 1980), 95.

The reason, then, why experience may challenge other sources and the interpretations of other sources is that moral truth must "make sense." When a deeply held conviction such as the equality of women and men, grounded in our experience, appears to be contradicted by information from other sources, it must be tested against them. But if it continues to persuade us, continues to hold "true" so that to deny it would do violence to our moral sensibilities, our affective capacity to respond to the good, and our very capacity for knowing, then it must function also as a measure against which the other sources are tested.

Experience in each of these senses — given but not primitive, immediate but not innocent of interpretation, personal but not isolated, unique but not without a social matrix — plays an important part in moral discernment. As such, it is the experience of concrete persons and groups, and it is to be taken into account in moral discernment. Like Scripture and tradition, it requires analysis, interpretation, and decision about its usefulness in determining attitudes and behavior. In other words, experience, like every other source, is not self-interpreting. We all have had experiences, the meaning of which we interpret differently today than we did ten or twenty years ago.

Love and Just Love

A final preliminary consideration remains. In order to situate an understanding of "just sex" in a larger framework of human and Christian morality, it is necessary first to introduce the notion of a "just love." To look briefly, but closely, at love in this respect will prevent us from assuming that love is the sufficient answer to all of our sexual ethical questions. It will not do, as some wish, to end all ethical discernment by simply saying that sexual relations and activities are good when they express love; for love is the problem in ethics, not the solution. As I suggested in the previous chapter, our experiences of love, and our loves, take multiple forms. Some thinkers prefer to reserve the name "love" for a love that has normative content — that is, for loves that they consider to be good loves. Yet we know that not all of our loves are good, though they are loves.

There are wise loves and foolish, good loves and bad, true loves and mistaken loves. The question ultimately is, what *is* a right love, a good, just, and true love?[40]

I have some worries about once again examining here the meaning of love. What I offer is a somewhat abstract analysis which as such may be a deterrent to our finding justice as the normative content of love. Taking this route, there is danger that we will lose sight of the object of love — of who and what we love. This is not my intent. Since I consider this analysis of love necessary for understanding the criteria of just loving, it is my hope and intention that, in the end, we will arrive at a stronger, not weaker, focus on who and what we love. I also worry that all we have seen thus far about the social construction of human embodiment, gender, and sexuality will seem to be ignored in a search for the meaning of "just" love and the nature of its objects. This also is not my intent. As I shall try to show along the way, insofar as our understandings of anything are socially constructed, this is important to know. Recognition of this is a part of our search for the meanings of love and its objects. Finally, my analysis of love (and its derivative, desire) is an effort to describe our experiences of love in some kind of ethically normative way. The test of the accuracy and adequacy of my description will be whether or not it actually does describe experiences that others can recognize. Hence, it is farthest from my mind to substitute abstract analysis for concrete experience. Description and analysis are here for the sake of entering more deeply into the experience of love and the requirements of justice.

---

40. For now, I am using the terms "right," "true," "just," and "good" interchangeably, and I am assuming a common sense or popular understanding of them. There are, of course, significant technical differences among them as they are used in moral theology and ethics. The primary meaning that I am giving to all of these at this point is most clearly visible in the terms "true" and "just." By "true," here I mean true in the sense that a carpenter might use it, as in to "true" a board in relation to a larger structure, or to balance, square something in relation to something else. And, as we will see below, by "just" I mean rendering what is "due." These two terms come very close to being synonymous as I employ them here. The term "right" is often used when considering a duty, as in right versus wrong, and it thereby refers to the quality of an action insofar as it accords with moral norms, requirements of a contract, or whatever it is that determines what is obligatory between persons or between persons and anything else. "Good," as opposed to bad, tends to mean something intrinsic to a being, or to an end. It relates to action insofar as action serves the good of a being or leads to that good; or even insofar as action reflects the goodness of God.

I have already given a non-normative description of love, in particular sexual romantic love, in chapter 4. In this description lie clues
for the norms (the criteria, requirements, standards) of right and good
loving. If love is an affective response to, union with, and affirmation of an object, it will be accurate and adequate insofar as it does
not "miss" the object, the beloved—that is, (1) insofar as it is not a
response shaped by an illusory, distorted, or falsified understanding
of what is loved; (2) insofar as it really is an interior uniting with
the beloved (which need not always imply mutuality of loves); and
(3) insofar as it affirms the beloved in ways that do not miss the
actuality and potentialities of the one who is loved.[41] Put positively,
love is true and just, right and good, insofar as it is a true response
to the reality of the beloved, a genuine union between the one who
loves and the one loved, and an accurate and adequate affective affirmation of the beloved. Perhaps the most basic example of this is to
be found in our recognition that *things* are not to be loved as if they
were *persons*, and *persons* are not to be loved as if they were *things*.
What is wrong with loving a person as a thing is that the person *is a
person, not a thing*.

But we can look at more specific examples: A romantic love will
be less accurate, true, and even less just if it sees and responds to the
beloved not for what he or she is but solely for the prestige he can add
to my name; if this is the shape of the love, it will fail as union with
the beloved, and it will affirm for him what may be destructive not
only of him but of our relationship. Or a love for a child will be inaccurate and potentially destructive if it takes no account of the fact
that this individual is, say, only five years old—with limited capacities and significant potentialities, both of which are to be respected
and nurtured, not cut off or stifled in their beginnings. Or again, love
of a spouse (at least in a contemporary Western context[42]) will be not

---

41. I have addressed these same considerations in *Personal Commitments: Beginning, Keeping, Changing* (San Francisco: Harper & Row, 1986), 29–32, 80–84. Similar
issues are at stake in my efforts to combine compassion and respect in *Compassionate Respect: A Feminist Approach to Medical Ethics and Other Questions* (New York:
Paulist, 2002), 21–43.

42. Our perceptions, and hence, our loves are indeed in many ways socially constructed. This does not mean that they are unimportant or that they cannot have moral
norms that take social construction into account. If, for example, we live in a society

only inadequate but distortive and unjust if it affirms the spouse only as an instrument for housekeeping or breadwinning or producing a child. In all of these examples we have loves, but in some sense they are "false" loves, or at least mistaken loves. Why? Once again, what are the norms or criteria by which we can judge a love to be "true" and good, just and even wise? If we look at the three examples I have just given, there are more clues for an answer to this question.

Regarding the first example: There are lots of ways in which romantic love can be wonderful, life-enhancing, a gift to be celebrated and treasured. But there are also lots of ways in which it can be inadequate, inaccurate, and harmful both to the beloved and to the lover. At the very least we expect it to be a response to and affirmation of the beloved as a person — which is eminently more than a token for one's own prestige.[43] In the second example: The fundamental reason why it is important when loving a child to take account of the fact that she is a child is because she is more than a projection of our own needs and more than a "little adult." She is unique, vulnerable, and in need of relationships that affirm her; she is destined to become more autonomous, worthy of respect as a human being who can grow into wholeness. To affirm her without attention to what she needs in order to grow from a five-year old to an adult can be to disrespect and to harm her. Regarding the third and last example: A spousal love can truthfully include what the spouse can be and do for the other, but if it is only this, it misses the reality of the spouse

where the expectations for marriage are different from other societies, then these expectations have to be taken into account when we are considering what will harm or help persons, and what the meaning is of their commitments.

43. It might be objected in relation to my example here that "romantic" love is never as calculating as assessing someone's value in prestige for the one who loves. I do tend to agree with this objection, although the example is at least clearer than some others one might create. It might be better to instance a romantic love that is so overwhelming that it does mistake the characteristics of the one loved — seeing him (or her) as more intelligent, more sophisticated, more talented that he really is. In this case, romantic love would be indeed "romantic," yet miss the real person by reason of mistaken perception of the person's characteristics. I do not, however, think that being attracted to and falling in love with someone because of his or her genuine intelligence, or some other attractive feature, need ultimately be a mistaken love. It might be an instance where there is an accurate perception of characteristics, and although the characteristics are not the whole of the person, they can be the conditions of falling in love. Moreover, this does not preclude that such a love can grow into an unconditional love.

as person, with all that makes her or him lovable, and with all that has been mutually pledged in marital union.

Moral Norms for a Just Love

What begins to emerge from these considerations is that the norm or criterion for a true and good love is the *concrete reality of the beloved* — of whoever or whatever is loved.[44] Just as in regard to knowledge we identify the possibilities of ignorance, mistakes, and lies, so in regard to love we can simply fail to love the other at all, or we can love with a mistaken love, affirming some aspect of the beloved's reality in a way that unintentionally distorts the whole or misses an important part of it. We can also love with a "lying" love, intentionally ignoring and distorting aspects of the reality of the one loved. A love is right and good insofar as it aims to affirm truthfully the concrete reality of the beloved. This is in large part what I mean by a "just love."[45]

I say "in part" because not only must love respond to, unite with, and affirm the one loved in her or his concrete reality, but it must also be "true" to the *one loving* and to the *nature of the relationship* between lover and loved. A love will not be true or just if there is an affirmation of the beloved that involves destruction of the one who loves. I do not refer to a justifiable "laying down of one's life" for the beloved, but rather to a letting oneself be destroyed as a person

---

44. One clarification may be useful here: to suggest that right loving depends on our affirming the concrete reality of a person does not mean that we affirm, for example, the fact that the person is a thief. Nor does it mean that we abstract from this aspect of the person. It means, rather, that we recognize the person as a person, and wish for the person to be whole as a person and as the individual person she is or can be. Hence, love may include anguish over an individual's thievery, and a yearning for this individual to change insofar as this is possible. Similarly, right loving does not mean affirming that a person who is desperately poor, even starving to death, remain in this situation just as it is. To affirm the actuality and potentiality of persons includes wanting for them what they need for well-being.

45. See Farley, *Personal Commitments*, 81–82. My position is not that, given *accurate knowledge* of its object, love will always be just and true. This would perhaps fit with a Socratic view of love and morality, but not with mine. This is why I say that love may intentionally as well as unintentionally ignore or miss its object. My comments about both knowledge and love may, however, elicit scorn as yet another version of a "correspondence" theory of truth. I do not and cannot here take on questions raised by the whole of epistemology. Nonetheless, what I say about "just" love does require a moral epistemology that at least incorporates a form of mitigated or humbled realism.

because of the way in which one loves another. This will be clear if we remember that love is an "affective" affirmation — which means that the lover affirms the beloved *with her or his own being*. As I have indicated before, if I love you, in addition to knowing you, I do not say simply "You are," but rather, "I want you to be, and to be full and firm in being." I say this with my very being. Loving, therefore, involves placing one's *affective self-affirmation in affective affirmation of the beloved*. It involves, in other words, placing my love of myself in loving affirmation of the one that I love.[46]

Similarly, love is false or mistaken when it does not accord with the nature of the *relationship* between lover and loved. Our relationships are part of our reality. They are part of who we are, but precisely because they are "relationships" they do not reside in the one and the other separately; they are "between" us; they are in us and beyond us, in us but transcendent of each toward the other; for we are transcendent embodied beings. Love, of course, *makes* and shapes relationships, and love can change relationships. Yet love cannot, and ought not to try to, make some relationships be whatever we want them to be. Thus, for example, a parent-child relationship requires that love on either side be qualified in some way by reason of this relationship, without denying the genuine equality that is its ultimate aim or the necessary role-reversals that may come in time or by reason of specific circumstances. Thus, also, if I love someone as my spouse when the other is espoused to someone else, it means I do not take account of the other's commitments, which are part of his or her concrete reality; I falsify the nature of the relationship

---

46. I do not here mean, as some people insist, that unless we love ourselves first we cannot love another. Whether or not this is true, psychological development is not what I am talking about here. I mean, rather, that the nature of love for another (or for whatever) involves simultaneous affirmation of ourselves *in and for* affirming the other. By this I do not mean to imply that it is "self love" in the ordinary sense of this term that is affirmed first and above all, and only secondarily affirmed for another. The self-affirmation that is involved in any love of either oneself or anyone or anything else is simply the form that affective affirmation takes. Using other language, we might say that to will is to affirm oneself willing. There are further complexities that I will not go into here, but they should be kept in mind. That is, I can love another ultimately for his or her own sake, or for the sake of myself. In the latter case, I can truly love the other, but with a love that is relative to (perhaps even instrumental to, conditional on) my love of myself. Most would agree that this is not the height of interpersonal love which involves other-centeredness, but it is nonetheless love.

between us. Realizing contingencies in these examples, they none-theless reflect what I mean when I say that love must be appropriate to the nature of the relationship between lover and loved.[47]

I am arguing that it is the concrete reality of the beloved that must be attended to if love is to be just. This will be shorthand, however, for my conclusion here that love is just and true, in the sense of "ac-curate," (1) when it does not falsify or "miss" the reality of the person loved (either as human or as unique individual), (2) when it does not falsify or "miss" the reality of the one loving, and (3) when it does not violate, distort, or ignore the nature of the relationship between them. With this shorthand, I shall always be including the whole of what love descriptively involves, but with primary attention given to the beloved. I also do not leave behind the correlative conclusion that love is more or less just in the sense of "adequate" insofar as it is more or less fitting, appropriate, to the relationship, and insofar as it more or less adequately reaches the full complex reality of the one loving and the one loved. There are not only complexities in the objects of love but degrees of loving and of loving justly.

All of what I have said about "just love" tells us that love as an emotion (as an affective internal responsive act) is not blind (al-though it can be mistaken, and it can ignore or abstract from what it does not want to see or is incapable of seeing). As I have argued and held in all of my writings, emotions contain not only an affec-tive element but a cognitive one. Just as desire, anger, compassion, and fear are dependent upon the beliefs we have about their objects, so it is with love. As Martha Nussbaum puts it, we may deceive ourselves about what is given in love, "about who; and how; and when; and whether."[48] But the possibilities of error, of illusion or delusion, do not eliminate the possibilities of accuracy, of receiving

---

47. In the first example, I in no sense want to rigidify the nature of a child-parent relationship; I only want to acknowledge that it *is* a relation that is important to the love of both child and parent. Regarding the second example, it is difficult without providing fuller detail to take account of marital situations of abandonment, or situations in which legal marriage is no longer viable, or where the death of one spouse cannot be determined, and so forth. It is possible, too, that one might understand "spousal" love in relationships that cannot be "institutionalized" for one reason or another.

48. Martha C. Nussbaum, *Love's Knowledge: Essays on Philosophy and Literature* (New York: Oxford University Press, 1990), 261.

and responding to what is real. "We also discover and correct our self-deceptions."[49] At least sometimes we do.

Despite the utter importance of knowledge in relation to love, our loves need not be limited by our understanding of their objects. As Thomas Aquinas noted, love goes more directly to its object than does knowledge.[50] We can love someone beyond what we can know of him or her. This is true even of our love for God. For the union that is possible in love can exceed our knowledge of the beloved, although its direction and form remain subject to the knowledge we have. We can, for example, love someone utterly, in a way that any new knowledge we gain (even if it is "disappointing") will not diminish our love. This is, indeed, what it means to love "unconditionally."

In summary, then, the emotion of love is not the same as "feelings" that come and go, whether we like it or not, in the mode of physiological disturbances and sensations, and that may importantly accompany emotions but are not required for them.[51] Love is spontaneously receptive but not a passive reaction; it is active in response, constituted in union, shaped by perceptions and understandings, and engaging of myself in affirmation of what I love. It is true and just when and insofar as it accords with the concrete reality of what is loved, the one loving, and the nature of the relationship between them. This does not mean that we have perfect knowledge of any created realities. And it certainly is compatible with the social construction of our perceptions and our loves in the contexts in which

---

49. Ibid.

50. Thomas Aquinas, *Summa Theologiae* I-II. 27. 2 ad 2; I-II. 66. 6; II. 23. 6.

51. See Robert C. Solomon, "Emotions and Choice," in *Explaining Emotions*, ed. Amelie O. Rorty (Berkeley: University of California Press, 1980), 254: "One can be angry without feeling angry: one can be angry for three days or five years and not feel anything identifiable as a feeling of anger continuously through that prolonged period." Yet as Martha Nussbaum has observed, "we should distinguish 'feelings' of two sorts. On the one hand, there are feelings with a rich intentional content — feelings of the emptiness of one's life without a certain person.... Such feelings may enter the identity conditions of some emotion.... On the other hand, there are feelings without rich intentionality or cognitive content, for instance, feelings of fatigue, of extra energy. As with bodily states, they may accompany emotion or they may not — but they are not necessary for it." Martha Nussbaum, "Emotions as Judgements of Value and Importance," in *Relativism, Suffering, and Beyond: Essays in Memory of Bimal K. Matilal* (Delhi: Oxford University Press, 1997), 247. See also Solomon, *The Passions* (Notre Dame, IN: University of Notre Dame Press, 1983).

we live. Insofar as our perceptions and convictions about any realities are socially constructed, so will our emotions be socially constructed. Deconstruction, one hopes, is about getting clearer about the realities we love, want to love, and choose to love.

Love and Freedom

There is one more observation that must be made about love if we expect the norms of love (the criteria for right and just loving) ever to govern our actions. That is, love *can be subject to choice.* In its first instance, its first awakening, love is not a matter of free choice. It is, as I have already said, receptive, but actively receptive as a spontaneous response to what is perceived as lovable.[52] Still, we can influence our loves even in their beginning by choosing to pay attention to certain realities or not, putting ourselves in a position to discover lovableness insofar as it is there, choosing to believe in (even if we do not yet "see," since faith is a form of knowledge) the value of

---

52. As I have said before, it is common, especially among Christians, to speak of love for the "unlovable," and to consider the height of Christian love, *agape,* to be either motivated by duty, or to be God's love flowing through us and not really our love at all. From this point of view, love would be wholly active, and not in the first instance responsive to beauty or lovableness. This seems only partly true to our experience. There are a number of things wrong with this construal of Christian love. First, if it implies that our loves are always, only, and in every way "creative," bestowing goodness and beauty ("lovableness") on the other, this is to make claims for human love that belong only to God's love — which is a loving-into-being, a love *ex nihilo.* Whatever or whomever we come to love, however, is already lovable in some sense, by reason of God's creative love. It is true (and we know this from experience) that human loves *are* or can be creative, but only partially. Although our loves are in the first instance *responses* to what is already lovable, nonetheless persons can blossom under anyone's love, including our own.

Second, to say that we should love what is in every respect "unlovable" or "not able to be loved" is literally a contradiction, though it is surely possible to do the deeds of love out of duty or on command. When we are the ones being loved, an expression of love for us that rises only from duty, or that does not really come in any sense from the person who expresses it, is hardly a love in which we could rejoice. On the other hand, the belief that God loves through us, *whether or not we love at all,* is not only plausible but consoling. It just does not seem the kind of love to which Christians or any other humans are ultimately called.

In our experience, love is awakened and specified by what we discover to be beautiful or good or lovable. Even if we are not touched, awakened in love, by someone who according to some standards appears to be quite unlovable, the view of love that I am suggesting yields an obligation to try to discover the beauty of the other; and short of this, to *believe* that all persons are lovable (loved at least by God) even though we do not "see" it, at least not at first.

persons or of anything in creation. Insofar as love is like a judgment of value (or at least is in response to and informed by a judgment of value), we can, as Robert Solomon says, open ourselves "to argument, persuasion, and evidence."[53]

Even more importantly, once a love is awakened, it can *offer itself to freedom.* It can give rise to the need and the desire to affirm itself, and to affirm its object, by our free choice. (I do not mean to speak of love as if it is a "thing." It is I who am awakened in love; it is I who can experience and understand my love as worthy or not worthy of my freely chosen ratification.) At the center of ourselves where freedom is a possibility, we can *identify* with our loves and freely ratify them — this love or that, this form of loving or that, this or that action to express love. We take responsibility for our loves, or at least we can do so. We can also repudiate, or defer, some of our loves by choosing *not to identify* with them. We do not have direct control over our loves, so that our choice is hardly ever a choice to "turn off" a love; but we can choose not to identify our deepest selves with some of our spontaneous loves and not to let some loves flow into action. Moreover, I repeat, we can shape our loves by our choices. We can choose to believe in, pay attention to, what we love — even if the feelings that accompany love come and go. We can choose to try to modify our emotions and feelings when they conflict with our chosen loves — by ignoring them, focusing them, giving them "free play" or not in our imaginations. We can choose to do love's actions, and order our lives in ways that are conducive to the continuance and growth of our chosen, ratified loves.

Desire

Desire, as I have described it earlier, is grounded in a more fundamental affective activity; it is grounded in and rises from love — ultimately for myself or another or in some mixture of love of self

---

53. Solomon, "Emotions and Choice," 270. See also my treatment of love in relation to choice and to commitment in Farley, *Personal Commitments,* chap. 3. What I am saying here should not be construed as meaning that we are incapable of Christian *agape,* that we "appraise" and "judge" the lovableness of who and what we love and restrict our loves to objects of which we approve. It does mean that love involves — as I have said again and again — a response to what is perceived as lovable.

and other.[54] *Desire grounded in love of ourselves* is the form love takes when it wants (or rather, *we* want) greater self-affirmation, or well-being, or acquisition of some sort, or even developed virtue. *Desire grounded in love of another* is the form love takes when we are not fully united with the object of our love — whether because we want greater union, or possession, or mutuality, or presence; or because we want our love to be greater, better, more true, for the sake of our beloved. Desire will be just and true if the love that is its source is just and true, but it can also be constructed in ways that influence, for good or ill, the love out of which it rises. Desire for another may outrun our love for another, so that our love becomes love primarily for ourselves. All of this means that desire, too, can have norms; and the norms, not surprisingly, have a lot to do with the concrete reality of what is loved.

In the previous chapter I spoke of romantic love, sexual love, and the corresponding romantic and sexual desires. When we turn to sexual ethical norms, what we are looking for, ultimately, are the norms for sexual love and desire. From all that I have said thus far, I hope it is now clear why I am looking for the norms of justice that will "norm" the loves and desires, relationships and activities, associated with human sexuality. What, then, will a justice ethic look like in the sexual sphere of our lives?

---

54. See my treatment of desire in general and as part of any object for free choice: Farley, "Freedom and Desire," in *The Papers of the Henry Luce III Fellows in Theology* vol. 3 (Atlanta: Scholars, 1999), 57–74

Chapter 6

FRAMEWORK
FOR A SEXUAL ETHIC
Just Sex

═══ ❖ ═══

I T IS NO SURPRISE that the ethical framework I propose for the
sexual sphere of human life has to do with justice and with love.
I have been moving steadily to this all along. It is also no surprise
that I propose, finally, a framework that is not justice *and* love, but
justice *in* loving and in the actions which flow from that love. The
most difficult question to be asked in developing a sexual ethic is
not whether this or that sexual act in the abstract is morally good,
but rather, when is sexual expression appropriate, morally good and
just, in a relationship of any kind. With what kinds of motives, under
what sorts of circumstances, in what forms of relationships, do we
render our sexual selves to one another in ways that are good, true,
right, and just?

Arguing that justice and love should be put together in the ways
I suggest may be counterintuitive. Indeed, strong objections could
be raised: many will say that to make justice a requirement for love
undermines too many understandings of love, especially romantic
and sexual love. It introduces a kind of "tyranny" of justice into the
glory of love. It reduces sex to a contract or to some kind of measure
that is unsuited to what sexuality is. It is too harsh a discipline for the
spontaneity of love, the passion of sexual desire, and the intimacies
marked by joy while safeguarded by privacy. We do not need one
more way for heavy-handed socially constructed norms to shape and
to control personal relations, to the advantage of some but perhaps
the detriment of all.

Yet the undermining of sex and love is not a necessary consequence of a "law" of justice. Like W. H. Auden we might demur:
"Law is the one all gardeners observe.... Law is the wisdom of the
old, The impotent grandfathers shrilly scold...Law, says the priest
with a priestly look...is the words in my priestly book....Law, says
the judge...is The Law." But lovers shyly propose that the law is
"Like love I say.... Like love we can't compel or fly, Like love we often
weep, Like love we seldom keep."[1] The law of justice need carry none
of these meanings, however, as I hope to show.

Justice

Justice, of course, can mean many things. My use of the term is
based simply on the classic fundamental "formal" meaning: to render to each her or his due. This is a more general notion of justice
than our usual focus on certain kinds of justice — for example, distributive justice, legal justice, retributive justice. But it is at the heart
of all forms of justice, and when it comes to sexual justice, this basic
meaning remains relevant.

"Formal" meanings, however, do not go very far in telling us what
really is just. They provide direction, but not sufficiently specific
content to be of much help in guiding our behaviors. They do not,
in short, tell us *what* is "due." This is why whole systems of justice have, in fact, been unjust. Without critical specification of what
"due" means, there can be — in the name of justice — systems in
which slavery is endorsed, certain groups of persons are marginalized, and women and men are "legitimately" treated unequally. It
is presumed and sometimes theoretically defended that it is "due"
some individuals to be treated as masters and "due" others to be
treated as slaves; it is right and just to place some persons on the
margins of society because this affirms what is due them and what
is due others; it is due women to be assigned certain roles and places
in social hierarchies because this accords with what they *are*.

Although I am aware that there are many ways to specify the
requirements of justice — through social contracts, longstanding

1. W. H. Auden, "Law Like Love," in *Selected Poetry of W. H. Auden*, 2nd ed. (New
York: Vintage Books, 1970), 62–64.

customs, certain kinds of noncontradictory reasoning — I move forward here with the perspective I have already introduced. I begin, then, by translating the formal meaning of justice (render to each what is due) into the following basic formal ethical principle: *Persons and groups of persons ought to be affirmed according to their concrete reality, actual and potential.* Depending on their circumstances and the nature of their relationships, the concrete reality of persons can include some particularly relevant aspect of their reality — as, for example, buyer or lender, parent or child, professional caregiver or patient, committed member of a voluntary association, and so on. But even a formal principle like this one is insufficient for discerning what really is just. We therefore need to go on to determine "material" ethical principles of justice — that is, principles that do specify and substantiate what is "due," that do give substantive content to a formal principle. If, as I have argued in the previous chapter, a formal principle for justice in loving is to love in accord with the concrete reality of persons, then material principles of justice will depend on our interpretation of the realities of persons — their needs, capacities, relational claims, vulnerabilities, possibilities.

The Concrete Reality of Persons

Our knowledge of human persons generally, as well as of individual persons, differs and changes, since our interpretations of human experience are historical and social. Moreover, there are differences (not just perceptions of differences) in the experienced concrete realities of individuals and groups — differences that are or ought to be of tremendous importance to us. And who can not notice the myriad nuances of humanity that appear in so many ways in the searching eyes of the lover?

> ... How many loved your moments of glad grace,
> And loved your beauty with love false or true,
> But one man loved the pilgrim soul in you,
> And loved the sorrows of your changing face....[2]

---

2. W. B. Yeats, "When You Are Old," in *The Collected Poems of W. B. Yeats* (New York: Macmillan, 1956), 40–41.

To acknowledge all of these difficulties and possibilities should make us cautious in our interpretations of the concrete reality of persons, but it does not contradict the requirement of discerning as best we can the reality that is part of what every person is or shares in some form, the reality of persons as persons. Love itself may lead us to examine our interpretations of the realities of persons and to test these interpretations with what is available to us in the sources of moral insight that we saw in chapter 5. In this way we can correct or embrace them again.

In general, what I propose is an inductive understanding of the *shared concrete reality of human persons* that includes the following: Each person is constituted with a *complex structure* — embodied, inspirited, with *needs* for food, clothing, and shelter, and at some point usually a capacity for procreation; but also with a *capacity for free choice* and the *ability to think and to feel.*[3] Human persons are also essentially *relational* — with interpersonal and social needs and capacities to open to others, including God, in knowledge, love, and desire, as well as all the emotional capacities that we experience, such as fear, anger, sorrow, hope, joy. Persons exist *in the world*, so that their reality includes their particular *history* and their *location* in social, political, economic, and cultural contexts. Further, persons have some sort of relationship to institutions — without total identification or limitation to systems and institutions, and sometimes

3. How we interpret this complex structure will make a great deal of difference in what we affirm for ourselves and others. As I noted in *Personal Commitments*, 141 n. 2: If, for example, we think that emotions are the primary element in the human personality, we will have a different view of human well-being than if we think that each one's reason or rationality is primary. Similarly, if we think that free choice is of central importance to every person, we will want for persons something quite different than if we think that persons have a place in an organic society where their roles are prescribed and the importance of freedom is negligible. I cannot resolve such differences here, though my overall theory in this book not only raises the questions but attempts to offer a coherent view of some moral requirements based on an interpretation of the reality of persons. I should add, also, that I am not addressing here the question of who should be treated as persons if not everyone we think of as a person has the possibility of exercising the capacities I am describing (such as thinking, choosing, procreating, etc.). To describe what belongs to "personhood" is a different task from identifying the pool of entities that are to be treated as persons. For the latter, all those born of persons can be included, whatever their present capacities or capacities for development. But this involves a discussion of another set of issues than the ones that I am addressing in this volume.

with only a rejecting relationship. And the reality of persons includes not only their present *actuality* but their *positive potentiality* for development, for human and individual flourishing; as well as their *vulnerability* to diminishment. Finally, every person is *unique* as well as a common sharer in humanity. A just love of persons will take all of these aspects of persons into account, though some will be more important than others, depending on the context and the nature of a relationship.

Obligating Features of Personhood

Contemporary understandings of the human person lead us to a special focus on at least two basic features of human personhood: features that can be called *autonomy* and *relationality*.[4] "Basic" here does not imply that we can understand fully what the "essence" of the human person is. There is a wariness in contemporary Western thought about even acknowledging that there are "essences" to be known, let alone essences that *we* can know. My attempt to delineate features of what it means to be a human person recognizes the partiality of our knowledge, the historical changeability of knowledge and the variations of human self-understandings from culture to culture and across time. Nonetheless, it seems to me that we cannot reasonably assert either that we know nothing at all about the human person as person, or that we have nothing of a shared knowledge in this regard.

It is not necessarily to abstract from the concrete reality of individual persons to consider what is central to the human personality.

---

4. My approach might at least meet the pragmatic level of "strategic essentialism," in the sense in which Serene Jones and others use this term. See Serene Jones, *Feminism and Christian Theology: Cartographies of Grace* (Minneapolis: Fortress, 2000). Yet my concern is not primarily with speculative knowledge; it is with the kind of knowledge that will tell us what is harmful and what helpful in human life. To some extent, this corresponds with Beverly Harrison's view of justice as a primary metaphor of right relationship, one that shapes the *telos* of a good community and animates Christian moral sensibilities. See Beverly Wildung Harrison, *Justice in the Making: Feminist Social Ethics* (Louisville: Westminster John Knox, 2004), 16. I may be even closer to Martha Nussbaum's delineation of human "functional capabilities" approach, since Nussbaum and I share not only a social ethical aim but a belief in some rock-bottom capabilities and needs for human beings that demand respect and affirmation. See Martha C. Nussbaum, *Sex and Social Justice* (New York: Oxford University Press, 1999), 41–42.

Indeed, such considerations may illuminate each one's concrete individual reality and may reveal some of the central requirements of love, and sexual love, of any person as a person. "Obligating features" of persons constitute the basis of requirement to *respect* persons, in whatever way we relate to them, sexually or otherwise. Autonomy and relationality in particular are "obligating features" because they *ground* an obligation to respect persons as *ends in themselves* and forbid, therefore, the use of persons as mere means.[5] This claim bears exploration. I could argue here that persons are of unconditional value, ends in themselves, because they are created so and loved so by God, who reveals to us a command and a call to treat one another as ends, and not only as means. My approach is in an important sense warranted by this belief, and I am attempting to provide a way of understanding it. Yet I also think that a plausible elaboration of what characterizes humans — created and beloved as we are — is also accessible to those who stand in diverse faith traditions or no faith tradition at all. So I continue to explore and to argue on the basis of experience and our systematic understandings of experience: First, persons are ends in themselves because they are autonomous in the sense that they have a capacity for *free choice*. Why? Because freedom of choice as we experience it is a capacity for *self-determination* as embodied, inspirited beings, which means a capacity to choose not only our own actions but our ends and our loves. It is a capacity therefore to determine the meaning of our own lives and, within limits, our destiny. It is a capacity to set our own agenda, whether it is one that is good for us and others or not. Hence, for me to treat another human person as a mere means is to violate her insofar as she is autonomous; it is to attempt to absorb her completely into my agenda, rather than respecting the one that is her own.

Secondly, a human capacity for *relationship* (or relationality) also grounds an obligation to respect persons as ends in themselves. Why

---

5. By identifying persons as "ends in themselves" I do not assume that they are sufficient in themselves or that we can understand them in a vacuum, all by themselves. My second obligating feature shows this explicitly. More than this, however, I consider it quite possible to exist as a being that is an end it itself and yet to exist relative to God. See Farley, "A Feminist Version of Respect for Persons," *Journal of Feminist Studies in Religion* 9 (Spring/Fall 1993): 183–98; also, Farley, *Compassionate Respect: A Feminist Approach to Medical Ethics and Other Questions* (New York: Paulist, 2002), 36–39.

again? It is generally acknowledged that individuals do not just survive or thrive in relations to others; they cannot exist without some form of fundamental relatedness to others.[6] This generally implies dependence on others, yet the *capacity* for relation is a capacity to reach beyond ourselves to other beings, especially to other persons. We are who we are not only because we can to some degree determine ourselves to be so by our freedom but because we are transcendent of ourselves through our capacities to know and to love. The relational aspect of persons is not finally only extrinsic but intrinsic, the radical possibility of coming into relation, into union, with all that can be known and loved — and especially with other persons, including God, where union can take the form of communion, knowing and being known, loving and being loved. As such, we are not bounded, not complete in ourselves once and for all, as if our world could be closed upon itself. We remain radically open to union with others, through knowledge and love; our interior world is transcendent of itself, though we hold also a whole world within ourselves. To respect the world that we are and the world we are becoming requires respecting ourselves and other persons as ends, not only as means. Whether or not pre-modern, modern, or postmodern philosophies find settled selves or unsettled selves (a series of selves with no continuity or anchor), it is awe before the world of the self that can generate respect and even reverence, if only we see it.[7]

Another way to say all of this is that as persons we are *terminal centers, ends in ourselves, because in some way we both transcend ourselves and yet belong to ourselves.* It is by our freedom that we transcend ourselves, introduce something new, beyond our past and present. By our freedom, we also possess ourselves; our selves and our actions are in some sense our own. Besides the place of freedom in self-transcendence and self-possession, it is also in and through our relationality that we as humans both transcend and possess ourselves; we belong to ourselves yet we belong to others to whom we

---

6. Although I am interpreting relationality to refer to relation by knowledge and love, I do not thereby deny the necessary relatedness that includes dependence on God for one's very existence.

7. See Farley, "How Shall We Love in a Postmodern World?" *Annual of the Society of Christian Ethics* (Society of Christian Ethics, 1994), 3–19.

have stretched our being through our knowing love and our loving knowledge. In knowledge and love, and in being known and being loved, we are centered both within and without — both in what we love and in ourselves, as we hold what we love in our hearts. The capacity to love one another and all things, and to love what is sacredly transcendent and immanent (that is, the divine), makes persons worthy of respect. Each and every person is of unconditional value. Each person is a whole world in herself, yet her world is in what she loves. This is what interiority means for human persons, and what it means in our relationships one with another.[8]

Freedom and relationality, then, are the obligating features that *ground* any norms we articulate for general ethics or sexual ethics. Beings with these features ought not be completely scooped up into someone else's agenda. They ought not be treated as mere means but *also* as ends in themselves. Moreover, freedom and relationality as features of human persons are profoundly *connected* with one another: we cannot grow in freedom except in some nurturing relationships; and freedom ultimately is for the sake of relationships — the loves, the relationships we finally choose to identify with in our deepest selves. Together autonomy (or freedom) and relationality also provide the *content* for most of the basic norms for right loving and the basic moral norms for sexual ethics. Norms for a general sexual ethic, then, must not only satisfy the demands of these two features of personhood; they must serve to specify more clearly the meaning of the features.

Despite all that I have said above, it may not be superfluous to draw one general conclusion here regarding norms for sexuality. In chapter 4 I spoke of the multiple meanings and aims, or motivations, that are possible for human sexual activity and relationships — some distortive and destructive, some accurate and creative. Now, given our explorations of just love and desire, just sexual love and desire, we can say that the aims of sexuality ought to accord with, or at the very least, not violate the concrete reality of human persons. If they

---

8. I do not deny a kind of interiority in all beings, or certainly in higher level animals other than humans. I am here, however, talking about human persons, for which there is a kind of interiority that appears to be distinctive to the species.

do so accord, they will not be destructive or distortive. Also in chapter 4 I identified elements that characterize and can belong to much of human sexual experience. These included not only embodiment and emotions, but pleasure, desire and love, language and communication, procreation, and power. Pleasure, communication, the union of love and its intimacy, empowerment, and a desire for offspring are each great human goods. If sex is an expression of love that is just, then each and all of these can be the aim or part of the aim of sexual desire and activity.[9] Whether they are so in a way that is just will be clearer when we identify more specific ethical norms for sexual activities and relationships. Power, especially in interpersonal relationships can be, but need not be, a great human good. Whether and when it is good in sexual relations must also be determined by more specific norms.

Norms for Just Sex

Some preliminary clarifications are important for understanding the specific norms for a sexual ethic. First, the norms that I have in mind are not merely ideals; they are bottom-line requirements. Second, and as a qualification of the first, all of these norms admit of degrees. This means that there is a sense in which they are stringent requirements, but they are also ideals. In both senses, they are all part of justice. That is, they can be understood in different contexts as norms of what I shall call "minimal" or "maximal" justice. While minimal justice is always required, maximal justice can go beyond this to what is "fitting." Maximal justice may, in fact, point to an ideal that exceeds the exacting requirement of minimal justice.[10] Third, the

---

9. I am not espousing the view that sexual activity can be justified only when it aims at or is at least open to the possibility of procreation. I discuss this again in the context of one of the specific norms that follows.

10. What I mean by "fitting" may not be completely clear. Both minimal and maximal justice have to do with the concrete realities of persons and what is "due" them. With minimal justice, what is due is a bottom-line stringent requirement; maximal justice incorporates minimal justice but goes beyond it. However, simply "going beyond" may not mean greater justice. There are ways in which we can think we are exceeding the demands of justice, but rendering "more" may no longer be justice at all; it may be injustice if it is not fitting or appropriate for an individual or group. It may in fact be destructive. Thus, for example, a teacher may go beyond what is ordinarily required by

specific norms are not mutually exclusive. Although each of them emphasizes something the others do not, they nonetheless overlap enough that, as we shall see, some sexual behaviors and relationships are governed by more than one norm. Fourth, since humans are embodied spirits, inspirited bodies, theirs is an embodied autonomy and an embodied relationality. The norms that I will lay out, therefore, are to be understood as requiring respect for an embodied as well as inspirited reality. I turn now to the specific norms that I propose for a contemporary human and Christian sexual ethic.

1. Do No Unjust Harm

The first general ethical norm we may identify is the obligation not to harm persons unjustly.[11] This is grounded in both of the obligating features of personhood, for it is because persons are persons that we experience awe of one another and the obligation of respect. "Do not harm" echoes through the experience of "do not kill" the other. To harm persons may be to violate who they are as ends in themselves.[12] But there are many forms that harm can take — physical,

---

some of her students in terms of assistance; but her "going beyond" may or may not be just. Everything depends on the concrete realities of the students, what is appropriate in a professional/student relationship, and what the teacher can reasonably do, taking into account the legitimate demands of other students. She may, if she provides "too much" assistance, be harming her students because she does not encourage their own creativity and development of skills. Hence, "maximal" justice "goes beyond" in ways that are appropriate or fitting — as when someone is in terrible need, with no particular further claim on someone else to meet that need, but someone helps out anyway. He goes the "extra mile" because it is both needed and appropriate; it is fitting for the persons involved, the situation, and his capabilities. Some might call this "supererogatory," above and beyond any real moral obligation; but there are some instances (for example, in the demands of friendship as opposed to ordinary demands in relation to anyone) where there really is another level of obligation, though not as strict as the obligation involved in minimal justice.

11. Harm "unjustly" helps to clarify that the injunction "do no harm" is not a general absolute prohibition. We do harm persons when the harm is necessary to bring about a greater good. An example of this is in the practice of medicine. Almost every medical treatment (especially surgery) involves some harm to a patient, but it is a harm that is "justified" for a significant greater good.

12. Of course, we also have obligations not to harm other beings besides persons. We consider some of them to have intrinsic worth — as, for example, nonhuman animals and the whole network of beings that constitute our "natural environment." I do not want here to engage the discussion of whether some of these beings are of "unconditional" worth, though when the lives of human persons conflict with the lives of nonhuman beings, I am ready to say that the worth of persons takes priority. This is a

psychological, spiritual, relational. It can also take the form of failure to support, to assist, to care for, to honor, in ways that are required by reason of context and relationship. I include all of these forms in this norm.

In the sexual sphere, "do no unjust harm" takes on particular significance. Here each person is vulnerable in ways that go deep within. As Karen Lebacqz has said, "Sexuality has to do with vulnerability. Eros, the desire for another, the passion that accompanies the wish for sexual expression, makes one vulnerable. . . . capable of being wounded.[13] And how may we be wounded or harmed? We know the myriad ways. Precisely because sexuality is so intimate to persons, vulnerability exists in our embodiment and in the depths of our spirits. Desires for pleasure and for power can become bludgeons in sexual relations. As inspirited bodies we are vulnerable to sexual exploitation, battering, rape, enslavement, and negligence regarding what we know we must do for sex to be "safe sex." As embodied spirits we are vulnerable to deceit, betrayal, disparity in committed loves, debilitating "bonds" of desire,[14] seduction, the pain of unfulfillment. We have seen in previous chapters the role sex can play in conflict, the ways in which it is connected with shame, the potential it has for instrumentalization and objectification. We have also seen human vulnerability in the context of gender exclusionary practices and gender judgments: "Terrible things are done to those who deviate."[15]

Actions and social arrangements that are typically thought to be harmful in the sexual sphere include all forms of violence, as

---

topic for another day, however. What I am concerned with here is not only that humans are ends in themselves, but that they are so because of the obligating features of their personhood. It is therefore precisely because humans are self-transcendent yet belong to themselves that I identify and ground my norm that prohibits unjust harming of them.

13. Lebacqz, "Appropriate Vulnerability," 436.

14. See Jessica Benjamin, *The Bonds of Love: Psychoanalysis, Feminism, and the Problem of Domination* (New York: Pantheon Books, 1988); and Benjamin, "The Bonds of Love: Rational Violence and Erotic Domination," in *The Future of Difference*, ed. Hester Eisenstein and Alice Jardine (New Brunswick, NJ: Rutgers University Press, 1985), 41–70.

15. Christine M. Korsgaard, "A Note on the Value of Gender-Identification," in *Women, Culture and Development*, ed. Martha C. Nussbaum and Jonathan Glover (Oxford: Clarendon Press, 1995), 401–3.

well as pornography, prostitution, sexual harassment, pedophilia, sadomasochism. Most of these are controversial today, so that they cannot be rejected out of hand, judged without assessment of their injustice or justice. Many of these are governed by other principles for a sexual ethic that we have yet to explore. I will therefore return to them again, though all too briefly, placing them in the whole of the framework for sexual ethics that I am proposing.

"Do no unjust harm" goes a long way toward specifying a sexual ethic, but not far enough. It is necessary to identify additional principles for a sexual ethic that aims to take account of the complex concrete realities of persons. I said above that autonomy and relationality, two equally primordial features of human persons, provide the ground and the content for sexual ethics. They provide a ground or basis, as we have seen, for the principle that forbids unjustifiable harm. Together they yield six more specific and positive norms: a requirement of free choice, based on the requirement to respect persons' autonomy, and five further norms that derive from the requirement of respect for persons' relationality.[16] Hence, we move from our first norm, "do no unjust harm" to a second norm for a sexual ethic: freedom of choice.

2. Free Consent

We have already seen the importance of freedom (autonomy, or a capacity for self-determination) as a ground for a general obligation to respect persons as ends in themselves. This capacity for self-determination, however, also undergirds a more specific norm. The requirement articulated in this norm is all the more grave because it directly safeguards the autonomy of persons as embodied and inspirited, as transcendent and free.[17] I refer here to the particular obligation to respect the right of human persons to determine

---

16. See below the diagram of all the norms on page 231.

17. In some approaches to medical ethics, for example, the principle requiring respect for persons reduces to respect for a person's autonomy, and the primary specific rule becomes the requirement for informed consent in relation to medical treatment. It is a mistake, however, to *equate* respect for persons with respect for autonomy. This need not lessen the importance of respect for autonomy as an essential part of what respect for persons as persons requires. See Farley, *Compassionate Respect: A Feminist Approach to Medical Ethics and Other Questions* (New York: Paulist, 2002), 22–44.

their own actions and their relationships in the sexual sphere of their lives.[18] This right or this obligation to respect individual autonomy sets a minimum but absolute requirement for the free consent of sexual partners. This means, of course, that rape, violence, or any harmful use of power against unwilling victims is never justified. Moreover, seduction and manipulation of persons who have limited capacity for choice because of immaturity, special dependency, or loss of ordinary power, are ruled out. The requirement of free consent, then, opposes sexual harassment, pedophilia, and other instances of disrespect for persons' capacity for, and right to, freedom of choice.

Derivative from the obligation to respect free consent on the part of sexual partners are also other ethical norms such as a requirement for truth-telling, promise-keeping, and respect for privacy. *Privacy*, despite contentions over its legal meanings, requires respect for what today is named "bodily integrity." "Do not touch, invade, or use" is the requirement unless an individual freely consents.[19] What this recognizes is that respect for embodied freedom is necessary if there is to be respect for the intimacy of the sexual self.

Whatever other rationales can be given for principles of *truth-telling* and *promise-keeping*, their violation limits and hence hinders the freedom of choice of the other person: deception and betrayal are ultimately coercive. If I lie to you, or dissemble when it comes to communicating my intentions and desires, and you act on the basis of what I have told you, I have limited your options and hence in an

---

18. I realize I am introducing yet another ethical term here: "right." It goes beyond the scope of this volume to try to clarify this. I am therefore going to assume some general understanding of a "right" as a claim — whether legal or moral, grounded in the law, in a social contract, or in what human persons are. In my context here I acknowledge moral rights, claims that place moral obligations on others to respect, secure, and protect. Some of these claims can and ought to be secured also by law.

19. A "do not touch" rule holds differently in the sexual sphere than in the medical (although they sometimes come together, of course). In the latter, it undergirds the requirement of informed consent for treatment, though it admits of exceptions in cases of emergency, public health threat, and so forth. As far as I know, the term "bodily integrity" was first used in relation to autonomy (to establish personal physical boundaries) by Beverly Wildung Harrison. See her "Theology of Pro-Choice: A Feminist Perspective," *The Witness* 64 (September 1981): 20; also, *A Right to Choose: Toward a New Ethic of Abortion* (Boston: Beacon, 1983); *Making the Connections*, ed. Carol S. Robb (Boston: Beacon, 1985), 129–31. Needless to say, while Harrison's appeal to the concept was frequently in the context of abortion, it has much broader meaning — for her and for others.

important sense coerced you. Similarly, if I make a promise to you with no intention of keeping the promise, and you make decisions on the basis of this promise, I have deceived, coerced, and betrayed you.[20] Along with the requirement of free consent, then, these other obligations belong to a sexual ethic as well.

Relationality, I have argued, is equiprimordial with autonomy as an essential feature of human personhood, and along with autonomy grounds the obligation to respect persons as ends in themselves. Like autonomy, relationality does more than ground obligations to respect persons as persons; it specifies the content of this obligation. To treat persons as ends and not as mere means includes respecting their capacities and needs for relationship. Sexual activity and sexual pleasure are instruments and modes of relation; they can enhance relationships or hinder them, contribute to them and express them. Sexual activity and pleasure are optional goods for human persons in the sense that they are not absolute, peremptory goods which could never be subordinated to other goods, or for the sake of other goods be let go; but they are, or certainly can be, very great goods, mediating relationality and the general well-being of persons.

Hence, insofar as one person is sexually active in relation to another, sex must not violate relationality, but serve it. Another way of saying this is that it is not sufficient to respect the free choice of sexual partners. In addition to "do no harm" and the requirement of free consent, relationality as a characteristic of human persons yields five specific norms for sexual activity and sexual relationships: mutuality, equality, commitment, fruitfulness, and what I will designate in general terms, "social justice." For an adequate contemporary sexual ethic, we need to explore the meaning and implications of each of these norms.

3. Mutuality

Respect for persons together in sexual activity requires mutuality of participation. It is easy for us today to sing the songs of mutuality in celebration of sexual love. We are in disbelief when we

---

20. This is different from making a promise and then being unable to fulfill it, either because of change in circumstances, weakness on the part of the promisor, or whatever.

learn that it has not always been so. Yet traditional interpretations of heterosexual sex are steeped in images of the male as active and the female passive, the woman as receptacle and the man as fulfiller, the woman as ground and the man as seed. No other interpretation of the polarity between the sexes has had so long and deep-seated an influence on men's and women's self-understandings. Today we think such descriptions quaint or appalling, and we recognize the danger in them. For despite the seeming contradiction between the active/passive model of sexual relations and the sometime interpretations of women's sexuality as insatiable, the model formed imaginations, actions, and roles which in turn determined that he who embodied the active principle was greater than she who simply waited — for sex, for gestation, for birthing which was not of her doing and not under her control.

Today we believe we have a completely different view. We have learned that male and female reproductive organs do not signal activity only for one and passivity for the other; nor do universalizable male and female character traits signal this. We can even appreciate all the ways in which, even at the physical level, men's bodies receive, encircle, embrace, and all the ways women's bodies are active, giving, penetrating. Today we also know that the possibilities of mutuality exist for many forms of relationship — whether heterosexual or gay, whether with genital sex or the multiple other ways of embodying our desires and our loves. The key for us has become not activity/passivity but active receptivity and receptive activity — each partner active, each one receptive. Activity and receptivity partake of one another, so that activity can be a response to something received (like loveliness), and receptivity can be a kind of activity, as in "receiving" a guest.[21]

Underlying the norm of mutuality is a view of sexual desire that does not see it as a search only for the pleasure to be found in the relief of libidinal tension, although it may include this. Human sexuality, rather, because it is fundamentally relational, seeks ultimately

---

21. See Gabriel Marcel, *Creative Fidelity*, trans. Robert Rosenthal (New York: Noonday, 1964), 89–91.

what contemporary philosophers have called a "double reciprocal incarnation," or mutuality of desire and embodied union.[22] No one can
deny that sex may, in fact, serve many functions and be motivated by
many kinds of desire. Nonetheless, central to its meaning, necessary
for its fulfillment, and normative for its morality when it is within
an interpersonal relation is some form and degree of mutuality.

Yet we have learned to be cautious before too high a rhetoric of
mutuality, too many songs in praise of it. Like active/passive relations, mutuality, too, has its dangers. Insofar as, for example, we
assume it requires total and utter self-disclosure, we know that harm
lurks unless sexual relations have matured into justifiable and mutual trust.[23] Insofar as we think that sex is just and good only if
mutuality is *perfected*, we know that personal incapacities large and
small can undercut it. We know that patience, as well as trust, and
perhaps unconditional love are all needed for mutuality to become
what we dream it can be. But what is asked of us, demanded of us,
for the mutuality of a one night stand, or of a short-term affair, or of
a lifetime of committed love, differs in kind and degree.

Indeed, the mutuality that makes sexual love and activity just
(and, one must add, that makes for "good sex" in the colloquial sense
of the term) can be expressed in many ways; and it does admit of degrees. No matter what, however, it entails some degree of mutuality
in the attitudes and actions of both partners. It entails some form
of activity and receptivity, giving and receiving — two sides of one
shared reality on the part of and within both persons. It requires, to
some degree, mutuality of desire, action, and response. Two liberties
meet, two bodies meet, two hearts come together — metaphorical
and real descriptions of sexual mutuality. Part of each person's ethical task, or the shared task in each relationship, is to determine the

---

22. The concept was originally Sartre's, although he used it to refer more to the
arousal of sexual attraction and desire. See Jean Paul Sartre, *Being and Nothingness*,
trans. Hazel E. Barnes (New York: Philosophical Library, 1966). For more contemporary
uses and adaptations of this, see Thomas Nagel, "Sexual Perversion," in *Philosophy
of Sex: Contemporary Readings*, ed. Alan Soble (Totowa, NJ: Littlefield Adams, 1980),
76–88; Solomon, "Sexual Paradigms," ibid., 89–98; Janice Moulton, "Sexual Behavior:
Another Position," ibid., 110–18.
23. For a discussion of this danger in a wider context, see Richard Sennett,
"Destructive Gemeinschaft," ibid., 299–321.

threshold at which this norm must be respected, and below which it is violated.

4. Equality

Our considerations of mutuality lead to yet another norm that is based on respect for relationality. Free choice and mutuality are not sufficient to respect persons in sexual relations. A condition for real freedom and a necessary qualification of mutuality is equality. The equality that is at stake here is equality of power. Major inequalities in social and economic status, age and maturity, professional identity, interpretations of gender roles, and so forth, can render sexual relations inappropriate and unethical primarily because they entail power inequalities — and hence, unequal vulnerability, dependence, and limitation of options. The requirement of equality, like the requirement of free consent, rules out treating a partner as property, a commodity, or an element in market exchange. Jean-Paul Sartre describes, for example, a supposedly free and mutual exchange between persons, but an exchange marked by unacknowledged domination and subordination: "It is just that one of them pretends . . . not to notice that the Other is forced by the constraint of needs to sell himself as a material object."[24]

Of course here, too, equality need not be, may seldom be, perfect equality. Nonetheless, it has to be close enough, balanced enough, for each to appreciate the uniqueness and difference of the other, and for each to respect one another as ends in themselves. If the power differential is too great, dependency will limit freedom, and mutuality will go awry. This norm, like the others, can illuminate the injury or evil that characterizes situations of sexual harassment, psychological and physical abuse, at least some forms of prostitution, and loss of self in a process that might have led to genuine love.

5. Commitment

Strong arguments can be made for a fifth norm in sexual ethics, also derivative of a responsibility for relationality. At the heart of

---

24. Sartre, *Critique of Dialectical Reason,* trans. A. Sheridan-Smith (London: NLB, 1976), 110.

the Christian community's understanding of the place of sexuality in human and Christian life has been the notion that some form of commitment, some form of covenant or at least contract, must characterize relations that include a sexual dimension. In the past, this commitment, of course, was largely identified with heterosexual marriage. It was tied to the need for a procreative order and a discipline of unruly sexual desire. It was valued more for the sake of family arrangements than for the sake of the individuals themselves. Even when it was valued in itself as a realization of the life of the church in relation to Jesus Christ, it carried what today are unwanted connotations of inequality in relations between men and women. It is possible, nonetheless, that when all meanings of commitment in sexual relations are sifted, we are left with powerful reasons to retain it as an ethical norm.

As we have already noted, contemporary understandings of sexuality point to different possibilities for sex than were seen in the past — possibilities of growth in the human person, personal garnering of creative power with sexuality as a dimension not an obstacle, and the mediation of human relationship. On the other hand, no one argues that sex *necessarily* leads to creative power in the individual or depth of union between persons. Sexual desire left to itself does not seem able even to sustain its own ardor. In the past, persons feared that sexual desire would be too great; in the present, the rise of impotency and sexual boredom makes persons more likely to fear that sexual desire will be too little.[25] There is growing evidence that sex is neither the indomitable drive that early Christians (and others) thought it was nor the primordial impulse of early psychoanalytic theory. When it was culturally repressed, it seemed an inexhaustible power, underlying other motivations, always struggling to express itself in one way or another. Now that it is less repressed, more and more free

---

25. I am not gainsaying Foucault's critique of the "repressive principle" here. In fact, I may be reinforcing it, since so-called "repression" may construct the sort of sexuality that is the opposite of what repression aims to do. Moreover, the sorts of waning sexual desire that I describe for today may signal a different kind of social construction of sexual desire and sexual possibility: it may be the result not of too much sex but of social and cultural emphasis on orgasm as the sign of acceptable and valued sex. Orgasmic and other expectations of sexual performance may actually undercut the power of sex.

and in the open, it is easier to see other complex motivations behind it, and to recognize its inability in and of itself to satisfy the affective yearning of persons. More and more readily comes the conclusion drawn by many that sexual desire without interpersonal love leads to disappointment and a growing disillusionment. The other side of this conclusion is that sexuality is an expression of something beyond itself. Its power is a power for union, and its desire is a desire for intimacy.

One of the central insights from contemporary ethical reflection on sexuality is that norms of justice cannot have as their whole goal to set limits to the power and expression of human sexuality. Sexuality is of such importance in human life that it needs to be nurtured, sustained, as well as disciplined, channeled, controlled. There appear to be at least two ways which persons have found to keep alive the power of sexual desire within them. One is through novelty of persons with whom they are in sexual relation. Moving from one partner to another prevents boredom, sustains sexual interest and the possibility of pleasure. A second way is through relationship extended sufficiently through time to allow the incorporation of sexuality into a shared life and an enduring love. The second way seems possible only through commitment.

Both sobering evidence of the inability of persons to blend their lives together, and weariness with the high rhetoric that has traditionally surrounded human covenants, yield a contemporary reluctance to evaluate the two ways of sustaining sexual desire and living sexual union. At the very least it may be said, however, that although brief encounters open a lover to relation, they cannot mediate the kind of union — of knowing and being known, loving and being loved — for which human relationality offers the potential. Moreover, the pursuit of multiple relations precisely for the sake of sustaining sexual desire risks violating the norms of free consent and mutuality, risks measuring others as apt means to our own ends, and risks inner disconnection from any kind of life-process of our own or in relation with others. Discrete moments of union are not valueless (though they may be so, and may even be disvalues), but they can serve to isolate us from others and from ourselves.

On the other hand, there is reason to believe that sexuality can be the object of commitment, that sexual desire can be incorporated into a covenanted love without distortion or loss, but rather, with gain, with enhancement. Given all the caution learned from contemporary experience, we may still hope that our freedom is sufficiently powerful to gather up our love and give it a future; that thereby our sexual desire can be nurtured into a tenderness that has not forgotten passion. We may still believe that to try to use our freedom in this way is to be faithful to the love that arises in us or even the yearning that rises from us. Rhetoric should be limited regarding commitment, however, for particular forms of commitment are themselves only means, not ends. As Robin Morgan notes regarding the possibility of process only with an enduring relation, "Commitment gives you the leverage to bring about change — and the time in which to do it."[26]

A Christian sexual ethic, then, may well identify commitment as a norm for sexual relations and activity. Even if commitment is only required in the form of a commitment not to harm one's partner, and a commitment to free consent, mutuality, and equality (as I have described these above), it is reasonable and necessary. More than this, however, is necessary if our concerns are for the wholeness of the human person — for a way of living that is conducive to the integration of all of life's important aspects, and for the fulfillment of sexual desire in the highest forms of friendship. Given these concerns, the norm must be a committed love.

6. *Fruitfulness*

A sixth norm derivative from the obligating feature of relationality is what I call "fruitfulness." Although the traditional procreative norm of sexual relations and activity no longer holds absolute sway in Christian sexual ethics in either Protestant or Roman Catholic traditions, there remains a special concern for responsible reproduction of the human species. Traditional arguments that if there is sex it must

---

26. Robin Morgan, "A Marriage Map," *Ms. Magazine* 11 (July–August 1982): 204. For further elaboration on the meaning of interpersonal commitments, see Farley, *Personal Commitments*. In this book, there are ways of describing commitment itself that could allow it to be thought of as at least part of an end — for example the end of love and friendship. It has or can have intrinsic value in that it is constituted by the one giving to the other her "word," with a new form of relationship now established.

be procreative have changed to arguments that if sex is procreative it must be within a context that assures responsible care of offspring. The connection between sex and reproduction is a powerful one, for it allows individuals to reproduce and to build families; it allows a sharing of life full enough to issue in new lives; and it allows the human species to perpetuate itself. Relationality in the form of sexual reproduction, moreover, does not end with the birth of children; it stretches to include the rearing of children, the initiation of new generations into a culture and civilization, and the ongoing building of the human community.

At first glance, it appears that "procreation" belongs only to, is only possible for, some persons; and even for them, it has come to seem quite optional. How, then, can it constitute a norm for sexual activity and relations? Even if it were recognized as a norm for fertile heterosexual couples, what would this mean for infertile heterosexual couples or for heterosexual couples who choose not to have children, for gays and lesbians, for single persons, for ambiguously gendered persons? For these other individuals and partners, would it signal, as it has in the past, a lesser form of sex and lesser forms of sexual relationships? Or is it possible that a norm of fruitfulness can and ought to characterize all sexual relationships?

It is certainly true that all persons can participate in the rearing of new generations; and some of those who cannot reproduce in traditional ways do even have their own biological children by means of the growing array of reproductive technologies — from infertility treatments to artificial insemination to *in vitro* fertilization to surrogate mothering. All of this is not only true but significant. Yet an ethically normative claim on sexual partners to reproduce in any of these ways seems unwarranted.

Something more is at stake. Beyond the kind of fruitfulness that brings forth biological children, there is a kind of fruitfulness that is a measure, perhaps, of all interpersonal love. Love between persons violates relationality if it closes in upon itself and refuses to open to a wider community of persons. Without fruitfulness of some kind, any significant interpersonal love (not only sexual love) becomes an *égoisme à deux*. If it is completely sterile in every way, it threatens the love and the relationship itself. But love brings new life to those who love. The new life within the relationship of those who share it may move beyond itself in countless ways: nourishing other relationships; providing goods, services, and beauty for others; informing the fruitful work lives of the partners in relation; helping to raise other people's children; and on and on. All of these ways and more may constitute the fruit of a love for which persons in relation are responsible. A just love requires the recognition of this as the potentiality of lovers; and it affirms it, each for the other, both together in the fecundity of their love. Interpersonal love, then, and perhaps in a special way, sexual love insofar as it is just, must be fruitful.

The articulation of this norm, however, moves us to another perspective in the development of a sexual ethic. There are obligations in justice that the wider community owes to those who choose sexual relationships. Hence, our final norm is of a different kind.

7. Social Justice

This norm derives from our obligation to respect relationality, but not only from this. It derives more generally from the obligation to respect all persons as ends in themselves, to respect their autonomy and relationality, and thus not to harm them but to support them. A social justice norm in the context of sexual ethics relates not specifically to the justice between sexual partners. It points to the kind of justice that everyone in a community or society is obligated to affirm for its members as sexual beings. Whether persons are single or married, gay or straight, bisexual or ambiguously gendered, old or young, abled or challenged in the ordinary forms of sexual expression, they have claims to respect from the Christian community as well as the wider society. These are claims to freedom from unjust harm, equal protection under the law, an equitable share in the goods and services available to others, and freedom of choice in their sexual lives — within the limits of not harming or infringing on the just claims of the concrete realities of others. Whatever the sexual status of persons, their needs for incorporation into the community, for psychic security and basic well-being, make the same claims for social cooperation among us as do those of us all. This is why I call the final norm "social justice." If our loves for one another are to be just, then this norm obligates us all.

There is one way in which, of course, this norm qualifies sexual relationships themselves, obligating sexual partners as well as the community around them. That is, sexual partners have always to be concerned about not harming "third parties." As Annette Baier observes, "in love there are always third parties, future lovers, children who may be born to one of the lovers, their lovers and their children."[27] At the very least, a form of "social justice" requires of sexual partners that they take responsibility for the consequences of their love and their sexual activity — whether the consequences are pregnancy and children, violation of the claims that others may have on each of them, public health concerns, and so forth. No love, or at least no great love, is just for "the two of us,"[28] so that even failure to share in some way beyond the two of us the fruits of love may be a failure in justice.

My focus in articulating this norm, however, is primarily on the larger social world in which sexual relationships are formed and sustained. It includes, therefore, the sorts of concerns I identified above, but larger concerns as well. A case in point is the struggle for gender equality and (in particular) women's rights in our own society and around the world. This is relevant to the sexual ethic I am proposing because it has a great deal to do with respect for gender and sexuality as it is lived in concrete contexts of sexual and gender injustice.

Here we could identify numerous other issues of utmost importance. Sexual and domestic violence might head the list, both at home and abroad.[29] But it would include also racial violence that is perpetrated on men and women and that all too often has to do with false sexual stereotypes.[30] Development, globalization, and gender

---

27. Annette C. Baier, *Moral Prejudices: Essays on Ethics* (Cambridge, MA: Harvard University Press, 1994), 147.

28. Mary McDermott Shideler, *The Theology of Romantic Love: A Study in the Writings of Charles Williams* (Grand Rapids, MI: Eerdmans, 1962), 115.

29. The many writings of Marie Fortune provide descriptive and normative analyses of these issues. See especially the new version of her earliest work on sexual violence as "the unmentionable sin," in Marie Marshall Fortune, *Sexual Violence: The Sin Revisited* (Cleveland: Pilgrim, 2005). For considerations of these issues internationally, see Mary John Mananzan et al., eds., *Women Resisting Violence: Spirituality for Life* (Maryknoll, NY: Orbis, 1996).

30. See, for example, the diverse essays in Emilie M. Townes, ed., *A Troubling in my Soul* (Maryknoll, NY: Orbis, 1993).

bias would be high on the list of the issues I have in mind.[31] The myths and doctrines of religious and cultural traditions that reinforce gender bias and unjust constriction of gender roles become important here as well.[32] Included, too, must be the disproportionate burden that women bear in the world-wide AIDS pandemic.[33]

We have already seen in the previous chapter the kinds of injustices inflicted on persons whose gender and sexuality do not fall into the usual categories. We should add issues surrounding the explosion of reproductive technologies — many of which have proven to offer a great benefit for individuals, but many of which remain questionable, such as technologies for sex-selection.[34] Other issues also require moral assessment, such as the availability (or not) of contraceptives, and the repercussions for some women of the marketing of male remedies for impotence. It is neither possible nor necessary to detail all of these issues here. My point is only that they, too, fall within the concerns of an adequate human and Christian sexual ethic. They signal social and communal obligations not to harm one another unjustly and to support one another in what is necessary for basic well-being and a reasonable level of human flourishing for all. These obligations stretch to a common good — one that encompasses the sexual sphere along with the other significant spheres of human life.

In summary, what I have tried to offer here is a framework for sexual ethics based on norms of justice — those norms which govern all

---

31. See, for example: Nussbaum, *Sex and Social Justice*; Nussbaum and Glover, *Women, Culture, and Human Development*; Amartya Sen, "Over 100 Million Women Are Missing," *New York Review of Books* (December 20, 1990): 61–66.

32. There are countless works by theologians on these issues now, but see, in particular, Howard Eilberg-Schwartz and Wendy Doniger, eds., *Off with Her Head! The Denial of Women's Identity in Myth, Religion, and Culture* (Berkeley: University of California Press, 1995).

33. See Farley, *Compassionate Respect*, 3–20; see also Linda Singer, "Regulating Women in the Age of Sexual Epidemic," in *Erotic Welfare: Sexual Theory and Politics in the Age of the Epidemic*, ed. Judith Butler and Maureen MacGrogan (New York: Routledge, 1993).

34. See Committee on Ethics, "Sex Selection" (Washington, DC: American College of Obstetricians and Gynecologists, November 1996). For a careful probing of reproductive technologies more generally, see Maura A. Ryan, *Ethics and Economics of Assisted Reproduction: The Cost of Longing* (Washington, DC: Georgetown University Press, 2001). See also Lisa Sowle Cahill, "The New Birth Technologies and Public Moral Argument," in Cahill, *Sex, Gender and Christian Ethics* (Cambridge: Cambridge University Press, 1996), 217–54.

Norms for Sexual Justice

Basis	Norm
Respect for the autonomy and relationality that characterize persons as ends in themselves, and hence respect for their well-being:	1. Do no unjust harm
Respect for autonomy:	2. Free consent of partners
Respect for relationality:	3. Mutuality
	4. Equality
	5. Commitment
	6. Fruitfulness
Respect for persons as sexual beings in society:	7. Social justice

human relationships and those which are particular to the intimacy of sexual relations. Most generally, the norms derive from the concrete reality of persons and are focused on respect for their autonomy and relationality. This is to respect persons as ends in themselves. It yields an injunction to do no unjust harm to persons. It also yields specifications both of what it means to respect autonomy and relationality and what it means to do no harm. Autonomy is to be respected through a requirement of free consent from sexual partners, with related requirements for truthtelling, promise-keeping, and respect for privacy. Relationality is to be respected through requirements of mutuality, equality, commitment, fruitfulness, and social justice.

Even more specifically, we may in terms of this framework say things like: sex should not be used in ways that exploit, objectify, or dominate; rape, violence, and harmful uses of power in sexual relationships are ruled out; freedom, wholeness, intimacy, pleasure are values to be affirmed in relationships marked by mutuality, equality, and some form of commitment; sexual relations like other profound interpersonal relations can and ought to be fruitful both within and beyond the relationship; the affections of desire and love that bring about and sustain sexual relationships are all in all genuinely to affirm both lover and beloved.

I recognize full well that it is not an easy task to introduce considerations of justice into every sexual relation and the evaluation of every sexual activity. Critical questions remain unanswered, and serious disagreements are all too frequent, regarding the concrete reality of persons and the meanings of sexuality. What can be normative and what exceptional — that is, what is governed by the norms I have identified and what can be exceptions to these norms — is sometimes a matter of all too delicate judgment. But if sexuality is to be creative and not destructive in personal and social relationships, then there is no substitute for discerning ever more carefully the norms whereby it will be just.

Special Questions

I hope that what I have delineated above as a justice ethic for the sphere of sexuality in human life already speaks of the practice of this ethic. It is not intended to be merely an abstract outline of ethical principles and rules. The chapter that follows will attempt to show what this ethic means in response to particular aspects of our lives. There are further questions that bear consideration, however, before I leave the substance of this chapter. Some of these questions challenge the ethic I have proposed; some of them expand it in ways that may be particularly important to the Christian community.

An Ethic Only for Adults?

Insofar as a justice ethic makes sense at all, can it make any difference to teenagers whose reported sexual practices today appear untouchable by traditional or new ethical frameworks? I am not here referring to the exploitation of the young by adults in the multiple forms that sexual harm is perpetrated. The ethical norms I have outlined are clearly intended to protect the young in special ways from the violence and manipulation of adults who would use the vulnerable sexuality of children and adolescents for their own (that is, the adults') pleasure or monetary gain. I am, rather, referring to the practices of teenagers among themselves. My focus is, of course, on practices that are no doubt time-bound and culture-bound, but I suspect there are analogues that will emerge again and again, at least in Western culture.

The phenomenon of "hooking up" is an example of a practice among teenagers that seems to elude any norms other than acceptance among peers.[35] "Hooking up" is precisely what it depicts: sex without any relationship and without any strings. "Friends with benefits" differs in that there is some form of friendship prior to sexual activity, but still, no strings. Dating still exists, but at least according to some reports, appears not to be the sexual relationship of choice. "We might date. . . . I don't know. It's just that guys can get so annoying when you start dating them."[36] "Now that it's easy to get sex outside of relationships, guys don't need relationships."[37] Many teenagers, according to these reports, are looking for anything but commitment — or even mutuality in any sense other than physical.

There may be a growing concern among teen-agers for "safe sex," in the sense of protection especially against sexually transmitted diseases. Whether or not this fuels the reported wide-spread practice of oral sex is hard to determine. What is clear, however, is that adolescents are misinformed about the health consequences of oral sex and other sexual practices, so that it is hard to believe that "concrete realities" of persons are much taken into account. If a justice ethic is to make any difference at all in the choices that young people make regarding their sexuality, the first step will have to be education about sex and its dangers as well as sexuality and the ways it may be not only harmless but good.

Whether or not published reports about the sexual lives of teenagers and even of pre-teen children actually reflect the majority of teenage experiences (and I do not assume that they do), it is clear

---

35. See, for example, Benoit Denizet-Lewis, "Friends, Friends with Benefits, and the Benefits of the Local Mall," *New York Times Magazine* (May 30, 2004): 30–35, 54–56; Donna Freitas, "Let's Talk About Sex," *Christian Century* (June 14, 2005): 29–31; Lauren F. Winner, *Real Sex: The Naked Truth about Chastity* (Grand Rapids, MI: Brazos, 2005); Caitlin Flanagan, "Are You There God? It's Me Monica: How Nice Girls Got So Casual about Oral Sex," *Atlantic* (January–February 2006): 167–82. See also the multiple studies reported by Barbara J. Blodgett in *Constructing the Erotic: Sexual Ethics and Adolescent Girls* (Cleveland: Pilgrim, 2002), chapter 4.

36. Quoted in Benoit Denizet-Lewis, "Friends, Friends with Benefits, and the Benefits of the Local Mall," 32.

37. Ibid, 34.

that they represent some. What can a justice ethic say to these particular practices and experiences? What can it say to adolescents for whom these practices are not part of their experience? What have we to offer young girls who, in the midst of this kind of sexual activity, or on the outside looking in, say that they do this or want this because their lives are boring? Or because they want relationships, though they seek them in vain in the practices that aim to make relationships unnecessary? And what can we say to young boys, who appear to enjoy these practices more than girls; who find in them a way to stay uncommitted yet have access to sexual partners almost without limit?[38]

I do not here, as I have said, attempt to assess how widespread these practices may be. Nor do I attempt to judge the practices themselves — at least not without longer term empirical studies of the consequences and not without a careful consideration of the total situation in which Western teenagers find themselves today. I do want to raise the modest but urgent question: Suppose these practices are harmful to young people. Suppose some of them enjoy these practices, but some do not. Suppose some of them feel used, but their partners have no understanding of this. Would sexual taboo morality change the situation? Perhaps so, perhaps not, but its lasting effect might have to do with developing shame and guilt more than wisdom and prudence about human sexuality.[39]

---

38. For some insights into these experiences, see Blodgett, *Constructing the Erotic*, especially chapters 4–5.

39. In 1994 the Sexuality Information and Education Council of the United States (SIECUS) convened the National Commission on Adolescent Sexual Health. This Commission developed a consensus statement that highlighted the need for adults to encourage adolescent sexual health by providing accurate information and education, fostering responsible decision-making skills, offering support and guidance in the exploration of young people's own values, and modeling healthy sexual attitudes and behaviors. It encouraged adolescents to "delay sexual behaviors until they are ready physically, cognitively, and emotionally for mature sexual relationships and their consequences." It supported education about intimacy, sexual limit setting, resisting peer, partner, social, and media pressures, and consideration of the benefits of abstinence of genital intercourse, as well as prevention of pregnancy and sexually transmitted diseases. In a balanced publication elaborating on these issues, it also provided positive assessments of adolescent behaviors in recent years. See Debra W. Haffner, ed., *Facing Facts: Sexual Health for America's Adolescents* (New York: SIECUS National Commission on Adolescent Sexual Health, 1995).

The real question here may be whether young people are capable of justice — whether their socially constructed interests and desires, and their still largely hidden and unrecognized (by themselves) desires and hopes, can respond to the challenge and call of justice. If justice matters to them at all in their other relationships (and I believe there is plenty of evidence that it does), can it come to matter in their sexual relationships as well? If and insofar as they want it to matter, or are even intrigued by what this would mean, then questions of respect — self-respect as well as respect for another — and questions of freedom, mutuality, equality, and benefit or harm, will not be uninteresting questions. We know the dangers as well as ineffectiveness of moralism, and the potential dangers of narrowly construed moral systems and rules. We do not yet know whether an ethic of just love and just sex will transform any young person's understanding or action. Insofar as we care about our children, it is worth a try.

Sexual Relations with Oneself

Most of the justice norms that I have delineated in this chapter derive at least in part from "relationality," one of the basic obligating features of human persons. The norms as I have presented them are clearly relevant to sexual relationships between persons, but it is not so clear how this justice ethic relates to sexual relations with one's self. I do not thereby want to dismiss the importance of questions about "self-pleasuring" (or masturbation), especially since general perceptions and attitudes regarding this form of sexual expression have changed radically in the latter part of the twentieth century. Perhaps the most important insight we need in this regard is that it, like other sexual activities, needs to be moved out of the realm of taboo morality.

Through centuries of Western thought masturbation was judged to be not only an immoral sexual practice, but one that should be particularly repugnant to human individuals and the human community. As Immanuel Kant insisted, it places humans "below the level of animals."[40] Christian traditions looked upon it as the "solitary

---

40. Immanuel Kant, *Lectures in Ethics*, trans. Louis Infield (New York: Harper & Row, 1963), 170.

sin," "onanism," "self-abuse," and judged it harshly until the twentieth century, although perhaps not so harshly in every prior century. Traditions of professional medical opinion undergirded and joined in the negative judgments made by religious authorities. Although there are theologians and church traditions that continue to consider masturbation immoral, many others (most, as far as I can tell, along with most medical practitioners) do not assess it in this manner anymore. Masturbation is more likely to be considered morally neutral, which could mean that it is either good or bad, depending on the circumstances and the individual. It could also mean that, while the practice may raise psychological questions (if it becomes obsessive, for example), it usually does not raise any moral questions at all.

Ever since the Kinsey studies, it has been impossible to claim with any credibility that masturbation is a practice of only a very few, or that past dire predictions about dangerous physical or psychological injury from the practice are accurate. Anecdotal reports today tend to show that any evil or injury involved is the result of misinformation, unsubstantiated myths, and experiences of defilement and guilt in what is perceived to be the breaking of religious or cultural taboos. It is surely the case that many women, following the "our bodies our selves" movement in the fourth quarter of the twentieth century, have found great good in self-pleasuring — perhaps especially in the discovery of their own possibilities for pleasure — something many had not experienced or even known about in their ordinary sexual relations with husbands or lovers. In this way, it could be said that masturbation actually serves relationships rather than hindering them.

My final observation is, then, that the norms of justice as I have presented them would seem to apply to the choice of sexual self-pleasuring only insofar as this activity may help or harm, only insofar as it supports or limits, well-being and liberty of spirit.[41] This remains largely an empirical question, not a moral one.

41. For a traditional view, see Germain Grisez, *The Way of the Lord Jesus*, vol. 3: *Difficult Moral Questions* (Quincy, IL: Franciscan, 1997), 134, 247. For critical contemporary analysis, including conceptual analysis and biblical and tradition viewpoints, see Anthony Kosnik et al., "Masturbation," in *Readings in Moral Theology No. 8: Dialogue about Catholic Sexual Teaching*, ed. Charles E. Curran and Richard A. McCormick (New York: Paulist, 1993), 349–60; Ronald Lawler, Joseph M. Boyle, and William E.

The Negative Potential of Sex

I have tried throughout this chapter and previous chapters to emphasize the positive meanings and values of sexuality. I have not, however, ignored its negative potential. Along the way I have noted serious instances of the injurious use of sexuality (such as rape) as well as problematic practices that have traditionally been challenged as more evil than good (such as prostitution and pornography). I have left some questions hanging, promising to return to them. I do so here, but with brief observations, less than the questions deserve, yet important to probing them more fully.

The framework for sexual ethics that I have presented clearly does not treat sex as evil in some intrinsic way — not evil because of an uncontrollable biological drive, not evil because pleasure-seeking is inevitably self-centered, not evil because the human body is a burden to the human soul. My proposed framework, as a way of thinking about sexual ethical questions, does not yield conclusions such as: Sex without openness to biological reproduction is evil because it involves unjustified "venereal pleasure."[42] It cannot yield conclusions such as: All sex as sex requires divine forgiveness, since it is inevitably tainted by a previous cataclysmic human "Fall."[43] It cannot yield conclusions such as: All sex is defiling and shameful if it is expressed

---

May, "Masturbation," ibid., 361–71; Alan Soble, "Masturbation: Conceptual and Ethical Matters," in *The Philosophy of Sex: Contemporary Readings*, ed. Alan Soble, 4th ed. (New York: Rowman & Littlefield, 2002), 67–94. For a critical essay from the standpoint of women's experience, see Jacqueline Fortunata, "Masturbation and Women's Sexuality," in *The Philosophy of Sex*, ed. Alan Soble, 1st ed. (New York: Littlefield Adams, 1980), 389–408.

42. I am convinced that this rationale is the unsubstantiated position behind, for example, the directions given by Roman Catholic hierarchical leaders forbidding the practice of tubal ligation in Catholic hospitals — even in circumstances where a woman may already have multiple children and, because of serious heart disease, be at risk of death should she have to sustain another pregnancy. See Margaret A. Farley, "Power and Powerlessness: A Case in Point," *Proceedings of the Catholic Theological Society of America* 37 (1982): 116–19; Richard A. McCormick, "Sterilization: the Dilemma of Catholic Hospitals," in *The Critical Calling: Reflections on Moral Dilemmas since Vatican II* (Washington, DC: Georgetown University Press, 1989), 273–88.

43. I do not hereby quarrel completely or only with Martin Luther's position that original sin has left all humans still sinful in a way that goes beyond sinful actions of their own. Insofar as Luther held the Augustinian position that it is sex that bears paradigmatically evil consequences of original sin, I oppose this, as I hope my norms imply and what I have said about Christian perspectives on sex articulates.

in forms outside of traditional categories of acceptability. It cannot yield conclusions such as: Sex is always an expression of human conflict, and inevitably contains some degree of violence.

Yet there are characteristics of some human relationships that, when expressed sexually, do wreak havoc on the vulnerable individual and disrupt the human community. Moreover, the harm that is done, for example, in sexual assault seems to be more potentially deadly than the harms of nonsexual assault, emotional abuse, exploitation. This may be so because of the lingering cultural connotations of defilement of which Ricoeur spoke. It may also be so because sexuality is uniquely intimate to human persons as embodied spirits, inspirited bodies. For whatever reasons, it does appear that to be violated so intimately in our bodied selves can entail harm in a distinctively terrible way. Hence, for example, the trauma of sustained sexual abuse of children is more injurious than other forms of physical and emotional abuse. It is perhaps here that we should at least note the significant difference in gravity between what have been called "sins of weakness" and "sins of malice."

Although there is some reticence to judge the use of sex in ways that involve violence and exploitation, there are not many who think positively about the stories that appear daily in newspapers regarding practices in our own and other parts of the world. The reticence is due largely to fear of critiquing practices from the standpoint of one culture against another. Yet these practices appear to occur across cultures, and a kind of moral repugnance seems fully justified. I refer here, for example, to the use of rape as an accepted form of modern warfare, or at least an accepted side-effect of it; the widespread trafficking of women and children for purposes of prostitution or sexual slavery; the millions of children used in prostitution whether trafficked from or simply used within their own lands; and on and on. A fall-out from some practices produces an unjust stigmatization of innocent victims — as, for example, in the sometimes lethal punishment of wives, but not husbands, for adultery; the stigmatization of women who have been raped and of children born from rape; the shunning and stigmatization of wives who have been infected with HIV by unfaithful husbands. I do not want or need to discuss these crimes or even these terrible but unwarranted stigmas in further detail, since studies of them are plentiful and readily available.[44] What is clear, however, is that they violate all of the sexual ethical norms I have identified above.

Pornography and traditional forms of prostitution are, as I have indicated, two issues that have become highly contested in the past twenty-five years. Feminists have found themselves on opposing sides of both of these issues, though often the debates are less about the practices themselves than about related issues. In regard to pornography, the debate is about freedom of speech versus censorship, although it inevitably involves some assessment of the consequences of pornography for gender relations, children used in pornographic films, the psychological outcome of sustained use of pornography over time, and what counts or does not count as pornography.[45] These are serious issues, and must be weighed carefully. Not all use of pornography is harmful to individuals, no doubt, and it is all too easy for zealots to lump even great literature and art into the category of pornography. Nonetheless, I have through the years been unable to forget the poignant story of a young man who told me of

---

44. In addition to ongoing newspaper reports, see, for example, Brian M. Willis and Barry S. Levy, "Child Prostitution: Global Health Burden, Research Needs, and Interventions," *The Lancet* 359 (April 20, 2002): 1417–21; Catherine Panter-Brick, "Street Children, Human Rights, and Public Health: A Critique and Future Directions," *Annual Review of Anthropology* 31 (2002): 147–71; Grace Wamue, "Gender Violence and Exploitation: The Widow's Dilemma," in *Violence Against Women: Reflections by Kenyan Women Theologians*, ed. Grace Wamue and Mary Getui (Nairobi, Kenya: Acton, 1996), 40–48; Jade Christine Angelica, *A Moral Emergency: Breaking the Cycle of Child Sexual Abuse* (Kansas City, MO: Sheed & Ward, 1993). I should note also that there are multiple other issues regarding emotional and physical violence associated with sex, such as sexual harassment, date rape, and so forth. The literature is voluminous on the former. On the latter, see Kristen J. Leslie, *When Violence is No Stranger: Pastoral Counseling with Survivors of Acquaintance Rape* (Minneapolis: Fortress, 2003).

45. See, for example, Catherine A. MacKinnon, "Pornography Left and Right," in *Sex, Preference, and Family*, ed. David M. Estlund and Martha C. Nussbaum (Oxford: Oxford University Press, 1997), 102–25; MacKinnon, *Toward a Feminist Theory of the State* (Cambridge, MA: Harvard University Press, 1989), chapter 11; Alan Soble, "Pornography and the Social Sciences," in *The Philosophy of Sex: Contemporary Readings*, ed. Alan Soble (New York: Rowman & Littlefield, 2002), 421–34; Martha C. Nussbaum, "Objectification," *Philosophy and Public Affairs* 24 (1995): 249–91; Jeffrey Rose and David B. Hart, "Pornography and the Internet: An Exchange," *New Atlantis* no. 6 (Summer 2004): 75–89.

his own introduction to an addictive use of pornography by his father and older brother, and who upon reflection bemoaned the distortions in his own abilities to relate to women as a result. Norms of justice are clearly relevant here, but the major task is to sort out what is harmful or not, what conditions people to distorted gender relations, whether and how pornography eroticizes sexual violence, and who is being exploited or coerced among those who work in the sex industry itself.

Regarding prostitution, the debate tends to be about situational issues — that is, the difference between, on the one hand, sex workers who argue that they are situationally free to choose this work for reasons related to their own interests and, on the other hand, sex workers who are coerced physically or economically into prostitution. This debate also incorporates assessments of the right or good of anyone's trading of bodily sexual favors for money. In a balanced moral evaluation of claims and counterclaims in these regards, Karen Peterson-Iyer has acknowledged the freedom of at least some prostitutes, but freedom within limited options. Calling for a fair hearing of the voices of prostitutes themselves, Peterson-Iyer nonetheless raises questions about the possibilities of genuine mutuality or equality in contexts that are all too conducive to the subjection of one sexual partner to another, objectification of both parties, commodification of sex, and the separation of sex from self-identity.[46] We are left not only with questions about the justification of prostitution as a practice but with a challenge to our own discernment of obligations in social justice to prostitutes and the world around them.

Character, Faith, and Sexual Justice

The justice framework for sexual ethics outlined in this chapter is, as I have said, for a Christian and a human sexual ethic. What is distinctive about a Christian sexual ethic is not that it offers something other than a justice ethic but that it is contextualized differently and,

---

46. Karen Peterson-Iyer, "Prostitution: A Feminist Ethical Analysis," *Journal of Feminist Studies in Religion* 14 (Fall 1998): 19–44. See also the excellent diverse set of essays in Ronald Weitzer, ed., *Sex for Sale: Prostitution, Pornography, and the Sex Industry* (New York: Routledge, 2000).

like other religious traditions, it will no doubt give significance to additional norms. For example, norms and ideals of faithfulness, loving kindness, forgiveness, patience, and hope that are important for any relationships within the Christian community will surely be relevant to sexual relationships as well. Insofar as any sexual ethic requires taking account of the person as a whole, a Christian sexual ethic will surely hold at its center an understanding of the person before God.

Christian traditions share an affirmation of the goodness of creation, the central significance of the incarnation of God in Jesus Christ, the redemption of humanity and all creation by the saving action of God through Jesus Christ, the command and the call of humans to love God with all their heart and soul and strength and to love their neighbors as themselves.

Christians affirm also the call of human persons to a destiny of friendship and ultimate communion with God and all persons in God. Christians (at least many Christians) affirm beliefs in the role of human persons as agents in cooperation with the ongoing creative activity of God; the importance of not only the individual but the community; the responsibilities of human persons to promote the health and well-being of one another; the shared task of working for justice in the world and the healing of creation; the equality of persons not only before God but before one another. Christians believe, too, in loves that, like the love of Jesus Christ, are stronger than death; and in the possibility that tragedy is not the last word in the meaning of human lives. To some persons, the whole world manifests something sacred — that is, the presence of God — so that human sexuality, too, has a sacramental dimension. A Christian sexual justice ethic is informed and sustained in the context of these beliefs.

Moreover, for Christians to love neighbors, near and far, as themselves is to love them justly, to love them on the model given by a God of compassionate justice. The questions of morality that Christians must address are, therefore, questions not only of what we must do, but what we must be and become. A human justice ethic, and surely a Christian justice ethic, must attend not only to action guides but to the kinds of persons we are called to be. In the sphere of sexual

morality, for example, what possible effect can norms for just relationships have in our lives if we do not attend to the "sort of person"
we want to be?[47]

When ethics addresses questions of what we ought to be, it is in the
realm of what is standardly referred to as "virtue ethics," or "ethics
of character." These questions presume that, in addition to all the
factors that go into making us "who we are" — such as genetic inheritance, temperament, environment, socialization, nurturance (or
lack thereof) — we ourselves have some sort of influence on what
we become. For Christians, these questions presume that in addition to divine grace — or better, with the power of divine grace — we
shape ourselves significantly by our freedom. Our capacity for free
choice, however limited or expanded, is after all a capacity for "self-
determination." To some degree, in some respect, we are responsible
not only for our actions, but for the kind of person we come to be.
In a Christian sexual ethic, therefore, we should not be surprised
to find guidance not only from norms of strict justice but from the
ideals and the challenge of the Sermon on the Mount.

Part of our concrete reality is that we live out our lives in time;
hence, our lives and our loves are in process. We are, as we say,
"developing." We develop physically and intellectually, culturally and
socially, but also spiritually and morally. We become generally kind
or unkind, honest or dishonest, compassionate or callous. In other
words, we may develop well or badly, in every dimension of our being.
Even when we develop well, however, a little reflection tells us how
complicated we are. Being a certain sort of person does not mean
that we are without contradictions in our selves, or that we have no
weaknesses to bear or faults over which we break our hearts.

Although religion in whatever tradition can function primarily as
a harsh reminder of duty, a source of shame and guilt, a producer
of timidity or zealous moralisms; it can also free us from the sort of
fear that keeps us away from God and fractures our selves. Christianity, like other religious traditions, has endured in part because
it helps people to make sense of their lives. It offers some response

---

47. This phrase is James Gustafson's in "The 'Sort of' Person One Is," *Can Ethics
Be Christian?: An Inquiry* (Chicago: University of Chicago Press, 1975), chap. 2.

to the large human questions of yearning and love, of suffering and death, hope and transcendence. Christianity itself offers hope in forgiveness, liberation from too narrow a view of human possibility, and the promise of a covenanted relationship with God that will not be broken. We know the partiality of our loves and the incapacities of our hearts. We know the fragility of all human relationships. Yet we are able to believe that some loves can be blessed with inexhaustible life, that some relationships can hold no matter what the forces of evil may threaten against them, that sexuality can become part of the highest forms of friendship, and that a call to justice remains.

The ideals of virtue that may motivate as well as shape our efforts to become just in our sexual expressions and relationships can be described in terms of wisdom, integrity, freedom, and great love. We need refined capacities of self-knowledge and knowledge of the other; we need capabilities for reverent discernment of what is just in every relationship. We can hope that the development of such capacities and abilities will make us more and more wise, though there are clearly degrees and limits to whatever wisdom we accrue. In turn, we hope that whatever the wisdom we attain or receive will make our discernments more thoughtful, more sensitive, and more just.

We who may begin with undisciplined loves, or find our desires in conflict along the way, can recognize our needs for wholeness. Wholeness in this sense may bring unity and peace for ourselves, but it will also allow us more and more to bring an undivided love to every beloved. For Christians, the ideal is to integrate our loves somehow in an utter love of God. Our desire is for an integration that destroys no desire but transforms it, that ignores no love but makes it just, that harms no one, not even ourselves. This is the kind of integrity that nourishes our sexuality and makes it just.

Little by little, wisdom and integrity bring freedom. They make liberty of spirit possible, and the creative use of free choice consistent. Virtue in its classical meaning, after all, has to do with the refinement of our capacities so that we exercise them with consistency, greater ease, and delight. This virtue is not the pinch-faced virtue of either the fearful or the self-righteous; nor is it the semblance of "purity" that is the enemy of generosity, humility, and full-hearted care. It is not the kind of freedom that is finally attained only by experimentation, keeping all options open, all forms of genuine relationship at bay. This freedom is, rather, the freedom of courage in the face of real risk and fear; perseverance in the face of weakness and distraction; trust in the face of self-doubt; faithfulness in the face of the furies or demons that would divert us both from the searches to which we are called and from our chosen and already anchored loves. It is a freedom that not only protects us from exploitation and harm, but that positively affirms and lifts our loves with the whole of ourselves. This, then, is the freedom that unleashes just love, desire, and sex.

Finally, wisdom, integrity, and freedom serve great love. Insofar as they all together approximate the conceptual core of the traditional "cardinal" virtues — prudence, temperance, fortitude, and justice — they serve a just love. I myself prefer these alternate names for central, comprehensive, and pivotal virtues (that is, alternate to the traditional concepts of prudence, temperance, fortitude, and justice); they garner the best of the traditional theories but jettison culture-bound connotations that do not serve well our new understandings of human sexuality. Great love is a love that is right, just, true, and good. It does not contradict the concrete reality of either lover or beloved; it is true to the nature of the relationship between them; it is whole and wise and brave and also humble, non-grasping, able to laugh and to mourn; it integrates multiple loves, even multiple great loves, in harmony with an utter love of God.

These virtues, or characteristics of persons, are admittedly ideals. Yet they, too, have a kind of bottom-line aspect. Without any degree of virtue, it is hard to imagine sex that is good; without growing maturity in virtue, it is difficult to imagine sex that is great. So faith, character, and moral growth belong to an ethics of sexual justice just as much as norms that guide our actions. Each illuminate the other, and each makes the other more possible.

Chapter 7

PATTERNS OF RELATIONSHIP
Contexts for Just Love

═══ ❖ ═══

I HAVE SAID REPEATEDLY throughout this book that my intention is not to address, certainly not to resolve, all of the pressing questions for sexual ethics. Rather, my aim has been to propose a framework for thinking about these questions. In this chapter, however, I do turn to particular patterns of relationship in the sexual sphere of our lives precisely in order to reflect on them in the light of the framework outlined in the previous chapter. The patterns to be addressed are marriage and family, same-sex relationships, divorce and remarriage. This means that I will not be focusing on alternative patterns such as cohabitation, bisexuality, celibacy, singleness, kinship (though they are all extremely important), except insofar as these relate in some way to marriage and family, same-sex relations, and divorce and second marriages. Although each of these three patterns requires much more attention than I offer in this one chapter, my hope is that they have enough in common to justify my bringing them together here. They are, in fact, interrelated in significant ways: they overlap considerably, so it may be that treating them together can provide insights not otherwise obvious when they are studied separately; they are all patterns that promise happiness and human flourishing, although each of them may also yield experiences of pain; they are all patterns that are complex; and they are all lived out in contexts that call for both justice and mercy.

Marriage and Family

Studies regarding marriage and family have multiplied astonishingly in recent years. No doubt this is in large part because forms of family

have proliferated and changed, producing confusion and concern —
to the point where the situation is called a crisis. My own approach,
however, to forms of family and to the possibilities for marriage will
not be in terms of response to "crisis," since I am persuaded by historians that "for thousands of years people have been proclaiming
a crisis in marriage [and family] and pointing backward to better
days."[1] For me, this relativizes the significance of "crisis," although
there are serious and new challenges for contemporary institutions
of marriage and family. Indeed, even those like Stephanie Coontz
and Nancy Cott who have looked long and hard at the sweep of historical developments have been inclined to observe that around the
globe "the current rearrangement of both married and single life is
in fact without historical precedent,"[2] and in the United States there
has occurred in recent years a "seismic shift" in marriage practices
which, of course, has had implications also for families.[3]

In response to current experiences of marriage and family, a
"turn to the family" has preoccupied not only secular historians,
philosophers, and social scientists but also religious historians and
theologians. The latter have engaged in interfaith studies as well
as major works on particular religious traditions. For example, the
massive projects on "Religion, Culture, and Family" and "Religion,
Marriage, and Family," led by Don Browning at the University of Chicago, have produced or in some way influenced nearly twenty books,
with more on the way.[4] Writings by Rosemary Radford Ruether, Lisa
Sowle Cahill, Christine Gudorf, and others have added significant insights into past and present Christian perspectives on marriage and
family.[5] My primary goal here is not to repeat what scholars have
already said, although I will surely draw on their work; it is, rather,

---

1. Stephanie Coontz, *Marriage, a History: From Obedience to Intimacy or How
Love Conquered Marriage* (New York: Viking, 2005), 1.
2. Ibid, 2.
3. Nancy F. Cott, *Public Vows: A History of Marriage and the Nation* (Cambridge,
MA: Harvard University Press, 2000), 201.
4. For an overview of these publications as of 2005 see the Web site:
http://marty-center.uchicago.edu/research/rcfp/.
5. See Rosemary Radford Ruether, *Christianity and the Making of the Modern
Family: Ruling Ideologies, Diverse Realities* (Boston: Beacon, 2000); Lisa Sowle Cahill,
Family: A Christian Social Perspective (Minneapolis: Augsburg Fortress, 2000); Lisa
Sowle Cahill and Dietmar Mieth, eds., *The Family*, 1995 special issue of *Concilium*

to see whether there are specific additional elements to be discovered or reinforced in a sexual ethic that takes seriously these patterns of relationship.

Historical and Cultural Contexts

The institutions of marriage and family have always been significant for society and for religious traditions. As Ruether observes, "Both the church and the state have a stake in stable, committed partnerships that provide the framework for child-raising, sustaining the well-being of related people over time, and caring for others in crisis, illness, and old age."[6] And Nancy Cott notes that even today, "No modern nation-state can ignore marriage forms, because of their direct impact on reproducing and composing the population."[7] Throughout history, of course, marriage and family have taken diverse forms and fulfilled diverse functions suited to the social and cultural contexts in which they were lived out. In many of these contexts, marriage functioned to determine relationships between families, establish inheritance lines, create and reinforce gender roles, circumscribe sexual activity, determine rights and duties in sexual relations, and provide for the legitimacy and rearing of children. A primary determinant of marriage was the need of families to gain in-laws, to establish or secure political and economic alliances between and among families.[8] Yet the history of the functions of marriage is a complex one that cautions us against too hasty interpretations of the past or its relation to the present.

(London: SCM, and Maryknoll, NY: Orbis); Adrian Thatcher, ed., *Celebrating Christian Marriage* (New York: T. & T. Clark, 2001); Christine E. Gudorf, "Western Religion and the Patriarchal Family," in *Feminist Ethics and the Catholic Moral Tradition*, ed. Charles E. Curran, Margaret A. Farley, and Richard A. McCormick (New York: Paulist, 1996). See also the review essay by Sondra Wheeler, "Finding Our Way Home: Theologians' Re-engagement with the Ethics of Family," *Religious Studies Review* 29 (October 2003): 337–41.

6. Ruether, *Christianity and the Making of the Modern Family*, 213.

7. Cott, *Public Vows*, 5.

8. Coontz, *Marriage, a History*, 32–33. Coontz observes that there has been only one society where marriage has not been a significant institution, and this was a society with only 30,000 members in which sibling relations were much more important than marriage. Moreover, among all the possible functions of marriage, Coontz sees the acquiring of in-laws as the most distinctive. This is the only function that cannot be performed, she concludes, by groups of brothers and sisters.

According to Coontz, polygyny has been the marriage institution of choice across more time and more cultures than any other.[9] In the West, monogamy became the preferred form of marriage, but more gradually than contemporary Christians might suspect. When Christianity spread beyond Palestine it encountered different laws and customs for marriage than it had inherited from either Jewish or Greco-Roman traditions. The practice of polygyny in some Western ethnic groups such as the Franks, Teutons, and Germans continued through the early Middle Ages.[10] Since then, however, wherever Western culture has encountered polygyny, it has tended to judge it to be "primitive," "uncivilized," and needing to be changed.[11] This has been true whether these encounters were within Western nations or in other parts of the world. In the United States, for example, this has been the response to Native Americans, Mormons, and immigrants with polygynous cultural backgrounds.

The narratives of marriage and family in Western civilization have been marked by particular trajectories that have changed the landscape of relationships in profound ways. Major shifts have taken place, for example, in the motivations for marriage, in who makes choices about marriage and who regulates its forms, and in the patterns of gender relations within both marriage and family. These shifts do not happen in a vacuum, however; they become possible and are in some sense driven by changes in the political and economic contexts in which they take place.[12] Although I turn now to those trajectories in Western history, there is plenty of evidence that what has happened in the West is now also happening around the world.

In the beginning of Western civilization and for a long part of its history, marriage was undertaken primarily to meet the needs of families and kinship groups — economic, political, and social needs. The

---

9. Coontz, *Marriage, a History*, 10, 27. Coontz cites in support of this George Peter Murdock, *Ethnographic Atlas* (Pittsburgh: University of Pittsburgh Press, 1967).

10. Ruether, *Christianity and the Making of the Modern Family*, 51–52. See also Margaret M. Mitchell, "Why Family Matters for Early Christian Literature," in *Early Christian Families in Context*, ed. David L. Balch and Carolyn Osiek (Grand Rapids, MI: William B. Eerdmans, 2003), 353–54. It should be said that the western Germanic tribes were barely Christian before the fifth century.

11. See Cott, *Public Vows*, 105–30.

12. Some of these changes have been charted in historical overviews I have already noted in chapter 2.

historical trajectory of the control of marriage — that is, the control shifting from families to church to monarchies to democratic states to individuals — is long and complex, but from our present vantage point, the most visible strand within this shift appears to be the gradual move to marriages chosen by individuals on the basis of the experience of love and the hope of personal happiness. As Coontz notes, in the past "some people fell in love, sometimes even with their own spouses,"[13] but the functions of marriage were too important to leave to the private determination of two individuals on the basis of private affections. Historians date differently the evolution of Western marriage from family-dominated arrangements to a choice of interpersonal love, but the major shift appears to have taken place in the seventeenth and eighteenth centuries. This process was therefore under way by the beginning of the history of the United States. Cott picks up the narrative in this new and expanding country with a deconstructive focus on the continuing roles of the nation, the state, and local communities in controlling the forms and functions of marriage. However much it looked to be otherwise, marriage was not a private but a public institution, a vehicle whereby the state attempted to organize, govern, and shape the populace in ways driven by religious, political, and economic concerns. Whether in spite of or because of government control, the narrative nonetheless proceeds through four centuries, ultimately to transformations of marriage into private choices, and the family into a haven apart from the world.

Changes in gender relations were ineluctably tied to changes in the functions and meanings of marriage. "In the beginning" it may

---

13. Coontz, *Marriage, a History*, 7. Coontz later notes that individuals might hope to find love, or at least "tranquil affection" in marriage, and a concern for the well-being of couples was not ignored in many family arrangements. Still, this was not what marriage was primarily for. Contrary to Coontz's conclusions, at least one historian is skeptical of the interpretation of arranged marriages as "unemotional" or "loveless." Suzanne Dixon has suggested that scholarly insistence on separating love from these kinds of marriages "may reflect contemporary Western revulsion at the idea of arranged marriages.... But it is a logical leap from the mode of arrangement to the expectations and content of a marriage." Suzanne Dixon, "Sex and the Married Woman in Ancient Rome," in *Early Christian Families in Context: An Interdisciplinary Dialogue*, ed. David L. Balch and Carolyn Osiek (Grand Rapids, MI: William B. Eerdmans, 2003), 115. Dixon adduces literary evidence through these centuries of "lovesick husbands" and other erotic motifs.

be simply that "flexible, gender-based division of labor within a mated pair" was important for human survival.[14] Gender roles and relationships, therefore, were functional, based on what needed to be done. The history of gender after this is also complex, as we have already seen in previous chapters. But it moves along a line that includes the subordination of women to men, the sometime consideration of women's bodies as the property of men, and the ongoing unequal partnership between women and men within marriage and family. Cott's sobering depiction of the way in which marriage has been a public institution in U.S. history includes the claim and strong evidence that, as such, marriage has been the instrument through which the state could and does shape gender roles.[15] Her argument is that in this nation's history there has been a "seamless" adaptation of Christian doctrine to Anglo-American law. Central to Christian understandings of marriage, as Cott interprets them, are the notions of *mutual consent* for the establishment of a marriage (more important than anything else in the gradual evolution of Christian thought between the seventh and the twelfth centuries) and *"two in one flesh."*[16] These notions blended well with Anglo-American ideas of *contract* and of the *legal oneness* of husband and wife. In addition, Christian understandings of the husband as the "head" of his wife and his family were in accord with English common law's conception of the legal, political, and economical "oneness" of husband and wife. Husbands, as the only full citizens in early American households, were their wives' political as well as legal representatives. And since a wife's domestic labor as well as her assets belonged to or were administered by her husband, she also became economically one with him. Marital unity meant enlargement of a husband's identity, but it more often than not required of a wife the relinquishment of hers.[17]

In Cott's analysis, the nature of the relationship between husband and wife was to mirror the relationship between the state and the

---

14. Coontz, *Marriage, a History*, 38. Coontz actually gives two possible renditions of the story of the beginning of marriage. The second one is that marriage began simply as a way for men to have access to women in a manner that fit the needs for exchange. Ibid., 41.

15. Cott, *Public Vows*, 3.

16. Ibid, 10–11.

17. Ibid., 11–12.

people. When in the eighteenth century the latter relationship was challenged in terms of its patriarchal model, a new way was sought to understand the analogy between the social contract that established the state and the marital contract that founded the relationship between husband and wife. Therefore, in the institution of marriage there were new concerns for equality between husband and wife.[18] The authority of the husband remained in place but only or primarily because the marriage contract was "rewritten economically."[19] This allowed for the equality gradually gained by wives' achieving legal and political agency, but at the same time, it strengthened beliefs that husbands were to be providers, and wives were thereby economically dependent upon them. The contract was still one to which both parties consented, but it remained a contract the terms of which they did not get to choose.[20]

Coontz traces something of a similar trajectory in Western Europe from the seventeenth century to the twentieth. As she sees it, the new marital economic contract was here closely tied to the developing notion that marriage is for love. What emerged, she argues, was the combination of the "love match" with the "male provider marriage."[21] For the first time marriage belonged to a private sphere in which the husband was the sole breadwinner, and the wife was responsible not only for domestic tasks and child rearing but for sustaining the emotional core of the marriage and the affective ties within the family. Gender relations indeed changed; they were now not based on supposed natural male superiority but on (again supposed) natural male/female complementarity. Marital love, it was presumed, could be nurtured through an emphasis on the differences between women and men.

Marriage as a "love match" was nonetheless destabilizing, since it began to challenge also the economic dependency of wives. Whether in Europe or the United States, something new began to emerge.

---

18. Ibid., 16–17.

19. Ibid., 157. Cott traces this development from the eighteenth to the twentieth century.

20. Cott refers throughout her study to this anomaly, but includes not only the gender relationship assumed and even stipulated for the contract but the additional fact that some persons were refused the right to marry at all (for example, slaves).

21. Coontz, *Marriage, a History*, chapter 9.

Gender relations, the structure of marriage and family, and identification of who controls the theory and practice of these institutions,
were now all problematized.

Christianity and Its Influences[22]

Woven through these histories is the substantial role of Christianity
in shaping political and cultural understandings of marriage and family, especially in the West. Needless to say, the history of Christianity
in regard to marriage is, like all histories of marriage, complicated
and subject to the perspectival interpretations of particular historians. We may begin by asking why, for example, did early Christians
adopt a commitment to monogamy? The reason closest to hand
is that this was what Christianity inherited. After all, as Theodore
Mackin notes, in its early years almost all married Christians were
adult converts who were married before becoming Christian. "As
long as the demographic center of early Christianity was Palestine,
the marriages of early Christians would be Jewish in social structure and motivation."[23] Christianity, as most scholars agree, was in
its beginnings a movement within Judaism. Nonetheless, the cultural context in which early Christian and Jewish families were
located included the larger Greco-Roman world. In the first century of the common era the preferred model for both Jewish and
Roman marriage was monogamy, although some, apparently atypical, polygynous marriages and households still existed for Jews and
others in this context.[24]

---

22. Some of what I discuss here can be found in Margaret A. Farley, "The Church
and the Family: An Ethical Task," *Horizons* 10 (1983): 50–71, and "Family," in *The
New Dictionary of Catholic Social Thought*, ed. Judith A. Dwyer (Collegeville, MN:
Liturgical, 1994), 371–81.

23. Theodore Mackin, *What is Marriage?* (New York: Paulist, 1982), 76.

24. See Ross S. Kraemer, "Typical and Atypical Jewish Family Dynamics: The Cases
of Babatha and Berenice," in *Early Christian Families in Context: An Interdisciplinary
Dialogue* (Grand Rapids, MI: William B. Eerdmans, 2003), 149. Kraemer observes:
"...whether [polygynous marriage] was more common than we realize is currently
impossible to say," since "we know little about the actual family practices of relatively
ordinary people." Kraemer and others also note that there seems not to be much that
is distinctively Jewish in Jewish families in antiquity. Citing Shaye Cohen, she reports
that Jewish families in their "structure, ideals, and dynamics seem to have been virtually identical with those of its ambient culture(s)"; Shaye J. D. Cohen, "Introduction,"
The Jewish Family in Antiquity, ed. Shaye J. D. Cohen (Atlanta: Scholars, 1993), 2.

It is not enough to say, however, that monogamous marriage was embraced by early Christians simply because it was "there." After all, Christians considered themselves "converts" in the sense of turning to a new way of life that marked them as disciples of Jesus Christ and that carried with it significant moral commitments. Concern for the avoidance of "passionate lust," while not unique to Christians of the time, made monogamous relations more suitable than polygynous ones for Christians.[25] Moreover, monogamy was incorporated more broadly into early Christian beliefs and theologies — in terms of its potential symbolic significance for understanding the relation of Jesus Christ and the church, and in terms of its amenability to Christian understandings of neighbor-love. Whether Christianity could have adapted to other patterns of marriage remains, in my view, an open but largely moot question — although not moot in interfaith and cross-cultural dynamics.

Roman law and custom regarding marriage, fashioned on mutual consent, also proved easily adaptable to Christian beliefs and commitments. Christians, like others in the culture in which they lived, thought marriage was a family matter — although the mutual consent of spouses established the marriage. The practice of having Christian pastors present at weddings grew only gradually and informally. Christians brought to marriage some new attitudes, however. As Mackin notes, the eschatological expectations of the early Christians made marriage appear somewhat irrelevant, though a major reason for marrying would continue to be the need of individuals for a context in which they could be sexually active. Marriage as such was not so important to the spreading of the good news.[26]

This, however, brings us to another important question regarding the place of marriage in the Christian church from its beginnings and through many centuries of its growth. Despite the fact that marriage could be structured and established in ways consonant both

---

25. See Wayne A. Meeks, *The First Urban Christians: The Social World of the Apostle Paul* (New Haven, CT: Yale University Press, 1983), 102.

26. This does not mean that marriage and family were not in some ways utterly important to the Christian churches, from the early church on. As original places of worship, sites of hospitality, centers for moral growth and education, it is hard to imagine that Christianity could have grown without them.

with the culture in which it grew and with its own faith commitments, the place of marriage and family in the Christian community
was ambiguous. There were a number of reasons for this. One was
the belief that Christians lived in the "end times," when marrying
was relativized by hope in the eschaton. Another was a skeptical
view of human sexuality that made sexual renunciation a reasonable choice for some. Christianity, as we saw in chapter 2, emerged
in the late Hellenistic Age when even Judaism was influenced by
pessimistic attitudes toward sex. As Ruether observes, "both the
Greco-Roman and the Jewish worlds of the first century knew of
movements and ideologies that were antifamily"[27] and, one might
add, in some sense anti-sex. Philosophies were abroad that challenged persons to live celibate lives in order to keep their minds free
for thought and their hearts unencumbered, especially by the burdens
of a household. There were even organized communities for celibates
among Jews. But in no other rapidly growing group did the notion
of leaving marriage and family behind in order to make a whole-
hearted commitment to God and to the service of the gospel take
hold so strongly as it did in the Christian communities. Although
early Christian writers and preachers affirmed sex as good, a part of
creation, they also believed it to be paradigmatically injured by the
destructive forces of a moral Fall. Hence, taking a lead from Paul,
those who could remain unmarried for the sake of the reign of God
were encouraged to do so.

Peter Brown's study of the practice of "permanent sexual renunciation" among men and women in Christian circles from 40 C.E.
to 430 C.E. provides a multifaceted view of this phenomenon.[28] One
thing is clear: not all choices of celibacy in this period were based on
a negative valuation of sex. Even Paul's rationale focused on freedom
to spread the gospel; his was a pragmatic motivation, not one that

---

27. Ruether, *Christianity and the Making of the Modern Family*, 21.
28. Peter Brown, *The Body and Society: Men, Women, and Sexual Renunciation in Early Christianity* (New York: Columbia University Press, 1988). See also Elizabeth Abbott, *A History of Celibacy* (Toronto: HarperCollins, 1999); Elizabeth Castelli, "Virginity and its Meaning for Women's Sexuality in Early Christianity," *Journal of Feminist Studies in Religion* 2 (Spring 1986): 61–88; Ross S. Kraemer, ed., *Maenads, Martyrs, Matrons, Monastics: A Sourcebook on Women's Religions in the Greco-Roman World* (Philadelphia: Fortress, 1988).

depended on a negation of sex. Beyond this, people chose celibacy on the basis of diverse and multiple reasons: the soul can transform the body; conversion of heart is helped by celibate integration of affections in relation to God; sexual nonavailability of women to men can overturn gendered expectations; friendship can be greater if it transcends sexual intimacy; rigorous asceticism includes the repudiation of sex; sexual renunciation provides what martyrdom once offered: a total self-gift to God; the death and resurrection of Jesus can be entered into in a way that makes sex irrelevant. Brown finds all of these forms and motivations for permanent celibacy — emerging, developing, competing among themselves and competing with a view of married chastity. None of them were lived in a social vacuum, and most of them were intensely debated.[29] Options for celibacy do not, however, by themselves account for the ambiguity surrounding the status of marriage for the early Christians.

Rowan Greer has argued that the church in late antiquity manifested at least three attitudes toward marriage and family, the combination of which yielded a deep ambivalence.[30] First, there was a seeming rejection of family ties, sometimes even open hostility toward the family. The Christian message was a sword of division, setting family members against one another (Matt. 10:34–39; Luke 12:51–53). All Christians were asked in some sense to leave all things, including father, mother, spouse, and children (Matt. 12:25, 22:30; Luke 20:35). Believers lived in anticipation of a new age which would exclude marrying and giving in marriage. Christian attitudes toward martyrdom sometimes manifested extreme forms of rejection of family responsibilities. Women left husbands and children to

---

29. See Margaret A. Farley, "Celibacy Under the Sign of the Cross," in *Sexuality and the U.S. Catholic Church: Crisis and Renewal*, ed. Lisa Sowle Cahill, John Garvey, and T. Frank Kennedy (Rowman & Littlefield, 2006), forthcoming. See also Farley, "The Church and the Family: An Ethical Task"; "Family," in *The New Dictionary of Catholic Social Thought*.

30. Rowan A. Greer, *Broken Lights and Mended Lives: Theology and Common Life in the Early Church* (University Park: University of Pennsylvania Press, 1986), 77–100. I am indebted to Greer for what follows in regard to early Christians and their perception of early Christian assessments of family life. Something close to, or at least in large agreement with, Greer's analysis is further elaborated in Ruether, *Christianity and the Making of the Modern Family*, 25–35, and in Cahill, *Family*, 18–47.

"run to martyrdom," and men were sometimes encouraged to forsake wealth, wife and children, brothers and sisters, with assurances that the renunciation of human ties would bring the achievement of spiritual ties and freedom to spread the gospel.

Second, and closely related to this, early Christians saw the church itself as a substitute for traditional families; the church was their new family.[31] For those who were previously without a family (for example, widows and orphans), now there was the protection of the church. For those who had to leave their former families because of the call of the gospel and the familial divisions it created, the church itself could be their new home (Matt. 10:29–30). The Christian community offered a kind of membership, way of belonging, that promised to abolish all barriers of nation, gender, or economic status. It offered a shared life and a communal identity that superseded any other groupings, even family units.

Finally, in tension with the first and second attitudes, Christians also believed that marriage and family in the ordinary sense could be affirmed, not abolished, within their new life of faith.[32] "Leaving all things" could have a different meaning for those called to live in traditional family households (Acts 10:2; 11:14; 16:15). It could mean the kind of unselfish love that is required in familial relations, the obligation for families to extend their goods to others in need, or a form of engagement-with-detachment on the part of Christians for a significant framework of life that was nonetheless part of a fleeting world.

Marriage was, of course, the choice of the majority of Christians. As such, it was a way of life in which the church had a stake. The household, for Christians as for Jews, Greeks, and Romans, was essential to early urban Christianity. It is not surprising, therefore, that some Christian leaders became alarmed at the real and potential consequences of family rejectionist attitudes that disrupted households and occasioned slanderous criticisms from outside observers. In order to moderate or prevent these consequences, Pauline leaders began to promote household codes in their churches (Col. 3:18–4:1; 1 Tim.

---

31. Greer, *Broken Lights and Mended Lives*, 97–99.
32. Ibid., 99–100.

2:8–15; Eph. 5:22–33; 1 Pet. 2:11–16; Titus 2:2–10). Based on an imperial model for the subordination of all in a household to the *paterfamilias*,[33] the codes supported slavery and reinforced patterns of the domination of husbands over wives. Although the household codes are sometimes interpreted as an affirmation of marriage and family, their imposition held none of the vision of a "new order" that was also important to the early Christians. The legacy of the codes was that Christian families were to adapt to the social order that was around them.

Overall, however, the message of the early Christians remains ambiguous and ambivalent. Attitudes of rejection, substitution, and affirmation regarding marriage and family continued in tension. In the third century all three attitudes contributed to a Christian stance that was in opposition both to the anti-marriage and anti-sex of some Gnostic groups as the church fathers presented them, and to the supposed libertine practices of others. Through many centuries, the Christian church continued to affirm marriage as good, although celibacy was considered better. Affirmation of the family was invariably based on its functional roles in socializing children or in keeping order in society.

It has been argued that Christian ambivalence toward marriage and family through so many centuries served as a critique of the general practices in the Roman Empire, and even worked to transform some traditionally limited versions of these institutions.[34] Apart from the household codes Christianity constituted an implicit judgment of the family as an expression of worldly power. Nonetheless, on one hand, the results of Christian teaching left the general standards and structure of Greco-Roman marriages and families little changed. The *paterfamilias* by and large still reigned, and the household remained ordered as the culture required. On the other hand, much of the eschatological relativization of marriage and family

---

33. See Mary Rose D'Angelo, "Colossians," in *A Feminist Commentary*, vol. 2 of *Searching the Scriptures*, ed. Elisabeth Schüssler Fiorenza (New York: Crossroad, 1994), 313–24.

34. See Greer, *Broken Lights and Mended Lives*, 111–16; Ruether, *Christianity and the Making of the Modern Family*, 5–6.

established in the early church also remained in place. Although marriage was given the dignity of a sacrament among other sacraments in the twelfth century, it was still seen as a lesser calling — still relatively less significant than celibacy — and still primarily instrumental in relation to church and society. Even key developments in the theology of marriage and family tended not to alter the basic assessment of its place in Christian life, even though they affected particular issues such as the nature of the marital bond and the purpose of sexual activity.

Only in the fourteenth century did there begin a significant enough shift in Christian self-understanding to allow a new evaluation of marriage and family life.[35] Subsequently, Renaissance humanists introduced a massive change in focus from otherworldliness to social responsibility, from sexual renunciation to self-discipline and achievement in a world where family and productive labor began to be combined. It was the Protestant Reformation that completed this movement and dramatically articulated a new understanding of the place of the family in Christian life. Marriage and family replaced celibacy as the center of sexual gravity and the primary unit of Christian life. As we saw in chapter 2, Martin Luther and John Calvin did not change the traditional Christian suspicion of sexuality, but they accepted whatever was wrong with sexuality simply as a part of human nature after the Fall.[36] Sex could not be "justified" by procreation or anything else, but only forgiven; and the context of forgiveness was heterosexual marriage. The cure for unruly desire was to be its domestication, its taming, through the burdens of maintaining a household and the rearing of children. More than this, for Luther the primary ethical demand made on Christians was love of neighbor. It was in the institutions of marriage and family that individuals would learn obedience to God, patience, and the required forms of neighbor-love. Through marriage, sexuality could be channeled into the meaning of the whole of life.

35. See John K. Yost, "The Traditional Western Concept of Marriage and the Family: Rediscovering its Renaissance-Reformation Roots," *Andover Newton Quarterly* 20 (March 1980): 169–80.

36. See relevant writings of Luther: *Two Kinds of Righteousness* (1519); *Sermon on the Estate of Marriage* (1519); *Treatise on Good Works* (1520); *Estate of Marriage* (1522); *How God Rescued an Honorable Nun* (1524); and *On Marriage Matters* (1530).

In the Reformation traditions thereafter, the early Christian ambivalence toward marriage and family disappeared. In and through the institutions of marriage and of family, Christians (with rare exception) were now believed to be called to holiness and to the service of their neighbor — the near neighbors of spouse and children and the far neighbors of the wider society. The removal of ambivalence was so effective that, for example, women were left with few alternatives to the life-style of wife and mother. Once the cultural shift of the nineteenth century led to the separation between the private world of the family and the public world of productive work, Christian interpretations of "female nature" were locked into the private, domestic sphere.[37]

The history of Christian marriage does not, of course, stop with the Reformation. But the beliefs and attitudes of the major Christian traditions were set. Although significant differences continued in Roman Catholic and Protestant beliefs and attitudes about marriage and family up until the last half of the twentieth century, both of their histories show a close parallel and interaction with the secular cultural shifts from the seventeenth century to the twenty-first. Hence, Christian families are now like almost all others in the West, with similar issues of gender relationships, diversity of familial forms, structural changes, and destabilization in a culture of ongoing change. I turn, then, from this thumbnail sketch of historical experiences of marriage and family to considerations of these institutions as we know them today.

Descriptive and Normative Questions

As in every time and place, no doubt, today some marriages are happy, and some are not. Sometimes relative levels of happiness or unhappiness correlate with beliefs about the nature of marriage, and sometimes they do not. Sometimes they have clearly to do with structural issues within families, but not always. Anyone who thinks carefully about experiences in families is in favor of transforming

---

37. See Beverly Harrison, "The Effect of Industrialization on the Role of Women in Society," in *Making the Connections: Essays in Feminist Social Ethics*, ed. Carol S. Robb (Boston: Beacon Press, 1985), 42–53.

practices that are oppressive, although there is not always a consensus about what counts as oppression or what transformation should look like. Both marriage and family have been caught in the so-called "culture wars" of today, and they sit in the middle of some volatile political battles. Just about everyone wants both marriages and families to generate human well-being and flourishing; Christians want the shape and the context of these institutions ultimately to be conducive to relationships with God.

Marriage, it is generally agreed, involves commitment; it involves undertaking particular kinds of obligations that we would not otherwise have. Life in a family also involves commitments and obligations, many of them "givens," as in obligations of children to parents and siblings to siblings. "Given" obligations like these are not initiated by a free choice, but they ultimately call for ratification by free choice and commitment. Both marriage and family entail commitments to persons — to love and to care for, to challenge and to support. Insofar as these commitments are understood and shaped by recognized expectations of society, the commitments are not just to love or to care. For the sake of love and the ones we love, we commit ourselves to institutional frameworks that will hold us faithful to our love. We therefore commit ourselves or ratify our obligations to whatever we understand to constitute these frameworks. As an institutional framework for love, marriage involves not only a framework for sex but for a whole fabric of life to be shared together — herein lie its glory and its troubles. As a framework for love, chosen or ratified, family involves relationships not just of loyalty but of growing together in a shared life that is intrinsically good in itself, even as it bridges generations and opens to the wider world — herein lie its treasures and its potential disasters.

Just as human relationships are or ought to be governed by certain norms or ethical principles — in particular, norms of justice; so also, institutional frameworks for commitment in human relationships ought to be subject to norms of justice. If they are not, we challenge them or forsake them, or we shrivel up within them. What can all of this mean for our understandings of and living within the frameworks of our marriages and our families?

Diversity in Family Forms

If there has never been only one form of family in the past, and if we ourselves live in a time of multiple forms of family, how are we to think about the diversity of forms in a way that recognizes them within the concept and the framework of "family"? Can we, for example, think of single-parent as well as two-parent families as "family"? Heterosexual marriages with children as "family"? Same-sex individuals, partners or spouses, with children? Blended families following divorce and remarriage? Families with parents whose children are not genetically related but also not legally adopted? Families where parents are not legally married but who raise children together? Families where there is multiple "mothering" or "fathering" of children not only by biological mothers and fathers but also by grandparents or aunts or uncles or cousins or close friends? Families that do not live together at all? Nuclear families and extended families? And on and on, in a wide diversity of families as "family"?

The general tendency among ethicists today is to advocate inclusiveness in the understanding and acceptance of what counts as "family." And despite some strong opposition not only from the religious right but from moderates as well, there is a growing tendency on the part of more and more people in the United States to accept diverse configurations of family. Lisa Sowle Cahill, for example, identifies the basic cross-cultural form of family as "an organized network of socioeconomic and reproductive interdependence and support grounded in biological kinship and marriage."[38] She nonetheless takes seriously other forms of "human alliance . . . for mutual economic and domestic support, as for reproduction and child-rearing" as analogous to the basic kin- and marriage-based families.[39] She concludes that it is probably not possible to identify the outer boundaries of family, and moreover not prudent to do so. Similarly, Rosemary Radford Ruether insists that a genuine clue to "family value" today involves "acceptance of and support for a diversity of family forms . . . and household patterns" which we are to honor and

---

38. Cahill, *Family*, x-xi.
39. Ibid., xi.

support.[40] Marifé Ramos González argues that "There is no such thing as 'the' Christian family. . . . The Christian 'family' has been over-simplified and excessively idealized. Unfortunately, each family's particular circumstances, which affect its moral decisions for better or worse, are often ignored."[41]

These views are extremely important. We do need not only to support but to celebrate every configuration that "works," that functions reasonably well in facilitating and undergirding a life for people together in mutual affection and flourishing, perhaps especially when it comes to the rearing of children. There is no one model that guarantees happiness and flourishing, at least not in our time. The range of possible models is wide, although perhaps not unlimited. What limits there are have to do less with our preferences for, or idealization of, a "best" model, than with the justice and love that a model makes possible. For example, Jean-Paul Sartre and Simone de Beauvoir developed an entourage of admirers, sexual partners, and protégées whom they liked to call "The Family." The fabric of this "family's" life, however, was apparently marked by deception, seduction, exploitation, prurient exchanges, and held together by a "pact" on the part of the two of them that intentionally included these ways of living together.[42] If the descriptions we have of this agreement and its consequences are accurate, it would be easy for me not to include the Sartre/Beauvoir model of "family" within my understanding of family. This does not mean that other forms or models of family, which may be included in the range of genuine families, do not sometimes have similar problems with intrigue, jealousy, competition, deception, and the like; they are, however, not models that are constructed and designed precisely to include, even savor, these negative forms of relationship. Models may miss or fall short of their goals, but as models they may still count as genuine "family."

---

40. Ruether, *Christianity and the Making of the Modern Family*, 212.

41. Marifé Ramos Gonzàlez, "The Family and Moral Decisions: How Should the Christian Family Respond to the New Moral Challenges of Today?" in *The Family*, ed. Lisa Sowle Cahill and Dietmar Mieth, *Concilium* (Maryknoll, NY: Orbis, 1995), 66.

42. Louis Menand, "Stand by Your Man: The Strange Liaison of Sartre and Beauvoir," *New Yorker* (September 26, 2005): 140–46. Menand is critiquing the four volumes of Beauvoir's memoirs published between 1958 and 1972.

Yet I, like others, will not attempt finally to define "family." What I will do is consider the nature of the relationships that are within a model of family, the goal of the model as a social institutional framework for commitment, and the possibilities it holds for a way to its goal.

Structures and Norms of Relationship

If marriage and family are to function in ways that contribute to the well-being and the flourishing of those who embrace and live within them, then their structures need to be just. This applies to the relationships between spouses, parents and children, siblings, and any others who belong to a "family," whether intergenerationally or horizontally extended to "relatives" of whatever kind. I begin with the relationship between spouses.

To "enter into" marriage is like any other commitment in that it means to yield to another a claim over oneself; it is to give one's word in a way that the word now exists in the other but remains within one's self.[43] But what is the word, the promise, the claim given, the obligation undertaken, in marrying? It is to love — in whatever degree, with whatever understanding of what love means, and with whatever capacity for love. It is to give love a past by giving love a future. It is also to enter into a framework for loving and for sharing a life.

If marrying is itself to be done justly, it must be done in freedom, with some degree of knowledge, and with an intention — again, in some degree — to share a life marked by mutuality, equality, and fruitfulness in the senses of these terms I have described in the previous chapter. Traditionally, the framework of Christian marriage has been marked by three elements: monogamy, sexual exclusivity, and permanence. Whether it has to continue to include just these elements is not quite the question I am addressing here. I have suggested already that polygyny might have been accommodated by Christianity, but there are good reasons for it not to be a considered choice in our time and place. Even where it continues to exist as a majority

---

43. What I give in brief form here is elaborated in my earlier work *Personal Commitments: Beginning, Keeping, Changing* (San Francisco: Harper & Row, 1986).

pattern for marriage, the critiques it receives, especially from women within it, grow louder and clearer.[44] Exclusivity, in terms of fidelity as a sexual partner to one's spouse, has been violated, of course, through time, but not without consequences and not without negative judgment. In the 1970s there were proposals for "open" marriages, in which the very marriage commitment, the agreed upon terms of the marriage, would allow for multiple sexual partners apart from the marriage relationship. Those who made these proposals abrogated them some years later on the grounds that they had proved unrealistic and unworkable.[45] As for permanence, marriage as a lifelong commitment has obviously come upon hard times, though it remains as an ideal and as the actual intention of most individuals who marry.

Reasons for each of these three elements have changed somewhat over the centuries, but they remain concerns both for spouses and for children. Monogamy is the model of choice for most persons in our culture, and certainly for committed Christians. It is thought to be the model that best serves marriage based on love, especially romantic love; it is a model that offers the possibility of intimacy and companionship as goods in themselves; it is a model that can provide the kind of affection that children need; it is a model that can nurture both sex and love in ways that lead to the highest forms of friendship; it is a model that can incorporate understandings of transcendent embodiment and a communion between spouses that partakes of and leads to communion with God. This is its rationale; this is what monogamy as a "framework" can promise. What monogamy promises is not always fulfilled, of course; even the limited degrees of fulfillment that are achieved are not always what was hoped for in the beginning. But institutional "frameworks" are like that, in every sphere of life's commitments. They never guarantee what they are designed for; they only shape, or can shape, the possibilities.

Sexual exclusivity is also both an ideal and a committed obligation in Christian understandings of marriage. It is what is presumed

---

44. See my reports of this in chapter 3.

45. For the most famous proposal, see Nena McNeil and George McNeil, *Open Marriage: A New Life Style for Couples* (New York: M. Evans, 1972). For a report of changed minds, see Arlene Skolnick, *Embattled Paradise* (New York: Basic Books, 1991), 139.

necessary for the goals of monogamous marriage just described. However blasé we have become about adultery in our culture, it remains a form of betrayal and almost always an experience, on the part of the one betrayed, of deep pain. It may not be the unforgivable sin — a marriage so injured can sometimes be restored — but it is not an insignificant breach in the commitment and framework of marriage. I do not need to detail the reasons why sexual exclusivity and fidelity are important to spouses. The reasons are myriad, having to do with embodied sexual bonding, intimacy, and the meanings of sexual exclusivity for all the other aspects of marriage and family. But I remember a woman student of mine once saying that the reason she thought sexual exclusivity belonged essentially to her marriage was that it represented one sphere of her life — a sphere of the utmost intimacy and importance — in which she did not have to be *competitive.*

Lifelong commitments appear much more difficult to sustain in our time and place for reasons that we all know: longevity in human life spans, multiple options in almost every sphere, inability to continue on paths once chosen without traditional structures in place, and so on. In regard to marriage, it is clear that unrealistic expectations and sheer unwillingness to put up with situations that are harmful, not life-giving, or destructive of others constitute the major reasons why permanence is an ideal but one that many cannot reach. Yet if permanence — lifelong faithfulness in love, in sex, in sharing of the multiple dimensions and circumstances of life — can be achieved, it is the path toward the goals of marriage that are most desired. As I have said in regard to the norm of commitment in the previous chapter, it has the possibility of nurturing love and sexual desire; and as I have suggested above, it has the possibility of bringing embodied and inspirited love to its greatest joy.

All of the goals and the realities of marriage as a social framework for love and for life depend, however, on whether the relationship it frames is just. This in turn depends to a great extent on whether the structures of the framework are just. Free choice, mutuality, equality, commitment, fruitfulness, and a responsibility for the wider world can be the measures of this justice. Structures of marriage, for example, that retain inequality between husband and wife — the one the "head" or leader, the other the "helper"; the one by stipulation the breadwinner, the other economically dependent; the one the representative of the family to society and church, the other only the "represented" — these are structures that can severely limit or prohibit the full functioning of marriage and the attainment of its goals. Of course, every marriage partnership is unique in some respects, so even breadwinner/domestic management roles can work however they are shared or divided. Role choices can be embraced in ways that are not universal, and depending on how they are lived, they *may* serve the needs and goals of marriage as long as the relationship between spouses remains just.

The structures of a marriage reflect to an important extent what the individuals believe they are doing when they enter into marriage. For example, a lot of the rhetoric surrounding marriage signals that what is called for in the commitment of marriage is the "total gift" of one to the other. This language is misleading if it means, first, that it is even possible for one person to give him or her self totally to another — except perhaps in forms of slavery where both actions and affections are submitted to the governance of another. If it suggests the theory I have noted before regarding individuals being like two halves who need to become one whole, it carries all of the inaccurate and harmful corollaries of one becoming more whole than the other, or of those who do not marry never being sufficiently complemented in love and in life to become whole.

Moreover, if this language is to be taken literally, it suggests a form of self-sacrifice that has never been good, especially for women. There are, at least for Christians, limits to the sacrifice that is required or even morally allowed for one person in relation to another. Self-sacrifice can destroy as well as contribute to true and just relationships. Some moral obligations are grounded in one's own reality as a human person like other human persons. Hence, one can give one's self in a just and true love, but one ought not obliterate one's self in the giving. Having said this, I do recognize the kinds of unfolding sacrifices — great and small, in the everydayness of ongoing married life and family — and the kind of crucified love, that any great love demands. To lay down one's life for another is perhaps the vocation of every Christian, but if it means genuine destruction of self — of the person whose deepest truth is still coming to be — it is not the kind of love that will build a marriage or a family that are filled with the signs of justice and life.

A just marital love and a just framework for marriage and family will go a long way toward facing one of the most distressing problems in families today — that is, the problem of domestic violence. It is difficult for us to comprehend the size of the problem when some form of violence, physical or emotional, is estimated to exist in up to sixty percent of marriages, and thousands of children are not only abused but die from family violence each year. Everyone can see the problem with harming one another, especially in the close situations of family relationships. But not everyone sees the relevance of power differentials in families, or how violence can rise from a sense of powerlessness effected by religiously inspired but unrealistic expectations placed on persons in family roles. We all face the task today — whether in society or in Christian community — of critically evaluating the import of beliefs regarding power in family relationships and the tolerance of physical and psychological violence as long as it is "contained" within the family. We all need to be concerned about modes of conflict resolution in intimate relations and the rights of persons to reciprocity of care as dependency roles change through a lifetime. I need not elaborate on these matters here, but only signal them as part of a sexual ethic for marriage and family.

One scholar who has taken seriously the need for justice in familial and marital relations is Susan Moller Okin.[46] Her starting point is the contention that contemporary theories of justice invariably assume the family as a social institution and assume that it is just. She argues, on the contrary, that all too often the family is not a just society, and its injustice has negative effects on every other form of society, as well as on the individuals in the family. It is a mistake, she says, to think of the family as a natural "given," anterior to society and with an internal meaning that needs no critiquing as to its justice or injustice. To move beyond this mythical account of the family, Okin proposes to use the strategy of John Rawls in his now

---

46. Susan Moller Okin, *Justice, Gender, and the Family* (New York: Basic Books, 1989).

classic theory of justice for societies;[47] that is, to assume a "veil of ignorance" over each member of a family such that no one knows what her or his role will be in the family. Given that one could be in any of the familial or marital roles, what would everyone want justice to look like once they are actually assigned a role? This is a form of "standing in one another's shoes," and it is a promising thought experiment or heuristic device for gaining critical distance in assessing marriage and family as frameworks for human relationships.

The Goals of Marriage and Family

So much is at stake in the spheres of marriage and family because they are the spheres in which so much of interpersonal love is lived and worked out. The goals of marriage are to some extent the goals of love: embodied and inspired union, companionship, communion, fruitfulness, caring and being cared for, opening to the world of others, and lives made sacred in faithfulness to one another and to God. I do not want rhetoric here to exceed reality, but it is important to ponder what we are doing in our marriages and in our families. Christianity has not always been a good articulator of this. As we have seen, in the early centuries of the church, there were worries that a commitment to these social institutions would leave one with little time for spreading the gospel or doing the deeds of a more universal love; worries that the heart might be divided between love of spouse and love of God; worries that preoccupation with the "things of this world" would distract from the "things of God." Today, in the light of Reformation insights as well as twentieth-century Catholic insights, these worries are not so much with us. Reminded that to love another human being with Christian love is to love that other in Jesus Christ and Jesus Christ in that other, we recognize that human love and divine love need not divide the heart. Although love of God and love of neighbor are not completely equatable, they can be significantly integrated, one with the other. Moreover, with a sacramental view of creation the "things of this world" are not separable from the "things of God," and all persons can be called to share

---

47. John Rawls, *A Theory of Justice* (Cambridge, MA: Harvard University Press, 1972).

in the mission of Jesus Christ, the mending of the world, the struggle to make the world a place where justice and neighbor-love flourish. Preferential love for spouse and family, although in danger of competing with larger loyalties to community and society, can expand to a great-hearted love and a sacrificial effort to care for the world and to build the reign of God. Finally, there is a universal call to holiness, one that is part of every Christian way of life; the challenge is to discern the meaning of this call in the context of marriage and family. It begins by discerning how this way of life can be lived justly.

Along the Way

I have said several times that rhetoric about marriage and family needs to be realistic and cautious — neither too high-flying nor too skeptical. Practically speaking, no one in this world has already attained the goal of their marriage or even of their family. We are all on the way. Issues of monogamy, sexual exclusivity, and permanence are issues of learning the ways of a faithful and enduring love. The story of commitments is not only in their beginning and their end; it is in their "in between."[48] Our lives are stretched out in time; they are not lived all at once. And human time is not like a clock; it is more like the rings in a tree; it is within us. Hence, in the everyday, our choices to ratify our commitments, our efforts to grow in simple patience, kindness, forms of presence, forgiveness, and the "little by little" of welcoming love: these can be part and parcel of the "in between" of lives marked not just by success and joy but by failure, irritation, confusion, and the need for radical hope. Every way of life is lived under the sign of the cross, but every way of life can also grow in its light.

About Children

So much has been written about parenting, about whether our culture loves children or is indifferent to them, about the needs of children and everyone's responsibility for future generations, that I can add little to this literature. We do have special questions about children today: about the size of families, childless marriages, reproductive

---

48. See my treatment of this in *Personal Commitments*, chapters 4–5.

technologies as ways to have children, population concerns, stages of parenting, raising children in a culture fraught with danger for them. In regard to every question, the issue of justice — to children, to parents, to society, to the world — is the central issue.

We live in an oddly conflicted time, especially when it comes to the use of reproductive technologies. These are the technologies that allow almost anyone to have children, whether women or men, whether fertile or infertile, whether single or married. Two things drive our pursuit of these technologies, and they exist at least in paradox. First, some reproductive technologies are used in ways that disconnect biological contributions to children from parenting them. Hence, for example, donor sperm, donor eggs, donor embryos, are often used with only minor concerns about the disconnection between donor and the child to be conceived. Second, reproductive technologies are also used in ways that express an almost insatiable desire to have one's own biological children. That is, a billion-dollar industry has arisen to insure genetically related offspring. I make this observation not to critique reproductive technologies, but as a way to provoke reflection on how it is we want to reproduce ourselves as humans. There are raging debates about all of this, but it may bear more reflection at this point than debate.

There are related questions. For example, when children are born, whose obligation is it to rear them? We now quite readily divide parenting roles into biological parenting, birthing, and social parenting. Even in what is still considered a "standard" form of parenting — that is, heterosexual conception, bearing, and rearing of a child — we debate about who should actually bear the major responsibility and burden of raising a child. Is it best for the child if a parent remains at home? Is it better if a parent remains at home for years, including in his or her tasks home-schooling? Or is it better to offer children more than one model and experience of mothering and fathering? Is it oppressive to children to be without much active presence on the part of parents? Is it oppressive for them to have too much active presence in terms of children not having the nurturing of grandparents and other family members, or of child care professionals and social situations in which they are mutually nurtured both by mentors and by peers?

I do not propose specific answers to all these questions. However, I do want to identify a principle to guide us in this area of human responsibility, a principle that incorporates the norms of a sexual ethic and that can perhaps be extended to the consequences of sex. I have already said enough about autonomy and relationality that it will not be surprising if I add the following: no children should be conceived who will be born in a context unconducive to their growth and development in relationships, or unconducive to their ultimately becoming autonomous, morally responsible for themselves. There is, of course, no real way to predict which of many contexts can provide what children need to experience relationality and to grow in freedom and the possibility of self-determination. Yet we can say that choices regarding the various forms of reproduction, and various configurations of parents, can be evaluated in terms of whether or not someone is sufficiently committed to each child to provide for the child's nurturance within an intimate relationship; and to provide for whatever the child needs to grow in the possibility of personal freedom. In other words, forms of reproduction and configurations of parenting can be assessed in terms of whether or not a child will be affirmed in her relationality and her development of a capacity for self-determination — whether or not she will be respected and nurtured in the features of her being that constitute the core of her humanity.

Same-Sex Relationships

Questions surrounding the ethics of same-sex relationships are in Christian communities as in Western society at large marked by ongoing controversy and, for many, ongoing anguish and anger. These questions are among the most volatile issues in churches and synagogues across the United States. They are ethical questions that must be addressed because they remain, for many, the heart of the matter regarding homosexuality — a major issue for church unity, a central factor in gay and lesbian individuals' continuing journey of faith, a challenge to a society that all too frequently tolerates discrimination and even violence against its gay and lesbian people. They are ethical questions that must be addressed also because they are questions about real persons — questions about identity, place in community, relationships, and callings.

The fundamental question pressed throughout this volume has been: when is sexual activity appropriate in human relationships? It is this same question that must be asked when we turn explicitly to same-sex relationships. This means that the key question here is not whether same-sex relationships can be ethically justified, but what must characterize these relationships when they are justified. To anticipate a conclusion regarding same-sex relationships that follows from the work of previous chapters: the ethical framework for sexual relationships and actions developed in chapter 6 is not different for heterosexual and homosexual relationships. Given the intensity of the debates regarding same-sex relationships, however, it is not sufficient to start and end with this conclusion.

The literature on homosexuality in recent years appears to be even more voluminous than publications on marriage and family. Multiple aspects of homosexual orientation and sexual activity have been examined — its history in Western societies, cross-cultural experiences of homosexuality, its etiology, religious assessments, social contexts, and more. Because of the rich resources for understanding same-sex relationships today, especially in Western culture and in Christian contexts and theologies, I attempt only three things here: first, a consideration of Christian sources used or available for use in the Christian community; second, an exploration of ways in which the framework for sexual ethics that I have proposed may open up possibilities for an ethics for same-sex relationships; and third, some reflection on whether or not it matters if a preference for same-sex relationships is a "given" for some people, but chosen by others.

Theological and Ethical Sources

In the Christian churches, debates about same-sex relationships tend to focus on the interpretation and use of the sources for Christian theology and ethics: Scripture, tradition, secular disciplines, and contemporary experience, as discussed in chapter 5. Insofar as debates have taken place not only in Christian circles but in the public forum, many of the arguments are surprisingly similar. In particular, arguments from natural law perspectives — or better, arguments about the concrete reality of same-sex orientation — overlap in secular and religious debates. It is therefore to some extent possible to combine an examination of Christian sources with an examination of arguments that appear in secular, especially political, contexts.

My own view is that none of the sources for Christian sexual ethics provides much light on the moral status of same-sex relationships if the question remains simply whether they are permitted or prohibited. For example, we have seen in previous chapters just how difficult it is to get answers to specific permission/prohibition questions in sexual ethics from Scripture. Similarly, historical studies of Christian traditions yield ambiguous results. Secular disciplines, too, have not offered sufficient evidence to settle the questions of the moral status of same-sex relationships and actions. Contemporary experience is more promising as a guide, but we need to look at it more carefully.

Scripture

In general, the very few biblical texts that deal explicitly with homosexuality must be read against the whole of the biblical witness.[49] As we have seen, there are two elements in Hebrew Bible perspectives on sexual conduct that influence almost all of its texts on sexual morality — namely, the obligation to marry and to procreate, and the patriarchal model upon which ideas of marriage and society were institutionally based. Given these perspectives, there is understandably little room for same-sex relationships. A third element influential in shaping the sexual rules of the Hebrew Bible is the concern to distinguish practices of the Israelites from what was considered the idolatry of neighboring nations. The Leviticus prohibition against males lying "with a male as with a woman" is associated with this concern (Lev. 18:22; 20:13). It is only later that interpretations tend to escalate specific prohibitions into paradigms of moral evil, thus obscuring the original intent of the laws.

---

49. It is a disputed question whether some of even these few texts are referring to anything like what is meant by "homosexuality" today. The term as such does not actually appear in any of the original languages of the Bible, and the concept appears to have different, or at least more narrow, content than is generally given to it today.

The story of Sodom and Gomorrah (Gen. 19:1–29), today popularly thought to present a threatened crime of homosexual rape at the heart of the sins of the cities (Gen. 1–11), has no such meaning when looked at more carefully. In its earliest interpretations — that is, in other Hebrew Bible and apocryphal texts — the extreme moral depravity of the citizens of Sodom and other cities of the plain was identified not with homosexuality but with violations of moral requirements of hospitality, as well as with injustice, arrogance, and hatred of foreigners (Ezek. 16:49; Sirach 16:8; Wisd. of Sol. 10:6–8; 19:13–15). In the Christian Testament, where Sodom is referenced, again there is no mention of homosexuality (Luke 10:12; Matt. 10:15). What influenced later Christians to introduce an identification of homosexual sins as central to this story was probably the interpretation of first century C.E. Jewish writers, in particular the historian Josephus and the Hellenistic philosopher Philo.[50]

The Christian Testament, like the Hebrew Bible, is also not a very helpful source if our question has to do with moral prohibitions or permissions regarding same-sex relationships. As we have seen before, it offers no systematic code of sexual ethics. The few texts that appear to refer to homosexuality offer problems of interpretation — whether because of ambiguity in the use of rhetorical devices and specific terms, or disparity between the meaning of same-sex relationships in the historical context of Paul (Rom. 1:26–27; 1 Cor. 6:9; 1 Tim. 1:10) and the meaning we assume for same-sex relationships today.

Contested interpretations of Romans 1:26–27 provide an interesting and important case in point. The contemporary debate about this text has gone on for years, and it can be tracked within, for example, the writings of John Boswell, Richard Hays, and Dale Martin. Boswell argues first that Paul's intention was not to stigmatize any particular sexual behavior, but rather to "condemn the Gentiles for their general infidelity."[51] Boswell adds that Paul's reference to same-sex

---

50. See Martti Nissinen, *Homoeroticism in the Biblical World: A Historical Perspective* (Minneapolis: Fortress, 1998), especially 93–95.

51. John Boswell, *Christianity, Social Tolerance, and Homosexuality: Gay People in Western Europe from the Beginning of the Christian Era to the Fourteenth Century* (Chicago: University of Chicago Press, 1980), 108.

relationships had to do with heterosexuals, filled with passion, acting against what was natural to them. This argument Boswell bases on the observation that same-sex "orientation" would not have been a recognized concept in the time of the early church. Hays rejects Boswell's interpretation, arguing instead that Paul would have held a notion of male/female complementarity as part of the created nature of human beings, and would therefore have judged any homosexual behavior as unnatural and a result of the Fall of Adam and Eve. Hays further charges, against Boswell, that it is anachronistic to argue for any interpretation of Paul's text in the light of more recent insights into homosexuality.[52] Martin counters that to place Romans 1 in the context of a reading of Genesis, whereby heterosexual desire is natural, ordained in creation, and homosexual desire is unnatural and disordered because of the Fall, is to miss and even distort Paul's point regarding not creation and fall but, rather, the invention of idolatry.[53] With this latter interpretation, Martin argues that Paul was referring not to "unnatural" desires but to the unleashing of excessive, out-of-control desires. "Degree of passion, rather than object of choice, was the defining factor of desire."[54]

Although in Paul's historical context the degree of passion did not make passionate desire unnatural, actions that violated convictions about gender hierarchy might indeed yield a judgment of "unnatural."[55] In the Greco-Roman world, any notion of a man taking on the lower role of a woman, choosing to demean himself by becoming

---

52. Richard B. Hays, "Relations Natural and Unnatural: A Response to John Boswell's Exegesis of Romans 1," *Journal of Religious Ethics* 14 (1986): 184–215; Hays, *The Moral Vision of the New Testament: Community, Cross, New Creation: A Contemporary Introduction to New Testament Ethics* (San Francisco: HarperSanFrancisco, 1996), chapter 16. The charge of anachronism here is a curious one, since Boswell's point is precisely that one cannot read back into Paul's writings a modern notion of sexual orientation. Hence, what is important is that this notion was *not* there. On the other hand, Bernadette Brooten argues, with Hays, that Paul would have had some idea of "natural" sexual expressions in terms of gender distinctions and orientations, but these would have been based on cultural assumptions of female inferiority — something of which Hays takes no account. See Bernadette J. Brooten, *Love Between Women: Early Christian Responses to Female Homoeroticism* (Chicago: University of Chicago Press, 1996), 245 n. 86.

53. Dale B. Martin, "Heterosexism and the Interpretation of Romans 1:18–31," *Biblical Interpretation* 3 (1995): 332–55.

54. Ibid., 342.

55. Ibid., 344.

"effeminate," engaging in sexual activity where the male is passive as a woman was thought to be, could be considered, "unnatural." In this case, however, the issue was male superiority, not the direction of erotic desire for male or female. Martin's concern for this element in a more adequate interpretation of Romans 1 is shared by other scholars whose focus is on the social construction of heterosexuality as the norm for sexual relationships. Mary Rose D'Angelo, for example, argues that "the biblical texts that have been read as condemnations of homosexuality originated in part as guardians of the kinds of sexual hierarchy that . . . is violated when a male is 'reduced' to the status of a woman."[56] Judith Plaskow observes that "we can read biblical prohibitions of homosexual behavior not as isolated injunctions but as part of the process of the construction of heterosexual marriage as normative."[57] And Diana Swancutt proposes a reading of Paul that subverts gender hierarchy by transforming it within the Body of Christ.[58]

If work on one text, such as Romans 1:26–27, can produce not only diverse interpretations but important insights into historical understandings of same-sex relationships, a continuing return to multiple texts may be warranted.[59] If we do not gain a final answer to questions of permission/proscription in this regard, this is important in itself. At the very least, it should keep us from entering the battle of proof-texting. Standing before the biblical witness as a whole, a

---

56. Mary Rose D'Angelo, "Perfect Fear Casteth Out Love: Reading, Citing, and Rape," in *Sexual Diversity and Catholicism: Toward the Development of Moral Theology*, ed. Patricia Beattie Jung, with Joseph Andrew Coray (Collegeville, MN: Liturgical, 2001), 175–97, at 181 and passim. See also John J. Winkler, *The Constraints of Desire: The Anthropology of Sex and Gender in Ancient Greece* (New York: Routledge, 1990); Brooten, *Love Between Women*, 239–53.

57. Judith Plaskow, "Lesbian and Gay Rights: Asking the Right Questions," *Tikkun* 9 (1992): 32.

58. Diana Swancutt, "Sexing the Pauline Body of Christ: Scriptural 'Sex' in the Context of the American Christian Culture War," in *Toward a Theology of Eros: Transfiguring Passion at the Limits of the Disciplines*, ed. Virginia Burrus and Catherine Keller (New York: Fordham University Press, 2006), forthcoming.

59. In addition to the works cited above, other studies of importance to the use of scripture in discerning a Christian stance regarding same-sex relations include: Robin Scroggs, *The New Testament and Homosexuality* (Philadelphia: Fortress, 1983); Jeffrey Siker, ed., *Homosexuality in the Church: Both Sides of the Debate* (Louisville: Westminster John Knox, 1994); Choon-Leong Seow, ed., *Homosexuality and Christian Community* (Louisville: Westminster John Knox, 1996).

modest conclusion to be drawn is that there exists no solid ground for an absolute prohibition or a comprehensive unquestionable blessing for same-sex relationships and actions today, not in the Hebrew Bible or the Christian Scriptures. Rather, discernment of the meaning and import of the scriptures themselves in relation to this particular ethical issue, as others, is part of the unfolding history of Christian understanding regarding human sexuality. But whatever the results of ongoing exegesis and interpretation, the Christian community must still discern, in the light of its other sources, just how relevant and useful are any isolated texts to the life of the community today.

Tradition

As far as I know, no one today is trying to argue that homosexual relationships or actions should be condemned simply because the Christian tradition has always thought about homosexuality in a certain way. To argue from this standpoint, in any case, would mean encountering problems with the view of tradition that I identified in chapter 5. Moreover, it is by no means certain that it is accurate to say that Christians have always judged homosexuality negatively. The historical studies of scholars like Boswell have uncovered a much less univocal teaching and understanding through the centuries.[60]

As I have said before, if today's Christians are to discern how to use the record of faith in the teachings, practices, theology, and prayer of the Christian community through time, it is necessary to engage in a process of exegesis and interpretation of this record, this tradition — no less than of Scripture. Even where in the Christian tradition homosexuality has been negatively judged — or positively judged, for that matter — we must come to understand and evaluate the reasons for these judgments, their social and cultural context, and the consequences of the judgments for Christians in the past and the present.

As noted in chapter 2, in the Christian tradition of sexual ethics there have been two dominant motifs: procreation as the fundamental purpose of sexual intercourse and male/female complementarity as the essential basis and framework for sexual activity. The former

---

60. Boswell, *Christianity, Social Tolerance, and Homosexuality*.

was predominant in the Roman Catholic tradition, and the latter came to particular prominence in mainline Protestant traditions with the insistence that the ordinary remedy for sexuality, disordered by original sin, must be heterosexual marriage. Both of these motifs are extremely relevant to the moral evaluation of homosexuality. So long as the tradition continued to justify sex primarily and even solely as a means for the procreation of children, or sex in heterosexual marriage primarily as a corrective to a disordered and indomitable sexual drive, there was, of course, little or no room for any positive valuation of same-sex relationships. Heterosexual marriage had to be not only the general norm for Christian life but, along with celibacy for those who could manage it, the only acceptable choice for Christians regarding sexuality.

Despite this longstanding general sexual ethical tradition, the twentieth century has seen dramatic developments in both Roman Catholic and Protestant sexual ethics. The dominant motifs have each undergone significant changes. In much of Catholic moral theology and ethics, the procreative norm as the sole or primary justification of sexual activity is gone. As we have seen, procreation is still extremely important as a goal for some sexual intercourse, and as giving meaning to some sexual relationships; but new understandings of the totality of the person support a radically new concern for sexuality as an expression and a cause of love. The values of sexual intimacy, pleasure, and companionship are lauded as important elements in human and Christian flourishing. This means that, above all, the kind of deep suspicion of sexual desire and sexual pleasure that characterized both Catholic and Protestant traditions for so long has largely disappeared. That is, the view of sexuality as fundamentally disordered is gone from a great deal of Christian thought. Moreover, in both Protestant and Catholic traditions, rigid stereotypes of male/female complementarity have been softened, so that equality and shared possibilities and responsibilities now appear in most Christian theologies of marriage and family.

All of these changes have made a significant difference for many Christians' evaluations of same-sex relationships. Still, however, the motifs of a procreative norm and gender complementarity continue to appear in, for example, evangelical Protestant views of marriage and family, and in official Roman Catholic negative assessments of homosexual activity. In the latter, the procreative norm is relativized for heterosexual relationships (following the acceptance of some forms of contraception such as "natural family planning"), but it is absolutized once again when homosexual relationships are at issue. For many Catholics and Protestants, the view of sexuality as an indomitable and chaotic drive needing above all to be tamed is gone for heterosexual sex, but it appears alive and well in judgments made about gay and lesbian sex. Construals of male/female gender hierarchy and complementarity are moderated for general social roles, but the importance of gender complementarity undergirds the final barrier against an acceptance of same-sex relationships.[61]

Nonetheless, important shifts have taken place regarding the moral assessment of homosexuality as well as heterosexuality. Despite ongoing tensions in the traditions, and intense debates, some Protestant mainline churches — notably the United Church of Christ — have developed positive statements and attitudes toward same-sex relationships. And despite what I have said about official positions in the Roman Catholic church, there are changes that should not be underestimated. Although homosexual genital actions are still judged to be intrinsically disordered, and hence "objectively" immoral, they can be "subjectively" moral depending on the state of mind and intentions of an individual person. Also, homosexual orientation in persons is not condemned; it is even accepted. Moreover, pastoral recommendations for welcoming gays and lesbians into the worshiping community are generally positive, although tensions remain.[62]

---

61. As instances of these sustained official Roman Catholic positions, see for example, Congregation for the Doctrine of the Faith, *Declaration on Certain Questions Concerning Sexual Ethics* (1975), #8; *Catechism of the Catholic Church* (Liberia Editrice Vaticana, 1994), #2357. For an unofficial but significant Protestant statement supporting traditional forms of gender complementarity, see John Piper and Wayne Grudem, "An Overview of Central Concerns: Questions and Answers," in *Recovering Biblical Manhood and Womanhood: A Response to Evangelical Feminists*, ed. John Piper and Wayne Grudem (Wheaton, IL: Crossway Books, 1991), 60–92; *The Danvers Statement* (Council on Biblical Manhood and Womanhood, 1990).

62. See, for example, U.S. Conference of Catholic Bishops, *Always Our Children: A Pastoral Message to Parents of Homosexual Children* (Washington, DC: 1973); Baltimore Archdiocesan Task Force, *A Ministry to Lesbian and Gay Catholic Persons*

What is clear is that the Christian tradition regarding homosexual persons and behavior is, at least in Western strands of the tradition, in a state of flux. This would be denied by many, but key developments are difficult to ignore. Without offering the last word for the tradition, another modest conclusion may be drawn: that is, just as it is certainly not possible to draw from the tradition at this point a comprehensive blessing for same-sex relationships, so it is also not possible to draw an absolute prohibition. The resources of the tradition require more examination if its best insights are to be brought to bear on contemporary questions of homosexuality.

Secular Disciplines

Various human sciences have contributed to contemporary understandings of homosexuality. Chromosomes and hormones, behavioral patterns and psychological adjustments, social forces and cultural differences have all been studied to some extent. As a result of such studies, there exists today a variety of theories regarding the etiology of homosexuality (genetic, biological, psychological, social, developmental, cultural) and its status as a possibility for human flourishing. Those who attempt to assess the history of biological and psychological research on homosexuality raise serious questions about the goals and results of much of this research.[63] From its serious beginnings in the nineteenth century, it has long been marked by a bias against homosexuality as a legitimate human variant. The goals of research were frequently based on the assumption that same-sex desires or orientation are pathological, and the research was therefore ultimately aimed at the development of therapies or

(Baltimore: Archdiocese of Baltimore, 1981). See also the extensive bibliography provided in *Homosexuality: A Positive Catholic Perspective* (Mt. Rainier, MD: New Ways Ministry, 2003). Recent concerns by church leaders about the ordination of gay men is disturbing but perhaps temporary, since these concerns are voiced in the context of past failures in institutional responsibilities regarding the sexual misconduct of clergy, heterosexual or gay.

63. See Timothy F. Murphy, *Gay Science: The Ethics of Sexual Orientation Research* (New York: Columbia University Press, 1997); Simon LeVay, *Queer Science: The Use and Abuse of Research Into Homosexuality* (Cambridge, MA: MIT Press, 1996). In addition to other biases in this research, both of these authors note the male bias visible in the fact that most studies of sexual orientation have been on male subjects.

disciplinary strategies. Philosopher of medicine Timothy Murphy observes that "The stigmatizing effects of sexual orientation science in the nineteenth and twentieth centuries are not to be denied insofar as some people did adopt views of homoeroticism as inferior sexuality precisely because of medicine's assertions to that effect."[64] This remained true even after medical organizations rejected the view of homosexuality as pathological.[65]

Yet ongoing research on homosexuality has to some extent served to correct the bias brought to research protocols and their social consequences. In recent years it has clearly contributed to the depathologizing of same-sex erotic orientation. For example, studies have provided significant evidence that gay men do not differ in fundamental psychological ways from heterosexually oriented men; that the children of gay parents are not more likely than other children to be gay themselves; that the inclusion of homosexuals in the military does not indicate that homosexuality is "contagious" or disruptive of the ordinary work and lives of military men.[66] Empirical research plays an important role in destroying myths regarding child molesters (the majority of whom are heterosexual married men); long-term studies are extremely important regarding the parenting success of gay or lesbian partners. While these studies do not by themselves settle the questions about the moral status of homoeroticism, they

---

64. Murphy, *Gay Science*, 53.

65. See American Psychiatric Association, *Diagnostic and Statistical Manual: Mental Disorders*, 4th ed. (Washington, DC: American Psychiatric Association, 1994). In 1952, the American Psychiatric Association considered homosexuality to be a sociopathic personality disturbance. In 1968, it changed this to a simple mental disorder. But in 1974 it declassified homosexuality as necessarily a disorder of any kind, retaining only the specific instance of ego-dystonic homosexuality. Later even this diagnosis was discarded, though the A.P.A. does continue to recognize "sexual orientation distress" in those who experience conflict with their homoerotic desires. The charge that the changes in the A.P.A. position are merely political, not based on sound medical opinion, tend to come only from those who oppose the change.

66. See, as cited in Murphy, *Gay Science*, 57, 238–39 nn. 25–29: Evelyn Hooker, "The Adjustment of the Male Overt Homosexual," *Journal of Projective Techniques* 21 (1957): 18–31; "Male Homosexuality in the Rorschach," ibid., 22 (1958): 33–54; "What Is a Criterion?" ibid., 23 (1959): 278–81; David W. Dunlap, "Homosexual Parents Raising Children: Support for Pro and Con," *New York Times* (January 7, 1996): A:13; Randy Shilts, *Conduct Unbecoming: Lesbians and Gays in the U.S. Military, Vietnam to the Persian Gulf* (New York: St. Martin's, 1993), 281–83, 647 and passim; F. D. Jones and R. J. Koshes, "Homosexuality and the Military," *American Journal of Psychiatry* 152 (1995): 16–21.

help to counter social bias and to provide significant input in future societal legislation. They should also give pause to those religious thinkers who continue to insist that homosexuality is both unnatural and a danger to society.[67]

The question of what is or is not "natural" continues to sit in the middle of debates about the value of the biological and social sciences for understanding homosexuality. Murphy, reflecting on the importance of ideas of nature for questions of the morality of homosexuality, asks what light can be shed on these questions by sexual orientation research.[68] Animal research shows that in the world of nature most animals engage in some same-sex behavior. Research on human sexual orientation shows the falsity of some popular beliefs as well as erroneous findings in previous research. Cross-cultural research provides evidence of same-sex relationships in virtually every culture and acceptance of it in many cultures. When it comes to biological research, however, Murphy observes that it is of "limited value in rebutting claims that homoeroticism is 'unnatural' in the usual sense of the term."[69] My own response to the search for biological factors undergirding sexual orientation is skeptical as well. If, for example, a "homosexuality" gene is identified, many people will not conclude from this that homosexuality is "natural" for those who have the gene. They will instead conclude that the gene is like a gene for alcoholism; that is, it is a genetic anomaly in the person who has it, and the response to it should be genetic or some other kind of therapy, or even the elimination of the gene altogether from the human gene pool. But we shall have to return to the issue of what is natural because it is "given," and what difference this makes in assessing the morality of same-sex relationships.

---

67. Some Christian psychologists argue that there is nothing in the conclusions of scientific and medical research that warrants a change in traditional Christian views of homosexuality, namely, traditional views that homosexuality is a violation of God's will, contrary to revelation about the created meaning of sexuality, and caused primarily by human brokenness and sin. See Stanton J. Jones and Mark A. Yarhouse, *Homosexuality: The Use of Scientific Research in the Church's Moral Debate* (Downers Grove, IL: InterVarsity, 2000).

68. Murphy, *Gay Science*, 166.

69. Ibid.

Much scientific research on homosexuality has focused on its determinants or causes. It may be asked, then, why research has not also addressed such questions as: What are the reasons that homosexuality has been seen as a danger to religion and society? Why has it been constructed as an object of moral opprobrium? How did it become a metaphor for degradation and lack of dignity?[70] These questions bring us once again to the issue of the social and cultural construction of the meanings of homosexuality. They are the questions raised by sociologist David Greenberg in his pursuit of the reasons for the intensity of feeling behind prohibitions against same-sex relationships.[71] It has been variously construed as a crime against nature, a sin against God, inherited physiological degeneration, and psychological illness; but also — at some points in time, including the late twentieth and early twenty-first centuries — as a special gift, or as simply an alternative orientation of human sexual desire. Depending on the favored construction, responses have ranged from recommendations for repentance, genetic therapy, psychoanalysis, or political advocacy for the rights and general welfare of gays and lesbians.

Greenberg traces the social and cultural influences on negative attitudes toward homosexuality in terms that he believes are not unique to homosexuality but common to the social construction of other forms of "deviance."[72] Social groups are labeled deviant by reason of social norms and devices that label them "outsiders," different in a way that is important to a given society for a variety of reasons. Tracing the patterns of response to particular outsiders includes taking account of multiple factors: what there is about the "offenders" that is considered deviant (for example, race, ethnicity, geographical origin, sexual orientation); the social and cultural context in which attitudes to these differences are formed (for example, increasing or decreasing population, economics, concern for familial conformity and cohesion); particular promotion of ideas about what counts as full humanity, qualities of leadership, acceptable behavior (as in those put forth by religious leaders, philosophers, or

---

70. See Murphy, *Gay Science*, 73.
71. David F. Greenberg, *The Construction of Homosexuality* (Chicago: University of Chicago Press, 1988).
72. Ibid., 499.

other professionals). Greenberg's sociological analysis of the history of Western civilization attends to these kinds of factors, providing different but plausible reasons in different times and situations for the sustaining, and the waxing and waning, of negative attitudes about homosexuality.[73] From kinship-structured societies to feudalism, and from the medicalization of homosexuality to "family values" politics, the reasons for identifying homosexuals as deviants changed, but one is tempted to conclude: once on the outside, for a long time on the outside. The intermingled factors are not predictable and not necessarily conspiratorial. Hence, for example, "The nineteenth-century inverts who argued that homosexuality was innate did not anticipate what the degeneracy theorists would make of their claim."[74]

Adrienne Rich's now classic essay on "Compulsory Heterosexuality and Lesbian Existence" reinforces and sheds new light on the social construction of homosexuality, especially lesbian experience.[75] She, too, focuses on the negative judgments about homosexuality, but in order to call for change. A poet and scholar in gender studies, Rich's aim and approach, therefore, differ from Greenberg's. Major goals for the essay are "to encourage heterosexual feminists to examine heterosexuality as a political institution which disempowers women — and to change it," and also to allow lesbian women to "feel the depth and breadth of woman identification and woman bonding."[76] This, she believes, can be a way to change and transform perceptions of lesbians as deviant. Her argument is that an initial tendency in women to identify with other "women as passionate comrades, life partners, co-workers, lovers, community," has been historically invalidated and forced into "hiding and disguise" by the social enforcement of heterosexuality.[77] Whether in the family, the workplace, or wider society, women are segregated into roles that are

---

73. For his summary of sociological methodology as it applies to his historical analysis throughout his book, see especially Greenberg, ibid., "Epilogue: Under the Sign of Sociology," 482–99.

74. Greenberg, *The Construction of Homosexuality*, 499.

75. Adrienne Rich, "Compulsory Heterosexuality and Lesbian Existence," in *The Lesbian and Gay Studies Reader*, ed. Henry Abelove, Michele Aina Barale, and David M. Halperin (New York: Routledge, 1993), 227–53. This publication adds a later Forward (1982) and Afterward (1986) to the original essay published in *Signs*, 5 (1980): 631–60.

76. Rich, in *Lesbian and Gay Studies Reader*, 227.

77. Ibid., 229.

"sexualized" in relation to men. Drawing on the work of Catherine MacKinnon as well as Kathleen Barry, Rich maintains that women in general are all conditioned to focus on men — for romance, security, leadership, and even their identity as the female "other."[78] The distortion in this is that they are prevented from establishing and sustaining the bonds between them that should have begun with their mothers and continued in some form in relation to all women. Rich is not proposing that every woman should or even can be in genital sexual relationships with another woman, but that there is a continuum of women-identified ways of existing — some lesbian in the usual erotic sense, but most a form of bonding that belongs to women in many kinds of relationships.

"Secular disciplines" as sources for theology and ethics include, of course, more than the biological and behavioral sciences and more than the kind of historical perspectives that Rich offers.[79] Nonetheless, at this point we can ask whether it is possible to draw any conclusions from what is available to us from the biological and behavioral sciences. In the interest of continuing, for now at least, only modest claims, here are some minimal conclusions: (1) The empirical sciences have not determined that homosexuality is of itself, in a culture-free way, harmful to human persons. Whether it is less conducive to human happiness is not a question that can be answered without an agreed upon idea of what happiness is. (2) Some rationales for religious and philosophical negative judgments of same-sex relationships — as well as popular beliefs that derive from these — have been shown to be false by empirical research. (3) Same-sex orientation may be natural for some persons if by "natural" is meant a given characteristic, impossible to change without doing violence to

---

78. See Catherine A. MacKinnon *Sexual Harassment of Working Women: A Case of Sexual Discrimination* (New Haven, CT: Yale University Press, 1979); Kathleen Barry, *Female Sexual Slavery* (Englewood Cliffs, NJ: Prentice-Hall, 1979).

79. My consideration of these sources draws also on such historical works as that by psychiatrist Francis Mark Mondimore, *A Natural History of Homosexuality* (Baltimore: Johns Hopkins University Press, 1996). I have found important and useful historical, sociological, and anthropological information also in collections such as: Martin Duberman, Martha Vicinus, and George Chancey, eds., *Hidden from History: Reclaiming the Gay and Lesbian Past* (New York: Meridian, 1990). In addition, I assume in this section on secular disciplines all that we have already seen of contemporary philosophical interpretations of sexuality in general.

the nature of a person as a whole. (4) Same-sex preference in sexual relations may be an option for many persons since human persons have generally a greater or lesser capacity to respond emotionally and sexually to persons of both the opposite or same sex. I return to all of these below.

The last word is not in from reason's efforts to understand sexuality or homosexuality. At this point, however, it is difficult to see how on the basis of sheer human rationality alone, and all of its disciplines, an absolute prohibition of same-sex relationships or activities can be maintained. On the other hand, the ambiguity of sex remains, so that it is equally difficult to argue that all sexual expressions are for the benefit of human persons. We are still pressed to the task of discerning what must characterize same-sex relationships if they are to conduce to human flourishing.

Contemporary Experience

The fourth source for Christian ethical insight is contemporary experience. Scripture, tradition, and secular disciplines all reflect on experiences, past and present. As I have said before, what differentiates "contemporary experience" as a discrete source is the unsystematic way we have access to it. In this context, I am referring primarily to the testimony of women and men whose sexual preference is for others of the same sex. Assuming all of the cautions I articulated in chapter 5 regarding experience as a source of moral insight, we cannot expect that experience alone will put to rest all of our questions regarding the status of same-sex relationships. We do, however, have some clear and profound testimonies — written, spoken, visibly lived — to the life-enhancing possibilities of same-sex relationships and the integrating possibilities of sexual activity within these relationships. We have the witness that homosexuality can be a way of embodying responsible human love and sustaining human and Christian friendship. We also have witness that obstacles raised to same-sex relationships and loves can bring deep and unnecessary suffering to the lives of homosexual persons and partnerships.

To understand the significance of concrete experience for theological ethics, let me point again to not one but two issues regarding

specific moral rules where experience appears to be an indispens-
able source. The first is the practice of "artificial contraception" in
heterosexual marital intercourse; the second is the issue of same-sex
relationships. I point to both issues in order to put the latter — which
is our direct concern here — in a broader perspective. The issue of
contraception is almost wholly particular to the Roman Catholic tradition today. One of the arguments currently offered in support of a
continued official prohibition of contraception is based on the supposed selfishness of married partners who use "artificial" means of
contraception. The claim is made that employing contraceptive tech-
nology to prevent pregnancy means that the love of the partners is
intrinsically selfish, even exploitative on the part of at least one of
them; it is a love that refuses to give or receive the "total gift" of
self. This description and claim, however, cannot stand in the face of
the reported experience of countless married persons. The counter-
descriptions from these spouses constitute genuine testimony from
persons who by their whole lives bear witness to a high degree of un-
selfishness — whether in raising the children they have or in serving
the church and society in other ways.

The same is true when it comes to homosexual persons and
same-sex relationships. Indeed, given the arguable inconclusiveness
of Scripture, tradition, and secular disciplines, concrete experience
becomes a determining source on this issue. And we do, as I have
said above, have clear and profound testimonies to the intrinsic goodness of same-sex loves and same-sex relationships. We do have strong
witnesses to the role of such loves and relationships in sustaining
human well-being and opening to human flourishing. This same witness extends to the contributions that individuals and partners make
to families, the church, and society as a whole.

I have acknowledged above in chapter 5 that experience is not a
"deposit" of truth that requires no criteria for its interpretation. For
it to matter in communal, institutional, or societal ethical discernment, it must cohere with general norms of justice, even though it
challenges specific rules as inapplicable or unjust. The reports of, or
the manifest visibility of, direct experiences need to be shared in ways
that make these experiences somehow intelligible in the light of central beliefs, even if they challenge less central and possibly erroneous

beliefs. Interpretations of experience need to take account of helpful and harmful consequences of the interpretations themselves, so that the good of some is not unfairly subordinated to the purported good of all. In the light of these criteria, we do have testimony and witness from women and men of integrity that should matter in human and Christian ethical discernment.[80] At the very least, without grounds in Scripture, tradition, or any discipline of human knowledge for an absolute prohibition of same-sex relationships, the witness of experience is enough to demand of the Christian community that it reflect anew on the norms for homosexual love.

Same-Sex Relationships and Justice

Early in my discussion of the ethical questions surrounding homosexuality I stated that the key question is not whether same-sex relationships can be ethically justified but what must characterize these relationships when they are justified. I anticipated a conclusion in this regard based on previous chapters, namely, that the justice ethic appropriate to heterosexual relationships is the same justice ethic appropriate to same-sex relationships. This sexual justice ethic is, in other words, an ethic for Christian — and perhaps all human — sexual relationships. Given my modest conclusions from the sources of a Christian same-sex ethic, we are now at a point where we can transcend the general question of permission/prohibition and look at specific norms for same-sex relationships. In doing so, I assume all that has been said in previous chapters about sexuality, love, and justice, and about the central features of human persons that ground and give direction for ethical norms in the sexual sphere. Hence, it comes as no surprise that an ethic applicable to and illuminative of

---

80. As has been pointed out by a number of persons, it is not necessary to demand that those whose experience is important to individual and communal discernment manifest exemplary lives in every way, placing upon them a greater burden than we do on others whose voice of experience we listen to without question. As D'Angelo says, many of those whose testimony we must hear are persons who have suffered deeply from homophobia, and whose voices have been silenced too long. "From these the Christian community should not ask or need the added testimony of an exemplary life or of Christian fidelity. Too often their inability to present such credentials is the first testimony to their tribulations." D'Angelo, "Perfect Fear Casteth Out Love," 193. I completely agree with this, although I would not necessarily consider this a sign of someone's lack of integrity.

same-sex relationships is based on an obligation to respect persons. To respect persons requires respecting their autonomy and their relationality—their capacity for self-determination by free choice and their capacity for relationships through knowledge and love. Since autonomy and relationality combine to make human persons ends in themselves, the first requirement in the sexual sphere as in any other sphere of human life is the requirement not to harm persons unjustly—whether they happen to be heterosexual or gay or lesbian.

Essential to relating to persons as ends in themselves, especially when their embodied selves are what is at stake, is a minimum but absolute requirement for the free consent of sexual partners. Everything that is ruled out for heterosexual relationships — rape, violence, harmful use of power, seduction and manipulation of individuals who have limited capacities of choice by reason of immaturity, intellectual disability, or special dependency—is ruled out for same-sex relationships as well. Derivately, truth-telling is required in same-sex relationships as well as an intent to keep any promises made.

In order to respect the relationality of homosexual persons, same-sex relationships ought also to be characterized by a significant degree of mutuality—of desire, action, and response. Similarly, reasonable equality is required in order to make free choice possible and to introduce an important qualification to mutuality. In addition, some form of commitment is expected and required by a Christian same-sex ethic, as is some form of fruitfulness. These latter two norms bear further consideration as they characterize same-sex relationships.

Many gay men and lesbians, like many heterosexual men and women, not only desire but consider necessary some form of commitment to relationships in which they are sexually active. Commitment today, of course, has become problematic, as much for homosexuals as for heterosexuals. If it is seen as a shutting down of one's life, a dampening of the possibilities of sexual expression, or as something that is almost impossible in today's world, it can hardly take the form of an obligation for sexual relationships. Moreover, if it is construed in terms identified with traditional forms of heterosexual marriage, with accompanying concerns for the procreation and rearing of children and for the domestication of sexuality, it can hardly be what gays and lesbians are obligated to embrace. Culturally conditioned expectations regarding gender roles, and assumed inequality in the power relations intrinsic to marriage, are not what either homosexuals or many heterosexuals find tolerable or just.

Yet commitment in sexual relationships that are just need not stifle either life or sexual love and desire; it may instead nurture, sustain, anchor, and transform sexuality. Its aim, at least, is to give a future to love and to a shared life, holding in continually ratified free choice what is otherwise fleeting and fragile. Commitment, or especially frameworks for commitment, are means, not ends in themselves. But they are means to the affirmation of persons as ends in themselves and the endurance of love that is an end in itself for those who want their relationships to hold. At its best, this is why the Christian community still recognizes commitment at the heart of an ethic for sexual activities and relationships. It prevents the use of sexual partners as mere means (for sustaining one's sexual desire and providing sexual pleasure), and it offers the possibility for the integration of sexuality into the whole of one's loves and one's life. It alone offers the possibility of sexuality as expression of transcendent embodiment in the highest forms of friendship.

Fruitfulness as a norm for sexual relations need not, as I said in chapter 6, refer only to the conceiving of children. It can refer to multiple forms of fruitfulness in love of others, care for others, making the world a better place for others than just the "two of us." It is the opposite of the sterility of an *égoisme à deux*. For those who object to same-sex relationships because they cannot be procreative, their objections represent either a failure of imagination or a narrowness of experience that disallows an appreciation of all the ways in which humans bring life into the world, and all the ways that the world needs new life from those to whom the gift of love has been given.[81] In the Christian community, the gift of love constitutes a calling, and it is a divine gift and divine call to lesbians and gay men, as it is to heterosexual women and men. Hence, fruitfulness is both an obligation and an appeal, a requirement and a graced opportunity.

---

81. It should also not be overlooked that many gay men and lesbians do conceive and raise their own biological children; just as many raise the children of their partners or the children of others.

The final norm for same-sex relationships, as for heterosexual relationships, is social justice. Here, too, some things must be added to what I have already said about this norm, for the social and ecclesiastical contexts in which homosexuals try to live faithfully in their relationships with one another and in the integrity of their own identity are still drastically different from the contexts that heterosexuals are used to and can expect. Social justice is the norm that identifies obligations in justice which others in the Christian community and the wider society have toward persons as sexual beings, and in this case, the obligations they have toward those persons who choose same-sex relationships. Just as gay men and lesbian women must affirm one another and themselves in terms of autonomy and relationality, so they have claims to respect from the wider society and the Christian churches. Homosexual persons, in other words, have the same rights as others to equal protection under the law, to self-determination, to a share in the goods and services available to all. Their needs for incorporation into the wider community, for physical safety, psychic and economic security, and basic well-being, make the same claims for social cooperation among us as do those of us all. The Christian community, in particular, is faced with serious questions in this regard. If, for example, a norm of commitment is appropriate for sexual relationships among Christians, and if such a norm belongs to a same-sex ethic as much as to a heterosexual ethic, then the problems of institutional support must be addressed anew.

Perhaps the first requirement under a social justice norm is to alleviate the social attitudinal consequences of maintaining a strong negative evaluation of homosexual activities and relationships.[82] For this negative evaluation, undergirded and proliferated through religious teachings and attitudes, constitutes in itself a social and political force. Though it is true, for example, that some and perhaps many church leaders have been persuaded at least not to oppose legislation that secures the basic civil rights of lesbians and gay men, the continuing significant societal resistance to this legislation and even more so to legislation regarding domestic partnerships is lodged

---

82. I have argued this point in "Response to James Hanigan and Charles Curran," in *Sexual Orientation and Human Rights in American Religious Discourse*, ed. Saul M. Olyan and Martha C. Nussbaum (New York: Oxford University Press, 1998), 101–9.

in the vehemence of the negative judgment that continues to be made regarding homosexual activity and relationships. This judgment is seldom a reasoned one, and its power as a social force is the power of an unreasoned taboo, lodged in and reinforcing the kind of unreflective repulsion that must be addressed if we are to move forward socially and politically on these issues.[83] As far as I can see, the primary way to address this unreflective negative response is for Christians and others to look again more critically (in the light of what has been learned regarding the sources for moral insight) at whatever reasons have been considered valid for prohibiting same-sex relations. Following this, education programs can be developed which will help to demythologize popular beliefs that create false fears regarding same-sex behaviors. Such programs can also examine the unsatisfactory yet in some ways helpful distinction between homosexual orientation and homosexual acts.[84] Finally, they can clarify what civil and welfare rights actually mean in the U.S. political tradition.[85]

---

83. An example of a philosopher who fuels the vehemence of negative judgments with inflammatory language is John Finnis. Arguing that sexual acts cannot be unitive unless they are marital, and not marital unless they have an openness to procreation, Finnis notes with approval what he takes to be a Greek assessment (much contested by Greek scholars) of homosexual acts as having "a special similarity to solitary masturbation, and both types of radically non-marital acts are manifestly unworthy of the human being and immoral." See John M. Finnis, "Law, Morality, and the 'Sexual Orientation,'" *Notre Dame Journal of Law, Ethics, and Public Policy* 9 (1995): 30. Like copulation of humans with animals, Finnis insists that genital coupling between humans with the same sexual organs must be repudiated as not only offensive but destructive of human character and relationships. Fearful, therefore, of the social influence of any seeming approval or even toleration of these activities, Finnis opposes any nondiscrimination legislation beyond the decriminalization of totally private actions.

84. Although emphasizing this distinction is unsatisfactory because it separates identity from action, and because it continues the assessment of homosexuals as somehow disadvantaged in their possibilities for full human flourishing, it is nonetheless a first step for many persons to reconsider their previous negative judgments of homosexual persons as persons.

85. Although education sounds like an uncontroversial recommendation, Greenberg may be right when he points out that what fuels the anti-gay rights movement is a fear of certain ideas influencing families and especially children. It is harder to communicate one's values to children if they are perceived to be undermined by teachers, the media, and so forth. "For conservatives the core concern is not protecting children from molestation . . . but shielding them from the knowledge that homosexuality exists and that it is not incompatible with intelligence and respectability." Greenberg, *The Construction of Homosexuality*, 471.

Legislation for nondiscrimination against homosexuals, but also for domestic partnerships, civil unions, and gay marriage, can also be important in transforming the hatred, rejection, and stigmatization of gays and lesbians that is still being reinforced by teachings of "unnatural" sex, disordered desire, and dangerous love. Gay bashing, as both church leaders and ethicists agree, is not a trivial matter; nor does it exist alone without attachment to multiple forms of avoidance as well as multiple forms of violence. Lodged in taboos and myths, the physical and verbal bashing of homosexuals is a greater danger to society — both as a violation of individuals' deep-seated human rights and a threat to human decency and the common good — than any feared approval or encouragement of homosexual lifestyles. A community's process toward a willingness to legislate regarding domestic partnerships of whatever form begins with, is premised on, and becomes the gradual extension of a stance against violence toward gays and lesbians. Its goal is the rendering of justice, a protection that is hardly separable from a provision for the meeting of basic needs.

Presently one of the most urgent issues before the U.S. public is marriage for same-sex partners — that is, the granting of social recognition and legal standing to unions between lesbians and gays comparable to unions between heterosexuals. This issue in some ways focuses the difficulties entailed in achieving respect for homosexual persons and for their incorporation into the ordinary life of the churches, while at the same time denying them communal and societal supports that are available to heterosexuals. The major argument against same-sex marriage has tended to be that it will weaken support for traditional heterosexual marriage and traditional notions of family. It is difficult to make sense of this reasoning, especially since the churches do not mount campaigns against laws that recognize divorce — arguably a greater threat to heterosexual marriage than gay marriages might be.[86] A more persuasive position is that

---

86. This is an argument that Charles Curran makes with particular attention to the Roman Catholic tradition. See Charles E. Curran, "Sexual Orientation and Human Rights in American Religious Discourse: A Roman Catholic Perspective," in *Sexual Orientation and Human Rights*, ed. Olyan and Nussbaum, 85–100.

the possibility of gay marriage would actually reinforce the value of commitment for heterosexuals as well as for homosexuals.

Many gay men and lesbians themselves oppose the idea of gay marriage on the grounds that the institution of marriage is already so frayed, so inadequate, and so rejecting of gays that it would be a mistake to mimic it in any way through legalization of gay or lesbian unions. Still, the important questions to be asked include whether or not those gays who wish to marry should be denied this possibility. They include also, as I have already said, questions for Christian churches: how do gay men and lesbians want to be incorporated as full participants in their faith communities, and how can practices be structured that will support them in the holiness of their own vocations within and beyond the community of faith?

Sexual Orientation: Given or Chosen

Understanding homosexuality as an inborn characteristic of some persons has been important to the achievement of tolerance and civil rights. Thus far science has not found the exact key to this inborn characteristic, but there can be no doubt that for many individuals who identify themselves as homosexual, there is their own clear experience of being attracted to those of the same sex from the time of their earliest memories. The inborn character of being gay would not have to depend on a biological cause; for even if it is the result of social and cultural construction, it may be as "unchosen," as unchangeable, and as basic to one's continuing identity as if it were biological. However we understand the givenness of homosexuality, this insight and conviction have helped religious traditions to accept the gay men and lesbians among them. As Judith Plaskow notes, this allows the view that "since homosexuality is not chosen, it cannot be immoral...[since] God would not demand of human beings something they cannot possibly obey."[87] Moreover, there is strength in recognizing oneself as a member of a group whose identity is clear, inborn, God-given.

Yet there are reasons to worry about the "givenness" of homosexuality as the primary or sole justification for the acceptance of

---

87. Plaskow, "Lesbian and Gay Rights," 31.

gays and lesbians.[88] For one thing, many lesbians do not report the same experience as most gay men — that is, that they always knew they were lesbian. Some women may consider themselves completely heterosexual, marry and raise children, and then fall in love with a woman. Or they may choose to self-identify as lesbian for political reasons in ways suggested by Adrienne Rich. Similarly, according to the sexual continuum theory (whether from Kinsey, other researchers, or Rich), some persons may be capable of emotional and sexual relationships only with those of the so-called opposite sex, others capable of emotional and sexual relationship only with those of the same-sex, and there may be many others at some point in between these poles on the continuum who are capable of relating to either the opposite or the same sex, the latter depending on how they encounter another of whichever sex, actualized and expressive in one or another gender. Moreover, the requirement of finding some biological explanation for innate homosexuality risks highlighting it as an anomaly — since we don't keep searching for the gene that explains heterosexuality. Finally, if the givenness of homosexuality is the mainstay of an ethic for same-sex relationships, there will always be the objection that no one needs to act on this tendency, and same-sex activity thus remains still outside the pale of justifiable sex.

My own view, as should be clear by now, is that same-sex relationships and activities can be justified according to the same sexual ethic as heterosexual relationships and activities. Therefore, same-sex oriented persons as well as their activities can and should be respected whether or not they have a choice to be otherwise. Insofar as this is true, it still matters a great deal to individuals how they come to realize their same-sex orientation or preference; but this is not what determines whether they themselves are whole human beings whose sexuality is justifiable when it accords with the norms of sexual justice. Everyone should look forward to the day when it will not matter in the course of human and Christian affairs whether one

---

88. These worries are succinctly expressed by Plaskow, ibid., 31–32, and Margaret R. Miles, "Beyond Biological Determination," *Anglican Theological Review* 72 (Spring 1990): 161–65. The possibilities of homosexuality being both given and chosen (being both an "orientation" and a "preference") are noted in Murphy, *Gay Science*, 233 n. 14; Greenberg, *The Construction of Homosexuality*, 481, 487–92; Mondimore, *A Natural History of Homosexuality*, 84–87.

is homosexual or heterosexual, and when one sexual ethic will help us discern the morality of all sexual relationships and activities.

Divorce and Remarriage

I turn now to the third pattern of relationship to be considered in the light of the sexual justice ethic I have proposed.[89] Questions of divorce and remarriage are not so easily seen to be questions regarding sexuality and its ethical determinants. Understanding them, however, does lead us into considerations of commitments and the breakdown of commitments in the sexual sphere. Moreover, issues addressed in previous chapters, including an understanding of sexuality, freedom, marriage, and commitment, have clear relevance for any probing of the questions of divorce and second marriages following divorce.

There is hardly a Christian family that has not been touched in some way in recent years by issues surrounding divorce. The reality or the possibility of the breakdown and loss of a marital relationship is close to hand in one way or another for almost everyone, whether for relatives, friends, or one's own self. Both divorce and remarriage have preoccupied theologians and church leaders frequently enough throughout the centuries that were we not faced with new and urgent situations we would weary of addressing them yet again. Perhaps contemporary experience is sharp enough, and history long enough, for us to gain a perspective not heretofore accessible regarding these questions. Yet the obstacles to new and needed insights remain formidable, especially but not only in the Roman Catholic tradition.[90] It is not easy to know even whether we are asking the

---

89. What follows is a revised version of a previous essay: Margaret A. Farley, "Marriage, Divorce, and Personal Commitments," in *Celebrating Christian Marriage*, ed. Adrian Thatcher (Edinburgh: T. & T. Clark, 2001), 355–72. Revisions include some additions from my earlier essays: "Divorce and Remarriage," *Proceedings of the Catholic Theological Society of America* 30 (1975), 111–19; "Divorce and Remarriage: A Moral Perspective," in *Divorce and Remarriage*, ed. William P. Roberts (Kansas City, MO: Sheed and Ward, 1990), 107–27; and "Divorce, Remarriage, and Pastoral Practice," in *Moral Theology: Challenges for the Future*, ed. Charles E. Curran (New York: Paulist, 1990), 213–39.

90. See Farley, "Divorce, Remarriage, and Pastoral Practice," for a close analysis of twentieth century changes in the opinions of Catholic moral theologians, developments

right questions. Life seems to have moved beyond issues of simply whether the churches should recognize divorce and accept remarriage, or even whether marriage can be in some sense indestructible no matter what. Our questions seem rather to be what are we to do about the fragility of contemporary marriages and the trauma and sometimes tragedy of their collapse, and what clarifying and healing words has the church to speak and what empowering grace to offer.

Debates until now have tended to focus on juridical, moral, and ontological interpretations of the bond that marriage entails. All of these dimensions are intrinsic to the problem, and they must continue to be addressed. Suppose we ask first, however, why the problem as a whole is so important to us. Why do we care so much that marriages are fragile, or that divorce and remarriage seem inevitable, even though they may not be our best remedy for the vulnerability of marriage itself? A number of answers can be given to this question, and their rich complexity is not captured by simple statements that something is right or wrong, or that certain patterns of behavior fit or do not fit an assumed pattern of Christian life. For example, Christians by and large believe that it is God's intention that marriage should be "for life." We also recognize that it is not only God's desire and intention that are at stake, but our own. When we reach a point in a relationship where we want to share our life with another individual, marriage, at least in some form, looks like our best option. The very nature of this love moves us to want to sustain it forever; our happiness seems to lie in this direction. And many of us still think that building a family is among the greatest of human enterprises. We also recognize the need for stability not only in our own lives but also in the societies on which we depend. And we still believe in the distinctiveness and importance of the bond of marriage as part of the fabric of the life of the church. Marriage, then, with permanence as one of its essential elements, is what God wants and we want and need — whether for ourselves or for others.

---

in church teaching and pastoral practice, and a description of the tensions between moral theologians and the hierarchical teaching church on these issues. For a brief description (not included below) of the current situation see Farley, "Marriage, Divorce, and Personal Commitments."

And yet it does not seem to work. The promises we make do not always hold; the desires we experience are not always fulfilled; the wholeness our love seeks is often elusive; the families we try to build are often fragmented and troubled; the stability we count on all too often disappears under our feet; and there is among us too much suffering and pain. Some analysts tell us that this is because ours is an era of radical individualism; we are not able to take responsibility for one another in the way past generations have done. Or ours is a hopelessly hedonistic culture, lost to the forms of discipline that human life requires. Or we belong to a sadly anxious and alienated set of generations, disturbed by too much war and death, too much ambiguous progress and change, too much expectation with too little wisdom about how to achieve what we yearn for and expect.

But maybe the explanation is both simpler than all of this, and at the same time more complex. What if our troubles regarding marriage and family are the consequence of real incapacities — not all of our own making, but part of our share in the "human condition"? The kinds of incapacities we experience are not lack of control of disordered lust, as many of our Christian predecessors thought, but our "almost inability" to live together. Whether because of some general human limitation or brokenness, or because in our social context we are weakened by one another's failings as much as we are strengthened by one another's virtue, the struggle "to live together" goes on, century after century, among peoples, nations, religions, classes. It goes on, too, in our most intimate lives, our most intimate relationships, especially when what is at stake is genuinely sharing our lives together on a day to day basis.

Our incapacities to sustain marriage and family are dramatically revealed at this point in our history for particular reasons. In the past, as we have seen, the institution of marriage sustained the relationship between partners in a marriage, and when necessary, it covered over the fragility and sometimes even terror of the relationship. It did not appear to matter so much whether husbands and wives loved one another or got along well with one another. If they did not, they could spend their time in other circles of men or women in which each could find strength, companionship, and even solace. Society, the church, culture, almost every other institution worked to maintain the institution of marriage because it served their aims. The goal was largely social utility, whether for the sake of the empire, the tribe, the nation, or the church. In turn, marriage as a social institution could for centuries on end sustain or circumvent marriage as relationship, and it could stabilize the intergenerational family that was most frequently formed. Today there is, in a sense, no similarly recognizable institution of marriage,[91] no institution that can be assumed to do for intimate relations what the marriage institution of the past could do.

What, then, can hold marriage as a relationship? What will hold the relationships that form our marriages? Not presently a strong and unquestioned institution, not the love itself, not the sanctioned "laws" of marriage, not even the children born of marriage. Love is notoriously fickle, waxing and waning in ways we cannot always control. And all the laws proclaimed, even reinforced by sanctions, do not save us from our inabilities to live together in peace and in joy. Children do hold us to one another and to them, but we have massive evidence that they alone cannot save our marriages.

We need not appeal to doctrines of original sin in the sense of "brokenness" or "fall" to understand all of this. We can appeal to our understanding of the concrete reality of human persons and a theology of human possibilities and limitations. One of the things revealed to us in the present experience of so much powerlessness in the face of the unraveling of a given marriage is that the efficaciousness of our free choice is limited. If freedom is our power of self-determination; if it is our capacity to take hold of ourselves by ratifying or refusing to identify with our own spontaneous desires, loves, judgments, obligations; then it is indeed the capacity to fashion ourselves according to the self we choose. Yet sheer free choice — the "grit your teeth and do it" sort of choice — is so limited. We want to remain loving and faithful, peaceful and strong, utterly self-forgetful and devoted, in a relationship of marriage. This may be easily said, but not so easily done. If life with a particular other becomes intolerable — as it can

---

91. I am not implying that the sea-changes in family structures are always a bad thing.

become — it will not be made tolerable simply by choosing it so — not by controlling the other or even by controlling one's own self. Freedom, along with relationality, may be our noblest feature, that by which we determine our own destiny in some kind of ultimate sense. Yet it has limited power to shape our own inner selves or our relationships with others.

In the face of limitation and powerlessness, what is there in the Christian tradition to strengthen us, to help us fashion our freedom and love? We have symbols and images, beliefs and convictions, memories and hopes; and what do they yield? Understandings of "covenant," of "sacrament," of Christian *agape* and unconditional fidelity; metaphors of Christ in relation to the church, and "two in one flesh"; interpretations of gender complementarity and the church as family. Insofar as we make all of these resources our own — elements in our faith, informers of our hope, reinforcements of our love — they do help us to sustain our choices and to remain loyal to our intentions. Yet these particular elements in our tradition have themselves come upon hard times, and not only because of our infidelities. As ideas, images, theological construals, they no longer offer sure remedies for our weaknesses of mind and heart, or sure bridges for our limited freedom. Even when lodged in genuinely sacramental realities, they do not by themselves solve our present inability to sustain our marriages in the ways we have wanted to sustain them.

A justifiable skepticism has undercut for us, as well it should, the past power of many of these notions in our traditions. We have learned, for example, that covenants were all too often, in the biblical tradition, between unequals; Christ's relation to the church has been all too often translated into gender assigned roles; "two in one flesh" covered over the frequent loss of identity and violation of an individual's, usually a woman's, own humanhood; the church's history regarding sexuality is so greatly flawed; and so on. All of these images and ideas may be retrievable, but not without passing through a clarifying critique.

So, where shall we go? Where is grace in all of this? How does grace "work" in these aspects of our lives? How does sacramental grace function, and how can it be recognized and nurtured? One place we might look is to the nature of the commitment that is at the heart of marriage. Probing its experience and its meaning may shed light on the ways of sustaining marriage as well as the ways of letting it go.

The Marriage Commitment: Making, Keeping, Changing

Like any other explicit, expressed, interpersonal commitment, marriage involves the giving of one's word.[92] But what do we give when we give our word, and why do we give it? First, we do something, or aim to do something, that relates to the future. We promise to do something or be something in relation to someone in the future. Giving our word has to do with an intention of action not only in the present but in the future. In the case of marriage, we give our word regarding interior actions (of respect, love, trust, and so forth) and exterior actions (regarding a way of sharing a life together) — promising these actions on into the future, indeed (at least in the Christian tradition) until we die. We do not simply predict our actions in the future, nor only resolve to do them. To give our word means, fundamentally, to give to another a claim over our selves — a claim on our doing and being what we have promised.

What happens, then, when we make a commitment, including a commitment in marriage, is that we enter a new form of relationship. We "send" (from the Latin, *mittere*) our word into another; we "place" ourselves in the other to whom we give our word. Frequently in human affairs we try to concretize, "incarnate," this, express it and symbolize it, by making the "word" tangible. For example, we sign our name on contracts; we give rings as signs of our word and ourselves; we exchange gifts to signal the exchange of our promises. And why do we do this? Precisely because our loves, our intentions, are fragile. Commitment in the human community implies a state of affairs in which there is doubt about our future actions; it implies the possibility of failure to do in the future what we intend in the present; it is our way of transcending the limits of our freedom in order to determine, in some way, our own future. The primary purpose, then, of interpersonal and social commitments is to provide

---

92. I adapt here an analysis of "commitment" made at much greater length in *Personal Commitments*, especially chap. 2.

some reliability of expectation regarding the actions of free persons whose wills are shakable.[93]

Commitments give us grounds for counting on one another, even on ourselves. The purpose of promising is both to assure the other of the future we promise and to strengthen ourselves in our intentions for the future. It does so because to give our word is to undertake a new obligation for which there will be sanctions should we fail in fulfilling it (we stand to lose the "word" we have given, to lose our reputation or our goods, even our happiness and sometimes perhaps even our salvation). By committing ourselves we give, as it were, a new law to ourselves; we bind ourselves by the claim we give to another. We make most of our commitments not because we must, but because this is what we want to do. We want to be held to what we most truly want to do and be. In some commitments, we want, against the threats of time, to make our loves whole. The "word" we give now calls to us from the one who holds it, the one to whom we have entrusted it. What commitment means, then, and what it entails, is a new relationship in the *present* — a relationship of binding and being bound, giving and being claimed; but the commitment points to the *future*. In the present, a new relationship begins, and the relationship is what moves into the future.[94]

This is true of all human commitments, but there are elements specific to the commitment to marry that are extremely important to our understanding of it and to our gaining any light on what it means and how it can be lived. For example, the commitment to marry is essentially mutual: two liberties meet, two words are given, two claims are yielded and held. Moreover, marriage involves a commitment to more than one person. At least in a Christian construal of what marriage is, a commitment is made not only to one's partner

---

93. When God makes promises to us, enters into covenant with us, it is not because God's will is shakable, but because God wants to give us a claim on God, and wants us to know and be assured thereby (as best we can understand) of the sort of unconditional love that is God's for us.

94. Our free choice cannot "settle" ahead of time our future. But through commitment it can influence our future. Commitment, or promise-making, is a device whereby we move into the future, changed because we are now obligated, not because we are necessitated. Hence, commitment changes our reality in the present, our relationships in the present, so that what we do in the future can — depending on what we do and under what circumstances — be accurately described as faithfulness, or betrayal.

but to God and to a community of persons (to the church and to the wider society). In addition, while a commitment to marry is made to persons, its content includes a commitment to a certain framework of life in relation to persons. That is, while those who marry commit themselves to love one another, they do so by committing themselves to whatever is still understood as the "institution" of marriage.[95] "Framework," of course, has more than one level of meaning in this context. There is a level at which "marriage" is a framework that structures a relationship into some generic form — for example, most generic understandings of marriage include the element of permanence. There is also a level where framework means a certain cultural or religious model of marriage — as, for example, when it includes sexual exclusivity, and either a hierarchical structure or one of equality between spouses. And finally there is a level of framework which is the particular structure implied or already worked out by particular participants in a given relationship of marriage — as, for example, the ways in which they will share their possessions, relate to one another's families, and educate their children.

In our own culture, as we have seen above, and certainly in the Christian tradition, an intention of permanence is included in the marital commitment. Given massive historical changes in social contexts, some of the reasons for incorporating the element of permanence in the framework of marriage have changed, though many remain the same. The importance of interpersonal reasons has grown, and institutional reasons have receded. Yet there have always been reasons for permanence that are intrinsic to the marital relationship itself and reasons of social utility beyond the relationship. Love itself can want to give its whole future, to bind itself as irrevocably as possible to the one loved and to express itself in this way. I have also argued in chapter 6 that sexuality may be best served in a context of permanent commitment, where it has a chance of being nurtured and integrated into the whole of one's personality and one's primary relationship. Further, an intention of and commitment to permanence is in the present as in the past considered

---

95. Despite the fact that we have so little of the "institution" left, there remains some content to what "marriage" means.

to be for the good of children and also for the good of the church —
in which marriage can function as a way of Christian life and a sign
of God's presence.

Yet here we meet the heart of a problem. If an intention of permanence is intrinsic to the meaning of Christian marriage, and if
marriage as a commitment is self-obligating, is it ever justifiable to
end a marriage short of the death of one's spouse? Can the claim
given to another in the commitment of marriage ever be released?
This is the central moral question for both divorce and remarriage.
And behind this, perhaps, lies the further question: If a marital
commitment to permanence cannot be released, should such a commitment reasonably be made in a time when our ability to sustain
it seems so compromised?[96] Or if we come to understand more fully
what is needed in order to live our commitments "to the end," will
we thereby learn better not only how to sustain them but also how,
if finally necessary, to let them go?

Divorce

We are used to acknowledging release from a marriage obligation
when it can be determined that some basic flaw marked the original marrying — a flaw in the procedure, a lack of full consent, a
situation of unfreedom of any kind (whether physical, psychological, or moral).[97] This kind of "release" is, of course, not really a
release from an obligation but a recognition that no marriage obligation was ever truly undertaken; the marriage did not really, validly,
take place. The much more difficult question is whether the obligation intrinsic to a genuinely valid Christian marriage, especially a
sacramental Christian marriage, can ever be ended without betrayal,
without the unjustified and unjustifiable violation of a claim that
was once yielded to another.

My own position is that a marriage commitment is subject to
release on the same ultimate grounds that any extremely serious,

---

96. I here call attention to, but do not discuss, proposals for "temporary" marriage trials, or graduated ceremonies in stages of marriage, or a return perhaps to older
notions of "betrothal." See, for example, Reg Harcus, "The Case for Betrothal," in
Celebrating Christian Marriage, 41–54.

97. This is at the basis of the Roman Catholic practice of annulments.

nearly unconditional, permanent commitment may cease to bind.[98] This implies that there can indeed be situations in which too much has changed — one or both partners have changed, the relationship has changed, the original reason for the commitment seems altogether gone. The point of a permanent commitment, of course, is to bind those who make it in spite of any changes that may come. But can it always hold? Can it hold absolutely, in the face of radical and unexpected change? My answer: sometimes it cannot. Sometimes the obligation must be released, and the commitment can be justifiably changed.

To understand situations such as these, it is useful to look at the generic grounds for discerning when a commitment no longer obligates.[99] Three grounds are defensible, it seems to me, and they can be applied in the context of marriage and divorce. A commitment no longer binds when (1) it becomes *impossible* to keep; (2) it no longer fulfills any of the *purposes* it was meant to serve; (3) another obligation comes into *conflict* with the first obligation, and the second is judged to *override* the first. Only one of these conditions needs to be in place — although often more than one characterizes the situation — in order to justify a release from the commitment-obligation. It is sometimes extremely difficult to discern when such conditions actually come to be, but that they do and that they can be identified, even in relation to marriage, seems to me to be without doubt. Some brief observations regarding each of these conditions may help to make this clear.

First, then, when it truly becomes *impossible* to sustain a marriage relationship, the obligation to do so is released. Impossibility — especially physical impossibility — has long been accepted as a general justifying reason for release from the obligation of a promise, as when in the Middle Ages a broken leg made it impossible to continue on a pilgrimage to which one had committed oneself. The kind of impossibility that is relevant for marriage commitments is not, of course,

---

98. See Farley, *Personal Commitments*, chap. 7. I do not want to imply that there can be no absolute commitments, unconditionally binding no matter what.

99. I provide a fuller description of these generic reasons or conditions in chapter 7 of *Personal Commitments*. I have also discussed in detail the adaptation of these in the context of marital commitment and divorce in the essays cited in note 86 above.

physical but psychological and moral.[100] Hence, recognizing it is less like perceiving an incontrovertible fact than like making a judgment or even a decision. Still, examples can be given — of irremediable and irreconcilable rupture in a relationship, or utter helplessness in the face of violence, or inability to go on in a relationship that threatens one's very identity as a person; and it seems true that a threshold of genuine impossibility does exist. We all do know of situations in which what was once love is now seemingly irreversible bitterness and hatred, so that to remain together threatens utter destruction to the partners themselves and to others. We know of situations where some aspects of the relationship may still survive but others prove so contradictory to marriage that at least one partner can no longer sustain it — as, for example, in a situation of relentless domestic violence. Or apathy and despair can burden a person and a relationship to a degree that, without drastic change, one is convinced one will, as a person, die. Or it may even happen that a new love arises, and it becomes too late to "turn back" (regardless of what one should have done about refusing this path in the first instance).

Second, a marriage commitment may reach a point where it has *completely lost its purpose*, its whole *raison d'être*, its intrinsic meaning. It is meant, for example, to serve love and life for spouses, for family, for society, for God. In order to do this it includes a commitment, as we have seen, to a "framework" for loving. But if the framework becomes a threat to the very love it is to serve, if it weakens it or contradicts it or blocks it, then the very commitment to love may require that the commitment to marriage as a framework must come to an end. Of course, marriage has multiple meanings and purposes, but it may be, in some circumstances, that all of these are undermined by the marriage itself — or some are so gravely

---

100. There is not space in this concluding chapter to include a discussion of what I have elsewhere called the "way of fidelity," although I have referred to it in terms of the "between" in the section on marriage and family above. I can only assume here the kind of effort and wisdom that is necessary to prevent the point of "impossibility" being reached. For this more positive treatment, see *Personal Commitments*, chap. 4. There as here, however, I acknowledge that circumstances can emerge — whether with or without anyone's culpability — when nonetheless it becomes genuinely impossible to sustain a commitment-obligation.

undermined as to jeopardize them all. If so, the obligation to the marriage commitment is released.

Third, if another obligation *conflicts* with and *takes priority over* the commitment to marriage, then the marriage bond may be released. Given the seriousness of the commitment to marry, there are not many other obligations that can supersede it. It is, after all, made with the kind of unconditionality that is meant to override other claims almost without exception. Yet there may be times when other fundamental obligations do take priority — fundamental obligations to God, to children, to society, even to one's spouse — when, for example, commitment to the well-being of the spouse conflicts with continued commitment to relationship within the framework of marriage. It is also possible for a fundamental obligation to one's own self to justify ending a marriage — not because love of self takes priority over love of another, but because no relationship should be sustained that entails the complete physical or psychological destruction of a person — including oneself.

When under certain conditions a marriage commitment ceases to bind, are there no obligations, human and Christian, that remain in relation to one's spouse? Clearly there are. Though commitment to a framework for loving is not completely unconditional or absolute, there are unconditional requirements within it. For example, there is never any justification to stop loving someone altogether — not a marriage partner or former marriage partner, any more than a stranger or even an enemy. When it is no longer possible or morally good to love someone within the framework of marriage, it is still possible to love that individual at least with the love that is universally due all persons. It may even be that an obligation to a particular love is required, one that is in *some* way faithful to the relationship that once existed. But let me turn briefly to what remains for some the most difficult question of all. That is, when the commitment to marriage no longer binds as such, when a true divorce is morally justified, is it also justifiable to remarry?

Remarriage

Despite the fact that a prohibition against remarriage after a valid marriage has ended in divorce is almost unique to the Roman Catholic tradition, there are many other Christians who are at least cautious about this possibility. Hence, it may be important to look to the arguments that have held sway in the Catholic community. The traditional Roman Catholic position has been and is that even if an end must come to a marriage in the sense of separation from shared "bed and board," there remains nonetheless an obligation not to remarry. The reason for this, of course, lies ultimately in a conviction that the original marriage in some sense continues to exist. Against the position I have just outlined wherein the original marriage may no longer exist, are serious arguments such as: (1) Christian sacramental marriage, unlike other commitments, is under the command of God and the interpretation of that command by Jesus Christ. Hence, the indissolubility of marriage remains absolute. (2) The "framework" or institution of marriage is under the governance of the church. There is, therefore, a special stipulation included in the marriage commitment whereby there will always be a juridical "remainder." Even if every other aspect of the commitment becomes impossible or meaningless or in conflict with a greater obligation, this much of the marriage commitment still holds. (3) A commitment to marriage, with valid consent and sexual consummation, changes the partners in their very being. No longer are they bound only legally or morally, but they are ontologically bound in an irreversible way.

I have elsewhere addressed these arguments, and I can here only summarize my responses to them.[101] Regarding the first, biblical scholars have shown effectively the exegetical difficulties of using New Testament texts to settle the question of an absolute requirement of indissolubility in marriage. In particular, the divergences among the command attributed to Paul in 1 Corinthians 7:10–11, and the various sayings about divorce in Mark 10:1–12, Matthew 19:1–12, and Luke 16:18, indicate that the early church was struggling with this issue. Hence, none of these texts can be used as the only basis for a Christian regarding divorce and remarriage.[102] This is why the Roman Catholic tradition has not argued that the issue can

---

101. See essays cited in note 86.
102. See, e.g., Mary Rose D'Angelo, "Remarriage and the Divorce Sayings Attributed to Jesus," in *Divorce and Remarriage: Religious and Psychological Perspectives*, ed. William P. Roberts (Kansas City: Sheed & Ward, 1990), 78–106.

be settled only on biblical grounds. Regarding the second, a purely ecclesiastical juridical basis has never been given as the incontestable and absolute ground for the indissolubility of marriage; human laws can be changed, or exceptions can be developed.[103] Moreover, were the church to demand an obligation not to remarry as a stipulation for marrying, this would make marriages that have ended in divorce a countersign in the symbol system that appeals to the relationship of Christ to the church. If the object of such a law were to secure a form of social stability, or the good of children, it would raise serious questions regarding the effectiveness of the law.

Traditional Catholic reasons for prohibiting remarriage after divorce rest primarily on some version of the third argument.[104] But even this argument, regarding the ontological union of spouses, is difficult to maintain with traditional warrants. Despite escalating language regarding the "two in one flesh" image — in terms, as we have seen, of an "ultimate gift" of spouses to one another" or the "nuptial meaning" of the body[105] — any concept of fusion between persons risks ignoring the realities of individual persons, and rests too often on symbols of purity/defilement (defilement if there is sexual union outside of the first marriage) that can no longer be sustained. Moreover, appeals to ontological union fail to acknowledge the limits of human freedom (as I have tried to articulate them earlier in this chapter).

This said, I am nonetheless inclined to acknowledge that some kind of bond of being is effected through marriage, and even that it remains in some form when the marriage commitment has come to an end. When two persons commit themselves to one another in the profound form of marrying; when they share their lives together for whatever period of time; they *are* somehow changed, united, in their beings. There are many ways in which this change continues, no matter what. After the marriage has ended, what remains may even include a "bodily" bonding — now experienced positively or negatively — as a result of the sexual relationship that once was part of

---

103. See, for example, John T. Noonan, *Power to Dissolve* (Cambridge, MA: Belknap Press of Harvard University Press, 1972).

104. See Theodore Mackin, *Divorce and Remarriage* (New York: Paulist, 1984), 516f.

105. See, for example, the many writings of John Paul II on marriage, including *Original Unity of Man and Woman: Catechesis on the Book of Genesis* (Boston: Daughters of St. Paul, 1981).

the marriage. There may also remain a spiritual bonding — positively or negatively experienced — as a result of months or years of shared history. If the marriage resulted in children, former spouses will be held together for years, perhaps a lifetime, in the ongoing project of parenting. In any case, the lives of two persons once married to one another are forever qualified by the experience of that marriage. The depth of what remains admits of degrees, but something remains. But does what remains disallow a second marriage? My own view is that it does not. Whatever ongoing obligation a residual bond entails, it need not include a prohibition of remarriage — any more than the ongoing union between spouses after one of them has died prohibits a second marriage on the part of the one who still lives.[106]

The sexual ethic I have proposed in this book is relevant to questions of divorce and second marriages. Divorce sometimes follows upon the failure of at least one partner to respect the other as an end; or it becomes inevitable when freedom, equality, and mutuality are nonexistent or in such low degree that the relationship is distorted. Sometimes it comes because there are failures in communal and societal support, so that the Christian concern for this dimension of marriage is played out in its absence. But as I have suggested, sometimes divorce does not follow from culpable failures on the part of either or both partners in a marriage. Sometimes it eventuates because of human limitation in the faces of the challenges of blending lives together. And when the commitment that establishes a marriage relationship can no longer hold without self-destruction or serious harm to another; or when the very purpose of the marriage in regard to all

---

106. I am aware of the responses given to this reasoning by those who argue that there is a critical difference between marriage after the death of a spouse and marriage after the "death" of a previous marriage. One response is that the original commitment was only "until death do us part," so a new marriage after the death of a spouse does not violate this promise. Yet clearly the intention of the promise is implicitly "forever," if there is a belief in the possibility of union after death. And in any case, if those who die do remain alive, but in another world, the *ontological* bond between marriage partners remains. A second response is that marriage is only intended by God to be for this world. Hence, the original marriage is dissolved when one of the spouses is no longer in this world. This is a difficult matter to sort out, however, given any belief regarding life after death and the ongoing fulfillment of relationships begun on earth. It is uncertain as to what the differences will be between "this world" and the "next." Hence, it seems unjustifiable to treat the prohibition against remarriage after divorce as if it were completely different from the allowance of remarriage after the death of one's spouse.

those affected by it is seriously compromised or lost; or when another commitment justifiably supersedes the marriage commitment; then the way in which a marriage ends should also be marked by mutual respect insofar as this is possible — mutual respect and all that this entails. New marriages, too, are subject to concerns of justice.

Christians believe that the grace of God is available in and through Christian marriage. The evidence of failed marriages suggests that this grace is not automatically effective. Our questions expand, then, to an exploration of how grace works in our loves, our incapacities, our promises, our ordinary efforts to live out our lives together, and even in our failures. I have not here probed the question of the "ways of fidelity," though this is of the utmost, indeed primary, importance. I have tried only to ask about the faithful ways of ending marriages and the faithful possibilities of beginning again. Insofar as we gain wisdom on all of these questions we shall find a healing word which may both strengthen marriages and, when it is necessary, ease the pain of their ending. Grace, I want to argue, can extend in all of these directions.

•

In the end, I have with this book attempted to contextualize and illuminate our understandings of sexuality and its possibilities for human fulfillment. Looking to the past and the present, to cultures far and near, I have tried to sort out the multiple meanings and goals of sexuality, sex, gender, and embodiment. Above all, I have asked and tried to respond to the question of when sexuality and its expressions are appropriate in human relationships. I have proposed a sexual ethic grounded in and specified by concerns for justice. Justice, I have tried to show, is not a cold notion apart from love; it is what guides, protects, nourishes, and forms love, and what makes love just and true. It concerns our loves and our actions; it concerns the sort or persons we want to be. I repeat what I have said before: it is not an easy task to introduce considerations of justice into every sexual relation and the evaluation of every sexual activity. But if sexuality is to be creative and not destructive, then there is no substitute for discerning ever more carefully whether our expressions of it are just.

INDEX